Springer Theses

Recognizing Outstanding Ph.D. Research

Aims and Scope

The series "Springer Theses" brings together a selection of the very best Ph.D. theses from around the world and across the physical sciences. Nominated and endorsed by two recognized specialists, each published volume has been selected for its scientific excellence and the high impact of its contents for the pertinent field of research. For greater accessibility to non-specialists, the published versions include an extended introduction, as well as a foreword by the student's supervisor explaining the special relevance of the work for the field. As a whole, the series will provide a valuable resource both for newcomers to the research fields described, and for other scientists seeking detailed background information on special questions. Finally, it provides an accredited documentation of the valuable contributions made by today's younger generation of scientists.

Theses are accepted into the series by invited nomination only and must fulfill all of the following criteria

- They must be written in good English.
- The topic should fall within the confines of Chemistry, Physics, Earth Sciences, Engineering and related interdisciplinary fields such as Materials, Nanoscience, Chemical Engineering, Complex Systems and Biophysics.
- The work reported in the thesis must represent a significant scientific advance.
- If the thesis includes previously published material, permission to reproduce this must be gained from the respective copyright holder.
- They must have been examined and passed during the 12 months prior to nomination.
- Each thesis should include a foreword by the supervisor outlining the significance of its content.
- The theses should have a clearly defined structure including an introduction accessible to scientists not expert in that particular field.

More information about this series at http://www.springer.com/series/8790

Daniel W. Ambaye

Land Rights and Expropriation in Ethiopia

Doctoral Thesis accepted by
the Royal Institute of Technology (KTH),
Stockholm, Sweden

Springer

Author
Dr. Daniel W. Ambaye
Institute of Land Administration (ILA)
Bahir Dar University
Bahir Dar
Ethiopia

Supervisor
Prof. Thomas Kalbro
Real Estate Planning and Land Law
Royal Institute of Technology (KTH)
Stockholm
Sweden

ISSN 2190-5053 ISSN 2190-5061 (electronic)
Springer Theses
ISBN 978-3-319-36788-0 ISBN 978-3-319-14639-3 (eBook)
DOI 10.1007/978-3-319-14639-3

Springer Cham Heidelberg New York Dordrecht London

Softcover reprint of the hardcover 1st edition 2015

Printed on acid-free paper

Springer International Publishing AG Switzerland is part of Springer Science+Business Media (www.springer.com)

Parts of this thesis have been published in the following journal articles:

Daniel W. Ambaye (2013) Compensation during Expropriation in Ethiopia and the UK: A Comparative Analysis, *Bahir Dar University Law Journal*, Vol. 3, No. 2, pp. 279–295.

Daniel W. Ambaye (2013) The History of Expropriation in Ethiopian Law, *Mizan Law Review*, Vol. 7, No. 2, pp. 283–308.

Daniel W. Ambaye (2012) Land Rights in Ethiopia: ownership, equity and liberty in land use rights, *FIG Working Week*, Rome, Italy.

Supervisor's Foreword

The World Bank, other institutions, and researchers have stressed on the utmost significance of defined and secured property rights in order to facilitate development in a country through access to credit, property transfer, and efficient resource allocation. Secure property rights necessitate clarity of rights, durability of rights, and the enforcement of such rights.

However, land law and land rights in Ethiopia have a less encouraging background history. Wars and violence have made the laws and rights unstable and insecure. Even today, land rights are unpredictable because of the continuous change and revision of land laws. Furthermore, there has been a lack of analysis to determine the nature and status of land rights in current Ethiopia. As a starting point in his thesis, Dr. Ambaye fills this gap of knowledge by reviewing and analyzing the current land rights.

Against this background, Dr. Ambaye enlightens us on the Ethiopian legislation and practice of expropriation/compulsory purchase from different angles. Firstly, the method and procedure of land acquisition by expropriation is investigated. Secondly, the concept of "public interest" as a requirement for compulsory measures is discussed. Thirdly, problems related to the absence and lack of scientific and uniform standards of valuation methods are covered. Fourthly, the thesis discusses the amount of compensation from a fairness perspective. Fifthly, the need for revision of the current legislation is addressed. The fifth theme focuses on areas of concern which need to be addressed by laws. For example, the city of Addis Ababa has been undergoing massive infrastructure development works—roads, underground cables, bridges, and water and sewage systems—resulting in the closure of businesses situated in the vicinity of the construction without any compensatory scheme.

Dr. Ambaye's thesis contains both theoretical and empirical research contributions of high standard, and he carries out the research objectives in a clear and precise manner. The operational recommendations for the development of the Ethiopian legislation of land rights and expropriation, as well as the legal practice, are scientifically underpinned in a relevant and valid manner.

As supervisor it has been a pleasure to see this thesis taking a form by the work of a very talented and creative scholar. I wish Dr. Ambaye all the best in the future.

Stockholm, October 2015

Prof. Thomas Kalbro

Acknowledgments

Many people have contributed to the completion of this study. First and foremost I would like to thank the Swedish Institute (SI) for providing me a scholarship for my education at the Royal Institute of Technology (KTH). My gratitude also goes to Sida for funding part of my travel costs and my research, which was conducted in Ethiopia during the past four years. This was made possible with the creative planning of Professor Hans Mattsson of KTH and the Institute of Land Administration (ILA) at Bahir Dar University.

I would like to express my profound gratitude to my supervisors, Prof. Thomas Kalbro and co-supervisor Prof. Annina Person, for their valuable comments and criticisms. I am grateful for their friendly approach and concerned readings of the thesis. I wish also to thank Prof. Hans Mattsson for his tireless effort to see the full realization of my Institute at Bahir Dar University. It was his suggestion in the first place that made me to apply for the SI Scholarship. Dr. Frew Tegegne and Ato Seid Hussien, the two previous directors of ILA, were also instrumental in the completion of the study. I am grateful for their moral support and friendly concerns.

I wish to express my appreciation to the KTH staff at the Department of Real Estate Planning and Land Law and ILA's staff at Bahir Dar University for their friendship and encouragement during the study period.

I am indebted to Dr. Tesfaye Dangew of Bahir Dar University for reading and editing the material before its submission for review.

Finally, I wish to express my heartfelt gratitude to my beloved wife, Seni, and my children Nebiyu, Arsema, and Henock for their generous love and support throughout my study. I am also grateful to my father Weldegebriel Ambaye and my Mother Birhan G. Anania for their love and prayers.

Contents

Acronyms and Abbreviations

Addis Ababa	The Capital City of Ethiopia
ANRS	Amhara National Regional State
Asrat	Tithe, tax amounts to one-tenth of the total produce
Axum	Ancient city of Ethiopia from First BC
BoEPLAU	Bureau of Environmental Protection Land Administration and Use
CSA	Central Statistical Agency
FDRE	Federal Democratic Republic of Ethiopia
Gebir	Royal feast
Gibir	Tribute, land tax, usually paid in kind
Gonder	Ethiopian Capital during seventeenth–eighteenth centuries
GTP	Growth and Transformation Plan
Gult	Land right that gives right to administer, collect tax, and adjudicate cases
Kebele	Administrative sub-district
Rist	Land use rights, inheritable from family
RLAUP	Rural Land Administration and Use Proclamation
SNNPRS	Southern National Nationalities and Peoples' Regional State
Woreda	Administrative district

Chapter 1
Research Background and Methodology

1.1 Research Background

1.1.1 Introduction

The Federal Democratic Republic of Ethiopia (FDRE) is a country located in the horn of Africa, bordering with Eritrea in the north, Sudan and South Sudan in the west, Somalia and Kenya in the south and Somalia and Djibouti in the east. Ethiopia covers an area of 1.1 km^2 of land and is home to 73 million inhabitants.[1] Ethiopia is one of the oldest nations in the world tracing back its history 3,000 years back. Archeological and Paleontological evidences also show that Ethiopia is the cradle of mankind.[2] It had been ruled for over two millennia by the house of rulers of the Solomonic Dynasty, except for a few centuries when the Zagwe Dynasty was in power.[3] The last descendant of the Solomonic dynasty, Emperor Haile Sellassie (1930–1974), was ousted from power in 1974, following the Ethiopian Revolution and was replaced by a military junta called *Derg*. The Derg ruled the country for the next 17 years, a period in which famine and civil war were its hallmark. Unlike

---

[1] Ethiopian Central Statistical Agency (CSA), http://www.csa.gov.et.

[2] Henze, P. B. 2000. *Layers of Time: History of Ethiopia,* London, C. Hurst & Co Publishers Ltd., p. 1; See also many reports published in both the respected scientific journals "Nature" http://www.nature.com and "Science" http://www.sciencemeg.org about the many archeological and paleontological findings in Ethiopia dating back to 4 million years, the famous one being "Lucy", a 3.2 million years of hominid discovered in 1974 by Prof. Donald Johanson (Johanson, D. C. & Edey, M. A. 1981. *Lucy, The Beginning of Human kind,* New York, Simon & Schuster.).

[3] Legend claims that the Ethiopian Queen of Sheba crossed the Red Sea to visit King Solomon of Jerusalem and bore a child from him by the name Menelik I, the first line of Ethiopian Solomnic Dynasty (see translated from Geez Budge, E. A. W. 1922. *The Kibre Negest: The Glory of Kings,* London. A modern translation is available by Miguel F. Brooks, 1995, *Kibre Negest (The Glory of Kings),* The Red Sea Press, Asmara). The Solomnic Dynasty had ruled Ethiopia for many centuries, except the time between ninth and twelfth century when power was controlled by the Zagwe Dynasty.

D.W. Ambaye, *Land Rights and Expropriation in Ethiopia*,
Springer Theses, DOI 10.1007/978-3-319-14639-3_1

other African countries, Ethiopia has never been colonized except for the 5 year Italian occupation during the Second World War. For this reason, the Ethiopian traditional land tenure system that survived until 1975 was unique in that it was not shaped or influenced by outside forces.

In 1974, there was a revolution that resulted in the removal of the old regime and the nationalization of all land and means of production. After the assumption of power by the Derg, civil war that lasted for the following 17 years ensued. The Derg was overthrown from power in 1991 mainly by the present incumbent party, the Ethiopian People's Revolutionary Democratic Front (EPRDF). The new government converted the previous constitution of the Derg and adopted a new one in 1995.[4] Unlike its predecessors, the new constitution created a federal administrative arrangement in the country.

The Federal Democratic Republic of Ethiopia (FDRE) comprises of the Federal Government and the State members.[5] There are nine State members governed by their own State Councils[6] and two chartered cities, Addis Ababa and Dire Dawa, which are accountable to the Federal Government. The Federal Government and the States have parallel legislative, executive and judicial powers.[7] The powers and responsibilities of the Federal and State[8] Governments are provided in the Constitution.[9] Except for those powers exclusively vested with the Federal Government, Regional States have full power to decide on their internal administrative matters.

Land has been the source of economic, political and social prestige in Ethiopia. The emperors and the elite controlled land to perpetuate and maintain their power by controlling the land users. Private ownership of land has never been known in the country, except in the case of urban land for limited period in the past. The king was considered to be the owner of all land and natural resources, and through his grant, citizens could become beneficiaries of the land. The highest beneficiaries were members of the ruling feudal class, while large portion of the society remained tenant and with unsecured land rights.

In the twentieth century, the issue of land access and tenure security emerged as one important question in the country. The annexation of the southern part of the country by Emperor Menelik II, during the second half of nineteenth century, left thousands of people landless. With the modernization of the country in the second half of the century, issues of land were raised not only by the rural masses but also

---

[4] Constitution of the Federal Democratic Republic of Ethiopia, Proclamation No. 1/1995. *Negarit Gazeta.* Year 1 No.1. (hereinafter cited as FDRE Constitution).

[5] Article 50(1) of the FDRE Constitution.

[6] The Nine Regional States are Tigray, Afar, Amhara, Oromia, Somali, Beni Shangul Gumiz, Southern Nation, Nationalities and People (SNNP), Gambella, and Harari (47 of the FDRE constitution).

[7] Id., Article 50(2).

[8] In this work the word "State or States" means "Region or Regions" both of which signify the member administrative territories in a federal structure. Therefore throughout this research work both terminologies may be used interchangeably.

[9] See Articles 50–52 of the FDRE Constitution.

by the urban elite and students of various levels. The Haile Sellassie regime tried to make some land reforms and introduced constitutions and modern civil code, among other, to address the land issue, although without success. The 'Land To The Tiller' slogan that triggered the 1974 revolution ended with the demise of the feudalistic regime. To date, regimes that followed have not yet answered the land issue in a satisfactory manner.

Modern day Ethiopia is depicted as a country in rapid economic development where massive construction of roads, building of hydropower and irrigation dams, renewal and redevelopment of urban centers, expansion of cities, transfer of large-scale rural agricultural land to investors, zoning of industrial lands, etc. are being carried out. Millions of hectares of land have been taken from farmers and transferred to foreign and domestic agricultural investors. Thousands of blight houses that rested on hundreds of hectares of land in the city center of the capital, Addis Ababa, have been demolished to redevelop the areas. Thousands of farmers who used to live on the boarders of the many cities around the country have lost their land for the establishment of newly emerging towns or for the expansion of the existing ones.

Since the existing land policy forbids land transfer through sale, the only mechanism of land acquisition left for the state and private developers is the use of expropriation procedure. Expropriation is used as a tool to supply land that is required for all the economic activities mentioned above. The question to be addressed is whether the system allows adequate compensation to those who give way to social interest, by sacrificing their own.

1.1.2 Research Problem

Secured property rights have long been identified by the World Bank and other researchers as key elements to bring about higher levels of investment and access to credit, easy property transfer, and to maximize resource allocation.[10] Secure property rights rely on the durability of rights, clarity of rights, strength of rights, and the enforcement of such rights.[11] Durability of rights has to do with the lifetime of the property right such as fixed period or limitless one. Clarity refers to whether the land right is clearly known, demarcated and registered. Strength of rights means whether the property right provides stronger rights such as ownership or weaker ones like tenancy. Finally, the enforcement of rights refers to the institutional setup, such as the court system.

Like the political history, land law and land rights do also have a chaotic history in Ethiopia. Ethiopian history has been full of wars and violence that made the laws

---

[10] See generally Deininger, K. 2003. Land Policies for Growth and Poverty Reduction. *A World Bank Policy Research Report.* Oxford: World Bank and Oxford University Press.

[11] Ibid.

and rights unstable and insecure. Even today, land rights are dynamic and unpredictable because of the continuous change and revision of land laws. The level and depth of Ethiopian land rights and the changes and developments thereto witnessed since 1991 are not properly analyzed to determine the nature and status of land rights in current Ethiopia.

The FDRE Constitution provides that land and all natural resources are the properties of the state and the Ethiopian people.[12] The state is also duty bound "to hold, on behalf of the people, land and other natural resources and to deploy them for their common benefit and development."[13] The argument is that the Constitution provides the people equal ownership right on the land, with the state. Even if the state is represented to hold land on behalf of the people, it must ensure its use and distribution to the best interest of the people. The issue is whether the present land rights, as enshrined in the urban and rural land laws, reflect the common ownership right of land of the people. This can only be answered positively if the land laws create and maintain equity to accessing land.

One of the sound arguments in favor of state ownership of land in contemporary Ethiopia is that it is of little significance as to who really owns the land; instead, greater precautionary weight is attached to whether there are enough rules and regulations in place which provide guarantees and security to the holders of the land. Inadequate land securities tend to discourage holders of land from making additional investments on their land.[14] It is important, therefore, to prove or disprove the merit of this argument by showing the security/protection accorded to such rights and the extent of freedom to exercise them.

The Ethiopian Constitution and other federal and regional land legislations provide rural land right without time limit. Urban land holders as well get the land for a fixed period of time on lease basis. The laws also provide a compensation scheme for those who lose their land for public interest. The FDRE Constitution, in particular, provides that a "commensurate" amount of compensation should be paid during expropriation. By determining the land rights (level of land rights, equity and liberty in land use) and using them as a background, this study will raise and endeavor to proffer answers to the following problems which surface in the present expropriation scheme.

The main problem in the present legal framework is whether the amount of compensation paid in the event of expropriation reflects the joint ownership of land by state and the people. This main research problem will be systematically discussed from five different thematic angles:

The first theme addresses problems related to the method and procedure of land acquisition by expropriation. Expropriation is a forced taking of private property, but justice demands that certain procedures, such as public discussion, provision of notice before eviction, prior payment of compensation, the right to negotiate on the

[12] Article 40(3) of FDRE Constitution. This shall be investigated in detail in Chap. 2.

[13] Id., Article 89(5).

[14] See generally Deininger, supra note 10.

amount of compensation, the manner of eviction, and the right to appeal in the event of dissatisfaction with the compensation or any other violation of substantive or procedural rights should be followed. There are also cases of non-payment of compensation or delays and protracted procedures for payment.

The second theme is concerned with the issue of public purpose. The term may also be understood as public use or public interest. The usual contentious issue is the extent of state power in expropriating land in the interest of society. This power hinges on two fundamental principles of sanctity of private property and the public interest. The Ethiopian law seems to give the government unlimited and ambiguous power that it can use, and this power has to be delimited through analysis of the laws since arbitrary and unlimited state power is a source of insecurity.

The third theme covers problems related to the absence and lack of scientific and uniform standards of valuation methods in the country. This leads to applying of different valuation methods and compensation procedures in different regions of the country. The argument is that the lack of using standardized methods and procedures results in unfair valuation and compensation regimes whereby the equal rights of landholders, provided under Federal and State constitutions, may be infringed upon.

The fourth theme relates to the fairness of the amount of compensation. The Constitution provides for payment of a "commensurate" amount of compensation in the event of loss of property by expropriation. Fair or just compensation can be attained through payment of "fair market price."[15] In consequence, just compensation has also occasionally been defined as "the fair market value of the property as of the date of the taking, determined by what a willing buyer and a willing seller would agree to, neither being under any compulsion to act."[16]

Generally, there are three primary valuation methodologies for arriving at the fair market value of real property taken by way of expropriation: the comparable sales method, the income capitalization method, and the replacement cost method. The first two are widely used to assess the market value of real property, while the third one is applied in rare occasions, where the property has a unique character. In Ethiopia, the third method is applied to value real property. The problem, therefore, revolves around the use of this method which is believed to be a defective means to assess market value of the property, since it pays only the cost of replacing the lost property, without particularly considering the location value.

The fifth theme focuses on areas of concern which need to be addressed by laws. These are problems which are not addressed by the current expropriation legislations. For example, the law does not compensate for loss of profit occasioned through public works such as roads, dams, etc. The entire city of Addis Ababa and a handful of other major cities have, for example, been undergoing massive infrastructure development works including roads, underground cables, bridges, and

---

[15] Kitay, infra note 14 in Chap. 3, p. 50.

[16] Ibid.

water and sewage systems, resulting in the closure of businesses situated in the vicinity of the construction without any compensatory scheme.

Further, the laws do not address the post expropriation scenario. In other words, lack of comprehensive resettlement and rehabilitation programs have left displaced farmers unaided and untended. Problems arise due to the lump payment of compensation to those who have lost their land. Onetime payment does not create a sustainable form of compensation, because the sum is often squandered by farmers with little experience in handling cash capital. In other words, money in the hands of farmers who have no idea of investment would be easily squandered away.

1.1.3 Purpose and Research Questions

One of the methods to ensure tenure security is to pay adequate compensation in the event of expropriation. Expropriation remains the main source of tenure insecurity in Ethiopia. This is attributed to the incomplete and faulty laws and legally incompatible practices. In this study, an investigation is made to determine whether the amount of compensation which is being paid is adequate as compared to the land rights one is entitled to by law. Peasant farmers have, for example, lifetime right to the land that includes use, lease, donation and inheritance. They are like owners, except that they lack the sole right of sale. Urban residents acquire land on 99 or less years lease agreement. The lease right can be freely transferable and lessees can reap the profit during sale of the lease right, except some situations. The people get this right because they are the joint owners of the land together with the government. The general objective of the thesis is, therefore, to analyze and describe the land rights and expropriation laws in Ethiopia and compare them with the practice in order to determine the fairness of compensation.

The general and overall research question to be addressed here is: are land laws in general, and expropriation laws in particular, faithfully practiced such that people get just compensation?

More specifically, the study is designed to address the following specific objectives:

- To review and analyze the current land rights, as envisaged in the FDRE Constitution and other land related proclamations, and determine the equity in land access and the liberty in land rights;
- To assess whether the expropriation procedures are strictly practiced by public officials and courts;
- To determine whether the amount of compensation paid during expropriation is fair or not;
- To assess and give general recommendation on the best parameters and tools to establish a standard valuation system which is now lacking in Ethiopia;
- To make recommendations on what improvements need to be made and how solutions can be effected to rectify them.

To accomplish these specific objectives, the following specific research questions are formulated:

- What are the rights and limitations associated to land in Ethiopia?
- Do the urban and rural land rights envisaged in the rural and urban land proclamations reflect the constitutionally sanctioned joint ownership of land of the people?
- What are the gaps and ambiguities in the current land laws in general and Expropriation Proclamation in particular?
- Are there differences in the laws and practices concerning expropriation, valuation and compensation?
- What is public purpose and to what extent does it allow the state to exercise it in Ethiopia?
- Who has the ability to carry out valuation of properties in Ethiopia? And what are to be considered for valuation?
- Is the amount of compensation paid in Ethiopia fair? What are the reasons attributed for unfair compensation?

1.1.4 Significance of the Research

The Ethiopian jurisprudence and legal research is at its infancy, especially when it comes to land law in general and expropriation in particular. Land law was given an obscure place in the Civil Code, which was effective for 15 years before the eruption of the Ethiopian Revolution, and was consequently suspended. The Derg had passed its own rural and urban land laws and nationalized all land in the country which in effect rendered the expropriation rules completely ineffective. Following the assumption of power by the Derg, civil war broke out and continued for the next 17 years. For this reason, expropriation procedure had not been utilized fully as development endeavors were hardly made in those years.

Recently, the government passed more laws on land and specifically on expropriation. The laws are usually passed hastily and without much public deliberation, partly because of lack of legal experts in the area. On top of that, land law is not a mandatory course in the Ethiopian legal education, and it is not difficult to observe that law trained judges and researchers are not comfortable in dealing with the subject. For this reason, it can be said that there is no serious research work made in recent years on issues related to land and expropriation laws and practices. On the contrary, there is a huge outcry about urban land inaccessibility, inadequacy of compensation, and eviction without compensation and so on.

This research work is, therefore, hoped to be an eye opener for future researchers and students. This research is limited in terms of empirical study of area coverage, and there is no doubt that future development works will come up with their own issues and problems worth investigating. Further, it is hoped that government officials and responsible organs would find the findings of this study worth looking and would initiate revision and amendments of rural and urban land laws as well as expropriation laws and procedures. As mentioned earlier, land law is currently very dynamic in Ethiopia, for we see new land laws being adopted and old ones being amended.

1.2 Research Methodology

A combination of two research methodologies, namely, case study and qualitative legal research are employed in this doctoral study. While the qualitative legal research analyses the law and determines its nature and thereby helps one to understand the property right and expropriation procedure as they stand today, the case study method aims at investigating the existing practices on the ground and thereby identifying the conflict between laws and practices and the general implications of the laws. This section briefly describes both methodologies and shows how and to what extent both of them are employed in this dissertation.

1.2.1 Case Study

1.2.1.1 Case Study-What

Case study as a methodology involves a systematic gathering of enough information about a particular person, social setting, event, or group to permit the researcher to effectively understand how it operates or functions.[17] Case study focuses on one (or just few) instances of a particular phenomenon with a view to providing an in-depth account of events, relationships, experiences or processes occurring in that particular instance.[18] As Stake observes, case study research is concerned with the complexity and particular nature of the case in question.[19] The use of case studies has become extremely widespread in social science research. Case studies are also commonly used in business and law curricula to help students bridging the gap between foundational studies and practice.[20] The idea of case study is that it focuses on one instance, although researchers may use more than one instance. So, as opposed to mass study that uses survey strategy, case study confines to selected

[17] Berg, B. L. 2001. *Qualitative Research Methods for the Social Science* London, Allyn and Bacon, p. 225.

[18] Denscombe, M. 2007. *The Good Research Guide,* Open University Press, New York, p. 35.

[19] Stake, R. E. 1995. *The Art of Case Study Research* Thousand Oaks, California, Saga Publication. As quoted in Bryman and Bell, infra note 21, p. 53.

[20] Berg, supra note 17, p. 225.

situations. Case study is not actually a data-gathering technique, but a methodological approach that incorporates a number of data-gathering measures.

One advantage of case study is that it investigates the case in sufficient detail and can unravel things which otherwise might not be discovered by survey study. The case study also focuses on the relationships of different parts of the case and the processes it passes through. In this respect, case study approach tends to be *holistic rather than deal with isolated factors*.[21]

The other strength of the case study approach is that it allows the researcher to use a variety of sources, a variety of types of data and research method as part of the investigation.[22] This means case study approach enables the researcher to use multiple data collection mechanisms. While investigating a given instance, the researcher may use personal observation, questionnaire, interview, group discussion, study of documents and the like. As suggested by Bryan and Bell, the case study provides a vehicle through which several qualitative methods can be combined, thereby avoiding too much reliance on one single approach.[23] This does not mean, however, quantitative data is not considered in case study approach. The use of variety of methods in case studies facilitates the validation of data through triangulation, which enables to look things from more than one perspective The principle behind this is that the researcher can get a better understanding of the thing that is being investigated. It also avoids bias and error of data.[24]

In a case study approach, a researcher needs to choose one or few instances from among many events, people or organizations. This means the choice must be made deliberately and with a justification.[25] Therefore, case studies are not just selected randomly but on the bases of some known attributes. And this warrants an explanation or justification for the choice made by the researcher.

One criticism against the case study approach is related to its representativeness. People may criticize the credibility of its generalizations, whether it is possible to generalize based on the findings of one or few cases. Another possible ground for criticism is that case study focuses on processes and relations rather than measurable end products, based on quantitative data.

Although there is some truth in the above criticisms, they can be minimized or averted through a proper selection of cases. Berg suggests that a properly selected case may be representative enough to other similar cases:

> When case studies are properly undertaken, they should not only fit the specific individual, group, or event studied, but generally provide understanding about similar individuals, groups, and events. This is not to say that an explanation for why one gang member is involved in drug dealing immediately informs us about why all drug-dealing gang members

---

[21] Denscombe, supra note 18, p. 36.

[22] Ibid.

[23] Bryman, A. & Bell, E. 2003. *Business Research Methods,* Oxford, Oxford University Press, p. 53.

[24] Berg, supra note 17, p. 5.

[25] Denscombe, supra note 18, p. 43.

> are also involved in this activity. It does, however, suggest an explanation for why some other gang members are likely to be involved in these behaviors. The logic behind this has to do with the fact that few human behaviors are unique, idiosyncratic, and spontaneous. In fact, if this were the case, the attempt to undertake any type of survey research on an aggregate group would be useless. In short, if we accept the notion that human behavior is predictable—a necessary assumption for all behavior science research—then it is a simple jump to accept that case studies have scientific value.[26]

The researcher is needed to stress the extent to which the particular example being investigated is unusual, and thus emphasize the limits to how far the findings should be generalized to others in the class. The two crucial tasks for the case study researcher are outlined by Denscombe as follows[27]:

a. To identify significant features on which comparison with others in the class can be made; and
b. To show how the case study compares with others in the class in terms of these significant features.

1.2.1.2 Case Study-Why and How

A case study is preferred compared to other methodologies because, on the one hand, it is believed that it enables one to collect different types of data at a time from one place, and on the other, it avoids redundancy of data collected from different places. Since one focus of this study is to investigate the compatibility of laws and practices, and since the practical procedures are known and specific, a study in one place was thought to be representative enough. The differences in the laws and practices are covered by employing different case scenarios, like urban land expropriation and rural land expropriation. Yet, this does not mean that the findings would be taken as perfectly conclusive to reflect the realities in all of the country. This, in other words, warrants the need for further studies in other places of the country. In the following sections, brief descriptions of the areas and cases are provided so that the reader can recall them whenever they are mentioned in the chapters that follow.

1.2.1.3 Data Collection Method

Documenting land rights and the comparison of the expropriation laws and practices is the main task of this research work. Therefore, to fully appreciate the practice of expropriation process and its implication in Ethiopia, qualitative data was collected from selected case study areas as fully described in Sect. 1.2.1.4.

---

[26] Berg, supra note 17, p. 232.

[27] Denscombe, supra note 18, p. 43.

In these studies, it was possible to employ multiple data collection methods such as interviews, personal observations, group discussions and document investigations. The data collected generally deal with the practical application and procedures of expropriation, such as notice, public discussion, inventory, valuation systems, payment of compensation, and the use of money thereafter. Triangulation method was applied to check the accuracy of data, which were collected through interview and group discussion of affected people, by interviewing experts and officials who were responsible for the expropriation, valuation and compensation. Archival and project documents and personal observations were also employed to refine and fully understand the practice on the ground.

1.2.1.4 Descriptions of Case Study Areas

This research uses data collected in various ways mainly from three regions in Ethiopia. The first one is Addis Ababa City, where wide expropriation practices are being carried out. At no time in its history has the city witnessed such a massive redevelopment and construction work as today. Addis Ababa city can adequately represent the expropriation practices of urban land. The second region is the Amhara region, which has ample expropriation cases of urban and rural scenarios. I especially focus on the expropriation practice of the rural land in this region. A third region employed in this research is the Oromia region, which is the largest region in the country. This region is included in the study, because of its peculiar cases and because of its incomplete laws, as shall be discussed in detail in this research. This section will provide only brief description of the cases to acquaint them with the reader. Detailed analysis and examples based on these cases shall be provided in different parts of this dissertation (Figs. 1.1, 1.2 and 1.3) (Chaps. 4, 5 and 6).

a. Addis Ababa

Addis Ababa, the capital city of Ethiopia, was established by Emperor Menelik II in 1886. Addis Ababa is also the diplomatic centre of Africa which hosts 30 % of the urban population and is one of the fastest growing cities on the continent. Based on the 2007 population and housing census, the 2012 projected population figure of the city is 3.04 million.[28] The city has been expanded from 22,360 ha in 1984 to 54,000 in 2010. Currently it is divided into 10 sub-cities (alternatively see map).[29] The land in the city is classified into three zones according to its proximity to the center: namely, central market zone, transitional zone, and expansion zone. Of the total land area, about 14,765 ha is slum area destined for redevelopment.[30]

---

[28] http://www.csa.gov.et/index.php?option=com_rubberdoc&view=doc&id=421&format=raw&Itemid=606.

[29] Arada, Kirkos, Gulele, Lideta, Bole, Yeka, Nefas Silk Lafto, Addis Ketema, Kolfe Keranio, and Akaki Kality.

[30] Interview with Ato Adem Nuri, head of valuation and compensation section at the Addis Ababa City Land Bank and Urban Renewal Project Office.

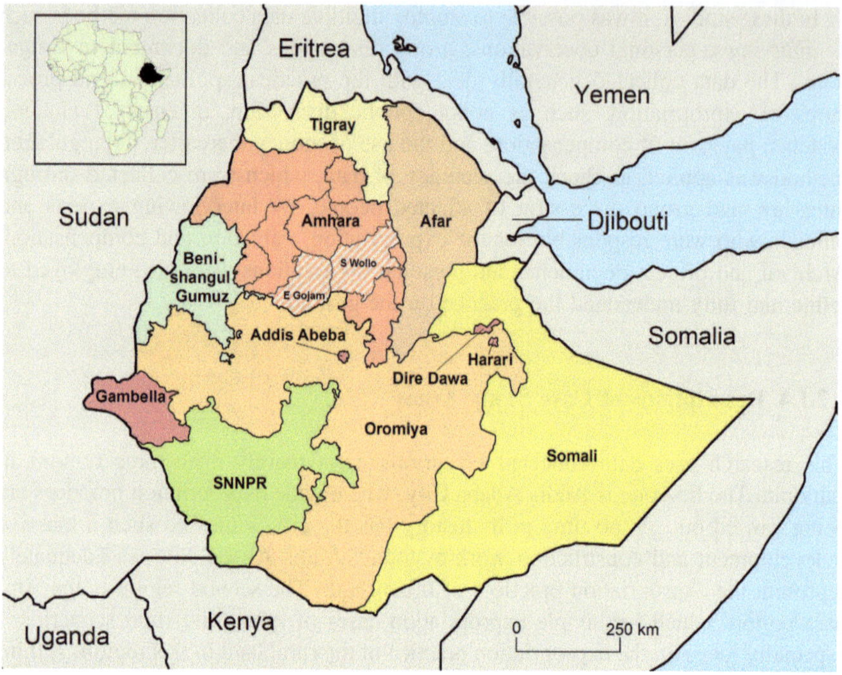

Fig. 1.1 Ethiopian regional map

The main reasons for land expropriation in the city are urban renewal/redevelopment, construction of condominium housing, and road construction. Land that is significantly subjected to expropriation is located in the center and the expansion zones of the city. Land expropriated in the city center is used for urban renewal, road and railway construction, private investment, construction of government offices and the like. Land expropriation in the expansion zone (the periphery) is used mainly for housing (condominium, private, and real estate) and investment (industry). Private housing includes land replacements for those who are relocated from the city center by expropriation. In the transition zone, found in between the center and the expansion, the rate of land expropriation is lower, and if any, it is used for roads and private investments, such as hotels.

Urban renewal and upgrading activities are being done in the slum areas of the city center, such as Arada, Kirkos, Lideta and Addis Ketema sub-cities. Most of the houses in these areas belonged to the government since they were nationalized by the Derg in 1975. Yet, there were significant number of private houses in the middle of them as well.

The area selected for case study in Addis Ababa is the "Basha Wolde Chilot" in Arada sub-city. The Arada sub-city is one of the most blight areas which has been highly affected by expropriation and urban redevelopment processes. The Basha Wolde Chilot, literally translated as the "Court of Basha Wolde", is found within

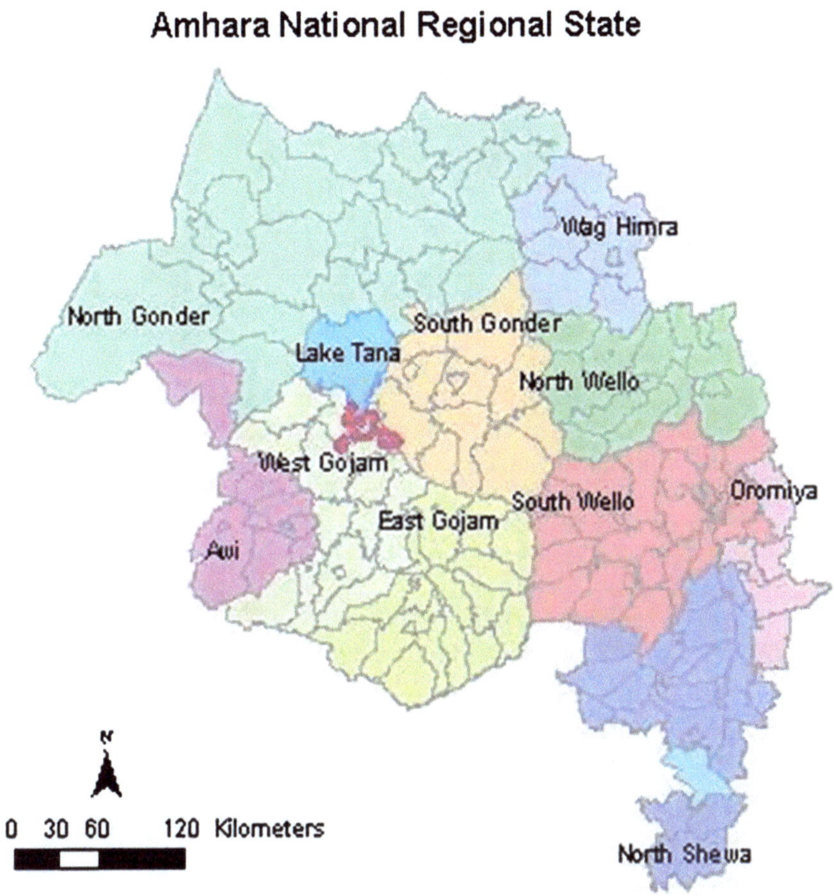

Fig. 1.2 The map of Amhara National Regional State

the heart of the Arada sub-city. This area was built in the late nineteenth and early twentieth century, during the reign of emperor Menelik II, which means during the establishment of the city itself. Almost all the houses were slums made of mud and wood, without proper toilet and sewerage systems. Paradoxically, the front side of the Menelik Palace, which houses the prime minister, and the most prestigious Sheraton Hotel, have been surrounded by slum and low esteemed houses.

In this area as well, most houses were government owned although there were many private houses in the middle of them. Land accumulated by expropriating and demolishing the area is used basically for two things: the upfront is transferred by lease to private developers and business entities and the other part is used for condominium housing constructions.

Arada sub-city and especially Basha-Wold Chilot was selected as a case study for different reasons. The first reason is convenience. The study area is found at the

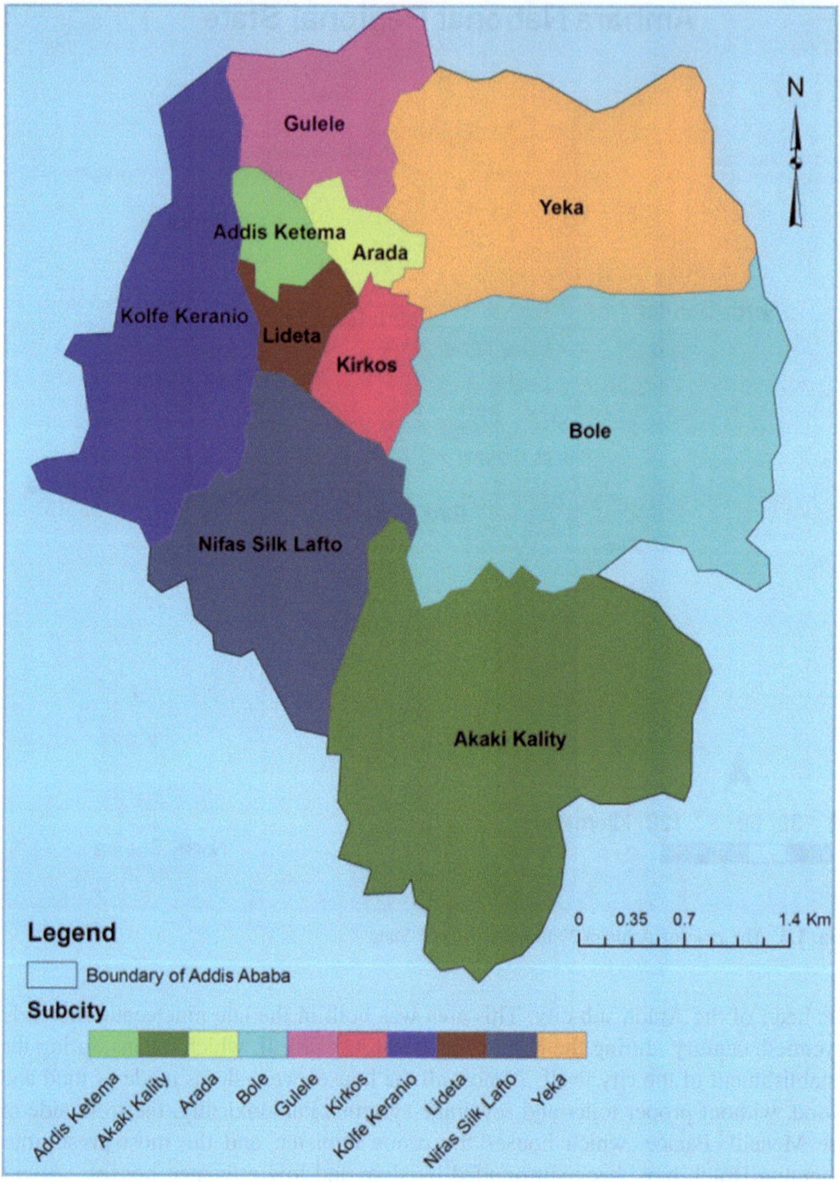

Fig. 1.3 The map of Addis Ababa City

heart of the city and is easily accessible to public transport and other offices such as the municipality and the city's office for land bank. City officials who work at the municipality and the office of the city's land bank were important subjects for the study not only because they were willing to be interviewed, but also for putting centrally collected data at the researcher's disposal. Another reason for selecting Arada sub-city was because the sub-city has been involved in the expropriation of large sector of the city's land, and hence it was believed that the built up experience would be beneficial to the researcher. A third reason is that it is believed that the Arada's practice would be a typical one. This means the case of Basha-Wolde Chilot is similar in many respects with other areas which could have been included in the study. This is because the expropriation process is carried out based on the same law and most probably the practice would also be similar. For this reason, Basha-Wolde Chilot could be taken to be a representative of other similar expropriation actions within the city. The only shortcoming of this case is that it does not represent the expropriation of farmlands, since it is located in the city center. This is covered by selecting another case in the expansion zone.

The researcher held group discussions with the affected people to learn all the processes they had been passing through. The discussion also aimed at understanding their feelings with regard to the adequacy of the amount of compensation they received. The discussion was held in two groups: the first group included subjects who were freshly receiving compensation, and not condominiums or replacement lands; and the second group comprised those who have been displaced earlier and had received compensation and replacement land. In addition, senior and junior valuation experts in Arada sub-city and Yeka sub-city, which is the host kebele for the displaced people from Arada, were interviewed. Senior land-bank and land-development experts and officials were also approached to learn about the general plan, problems and developments in the city's undertakings. The researcher was also allowed to review the documents containing the valuation figures.

b. Amhara Region

The Amhara National Regional State (ANRS) is the third biggest region in Ethiopia and covers a total land area of 170,152 km^2. In terms of population, the region is home to 17.2 million inhabitants. About 89 % of the region's people are rural farmers who are principally engaged in small-scale subsistence farming activities, while the remaining 11 % are urban dwellers engaged mainly in industry and services sectors. There are about 3.6 million rural properties in the Amhara Region employing more than 89 % of the region's population. Three cases are considered from this region as described below.

Rib Irrigation Dam Project

The Rib Irrigation Dam Project is found in South Gondar Zone, Ebinat and Farta *woredas*, Amhara Regional State. The dam is being constructed on the Rib River, one of the tributaries of the Blue Nile River. The World Bank financed 100 million USD for the project, as part of the Nile Initiative Program. The Ethiopian government has allocated 10 million USD for the irrigation projects on top of the 100 million dollars soft loan extended by the Bank. The Rib dam will have a capacity to hold 234 million m^3 of water. Upon going fully operational, the dam will develop

14,000 ha of land and benefit more than 28,000 households. The government believes that introducing the irrigation system creates permanent food security, helps soil conservation and increases food production. The Rib project which displaces 463 households, having a total of 1,672 family members, needs 306 ha of land. All the land under expropriation was used for crop production, tree plantation and grazing common lands.[31]

I visited the dam area in November 2012 and interviewed 45 people who lost their land for the construction of the dam site. It was not possible to involve other people in the interview, because they were not yet displaced from their land. However, they would be moved soon since their land is needed for the reservoir, drainage and other similar construction purposes. In any case, since the basic expropriation and valuation procedure was one and the same, it was believed that the 45 sample interviewees were representative enough. I have also looked into the valuation of properties of all the affected farmers, moved or not moved, which is based on the same rule. Besides, detailed discussion in the form of interview was held with the senior valuation expert of the Amhara Region who is in charge of all the expropriation, valuation and compensation tasks.

Bahir Dar

Bahir Dar city is the capital of the Amhara National Regional State (ANRS) inhabiting about 230,000 people, and is located on the southern shore of Lake Tana, the largest lake in Ethiopia. The Blue Nile (*Abay*-as called in Ethiopia) starts to flow from Lake Tana. The expansion of Bahir Dar city highly relied on the expropriation of land from the nearby rural farmers. Equally, the city has also been expropriating slums within the city and carrying out urban redevelopment and renewal programs. The case study chosen from Bahir Dar is the *Abay*-River-bank neighborhood case.

In 2011, the city administration haphazardly removed 54 households who had settled on the eastern side of the city along the *Abay* River and relocated them to the outskirt of the city. The land was needed for the construction of the office of the governor, the regional council and a modern conference hall. The people in this area were poor and lived in small and deteriorated houses. Most of the women in this neighborhood had been earning their income from small, home based, businesses such as selling *Tella*, a traditional beer. The other source of income for the women was the processing of lentil, bean and peas for the local grain stores. I have managed to conduct group discussion with randomly selected men and women heads of families and community leaders of the area, between January and February 2013. Moreover, a group discussion with three valuation experts at the Bahir Dar City municipality was held to get insight into the procedures followed. Further, municipal judges were also asked about the process so as to understand their version.

---

[31] Beza-Consulting 2011. Ethiopian Nile Irrigation and Drainage Project. Ministry of Water Resources. Available: http://www-wds.worldbank.org/external/default/WDSContentServer/WDSP/IB/2011/04/13/000333037_20110413030830/Rendered/PDF/RP11310V30AFR1110Same0info0as0RP526.pdf.

Road Construction Cases

The Ethiopian government has adopted a 5 years (2010/11–2014/15) Growth and Transformation Plan (GTP), which among others includes, the construction of 71,000 km rural roads all over Ethiopia.[32] The 5 years' plan of the Amhara region in this regard is to build 18,000 km of rural gravel roads having 4–10 m width. This program is known as Universal Rural Roads Access Program (URRAP). The construction of the roads also needs additional land for ditches and shoulders which extends the required land to 30 m in width. In the year 2011/12 only, the authority built 2,280 km of rural gravel roads across the region.[33] The basic characteristic of rural roads construction in the Amhara region is that compensation is not paid for the land taken from farmers.

To investigate the practice in this sector, three woredas from the region were selected. The three road projects are found in Qunzila (28 km), Fagita (19 km), and Denbecha (31 km) woredas. These cases were proposed for the study by experts from the Regional Rural Roads Authority since they were about to be completed and involved the acquisition of large size of land.

I have visited part of the roads construction and able to hold group discussion with affected farmers. Besides, responsible officials of the Rural Roads Authority and the woreda administration heads of the three woredas were interviewed in different dates between September and December 2012. The gist of the interview was, as shall be discussed in detail, to get an idea as to why the government refused compensation for the land expropriated for the roads construction.

c. Oromia Region: Tulu Kapi Case

The Oromia National Regional State is the largest region in Ethiopia in terms of population size and area coverage. It is rich in natural resource and coffee production. I was interested in one peculiar case in this region. The case involves a mining project found in the West Wellega Zone of the Oromia Region. This mining project is known by its local name, Tulu Kapi Gold Mining Project. The Tulu Kapi Gold mining project belongs to Nyota Gold Mining with its headquarter in London.

The Tulu Kapi Gold Mining project rests on 11.3 ha of land and has affected 485 heads of family. All the farmers were engaged in both crop production and coffee plantation. Because of the toxic nature of the project, every person would be relocated and every house and religious site should be demolished. Unlike other public or private investments, this gold mining project has a World Bank's stake in the business. The World Bank, through its private sector arm (IFC) involves in private projects that are considered by the Bank as robust ones. The Bank's involvement creates additional obligation on the company concerning, among others, compensation and resettlement programs during land acquisition. Therefore, Nyota was considering additional packages of compensations and resettlement

---

32 See MOFED, GTP, infra 66 in Chap. 5, p. 33.

33 Interview with Ato Akane, head (represented) of the URRAP of the Amhara National Regional State, January 2013, Bahir Dar.

programs in addition to what is stated in the Ethiopian expropriation and compensation legislations.

As shall be seen in due course, this same rule was also followed by another international mining company in the Afar region in Ethiopia. This company which is known as Allana Potash is interested in the extraction and export of potash and again the World Bank has a stake in it. Allana Potash is a Canadian Mining company, which is currently about to start the extraction of potash from the Dallol area of the Afar Regional State in Ethiopia.

I visited the Tulu Kapi area during September 24–27 of 2012. During this time, there was a workshop taking place in Nekemt, the capital of West Wolega Zone, in which the mining company, regional, zonal, and woreda land administration offices, zonal and woreda administrations, the Ministry of Mining, judges and other stakeholders participated. Most of the data concerning the project was collected during this time. But additional interview was also held with woreda administrators and the region's senior valuator. Besides, the researcher was given further information from the company concerning its obligations under the IFC land acquisition and resettlement rules.[34]

1.2.2 Legal Research Method

A legal research may be either doctrinal or non doctrinal. Doctrinal research is also known as legal dogmatic in the continental legal system. Doctrinal or legal dogmatic research can be defined in simple terms as research which asks what the law is in a particular area.[35] Legal dogmatic research concerns with researching current positive law as laid down in written and unwritten (inter)national rules, principles, concepts, doctrines, case law and annotations in the literature.[36] Its sources are predominantly those that are "thrown up by the legal process: principally statutes and decided cases, supplemented where possible with lawyers' literature expounding the rule and occasionally reflecting on them."[37] This current positive law needs to be "treated" within its own limits—often described from an internal perspective—meaning that its own sources are used as a basis for study, description, explanation and analysis into (conflicting) underlying values, presuppositions and principles, as well as for criticism and any needed proposals for improvement.[38]

---

[34] IFC, infra note 37 in Chap. 4.

[35] Dobinson, I. & Johns, F. 2007. Qualitative Legal Research. *In:* McConville, M. & Chui, W. H. (eds.) *Research Methods for Law*. Edinburgh: Edinburgh University Press, p. 18.

[36] Vranken, J. 2012. Exciting Times for Legal Scholarship. www.bjutijddschriften.nl/tijdschrift/rem/2012/2/ReM_2212_002_002_004.pdf, p. 43.

[37] McCrudden, C. 2006. Legal Research and the Social Sciences. *Law Quarterly Review*, 632–650, p. 634.

[38] Ibid.

All this primarily serves judicial practice, although proposals for improvement are also addressed to legislators or policy-makers.

Non doctrinal legal research includes those researches which are based on problem, policy or law reform.[39] Problem, policy and law reform research often includes a consideration of the social factors involved and/or the social impact of current law and practice. In this regard, the type of research done is descriptive or evaluative and its main task is to provide a recommendation for legal or policy reform or an amendment of the existing laws and procedures. The type of research done might include surveys and interviews with various individuals and groups affected. Such research is often referred to as socio-legal research.

These broad categories of legal research, which are grouped into doctrinal legal research and non-doctrinal legal research, obviously are not mutually exclusive. They overlap each other. In fact, all four categories of research, doctrinal, problem, policy and law reform could be part of a large scale research project. A researcher, for example, could begin by determining the existing law in a particular area (doctrinal). This may then be followed by a consideration of the problems currently affecting the law and the policy underpinning the existing law, highlighting, for example, the flaws in such policy. This in turn may lead the researcher to propose changes to the law (law reform).

While the doctrinal component of the above example could be seen as non-empirical, the assessment of the problem, evaluation of the policy and the need for law reform would require an empirical approach which could be quantitative, qualitative or a combination of the two.[40]

While legal sources can be accessed to determine what the law is, in terms of case law and legislation, the application of the law is contentious. Indeed, this may be the very reason for why the research was undertaken in the first place. The Ethiopian land law is exposed to problems of legal ambiguity, inconsistency and legal gaps. Further, there are inconsistencies between law and practice. But determining the nature of the law and its proper application only does not solve the kind of problem raised in this research. Therefore, this research includes also non-doctrinal research methods in that it does not only analyze and determine what the law is, but also tries to look into the implication and implementation of the law. The implementation of the law definitely affects society in some way, and when the effect is damaging and undesirable, a law reform is necessary.

As far as legal matters are concerned, this research mainly focuses on the analysis of the Federal Constitution and federal and regional land laws with particular emphasis on property rights and expropriation procedures.

Concerning theoretical issues, different books, journals, and articles focusing on historical and present land tenure and property rights in Ethiopia have been consulted. The concept and nature of expropriation, valuation and compensation as understood internationally has been reviewed by making references to relevant

---

39 Dobinson and Johns, supra note 35, p. 19.

40 Id., p. 20.

books and journals. Ethiopian sources are relatively better available on the historical part of Ethiopian land tenure system. Unfortunately, there is scant information or written material on the expropriation aspect. For this reason, there has been heavy dependence on western sources, books and journals, to establish and justify its nature.

Furthermore, government land policies and strategies were considered in a bid to evaluate their merits and their rationales. Key among those are the current agriculture and rural land policy and the existing urban land and housing policy of the Federal Government.

1.2.3 Descriptions of the Judiciary, Sources and Hierarchy of Laws

This section describes the Ethiopian laws employed in this work. It is important to understand the hierarchy of the laws in order to avoid confusion of laws, enacted by different organs of the Federal and State Governments.

1.2.3.1 Hierarchy of Laws

A hierarchy of laws refers to the ranking of laws on predominance basis. Primary laws have primacy and prevalence over subsidiary laws. In Ethiopia, the FDRE Constitution is the supreme law of the land. It has primacy over all Federal as well as State laws. Article 9(1) of the FDRE Constitution proclaims that any law, customary practice, or a decision of an organ of state or public official, which contravenes the Constitution, shall be of no effect. At the federal level, international agreements and proclamations have the same status as they are issued by the Federal legislature. These are followed by Regulations and Directives respectively. The same order applies to State laws.

The hierarchical order of the laws depends on the seniority of the law makers. For example, the Constitution is believed to be an expression of the will of the people, who are the sovereign power holders in Ethiopia (Article 8), and hence, the Constitution is considered as the supreme law of the land (Article 9.1). The people are represented in the government functionary through their representatives at the House of Peoples' Representatives (HPR) or the parliament (Article 54), which holds the second most important power in the nation.[41] Therefore, a *proclamation,* enacted by the parliament, becomes second in the hierarchy of laws next to the

[41] See for example, Article 50(3) of the FDRE Constitution which declares, "The House of Peoples' Representatives is the highest authority of the Federal Government. The House is responsible to the People. The State Council is the highest organ of State authority. It is responsible to the People of the State."

Constitution. International treaties have binding effect only after they are approved by parliament; thus, they are equal in status with proclamations.

Laws are also enacted by the executive branch of the government through delegated legislative power given by the HPR. The central body of the executive branch is the Council of Ministers, chaired by the Prime Minister. The Council of Ministers is responsible to the HPR which means that its power is secondary to the parliament. The law enacted by the Council of Ministers is known as *Regulation* and its usual purpose is to outline detailed rules to implement the proclamation passed by the parliament.

The fourth order of laws at the federal level are enacted by an individual ministry or agency with further detailed rules to implement the proclamation and regulation adopted by the parliament and the Council of Ministers respectively. This type of law is known as *Directive.*

When one looks into the nature of State (regional) laws in relation to the Federal laws, the FDRE Constitution still holds its supremacy over both laws. The power of the Federal Government and that of the States is clearly envisaged in the FDRE Constitution. Article 51 of the FDRE Constitution lists down the areas in which the Federal Government may enact laws. Under Article 52, States are given residual power that they can exercise. This means all areas of governance which are not exclusively vested with the Federal Government will be State powers.

With regard to land and natural resources, the power to enact laws on the utilization and conservation of land and natural resources and other historical sites and objects is provided to the Federal Government.[42] Yet, regional States are entrusted with the power to "administer land and other natural resources in accordance with Federal laws."[43] This means, concerning land, both the Federal Government and States have stakes and roles to play. The Federal legislator enacts a proclamation concerning land, and States followed by enacting their respective State proclamations, regulations and directives to effectively implement the Federal proclamation. However, in areas where regional states are considered as having exclusive power, they can enact laws without a need to refer to the laws of the Federal Government.

1.2.3.2 Sources of Law

It is important to give highlight about the type and nature of Ethiopian laws which are used in this dissertation. Accordingly, these relevant laws are briefly discussed below.

a. Constitutions

Ethiopia has witnessed four constitutions in its history. The first constitution was adopted in 1931 in the image of the Japan's Meiji Imperial Constitution. Then, this constitution was revised and adopted in 1955.[44] After the demise of the imperial

---

[42] Article 51(5) of the FDRE Constitution.

[43] Article 52(2)(d) of the FDRE Constitution.

[44] The Revised Constitution of the Empire of Ethiopia. Negarit Gazetta, 1955.

regime, the Derg passed the long awaited constitution of the People's Democratic Republic of Ethiopia (PDRE) in 1988.[45] Following the removal of the Derg from power in 1991, the current government adopted another constitution in 1995, which operates today. The first three constitutions are used in this dissertation to highlight the history of land rights and the expropriation practice in Ethiopia, while the current FDRE Constitution is used as a base of the discussion.

b. Proclamations

Different proclamations, starting from the imperial period (as early as the late 19th century), are examined in this dissertation. All are related to land in terms of land taxation, land entitlement, land distribution, and land expropriation. But the discussion is usually brief since the purpose is to trace the genesis of the property rights and expropriation. The main focus is made on the current Federal Rural Land Administration and Use Proclamation (FDRE RLAUP)[46] and regional Rural Land Administration and Use Proclamations (RLAUP) as well as the Federal Expropriation Proclamation.[47] Whenever comparison is necessary, regional State's RLAUPs are also used. Starting from 1908 urban land has been administered by a different law which over time was improved. All such proclamations concerning urban land are also raised at various levels of details in this dissertation, although the main focus is again on the existing Urban Land Lease Proclamation.[48]

c. The Civil Code

Adopted in 1960 and mainly based on the French Civil Code, the Ethiopian Civil Code[49] includes provisions pertaining to issues of land. Especially, allocation and administration of urban land as well as the issues of expropriation of land were well addressed in the Code. Although still operational on all other aspects of law, parts of the Code dealing with land and land expropriation were suspended starting from the Derg's period, because other laws on the same subject were enacted. Even today, the Civil Code provisions on urban land and land expropriation are not fully restored. In fact, other laws have replaced the urban land law and the expropriation rules of the Civil Code. But, since the Code was not expressly abrogated by any law, so far, efforts are made to use the Code whenever it becomes necessary.

---

[45] The Constitution of the People's Democratic Republic of Ethiopia, Proclamation 1 of 1987. Negarit Gazetta: Year 47, No. 1.

[46] Federal Democratic Republic of Ethiopia Rural Land Administration and Land Use Proclamation, Proclamation No. 456/2005. *Negarit Gazeta.* Year 11, No. 44. (Cited hereafter as FDRE RLAUP).

[47] FDRE Expropriation of Landholdings for Public Purposes and Payment of Compensation Proclamation, Proclamation No. 455/2005. Ibid.: Year 11, No. 43. (Hereinafter cited as Federal Expropriation Proclamation).

[48] Urban Lands Lease Holding Proclamation, Proclamation No. 721/2011. *Negarit Gazeta.* Year 18, No. 4.

[49] The Civil Code of Ethiopia. *Negarit Gazeta: Gazette Extraordinary.* Proclamation No. 165/1960.

d. Decrees
During the Imperial period, the Emperor had the power to pass his own law, called Decree. Of course, after the 1955 Revised Constitution, this power was restricted to situations wherein emergency cases occurred and the parliament happened to be in recession; even in such cases, the decree was supposed to be approved by the parliament upon its resumption of work. The emperor had passed many decrees before and after the Second World War pertaining to traditional land tenure and land taxes relevant for our discussion.

e. Regulations
Throughout the legal history of the country, the executive branch has been playing the main role in the implementation and execution of laws. It has also been passing a great body of laws in the form of Regulations. Starting from 1955, the council of Ministers was entrusted with the power to legislate its own laws. The main targets of this dissertation are those regulations adopted after 1991, the year when the incumbent government assumed power. Regulations dealing with the valuation and compensation processes of the Federal Government and that of the Regional States are more specifically the subject matter of this discussion.

f. Case Law
A decision of any court in Ethiopia can be reviewed by the Cassation Division of the Federal Supreme Court if it manifests a prima facie case for basic error of law and if it is a final decision.[50] Ethiopia is a follower of the Civil Law tradition and hence decisions of the Supreme Court were rarely taken as binding rules by lower courts. But since 2005, the interpretation of a law rendered by the Federal Supreme Court Cassation Division with not less than five judges became binding on federal as well as State courts of all levels.[51] It has to be noted here that the Cassation Division has no law making power as the courts of the Common Law. Rather, the interpretation it gives on account of errors of law shall be binding. In more recent times, the Cassation Division is able to publish its decisions which are now considered as binding rules and this research as well analyses some of these decisions. Besides, other cases from lower courts are also considered to exemplify the nature and kinds of cases raised by affected people.

1.2.3.3 The Judicial System

a. Regular Courts
According to Article 79(1) of the FDRE Constitution, "Judicial Powers, both at Federal and State levels, are vested in the courts." The Constitution creates parallel

---

[50] Muradu-Abdo 2007. Review of Decisions of State Courts over State Matters by the Federal Supreme Court. *Mizan Law Review,* 1, 61.; FDRE Constitution, Article 80(3)(a).

[51] Federal Courts Proclamation Reamendment proclamation No 454/2005. *Negarit Gazetta.* Year 11, No. 42.

governments, and hence a parallel judicial system at the federal and the state levels. Federal courts shall have jurisdiction on all issues that fall under the power of the Federal Government. While the jurisdiction and the rank of the three levels of the federal courts are basically determined by Proclamation 25/1996,[52] in States, it is determined by the Ethiopian Civil Procedure Code.[53]

Both at Federal and States, there are three levels of court systems. At State level, the courts are arranged, from below, as State Woreda Court, State High Court and State Supreme Court. At federal level, the names are Federal First Instance Court, Federal High Court and Federal Supreme Court. According to FDRE Constitution Article 80(1), (2), the Federal Supreme Court shall have the highest and final judicial power over Federal matters, while the State Supreme Courts shall have the same power over State matters. As already mentioned, the Federal Supreme Court has a Cassation Division with the highest appellate jurisdiction on all Federal and State Supreme Court final decisions on grounds of error of laws.

b. Municipal Courts

Urban land matters usually fall under municipal courts in Addis Ababa and other bigger cities. The Addis Ababa City Charter creates two levels of City Courts exercising municipal jurisdiction: First Instance and Appellate Courts.[54] There is no Supreme Court in the municipal system, although a cassation bench is included within the Appellate Court. Cassation review of the Appellate Court decisions can be brought before the Federal Supreme Court, which also decides jurisdictional conflicts between the city and federal courts. The Addis Ababa City Courts have civil, criminal and petty offence jurisdiction. Most Regional States as well established a two level municipal court with the task of hearing civil and criminal matters of smaller nature. Complaints related to inadequacy of compensation are usually heard by municipal courts before they go by appeal to the regular courts.

c. Social Courts

Social Courts are established at a kebele level, a fourth or third sub-stratum level of administration. From political administration perspective, kebeles are the last grass root level administration posts. In each kebele, there is an administrative council and a judicial committee known as Social Court. Social Courts have jurisdiction on minor issues (less than 5,000 birr in Addis Ababa and less than 1,500 in States). In some regions, rural land dispute are the jurisdiction of the social courts, but in others, like the Amhara Region, they fall under the jurisdiction of regular woreda courts.

52 Federal Courts Proclamation No. 25/1996. *Negarit Gazetta.* Year 2, No. 13. Minor changes have been added through amendments to this proclamation, but the basic nature is the same.

53 Ethiopian Civil Procedure Code. *Negarit Gazeta-Extraordinary.* Decree No. 52/1965, Year 25, No. 3.

54 Addis Ababa City Government Revised Charter Proclamation 311/2003, Articles 39(1) and 43.

1.3 Outline of the Dissertation

A brief description of the research problem, purpose and methodology is provided in this chapter. Chapter 2 examines the land rights in Ethiopia. It starts by describing the historical land tenure system in the country and analyses the existing land laws in detail so as to identify the gaps and ambiguities of the laws. It also shows the changes and developments witnessed throughout the ages by focusing on the equity of access to land and the liberty to use ones land. The major emphasis in this chapter is to examine whether the existing land laws give the people land rights as duly provided in the Constitution. In this chapter, extensive Ethiopian written material and laws are used to fully describe the history and grasp the laws. The chapter is used as a stepping stone to the discussion of the rest of the chapters. Introducing the nature of land rights and the scope of their exercise is important to determine whether the compensation paid for land taking is adequate or not.

Chapter 3 introduces the topic of expropriation. Expropriation even if it is well developed in other countries, in Ethiopia it is still an obscure subject which is not well known and researched; and hence, there is no developed jurisprudence on the subject in the country. Therefore, it is found to be ideal to introduce it by way of providing its definition, rational and justification. Various sources are used to establish the meaning, history and justification of expropriation in Ethiopia. An attempt is also made to trace its development in Ethiopia by referring to historical materials. The gist of the purpose of this chapter is found in its discussion on justification. It answers why expropriation should be used as an alternative method of land acquisition and how its direct antagonism with the principle of private ownership can be solved.

Chapter 4 is dedicated to the discussion of procedures that should be followed during the expropriation process. Expropriation is about taking one's land and property and converting it to some other different purposes. In other words, it causes physical and, perhaps, economic displacement on the person, leaving aside the emotional distress. Therefore, there are some procedures which should step by step be followed to minimize the general loss caused to the displaced person. For example, prior public discussion and notification, valuation of assets and advance compensation are required before the person is displaced from his place. This chapter tries to answer whether this is being done by examining actual practices. It also investigates the post facto situation of displaced people who are left without any rehabilitative and resettlement supports.

Chapter 5 has to do with the issue of public purpose. Public purpose is one limitation on the expropriation power of the government. It means the government cannot resort to expropriation whenever it wishes and for whatever purpose it wants the land. Land may only be expropriated if the intended project is found to be in the interest of society. The question is what constitutes public interest, or purpose? To determine the meaning of this very question is very important, because the government's power of expropriation highly depends on the answer to this question. To investigate the extent of the Ethiopian government's power in expropriating land property is the very mission of this chapter.

Chapter 6 focuses on the most sensitive areas of valuation and compensation practices. Payment of compensation is the second limitation on the power of government, besides the question of public purpose. Justice demands that society should reimburse the individual for what it gets in exchange from the individual. There is no justification for an individual to be sacrificed in the interest of society. Although this is the main thesis of the chapter, it also addresses the methods of making fair compensation. Therefore, valuation techniques and principles are examined in this chapter. To some extent, economic terminologies are employed to describe the principles. The purpose of this chapter is in general to assess whether fair compensation can be and is paid in Ethiopia in the event of expropriation.

Chapter 7 provides an analysis of the findings and a set of recommendations. The analysis is based on the findings of each chapter and it gives a synthesis of land rights and expropriation in current Ethiopia. In a bid to make it important to policy makers and responsible officials, the recommendations are grouped into two: recommendations that may be useful for policy and legal revision, and those that can improve the expropriation practice such that it complies with the laws and regulations.

Chapter 2
Land Rights in Ethiopia

2.1 Introduction

Land is the source of all material wealth; it provides us with all our needs to sustain on. It is also a major economic asset from which people and nations get significant profit. In many developing countries, land has been considered as an important economic and social asset where the status and prestige of people is determined. Because of such a high importance given to land, as compared to other properties, the legal protection accorded to land is always strict in nature.

Land is one form of property that is a subject of ownership or other form of use rights. Property is everything that has material or moral value for human beings… and guaranteed and enforced by law.[1] For legal scholars, "property" refers to entitlements to resources protected by formal legal institutions.[2] Property in the sense of legally protected entitlements comes in a variety of forms. The paradigmatic legal property right would be full title to a parcel of land or an object like a car, real property and personal property (or "chattels"), respectively. But, the law also affords legally enforceable claims to intangible resources such as intellectual property.

Different disciplines define "land" differently, in a manner that suits their objectives. In legal documents, mostly, it is considered as the surface of the earth and any fixtures on it, such as buildings, fence, tree plants, and improvement to the land.

For instance, according to Articles 552–554 of the French Civil Code, ownership of land "involves ownership of what is above and below it." Unless restricted by statutes, the owner of a land is considered as owning also the minerals inside the

---

[1] Aubry & Rau 1966. *Droit Civil Francis-Property-,* Translated by the Louisiana State Law Institute West Publishing Co. Vol. II, p. 1.

[2] Merrill, T. W. & Smith, H. E. 2010. *The Oxford Introductions to U.S. Law: Property,* New York, Oxford University Press, p. 3.

D.W. Ambaye, *Land Rights and Expropriation in Ethiopia*,
Springer Theses, DOI 10.1007/978-3-319-14639-3_2

land and the airspace above the land.[3] The basic feature of the above rule is that the term "land" signifies not only the surface of the earth, the ground, but also things found beneath the surface and fixtures above, and sometimes the airspace, above the ground. Of course, the details of ownership beneath and above the ground may be limited by different legislations. But fixtures, such as trees and buildings are always considered as part of the land.

Under Ethiopian law, property is either movable or immovable (Article 1126 of the Civil Code).[4] Land and buildings are considered as immovables (Article 1130 Civil Code). Hence, unlike the French one, where "land" includes "the ground and any fixture on the land", the Ethiopian Civil Code treats "land" and "buildings" as two separate types of immovables. Whether buildings should be considered as part of the land is not clearly envisaged as its French Counterpart Ethiopian law, of course, follows the French Civil Code, Article 518 which also says "land and building are immovable by their nature." But, as already shown above, in another section of the law, the French Civil Code declares that ownership of surface of land means ownership of all things above and below the land. In Ethiopia, however, there is no such kind of encompassing provision in the Civil Code. On top of that, today, as envisaged under Article 40(3), (7) of the FDRE Constitution, ownership of land is vested in the state and the people, while ownership of building is given to the individual. It means, the land surface and the building over the land are owned by two separate bodies. On the other hand, unless and until they are separated from the land, trees and crops are considered as part of the land (Article 1133 Civil Code). In other words, "land" signifies the ground and other fixtures to the land such as trees, grass, crops, excepting buildings and other similar erections.

In this chapter, land rights are referring to set of legally guaranteed entitlements or privileges which emanate by being an owner of the land. They may also be referred to as *bundle of right* or attributes of ownership. Ownership has not been defined in the Roman law or the French Civil Code, which is the main source of the Ethiopian Civil Code. The Romans were not concerned with theoretical definitions, and as Johnston, in his book, *Roman Law in Context*, remarked, "The best approach (taken by the Romans) seems to deal with the main attributes of ownership and from that allow the meaning of the term to emerge."[5] The attributes of ownership, according to the Roman law, are *usus*—the right to use the thing; *fructus*—the right to collect benefit offered by a thing; *abusus*—the right to dispose of a good either physically (destruction), or from a legal point of view (alienation-transfer gratuitously or for consideration).[6] In Anglo-American legal system, ownership is best described as bundle of rights, lists of loosely attached and transferable rights.

---

[3] Aubry and Rau, supra note 1, p. 182.

[4] 1960. The Civil Code of Ethiopia. *Negarit Gazeta: Gazette Extraordinary.* Proclamation No. 165/1960. Hereinafter Civil Code.

[5] Johnston, D. 1999. *Roman Law in Context,* Cambridge, Cambridge University Press, p. 22.

[6] Munteanu, C. 2005. Historical Remarks on the Legal Notion of Property. *Acta Universitatis Lucian Blaga,* 54, p. 58.

Some of the land rights which emanate from ownership are the right of use and enjoyment, right of collecting benefit by renting and leasing, right to give as mortgage, alienating for consideration such as exchange or sale, and alienating for free such as inheritance and donation.[7]

2.2 Land Ownership Regimes

Before proceeding to the discussion of ownership, it is important to provide an explanation on the nature of land ownership in Ethiopia first. As shall be raised and discussed in different parts of this dissertation, the Ethiopian land is governed under two proclamations and provides two classes of land rights. From the outset one needs to know that land belongs to the common ownership of the Ethiopian people and the state, and hence it is not subject to sale or other means of exchange. For this reason, rural farmers and pastoralists are given a right called "holding right" that provides rights of use and enjoyment, lease/rent, and bequeath (donation or inheritance). Obviously, this right is short of ownership because of the absence of the sole right of selling the land. Similarly, urban residents can get land under lease agreement that guarantees a 99 years use right on the land. Even if the land may be transferred by sale together with the development or without it (bare land only), it is highly restricted which makes it also short of ownership (details are presented under Sects. 2.6.4 and 2.6.5).

Therefore, when it comes to the classifications of the land regimes in Ethiopia, it is not made from pure ownership right perspective, but from the "holding right" perspective.

Honoré, in his seminal article, *Ownership*, conceives ownership as "the greatest interest in a thing which mature systems of law recognize."[8] Looking into existing Civil Codes one may find similar expression in the renowned French Civil Code. The Code under Article 544 describes "Ownership" as "the right to enjoy and dispose of things in the most absolute manner, provided they are not used in a way prohibited by statutes or regulations." Similarly, the Ethiopian Civil Code under Article 1204 explains ownership as "the widest right that may be had on a corporeal thing;" and "such right may neither be divided nor restricted except in accordance with the law." In other words, of all property rights a person has over an object, ownership is the widest and most complete one; and yet, this right may be restricted for public health, safety, security etc. reasons sanctioned by law.

---

[7] See for example Honoré, A. M. 1961. Ownership. *In*: A.G. Guest (ed.) *Oxford Essays in Jurisprudence*. Oxford: Oxford University Press. He provides list eleven attributes (property rights) found in any advanced legal system which may also be called bundle of rights: the right to the possess; the right to use; the right to manage; the right to the income; the right to the capital; the right to security; the right to transmitting; the absence of any term on possession; a duty to prevent harm; and the liability to execution, p. 165–179.

[8] Ibid., p. 108.

Land may be held in one of the following four ownership regimes: private, communal, state or open access. The physical characteristics of the natural resource, social circumstances, technology change, or population growth dictate one of the above forms of property ownership solution.[9] The idea is to own some land in one form (e.g. Private, common, state or open access) may be more appropriate perhaps from ensuring economic efficiency, for conservation/management of resource, for avoidance of conflict(ensuring justice) or for other reasons instead of another one.

For instance, to hold grazing land in common may be wise than using it privately (to avoid conflict and ensure justice) or in open access (to conserve the resource). Assume the grazing land in a village is owned by one individual while other villagers have no access or alternative food for their cattle. Obviously, people will feel that the arrangement is unjust and they may resort to violence to get access. As Anthony Scott has noted, "The mere existence of the institution of private property is not sufficient to ensure the efficient management of natural resources; the property must be allocated on a *scale* sufficient to ensure that one management has complete control of the asset."[10] As argued by most property right theorists, the cost of preserving the asset (grazing land) may be higher than the benefit gained from it, and this makes the ownership unworthy.

On the other hand, if the land is open to all, then the result will be the immediate depletion and exhaustion of the resource, in this case the grass. In a word, there is always some kind of rationality behind some form of property ownership arrangement. In the following sub-topics, an attempt is made to discuss the nature of the four types of property regimes mentioned above. Based on the current Federal Democratic Republic of Ethiopia (hereafter FDRE) Rural Land Administration and Use Proclamation (hereafter RLAUP) and the Civil Code, we shall also identify what kind of land falls under which regime in Ethiopia.

2.2.1 Private Ownership

Private ownership is a property arrangement in which full and exclusive rights to decide about the property are given to a single person (natural or artificial) or group of persons. The owner shall have the right to use, possess, receive income from it, or alienate it gratuitously or for consideration. As mentioned earlier, in countries following the Roman law system, the usual way to describe ownership rights is of *usus, fructus*, and *abusus*. Modern writers add one important element to these rights: the right to exclude others from using and possessing the property.[11]

---

[9] Stevenson, G. G. 1991. *Common Property Economics: A General Theory and Land Use Applications*, Cambridge, Cambridge University Press, p. 4.

[10] Scott, A. D. 1955. The Fishery: The Objectives of Sole Ownership. *Journal of Political Economy* 63, 116–124, p. 116.

[11] Snare, F. 1972. The Concept of Property. *American Philosophical Quarterly*, 9.

The experiences of many countries concerning land show that farming plots, residential land plots, buildings, easements (streets to serve the land property) are owned privately. In western countries, forest land, small lakes, streets and rural roads are also subject to private ownership.

The current governing land legislations in Ethiopia are mainly the FDRE Rural Land Administration and Use (RLAUP) 456/2005 and the Urban Land Lease Proclamation 711/2011, which are in place to govern rural and urban land respectively. Besides, the FDRE Constitution, FDRE Expropriation Proclamation 455/2005, and the Ethiopian Civil Code are relevant. Based on the above review, when one looks at the land ownership in Ethiopia, the ground (surface earth) is not subject to private ownership (see Article 40(3) of FDRE constitution). Land belongs to the state and the people, and is not subject of sale and exchange. This means that it is futile to classify the land paradigms in Ethiopia from pure ownership perspective. Rather, the land right provided, as termed in the RLAUP, is known as "holding right." It is less of ownership in that the holder lacks the power of sale and exchange[12] (details are given in Sect. 2.6).

Based on the above information, when one looks into the FDRE RLAUP 456/2005, one finds under Article 2(11), "private holdings" referring to private farming plots given to peasant farmers, pastoralists and semi-pastoralists. It is not clear about the private plots to be given to pastoralists, though. But, the assumption is that the plots may be those which the pastoralists will use for settlement or housing, rather than for grazing, which is communal in nature. Private land plots that are provided to peasants in the highlands are used for farming and housing. In urban area, land that is acquired through lease or government grant is considered as a private possession.

2.2.2 *Communal Property*

As opposed to private ownership, communal ownership is a property right allocation made in the interest of group of users. Here, there is no single individual in a privileged position to control and have command over all of the resources. In a system of communal property, rules governing access to and control of material resources are organized on the basis that each resource is, in principle, available for the use of every member alike. As noted by Clark and Kohler, writers on property

[12] FDRE Rural Land Administration and Land Use Proclamation, Proclamation No. 456/2005. *Negarit Gazeta*. Year 11, No. 44. (hereinafter FDRE RLAUP) Article 2(4) defines "holding right" as "the right of any peasant farmer, semi-pastoralist and pastoralist… to use rural land for purpose of agriculture and natural resource development, lease and bequeath to members of his family or other lawful heirs, and includes the right to acquire property produced on his land… by his labour or capital and to sale, exchange and bequeath same".

law, "The defining characteristic of communal property is that every member of the community has the right not to be excluded from the resource."[13] In principle, the needs and wants of every person are considered, and when allocative decisions are made they are made on a basis that is in some sense fair to all.[14]

The most usual types of properties owned in common are grazing lands, forest lands, fisheries, irrigation systems, underground water, water wells, village roads, neighborhood streets, and so on.

The common feature of such properties is that they are not destined to an exclusive use of an individual person; every member of the community wants them equally. The other feature is that most of them are exhaustible, if left to anybody as open or free access. Even in case of allocation of such properties to specific part of society, the resources may be quickly depleted and individual members may not be encouraged to conserve unless the use and enjoyment is regulated by an internal sets of rules.

This is because people tend to care less for what is common as compared to what is their own. As modern economists argue, when the incentive to care and conserve is less than the cost of so doing, people will not go for conservation. One such modern economic theorist is Harold Demsetz, who argues that people give less care to what is common property, since the cost of taking care is higher than the benefit gained. The primary function of private property becomes a guiding incentive to achieve a greater "internalization of externalities."[15] In this way, individuals are made to bear the costs and benefits of their own activities, and to absorb the costs of inflicting spillover effects upon others.

According to Demsetz, if land is held in common, it is likely each user will not feel the full impact, in terms of the benefits but particularly the costs of his use. When, for example, many individuals use a forest to produce wood, no one has an incentive to increase the forest population (e.g. by replanting when a tree is cut), since the benefits of his doing so will redound to others as well as himself. In other words, while he internalizes (suffers from or is burdened with) the costs of planting trees, it will be others who will reap the benefit. If this is the case, any rational person will not invest his money and time for the care of the forest land, unless he is sure that the benefit of his doing is by far greater than the cost he incurred; or at least that he is sure that others will also do the same.

In the absence of such assurance, the common property will be depleted quickly and will face what Hardin called "The Tragedy of the Commons", a situation where common or open access resources exhausted quickly by unregulated

[13] Clarke, A. & Kohler, P. 2005. *Property Law: Commentary and Materials,* Cambridge, Cambridge University Press, p. 36.

[14] Waldron, J. 1988. *The Right to Private Property,* Oxford, clarendon press, p. 41.

[15] Demsetz, H. 1967. Toward a Theory of Property Rights. *The American Economic Review,* 57, 347–359, p. 348.

overexploitation.[16] For this reason privatizing the land resource or setting internal rules are usually come up as solutions to the problem.

The difference between private ownership and communal ownership is that while in the former case the owner can sell his property, in the latter case, owner members may not be able to transfer their right by way of sale, especially to non-members.

Furthermore, in a well-functioning communal property situation, the users have certain rights and duties among themselves with respect to possession, use, and enjoyment of benefits from the resource. For example, in a regulated irrigation system, all participants have the right to divert water for specific time; they also have the correlate duty of not exceeding their assigned rate so as not to interfere with others' water flow. Although by and large the internal rules governing the use of the common property are prepared by the members themselves, their enforcement or implementation may need state intervention.[17]

In Ethiopia according to Article 2(12) of the FDRE RLAUP 456/2005, "communal holding" is "rural land which is given by the government to local residents for common grazing, forestry and other social services." This list is just an illustrative one and what are given are only examples. The government may allocate additional land as communal ones, if the local community needs it for some social or economic activities. Thus, land necessary for religious ceremonies, cultural festivities, or social gatherings may be permanently allocated to the village community in common. Besides grazing and forest land, one may also add irrigation systems (although the irrigable land may be private holding), water wells (especially in pastoralist areas), small rivers, hills,[18] etc. to the list of communal lands.

2.2.3 State Ownership of Land

To describe "state ownership" of land, terms like "public ownership", "collective ownership" or "government ownership" are also employed. Under the 1960 Ethiopian Civil Code, the term "public domain" is used for the same purpose. In any case, in this discussion, they shall be used interchangeably as the need arises.

---

[16] Hardin, G. 1968. The Tragedy of the Commons. *Science,* 162, 1243–1248. The concept has further been used to explain overexploitation in fisheries, overgrazing, air and water pollution, abuse of public lands, population problems, extinction of species, fuel-wood depletion, misallocation in oil and natural gas extraction, groundwater depletion, wildlife decline, and other problems of resource misallocation.

[17] For a better understanding on the nature of a well functioning communal property see generally Ostrom, E. 1990. *Governing the Commons: The Evolution of Institutions for Collective Action,* Cambridge, Cambridge University Press.

[18] For example in the past 2 years the government has been transferring holding right of hills and small mountains to the local people in order the hills to be forested and protected.

In order to give additional explanation on the subject, it is proper to see the usage of the terms in some literature and legislations. The terms "state or government ownership" seem to denote the ownership of land by the political body, a central or municipal level, while "public or collective ownership" seems to signify the ownership of land by all the people or by the local community. It does not mean, however, that this definition would be fully acceptable; one has to rely on the legislation of the respective country to decide the actual meanings. Writers on property and land ownership, though, use the above terms interchangeably.[19] Equally, others give different meanings. For example, the Chinese Land Law treats "collective ownership" and "state ownership" differently. Collective is understood as a village land committee, and farmers are forced to lease farm lands from these committees:

> According to the 1982 Constitution…the structure of land ownership seems relatively clear that, in principle, natural resources and urban land are state-owned, while suburban and rural lands are collectively owned.[20]

In any case, what is important is to know that material resources are answerable to the needs and purposes of society as a whole, irrespective of the fact that the decision maker is the central government, a special national committee, or a village committee. The assumption is that even though it is the state which owns the land, the objective is to use it in the best interest of society in general. For example, in many countries[21] urban land owned by city municipalities or local governments is used to benefit society, such as the provision for low cost housing.

Practically, there are no real differences between the dichotomy of the "state or government" on one hand, and the "collective or public" ownership of land on the other. My argument is that since the government, as a political body, puts itself as the representative of the people, the power of administration and allocation of land property is, most of the time, vested in the hands of the state, and hence the state becomes the sole decision maker. If, for example, we look into the land ownership

---

[19] For instance Philip Kivell, in his writing on the English and other European countries land ownership by central or municipal governments, uses the term "public ownership" of land to replace "state ownership" of land (see generally Kivell, P. 1993. *Land and the City: Patterns and processes of urban change,* London, Routledge.; Kivell, P. & McKay 1988. Public Ownership of Urban Land. *Transactions of the Institute of British Geographers, New Series,* 13, 165–178.). Similarly Jeremy Waldron, fuses both "collective ownership" and "state ownership" as giving the same meaning when he comments: "sometimes, collective property is presented as special type of private ownership with the state as the equivalent of a private owner" (Waldron, supra note 14, p. 40.). Further in her critical work on *Property*, Margaret Davies, employed "government" and "public ownership" equivalently (Davies, M. 2007. *Property: meanings, histories, theories,* New York, Routledge-Cavendish, p. 64).

[20] Ho, P. 2005. *Institutions in Transition: Land Ownership, Property Rights, and Social Conflict in China,* New York, Oxford University Press, p. 28.

[21] See generally Kivell: 1988, 1992, supra note 19; Bourassa, S. C. & Hong, Y.-H. 2003. Leasing Public Land: International experiences, Cambridge, Massachusetts Lincoln Institute of Public policy. The writers raise many European, Asian and Australian cities where in urban land is owned by the city municipalities or local governments.

system in former socialist countries, land was owned by the collective or the public, but the state was the real decision maker; citizens had use right only.[22] In Ethiopia we find the same approach in reading Articles 40(3) and 89(5) of the FDRE Constitution, where the "state" and the "people" are considered as two joint owners of land and natural resources, but the state is represented to administer it on behalf of the people.

The FDRE RLAUP identifies, under Article 2(13), "forestlands, wildlife protected areas, state farms, mining lands, lakes, rivers and other rural lands," as state holding lands. In this case, "other rural lands" means all land which is not held privately or communally. State land in Ethiopia means, land held by Federal or Regional government or by city municipalities. Rural land held by Regional governments is administered by *woredas*, while urban land is administered by respective city/town administrations. This means *woreda*s and city administrations have the power to give and take land. The Federal government holds vast tracts of land found in lowland rural areas of the country destined to be transferred for large-scale agricultural investments.

All urban land which is not occupied by private lessees is held by the government/municipality. Although it is not mentioned in the current lease proclamation, one can assume that all city streets, sewerage systems, parks, highways, and empty spaces must belong to the state.

One question that may be raised is that what can be done if the new land proclamations (urban and rural) fail to address all the issues? Definitely, we go to the Civil Code. It must be stressed that the land legislations must be considered as supplements or modifications to the Civil Code. Further, since in no where the Civil Code is clearly abrogated, as far as its provisions are not contrary to the existing land legislations, it must continue its function. The concept of public property of urban areas, both in the Civil Code and the current land legislations is basically similar. Based on this argument, we may apply the Civil Code provisions on "public domain" to determine the situation of public/state lands in urban areas.[23]

The Ethiopian Civil Code under Articles 1444–1459 presents the nature and status of public lands in urban areas. To see the details, all [urban] lands owned by the state or administrative bodies are to be treated as "private lands" or as "public domains" (Article 1444). Although the provision lacks clarity, it must be understood as follows. All land owned by the state (centrally or through its various branches) is treated either as "private" or as "public." "Private" means the state organ that owns (holds in today's situation) land will have the right to exclude others from access and use. For example, state business enterprises (such as, banks,

[22] See generally Wegren, S. K. (ed.)1998. Land Reform in the Former Soviet Union and Eastern Europe, London, Routledge. For example it is said that in Ukraine, like any other place in the then Soviet Union, in theory, land farmed by agricultural collectives was owned by the collective. In reality, because Ukrainian farms were subject to the USSR land code and the Model Charter for collective farms, land was state-owned and workers on these farms assumed the same role as wage labor in industrial enterprises, p. 49.

[23] See Civil Code, Articles 1444–1459.

insurances, transport companies, telecom companies or energy companies) or administrative bodies (such as ministry of agriculture, ministry of finance) all happen to hold land and buildings. There is no reason that they should make their property open to all, and such land holdings will be treated as private holdings and governed by the civil code part that governs private property.

On the other hand, there are other types of state lands whose use and enjoyment are put at a "public disposal", or by their nature they are "destined to a public service". These are the type of land or buildings that are termed as "public domain," (Article 1445) and the law tries to define their character. Since the definition of their character is not enough to identify them, the Code, under Article 1446, provides an example of such properties: roads, streets, canals, railways; seashores, port installations and lighthouse; buildings specially adapted for public services such as fortifications and churches. Thus, roads, streets, railways, canals are examples of properties put at public disposal.

2.3 Land Tenure and Ownership in Ethiopia

Under the general label "land tenure," we are concerned with the complex relationships that exist between categories of individuals and groups in reference to land and other natural resources. These relationships can be analyzed in terms of sets of rights and obligations held by these categories of people with regard to the acquisition, exploitation, preservation, and transfer of land and related resources.[24] A recent document published by United Nations Food and Agriculture Organization (FAO) defines land tenure as a "relationship, whether legally or customarily defined, among people, as individuals or groups, with respect to land."[25] Rules of tenure define how property rights to land are to be allocated within societies. They define how access is granted to rights to use, control, and transfer land, as well as associated responsibilities and restraints. In simple terms, land tenure systems determine who can use what resources for how long, and under what conditions.[26]

For a lawyer, as discussed above, what property right implicates is an entitlement that is enforced by law. Yet, tenure or property rights are wider than those written down in law books and enforced by law enforcements. Land tenure also encompasses those property rights recognized and enforced under customary systems. Customary land rights typically include communal grazing lands, private agricultural and residential houses. These rights are evolved indigenously within the local people. These traditional societies or groups have developed various ways of

[24] Clawson, M. 1968. Land. *In*: Sills, D. L. (ed.) *International Encyclopedia of the Social Sciences*. USA: The Macmillan Company & The Free Press. Id., p. 562.

[25] FAO 2002. *Land Tenure and Rural Development,* Rome, United Nations Food and Agriculture Organization, p. 7.

[26] Ibid.

controlling land rights in different situations. These cover how land is managed in relation to members of communities; how land rights can be transferred within the group; and how land rights can be transferred to other persons outside the group.[27]

In Ethiopia, in Afar and Somalie Regions customary land tenure is still operational. Most of the time, community leaders and clan chiefs are at the center of the allocation and enforcement of rights.[28] For generations, land rights in Ethiopia were governed and enforced by customary system. It was only after the 1960s and 1970s, that some legal measurements that changed the old system were introduced, especially with regard to rural land. In this section, an attempt is made to discuss the three types of tenure systems in Ethiopia, based on the historical, legal and political ideologies of the periods.

2.4 Tenure Systems in Pre-1975 Ethiopia

Pre-1975 Ethiopia is generally characterized as a feudal state, where most of the land was controlled by the state and feudal lords, and in which citizens were using land under different tenure arrangements. Such tenure arrangements were customary by nature and numerous in numbers. Before 1975, there were several types of land tenure systems which differed from province to province. For the sake of convenience and because of historical factors, the land tenures will be classified as northern and southern following the geography of the country. But, before that, let us see the powers and prerogatives of rulers and emperors of the time.

2.4.1 Land and Imperial Prerogatives

As quoted in Pankhurst, Job Ludolf, a seventeenth century German historian, is said to summarize the power of Ethiopian kings as follows: "The power of the

---

[27] Arko-Adjei, A. 2011. *Adapting Land Administration to the Institutional Framework of Customary Tenure: The case of Peri-urban Ghana,* Amsterdam, TUDelft, p. 20.

[28] See generally, Kabtamu-Niguse. 2012. *Land Tenure and Tenure Security Among Somali Pastoralists: Within the Context of Dual Tenure System.* LL.M thesis, Bahir Dar University, School of Law. As quoted in Kabtamu's thesis, the government land policy of the Somalie Regional State confirms the complete control of land by traditional chiefs rather than by government organs: "Because of the fact that all rural land in the region is administered by clan leaders under the traditional land administration system, government institutions, investors and others who are in need of rural land should negotiate with clan leaders who determine the amount of compensation. Thus, the willingness of clan leaders are necessary as both the access to land and the amounts of compensations are determined by the clan leaders and not by government agency," p. 128.

Abyssinian Kings is absolute, as well in Ecclesiastical as Civil Affairs."[29] Other travelers and writers also testified that Ethiopian monarchs had been absolute over the people and their objects.[30] Concerning land, the general claim, in the feudalistic Ethiopia, was that all land belonged to the king. Thus, all land rights emanated from the benevolent gift of the king to his subjects and the Church. The ideological background behind such claim was that land was acquired through conquest of local tribes by the Ethiopian kings to whom the land of the conquered was transferred in ownership as spoil of war. The state demanded an obligation of tribute from all land (except those which belonged to the church), as tax obligation was attached to land rather than a person.[31] The idea of royal ownership of all land in Ethiopia was documented by royal chroniclers of different kings.[32] For example, upon the purchase of land by king Lalibela (1200–1250) to construct his well known rock hewn churches in Roha, his hagiographer asked rhetorically to show the traditional power of the monarch in the distribution of lands: "who would have forbidden the king if he had decided to take the land [without purchase]?"[33] In his famous conflict with the monastic leaders, Emperor Amda-Sion (1314–1344) is said to have demanded their absolute obedience to him because they lived 'on the land of the king'. His son and successor, Sayfe-Arad (1344–72), is also said to have made the claim that 'God gave (all the) land to me'.[34] A more practical example of this royal prerogative over land is furnished by the abundant records of land grants made by Ethiopian kings in their name to various churches and monasteries.[35]

---

[29] Pankhurst, R. 1966. *State and Land in Ethiopian History,* Addis Ababa, The Institute of Ethiopian Studies and the Faculty of Law, Haile Sellasie I University, p. 1.

[30] During his stay in Ethiopia in the 16th century, the Portuguese priest, Francisco Alvarez, testifies that the power of the king was absolute (Alvarez, F. 1970 (Originally translated by John Stanley in 1881). *Narrative of the Portuguese Embassy to Abyssinia During the Years 1520–1527,* London, The Hakluyt Society.). A 100 years latter Almeida (a Jesuit priest) said "the Emperor confiscates and grants all the lands as and to whom he chooses." (See Pankhurst: 1966 (Ibid), p. 121.) James Bruce a 17th century Scottish traveler to Ethiopia has also declared that "all the land is the king's; he gives to whom he pleases during pleasure and resumes it when it is his will; but the crown makes no violent use of its power in that respect" (Paul, J. C. N. & Clapham, C. 1972. *Ethiopian Constitutional Development I, a Source Book,* Addis Ababa, Haile Sellassie I University and Oxford University Press, p. 290.). An Ethiopian writer and Minister during the Imperial period also noted: "the Ethiopian Emperor has an uncontested and boundless power over the territories he rules. He is both the temporal and spiritual ruler" (Id., p. 58).

[31] Ras Alula and Ras Gugissa, two famous governors of different part of the country, have once said to be declared that "Man is free, land tributary".

[32] Generally see Pankhurst: 1996, supra note 29.

[33] Taddesse-Tamrat 1972. *Church and State in Ethiopia, 1270–1527,* Oxford, Clarendon Press, p. 98.

[34] Ibid.

[35] See for example Huntingford, G. W. B. 1965. *The Land Charters of Northern Ethiopia,* Addis Ababa, Institute of Ethiopian Studies and the Faculty of Law, Haile Sellassie I University.; Crummey, D. 2000. *Land and Society in the Christian Kingdom of Ethiopia: From the Thirteenth to the Twentieth Century,* USA, University of illinois Press.

2.4.2 Land Tenure System in Northern Ethiopia

The northern part of Ethiopia is the cradle of Ethiopian civilization. It is believed that after the establishment of the state at the northern city of Axum, around 100 B.C, it slowly expanded southward until it took its present shape during the late nineteenth century.[36] As shown above, although all land was considered property of the emperors, it was distributed to different users on different conditions. Hence, the land tenure system in the northern part of feudalistic Ethiopia may generally be classified as private holdings, church lands and state lands.

2.4.2.1 Private Holdings (*Gult* vs. *Rist* Land)

For centuries, Ethiopian rulers had been distributing land to the nobility and peasants in the form of *gult* and *rist* rights respectively. The natures of *gult* and *rist* rights are fully addressed by the definition that Hoben, an anthropologist, gives to the terms in his widely read book.[37] Hoben writes that *gult* rights entail "fief-holding rights" whereas *rist* rights confer "land-use rights."[38] Other writers,[39] as well, agree that *gult* (fief) rights confer the ruling class (*bale-gult*) rights of collecting tribute, judicial and administrative powers as well as military mobilization over the people occupying the land. And those people who actually occupy and farm the land had a *rist* (use) right to the land.

The recorded history about *gult* shows that it started at least during the fourteenth century.[40] A lord who is provided a vast tract of land (3–4 square miles according to Hoben) as a *gult* will administer the people occupying it as holders of *rist*, collect tribute from them, adjudicate cases arising among them, and use the able bodies as soldiers during war times. He would retain part of the tribute as a fee for his services and fully use fees and fines he imposed in his power as a judge. However, the *gult* holder had no rights of produce over the land although he may cultivate part of the land for his private purpose using free local labor.

Referring to a 1917 book, *Handbook of Abyssinia,* written by an anonymous writer about the *gult* system in *Tigray*, the Northern part of Ethiopia, the historian Shiferaw Bekele describes the job description of *gult*-holder as follows:

---

[36] See for example Marcus, H. G. 1994. *A History of Ethiopia,* Los Angeles, University of California Press, pp. 10–11, it is said that the drive southward was characterized by the implantation of military colonies followed by feudal like social order, and priests and monks acted as instrument of pacification and acculturation.

[37] Hoben, A. 1973. *Land Tenure Among the Amhara of Ethiopia: The Dynamics of Cognatic Descent* Chicago, University of Chicago Press.

[38] Id., p. 5.

[39] See for example Markakis, J. 2006. *Ethiopia: Anatomy of a Traditional Polity,* Addis Ababa, Shama Books.; and Crummey: 2000, supra note 35.

[40] Taddesse-Tamrat, supra note 33, p. 98.

> The gult-holder, assisted by the local official (shum-adi), fixes the proportion of the state due which each adi (parish) must pay; he also acts as a court of appeal in civil and criminal matters from judgments of the shum-adi; he is responsible for peace and order in his gult and is, of course, the military chief of the district. In return for this he (a) has his land cultivated free of charge by the ristenyatat (rist holders); (b) receives all of the fines which he may impose in his judicial capacity; keeps a part, generally one-tenth, of the tribute collected by him; and (c) receives certain presents, example a sheep from each parish at Easter.[41]

Since *gult* was a kind of public office instead of land right, as a matter of principle, it was not transferable by inheritance or by sale. Of course, when the ruler/emperor wishes, the office might be passed to descendants. As exception, however, the historian Donald Crummey argues otherwise, based on his study of the seventeenth century Gonderine era. Without abandoning the view that *gult* was essentially a tribute right, Crummey argues that *gult* rights were transferred by sale and inheritance without necessarily involving the state.[42] This is, however, an exception to the Ethiopian history of property right.

Rist rights, in contrast to *gult* rights, were land-use rights. In principle, they were hereditary and could be held by lords and peasants alike. *Rist* rights were land use rights claimed by a member of a kin from members of his/her generations of same ancestor. As described by Hoben, a single estate of *gult* land, comprising a few square miles, included within its boundaries strip fields, held as *rist* by scores or even hundreds of farmers. The *gult* holder might also hold some fields as *rist* within his estate of *gult* land.[43]

For all practical purposes, *rist* land was like private ownership except the holder lacked the right to sell the land. The peasant could be able to use, rent, and inherit the land to family members. In exchange, peasants were obliged to make payment for variety land related taxes. Selling the land to non-family members was prohibited. Land was then transferred in the form of inheritance from family to children for generations, which over time reduced the size of the farm lands.

In north Ethiopia, the *rist* land may have originated with ancestral first holders through government grant for a loyal service, clearance of forest, or perhaps purchase. Then, the land remained within the family forever and descendants would get a share of it irrespective of their presence or absence in the area. This land was held communally by the lineage and was not subject to sale and alienation. It was a common custom in many places that a person wishing to sell his share must transfer it to one of the lineage members; outsiders were not allowed to buy the land. In the north, thanks to this kind of land-holding system, a peasant could claim a plot of land as long as he could trace his descent. Tenancy in this part of the country was very minimal compared to the southern part. Some argue that the use-right was secured in the sense that political authorities, including the Emperor, or landlords

---

[41] Shiferaw-Bekele 1995. The Evolution of Land Tenure in the Imperial Era. *In*: Shiferaw, B. (ed.) *An Economic History of Ethiopia: The Imperial Era 1941–1974*. Dakar: CODESRIA, p. 97.

[42] See generally Crummey: 2000, supra note 35.

[43] Hoben, supra note 37, p. 5.

refrained from interventions. As a result, "there was less tenure insecurity or fear of being evicted from the *rist* land."[44] The other character of *rist* in the north was that the land became highly fragmented because of the ad infinitum division of family land for many generations. Land disputes related to *rist* land claims were rampant in that they constituted 45 % of civil cases in court.[45]

The obligations of the *rist* holders were mainly two. The first was *giber* (land tax), which mostly amounted to one fifth of the produce or some form of fixed obligation delivered in kind that would be shared between the local *gult*-holder and the central state; and second, *asrat* (tithe) in which one-tenth of all crops grown had to be paid to the state.[46] These are the two known legal obligations of the peasants although there were other informal obligations claimed by the nobility.[47] According to the historian Bahru Zewde, the peasant's "control over his produce and labor time, was limited by the claims of the nobility, both lay and clerical."[48] The peasant was forced "to undertake courvéé (forced labor) such as farming, grinding corn, and building houses and fences that claimed up to one-third of his time."[49] The *rist* holder or the peasant was also known as *gabbar* (which comes from the root word *gibir*, tax/tribute) which means tribute/tax payer.

2.4.2.2 Government Land

In the socio-political system of the time, institutions did not have any mechanism of collecting tributes in kind or cash and redistributing them to their staff in turn. What was done was to parcel out the land and give it to the individuals who would keep the institution going.[50] As we shall discuss below, land was distributed to soldiers, priests, local administrators, judges, and state servants at various levels as remuneration for their service throughout the country. Modern state machinery with salaried soldiers and civil servants is of recent origin; it came after the Second World War. Therefore, land owned by the government was distributed to different people on the condition of serving the state at different levels. Such land might be reverted to the state in the event of non fulfillment of the obligation by the holder of the land.

---

[44] Clapham, C. 1988. *Transformation and Continuity in Revolutionary Ethiopia,* Cambridge, Cambridge University Press.

[45] Ministry-of-Information 1968. *Yemeret Yizota be Hibretesebawit Ethiopia (Land Possession in the Republic of Ethiopia),* Addis Ababa, p. 51.

[46] Hoben, supra note 37, p. 77.

[47] For instance Gebre-Wold-Ingida work, infra note 52, p. 306, listed down 24 types of duties paid or carried out by the peasant to the state or local authorities. Some of those duties had been abolished during the early 21st century.

[48] Bahru-Zewde 1991. *A History of Modern Ethiopia, 1855–1974,* Addis Ababa, Addis Ababa University Press, p. 14.

[49] Id., p. 15.

[50] Shiferaw-Bekele, supra note 41, p. 94.

Shiferaw Bekele[51] argues that the whole land tenure arrangement was designed on some kind of implicit condition. Peasants were obliged to pay tax and to render manual services to the local gentry in exchange for the land rights they received. A peasant who failed to pay tax would loss his land. Church land had been distributed among member of the clergy and lay people on the condition that they would serve the church in different capacities, and failure to fulfill these obligations would cause the forfeiture of the land rights. Government land had also been distributed among different people on condition that they would continue to serve the state. The grand design in the whole property arrangement was that land was serving as a means to run the state functionary. In the old days since gold and silver was not found in abundance,[52] the government had heavily relied in the land under its control to run the state.[53] This is done in two ways, by giving land in lieu of salary to those who directly serve the state and by collecting tax tributes in kind from those who farm the land, which it may use for different purposes.

Generally speaking, state land is one which is categorized neither as private *rist* land nor church land. The two Ethiopian writers on traditional land tenure, Mahteme-Sellassie[54] and Gebre-Wold-Ingida Work,[55] provided us with various types of state land tenure. The list is long but, here, we reproduce few of them in order to show its nature. As stated above, land was provided to different people based on the service they rendered to the state and the names given to the land rights correlated to the obligations attached to them.

a. Melkagna Rist/riste-gult/siso-gult

According to this system, *rist* land was given to the *malkagna* or *balabat,* local gentry, because he cleared the forest and started to cultivate it. In other situations, a *balabat* who fought local tribes together with the king and brought about a lot of land to the state was given a *rist* as a reward, which should remain in his generation permanently, a semi-freehold right. In addition, such a person was also given a larger area as his *gult*. It means, out of the vast area of land given to him as his *gult* land, he also got some land as his *rist* land. Hence, the *rist-gult* holder would have the right to the whole produce from his land, and also a right to claim a third as tribute and a tenth (as tithe) from those who cultivate on the rest of his *gult* land.

b. Maderia Land

Maderia land was land granted for life, mainly, to government officials, war veterans, and other patriots in lieu of a pension or salary, but the state possessed a

[51] Id., p. 94–96.

[52] Gebre-Wold-Ingida, W. 1962. Ethiopia's Traditional System of Land Tenure and Taxation. *Ethiopia Observer,* 5, pp. 302–339.

[53] Shiferaw, supra note 41.

[54] Gebre Wold Engida, W., supra note 52.

[55] Mahteme-Selassie, W. M. 1957. The Land System of Ethiopia. *Ethiopia Observer,* 1.; Mahteme-Sellassie, W. M. 1970. *Zekre Neger,* Addis Ababa, 2nd ed., pp. 107–119.

reversionary right over these land grants. In other words, it was temporarily given to government civil servants who were assigned to work in some locality in lieu of salary and it was returned to the state or given out to others when the civil servant was transferred or sometimes dismissed from his position.

c. Ginde-Bel Land

Ginde-bel Land is land given to persons who maintain government works of various types, such as *ye-zemach meret*, land belonged to soldiery, *beklo kelabi meret*, land given to those who look after government mules and horses, *dingay felach meret*, land given to those who work in the production of quarry for the construction of palaces, *medf chagn meret*, land given to those who carry and transport guns and cannons to battle front, *dinkuan chagn meret*, land given to those who carry and transport imperial tents, *atkilt tekay meret*, land given to those who plant trees and others in the compound of the royal palace, *postegna meret*, land belonging to those who transport mails and posts. These people were free from payment of land tax, but responsible for the *asrat* (tithe) one. The idea is that land was given for their services to the state and that they would be allowed to own it as far as they continue providing the services.

d. Were-genu, Balderas meret

Were-genu is land used for the raising of government cattle. The persons looking after such livestock were allowed to have *maderia* land of their own. In other words, the *Were-genu* land is dedicated to the feeding and raising of cattle and production of butter, both for the consumption of the royal palace. Similarly, *Balderas meret* is land held by peasants and reserved for the raising of government horses and mules.

e. Ganne-geb/maad-bet meret

Gann is a large container of Ethiopian local beer made of clay and *maad-bet* means kitchen, indicating that this type of land is related to the land selected for the production of food to the imperial palace. Since it was a custom for the monarchs to throw (hold) a big traditional feast (*gebir*) now and then, the palace needed a huge amount of food, either produced on such land or collected in the form of tax. Soldiers or peasants who worked on these lands were expected to supply the royal household with grains grinded once every year.

2.4.2.3 Church Land

The Ethiopian Orthodox Church had been the biggest beneficiary of state land grant since its establishment in the early fourth century at Axum (Ethiopian capital from 1st BC–8th AD). There is certain amount of evidence to suggest that the Cathedral of the Saint Mary at Axum, the monasteries of Abba Garima, and Debre Damo and several other religious establishments received grants of land at this time from the state.[56] The traditional practice was for the sovereign to endow cathedrals, churches and monasteries with land as well as to give land to the ecclesiastics in attendance upon them.[57] The historical records also show that such grants continued well up to the 21st century. Until the coming of the revolution in 1974, the church was said to be controlling one third of the land in the country.

This generous benefaction of the state was later on incorporated into the *Fitha Negest* (Law of the Kings), which in Ethiopian legal history, was considered as the first written legal document.[58] Concerning land grants and the waiver of tribute/land tax, Section 40, No. 1540 cum. 1541 of the Fitha Negest reads as follows:

> Let the king give honor to the order of the clergy, as did Constantine the Elect, faithful and righteous king; and as did others who followed him. Let the king be generous with his wealth. Let he give to each of them according to their ranks. First of all, the king shall give presents to the bishops; then to the priests, next to the deacons, and then to those who are below them. He shall exempt them from tributes, presents, and the other favors to be paid to the rulers. Let him assign something to the churches for the maintenance of the widows, the orphans and the poor, so that they may entreat God to reaffirm the true faith with the benefit in the Holy Trinity…[59]

Church lands were thus the most privileged since they were free from payments of tributes and land taxes.[60] This doesn't mean, however, that the cultivators of the land would be exempted from payment of land tax; on the contrary, they were equally responsible like any other peasant. This means, tax and tributes collected from the person who cultivated the land would be going to the church coffer instead of that of the government. In this way, churches were expected to support themselves.

Usually, the land given to the churches and monasteries, as *gult* land, was vast[61] and the church was not expected to cultivate it. Rather, the church land was

---

[56] Pankhurst: 1966, supra note 29, p. 22.

[57] Ibid.

[58] The *Fitha Negest* (Law of the Kings) is a sophisticated compilation of legal prescriptions concerning both religious and secular matters written in approximately the 13th century in Egypt as a guide to Christian population living within the Moslem society. Originally written in Arabic, and incorporating laws from Old and New testament, Roman law, and some Moslem principles and the proceedings of the early councils of Nicaea and Antioch, it is believed that it was translated to *Geez* (official state and church language of ancient Ethiopia) in the 15th century, during the reign of Emperor *Zera Yaqob* (1434–1468).

[59] Fitha Negest (Amharic and Geez Version). Addis Ababa: Tesfa-Gebre-Sellassie Printing Press. 44: 1540–1541, p. 380.

[60] Of course, this right was revoked in 1942 by Decree for the Administration of all Church Lands (Decree No. 2 of 1942), which ordered that church lands should pay tax (to the government) at the same rate as secular lands. See the full text in Mahteme-Sellassie: 1957, supra note 55, pp. 300, 301.

[61] See for example, Crummey, D. & Shumet-Sishagne 1991. Land Tenure and the Social Accumulation of Wealth in Eighteenth-Century Ethiopia: Evidence from the Qwesqwam Land Register. *The International Journal of African Historical Studies,* 24, 241–258, p. 247, where it is mentioned that Emperor Iyasu II (1730–1755) and Etege Mentewab, the dowager empress, granted

distributed among the people who served it. These people could be from among the clergy or lay men who supported and served the church in different capacities. Just like the peasant paid his tax to the government, they paid their taxes to be used by the church. The general name used for such type of tenure arrangement was *Samon* Land. Such land use was, however, as emphasized by Shiferaw above, conditional in that they had to continue to serve the church by themselves or through proxy. In most cases, priestly families had to see that one of their children became a priest. As Alvarez, the sixteenth century Portuguese traveler to Ethiopia, observed: "the sons of the priests are for most part priests…"[62] This fact has survived even in modern history, as summarized by Markakis as follows:

> There is a tendency among the clergy to preserve continuity and privilege within the family by passing on the priestly office from one generation to the next. A priest family will normally train one of its sons to enter the service of the church. Since the church provides traditional education, it is not difficult to get it. In this manner, the family preserves its rights over church land. Even if a family does not produce a priest from among its members, it seldom surrenders the land it holds under Samon rights; it simply arranges for a priest to discharge its obligations to the church, or may even pay a certain amount regularly to the administrator of the church in lieu of services.[63]

Concerning the proxy service, Shiferaw, in his study of land grants of five big churches in Addis Ababa, discussed some interesting facts: that six of the holders of *Samon* land, provided to the church of *Enteto Mariam* were Moslems.[64] This means that although the original holders of the land might be Christians and probably priests, their descendants had changed their faith to Islam, and have continued to maintain the land by fulfilling their obligation to the church through proxy services.

2.4.3 Land Tenure System in Southern Ethiopia

The southern, south eastern and south western provinces of Ethiopia were brought under Emperor Menelik's rule during the last third of the nineteenth century, above all between 1875 and 1889,[65] and most land of the southern people was expropriated/confiscated and alienated to northerners. In areas where the people accepted Menelik's rule voluntarily, traditional chiefs were allowed to retain their position

(Footnote 61 continued)
to the Quesquam church in Gonder a sum of 755 *gashas* (1 *gasha* is 40 ha) of land to be distributed among 260 *debteras* (church scribes).

[62] Alvarez, supra note 30, p. 57.

[63] Markakis, supra note 39, p. 123.

[64] Shiferaw, supra note 41, pp. 93, 94.

[65] Pankhurst: 1966, supra note 29, p. 136. These territories were, of course, under Ethiopian rule up to the 15th century. Then after, because of civil war and expansion of the Oromo people from the south, the emperors were pulling back to north and established their permanent city at Gonder.

and land.[66] Landed property continued to belong to the inhabitants exactly as in the older autonomous provinces of the northern part of the country.[67] The most successful, among these, were the present Wollega, Jimma, and Benishangul regions. On the contrary, the land of the rebels who resisted the entry of Menelik's forces, after being defeated, was confiscated and distributed to nobles, the church, Menelik's generals and soldiers, while the people remained landless *gabbars.*[68] The upper elites were empowered with appropriation of all taxes for themselves by passing a fraction of it to the sovereign. They were also given estates to cultivate for their own use.[69]

Land acquired through confiscation was then distributed on three-thirds or four quarter basis. The new rulers took either two-third or three-quarters of the land and left the remaining fraction (one third or one quarter) to the local chief who was then known as *balabat* (gentry). This last part of land is known as *siso* (a third) land. The big portion of land taken by the new settlers was shared between the church and the military based on the same principle applied in the Northern provinces. The amount of land distribution was 1–3 *gasha* (1 *gasha* is 40 ha) for a soldier, 10 *gashas* for *hamsa-aleqa* (commander of fifty), 20 *gashas* for *meto-aleqa* (lieutenant), 30 *gashas* for *shamble* (captain)[70] and so on.

Such land was granted on the basis of different conditions or names. Some are given as *rist-gult* or *siso–gult,* such as those given to the local chiefs; some as *maderia* (in lieu of salary for civil servant, war veterans, on condition of serving the state in time of war), and some as *ginda bel,* on condition of carrying tents, cannons, guarding prisoners and so on. The land given to the church was parceled out as *samon* land in the same fashion as had been done in the north.

A major characteristic of the development was, thus, the allocation of land to the new administrators and their followers, while leaving the natives landless. People from the north were encouraged to settle in these new areas and became beneficiaries of land grant or land purchase. This was done for two reasons: first, to recompense for their service in the war, and second, in order to create "effective occupation"[71] of the newly annexed territories.

The native people, who now became landless, were paradoxically given the name *gabbars*. This name did not connote the same meaning as it had in the north; in the north the name was given for a landed peasant who paid his tax, while in the

---

[66] The Ethiopian method for dealing with their enemies were based on the guidance offered in the *Fitha Negest*: "When you reach a city or a land to fight against its inhabitants, offer them terms of peace. If they accept you and open their gates, the men who are there shall become subjects and shall give you tributes, but if they refuse the terms of peace and offer battle, go forward to assault and oppress them, since the Lord your God will make you master of them." (Markakis, supra note 39, p. 131); Fitha Negest, supra note 59, 44:1552–1555, p. 383.

[67] Pankhurst: 1966, supra note 29, p. 136.

[68] Shiferaw, supra note 41, p. 151.

[69] Ibid.

[70] Id., p. 104.

[71] Crummey: 2000, supra note 35, p. 223.

south the person was landless. The *gabbars* in the south, rather, became servants of those who took their land.[72] Quoted by Pankhurst, C.F. Ray, a traveler to Ethiopia by that time, reflected that the nobles and their followers had considerable dependents upon them. The *gabbar* was a tenant subjected to more onerous burdens than existed elsewhere. The *gabbar* was obliged to look after the settlers by cultivating their land, providing labor, building houses and so on for free.[73] The general practice was that a person who got land in the south, reserved some part of the land for his private use (cultivated by the *gabbars* for him), and distributed the remaining part of the land to his *gabbars* and collected tribute (one third for himself) and tithe (to the government) and allowed them to subsist on the remaining produce. A study made by Markakis on Kembata district in the southern provinces vividly shows the circumstances that existed at the time:

> Kenyazmach (commander of right wing) Arado was allotted forty gashas (1,600 ha) of land for his service in Kambata district. He kept twelve gashas and distributed the rest among his lieutenants and soldiers. One of these, a man from Gojam named Ayele, was given a total of four gashas. The native people who found themselves on the land granted to Ayele became his gabbars (the total family member was 40 people). Ayele settled in the nearby town of Hosana, the capital of Kembata district. Ayele divided his land into hudad (good land reserved for him) and other which was distributed among the gabbars. The gabbars cultivated the hudad and delivered the entire produce to Ayele. Ayele also collected a third of the produce from the other land as a tribute for himself, and another tenth which he turned over to the state as tithe. The gabbars were also required to provide Ayele with firewood, to grind his share of the grain and deliver it to his home in town, and to repair his house and warehouses. In addition, they had to offer him obligatory gifts on Christmas, Easter, and Maskal. Ayele acted as the judge for his gabbars, and in his capacity imposed fines and collected fees. Whenever he visited his land, the gabbars were obliged to provide him with a feast.[74]

On the other hand, the rights of local gentries were remained unaffected because of Menelik's decree passed in 1905 (1897 E.C), which declares that in every land allocation to northern nobles, a third or in some cases half of it should be kept to the local *balabat,* gentry.[75] This is, as already mentioned above known as *siso-gult.*

The other characteristic of the southern land tenure was that the introduction of private ownership of land tenure. It is generally held that private land ownership in the south evolved out of Menelik's expropriation and redistribution of land after his conquest.[76] Many evidences and the wordings of the then laws showed that land was transacted through sale from state to individuals and among individuals. Emperor Menelik also introduced new land measurement (*qelad*) and a tax system, based on the measured lands in the southern regions. The new land taxes imposed

---

[72] Ibid.

[73] Pankhurst: 1966, supra note 29, p. 137.

[74] Markakis, supra note 39, pp. 162, 163.

[75] See as reproduced in Mahteme-Selassie: 1970, supra note 55, p. 109.

[76] Pausewang, S. 1982. *Peasants, Land and Society: a Social History of Land Reform in Ethiopia,* Munchen, Weltforum-Varlag, p. 36.

on *siso* land, *maderia* land and *rist* land were actually paid by the actual cultivator, the *gabbars,* instead of the owner of the land which increased yet the burdens of the *gabbars* and tenants.

2.4.4 Modernization and the Declining Role of Traditional Land Tenure System

The coming of Emperor Haileselassie I, in 1930, to the throne in the early twenty first century and his modernist approach of governance started to contribute to the declining role of the traditional land tenure system, especially to the abolition of the *gult* system in 1966. The traditional tax collection system (in kind) did not enable to generate enough money to the state to create the much needed modern state, with modern salaried military and bureaucracy. As discussed above, land tax in the form of tribute and tithe was collected by the *gult* holder in the northern provinces and the land owner/holder in the southern parts. Because it was difficult to find enough gold and dollars, tax was paid in kind[77] (grain, salt, honey, cattle and so on). As a result, government agents were forced to take it to market to change it to cash money. The system was not efficient and there was no strong bureaucracy to control its proper collection; land owners used to squander it. Studies show that the share of land tax was declining compared to indirect taxes (customs tax) throughout the 1940s–1970s.[78] To rectify such problem and in order to collect enough money from land, successive decrees concerning land tenure and land tax were promulgated well up to the 1970s.

As noted by Hoben, traditionally there was relatively little separation between political power, the control of land, and wealth. Men who enjoyed high positions of secular authority usually controlled much land. They were also at the apex of a redistributional economic organization. They collected tax and tribute from those over whom they held authority and expended a large portion of it again on the feasts and followers that were essential to the maintenance of their political power and their legitimacy in the eye of their subjects.[79] So, it was not easy for the government to weaken the power of the landed autocrats by eroding their traditional power of tax collection, administration and adjudication. That is why, as we shall see soon, the reformative process encountered strong resistance not only from the landed aristocrats but also, ignorantly, from the peasant farmers as well.

Hoben provides four reasons that weakened the traditional power of *gult* holders[80]: the growth of bureaucracy that replaces their administrative power, tax reform

[77] Gebre-Wold-Ingida, supra note 52, p. 302, 303.

[78] See for example Gilkes, P. 1975. *The Dying Lion: Feudalism and Modernization in Ethiopia,* London, Julian Friedman Publishers.; Also see Crummey: 2000, supra note 89, p. 239.

[79] Hoben, supra note 37, p. 209.

[80] Id., pp. 205–209.

that demands the direct payment of tax to government rather than to *gult* holders, emergence and establishment of modern court system that replaces their adjudication power, and finally the establishment of modern military that took away their power as collectors of local soldiers. In here, we will briefly look into the tax reform that had directly affected the land tenure system.

Before the Italian invasion and occupation of Ethiopia (1936–1941), the government tried to come up with two decrees[81] that tried to reduce the burden of the *gabbars* of the southern people. Especially, a decree promulgated on May 9, 1935 tried to reduce the burden of the peasantry by replacing all duties with payment of 30 thalers per *gasha*.[82] But, of course, this was the eve of the Italian invasion and the rule was not implemented. The government came up with series of laws related to land tax after the expulsion of the Italian forces (after the Second World War) which we shall see hereunder. The Italians, during their 5 years occupation, had abolished all informal taxes and burdens except the land tax (tribute) and the tithe (*asrat*). After liberation, the government took advantage of this situation and continued the process without restoring the previous system. The major laws enacted after this period are discussed below.

2.4.4.1 The 1941 Land Tax Decree

Shortly after he restored his power, Emperor Hailesellassie passed a land tax decree[83] in 1941 that mainly contains three things: first, the law entitled all government officials and agents to salaries; second, all the taxes paid by the gabbars were to be sent directly to government treasury. In other words, it abolished the intermediary role of land owners and gult holders.[84] Land tax was to be collected by government agents rather than landlords. Thirdly, it abolished all 'manual labor, firewood, grass and miscellaneous dues and taxes' imposed on the cultivators. This did not include, however, ginda bel and desta in which tax was paid in the form of manual labor.

---

[81] These are the law of September 1930 that deals with tax concerning excess land, and the law of May 1935 that established single land tax. Both are reproduced in Gebre-Wold-Ingida, supra note 52, p. 295–298.

[82] Mahteme-Selassie: 1957, supra note 55, p. 297.

[83] As reproduced in Gebre-Wold-Ingida, supra note 52, p. 325.

[84] For example an Order passed by the Emperor after a year or two reads: "The Ministry of Finance has submitted that the Asrat and trade or marketing tax which has hitherto been collected by *rist-gult* holders shall in future be collected by officers of the Ministry of Finance, and that the *rist-gult* holders shall give to the Ministry of Finance any money they hold at present. These *rist-gult* holders must also submit in writing the amount left in their hands." Gebre-Wold-Ingida, supra note 52, p. 331.

2.4.4.2 The Land Tax Proclamations of 1942 and 1944

Proclamation 8 of 1942,[85] promulgated on 30th of March 1942, but had been put into effect starting from 11 October 1941, brought one important change to the Ethiopian land tax system; it proclaimed that henceforth all land tax should be paid in Ethiopian printed dollars rather than in kind. Article 3(ii) of the proclamation put the amount of taxation based on the size of land area in *gasha* and its fertility rate. It classified the land into fertile, semi-fertile and poor, and imposed 15, 10, and 5 Ethiopia dollars respectively for each *gasha* land holding.

This proclamation lacked clarity in that it was confusing whether or not it replaced the previous two land taxes (tribute and tithe). In any case, a second proclamation (Proc. No. 70/1944) that repealed this proclamation was promulgated in 1944. This was also known as Land Tax Proclamation. This proclamation[86] under Article 4 provided a different tax rate for each of the three types of land fertility. Besides, it provided tax payments in lieu of tithe and tribute tax. For example for some provinces (Shoa, Arusi, Harar and Wollo) the amount set for fertile land was $35 in lieu of tithe and $15 in lieu of tax, for semi fertile land $30 in lieu of tithe and $10 in lieu of tax, and for poor land $10 in lieu of tithe and $5 in lieu of tax. In effect, this law had doubled the tax obligations of peasants as compared to the previous law. The other character of this proclamation was that it did not impose same tax rate for all parts of the country. The Northern provinces were even allowed to continue with their old system as their land was not yet measured in *gashas*. Once again, the law under Article 4 repealed "any other taxes, services and fees heretofore payable".

2.4.4.3 Education Tax and Health Tax

In spite of the state efforts, the above two proclamations could not greatly enhance the revenues of the central government, although they did effectively eliminate the possibility of tax collection by organs other than the state. Hence, to increase the revenue from the land the government introduced Education Tax in 1947 (Proc. No. 94/1947) and Health Tax in 1959 (Decree No. 37/1959)[87] based on the amount and fertility of land holdings. This shows that the state was desperate to increase its tax collection from the land, which in turn aggravated the burdens of the peasant.

---

[85] Full text is reproduced in Gebre-Wold-Ingida, supra note 52, p. 327.

[86] Land Tax Proclamation, Proclamation No. 70/1944. *Negarit Gazeta.* Year 4, No. 2. Also available in Ewing, W. H. (ed.) 1972. *Consolidated Laws of Ethiopia, V. I,* Addis Ababa: The Law Faculty of Haile Sellassie I University, pp. 538–543.

[87] Both are reproduced in Ewing, W. H. (ed.) 1972. *Consolidated Laws of Ethiopia, V. I,* Addis Ababa: The Law Faculty of Haile Sellassie I University, pp. 473 and 477 respectively.

2.4.4.4 Abolition of *Gult* and Tithe and Introduction of Income Tax

The government took things one step further to their logical conclusion, in 1966 and 1967, with proclamations which abolished both secular *gult* and tithe.[88] Proclamation 230/1966 that amended the previous land tax, proclamation 70/1944, clearly dictated those people who cultivate on lands subject to *rist gult* or *siso gult* directly to pay their tax to the Government treasury.[89] The same amendment eliminated the special tax status of those holding *rist gult* or *siso gult* rights with respect to land which they also own.[90] Since traditionally *gult* provides tribute collection power over *gult* holders, the transfer of the tribute collection power to other body eliminates the traditional institution of *gult* system. If a person whose land has been subject to *rist gult* rights had henceforth to pay the land taxes directly to the Government treasury, there was nothing left for the *gultenga,* the holder of the *gult* rights. His rights had, at a stroke, been eliminated. *Gult* holders were allowed to change certain part of their holding to private tenure and the remainder was divided among the *gabbars.*

The next step taken by the government was to amend the income tax in 1967 by introducing agricultural income tax. One of the characteristics of this proclamation was that it abolished the payment of tithe. As discussed before, cultivators used to pay a tenth of their produce to the government through the *gult* holder. Now the removal of this tax meant again eroding the power base of the *bala gults* and thereby reducing the burdens of the peasantry.

Although it cannot be denied that all these steps to some extent alleviated (especially the last two proclamations) the burdens of the peasantry of the south, they were not equally appreciated in the northern part of the country. For example, among the three peasant rebellions that took place in between 1940s and 1960s, the two that happened in the northern provinces of Tigray and Gojam were made against tax and land measurement activities of the state. Generally, the land tax proclamations and land measurements which were meant to enhance the amount of tax, initiated peasant rebellions in Tigray (1943), in Bale (1967–1970) and in Gojam (1968).[91]

---

[88] Crummey: 2000, supra note 35, p. 241.

[89] 1966. A Proclamation to Amend the Land Tax Proclamation of 1944. *Proclamation No. 230/ 1966.* Negarit Gazeta: Year 25, No. 9. Article 2(a).

[90] Id., Article 2(b).

[91] For more discussion on the subject, see Gebru-Tareke 1991. *Ethiopia: Power and Protest: Peasant Revolts in the Twentieth Century,* Cambridge, Cambridge University Press.

2.4.5 The Question of Land Reform and Inadequate Government Response

Over the years, the land holding in the southern provinces had slowly changed into private (freehold) holdings through different decrees. As opposed to the north, land in the south was freely transferable by way of sale. Like his predecessor, Haile Sellassie also continued to grant land to different groups. Immediately after the Italian war, he granted extensive land to patriots, exiles, soldiers and civil servants as private property. This policy, however, was of little benefit to tenant gabbars. Indeed, from the nearly 5 million ha of land allocated after 1941, only a few thousand reached the landless and the unemployed gabbars.[92] The concept of rist, as lineage land property, was not known in this part of the country. Hence, in the 1950s and 1960s extensive land sale was witnessed, especially the transfer from land owners to new investors.[93] But the effect of such measures made the existing gabbars once and for all landless tenants. Tenants, thus, were forced to cultivate on share-cropping arrangement which was said to be unjust in that it claimed 75 % of the produce to the landlord.[94]

As already mentioned above (Sect. 2.4.4), in spite of the fact that the government passed laws that forbid other burdens, tenants were subjected to feudal dues like working on the landlord's farm and giving him presents on special occasions for fear of eviction. Powerful lords of the land continued to confiscate peasant's property at will and to evict tenants arbitrarily even on the eve of the Revolution.[95] In addition to the fact that the system was seen as unjust, it was considered inefficient and unproductive for it did not give the tenants incentive to produce more because, it was alleged, they lost a lot of the increased produce to the landlord.[96] The most radical criticism of the land-tenure system came from the student movement, which, since the middle of the 1960s, made the slogan "Land to the Tiller" its main rallying call and the attainment of land reform its main target. When, as of 1969, the issue surfaced concerning whether the southern part of the country was not a case of settler colonialism by people from the north, and whether, therefore, the southern tenants were reduced to this status on land which had once been their own, land reform acquired a much greater political poignancy than ever

---

[92] Bahru-Zewde: 1991, supra note 48, p. 191.

[93] Dessalegn-Rahmato 2006. From Hetrogeneity to Homogeneity: Agrarian Class Structure in Ethiopia since the 1950s. *In*: Dessalegn-Rahmato & Taye-Assefa (eds.) *Land and the Challenge of Sustainable Development in Ethiopia.* Addis Ababa: Forum for Social Studies, p. 9. During the 1960s land was transferred by sale to civil servants, small scale traders and the like who anticipate profit from export of agricultural products.

[94] For example, according to different studies, the tenancy rate was 75 % in Hararge, 67 % in Showa, 62 % in Kaffa, all from the south. On the contrary, in the north was 15 % in Begemder, 20 % in Gojam and 25 % in Tigre.

[95] Dessalegn-Rahmato: 2006, supra note 93, p. 8.

[96] Andargachew-Tiruneh 1993. *The Ethiopian Revolution, 1974–1987: A Transformation From an Aristocratic to aTotalitarian Autocracy,* New York, Cambridge University Press, p. 97.

before.[97] Also, academics, foreign governments and aid agencies were very critical of the existing land-tenure system and urged for some kind of reform to be adopted.

One of Haile Sellassie's government responses to these criticisms was the establishment of a Ministry of Land Reform and Administration to deal with the matter.[98] One notion promoted by that ministry, well before 1974, was the redistribution of individually owned land in excess of 20 ha. A draft proposal to that effect was shelved for lack of support in government circles. The fact that the government officials and members of parliament had their economic and hence political power based on land was often attributed as a cause for the obstruction of the adoption of the draft proposal. Harold Marcus, a prominent historian on Ethiopia, claims that after the 1960 *cope d'état,* the Emperor was forced to "rely increasingly on overt military power for authority and on the aristocracy and oligarchy for administrative support. Since the last two represented the property-owning classes, Haile Sellassie was unable to implement significant land reform, in the absence of which the intelligentsia and the students, at first quietly and then stridently, opposed the regime."[99]

The emperor was generally said to be slow in taking a radical and important land reform that would have a socio-political effect. A contemporary researcher and professor at the then Faculty of Law at the Haile Sellassie I University, Harrison Dunning observed that:

> Beyond the elimination of personal services, it is difficult to name an objective related to land and designed to improve the social and political position of the Ethiopian peasantry toward which even partial action has been taken in the past quarter century. Even public discussion of such objectives has not occurred. With guidelines so unclear, it is fruitless to attempt to evaluate the contribution which land reform could make in these areas of national development.[100]

By way of conclusion, it can be said that the resistance of the peasantry population (because of ignorance on the advantage of land measurement and registration), internal resistance for land reform from the landed aristocrats, most of whom sate in both chambers of the parliament,[101] and the lack of action by the government[102] itself to bring about change in the tenure system were the reasons for absence of meaningful change in the property right arrangement during the eve of the downfall of the imperial regime.

---

[97] Ibid., p. 98.

[98] Ibid.

[99] Marcus, H., supra note 36, p. 173.

[100] Dunning, H. C. 1970. Land Reform in Ethiopia: A Case Study in Non-Development. *UCLA L. Rev,* 18, p. 306.

[101] See Shiferaw, supra note 41, p. 128, who told us that bills concerning land reform tabled to parliament in 1963, 1970 and 1972 were rejected by both parliaments.

[102] Dunning, supra note 100, at foot note 152, for example says: "Three draft proclamations had been submitted to the Council of Ministers by July 1, 1969: a Proclamation to provide for the Registration of Immovable Property; a Proclamation to provide for the Regulation of Agricultural Tenancy Relationships; and a Proclamation to provide for a Tax on Unutilized Land. As of October 1, 1970, none of these drafts had been submitted to Parliament".

2.5 The Derg Era: A Radical Shift in Land Policy

Frustrated by the lack of meaningful land reform and driven by the then Marxist ideology, practiced in some parts of the world, university students started demanding social, economic and political reforms with the leading motto "Land to the Tiller." The demand for change got momentum when the general public and finally the military and police force followed suit and resulted in the 1974 revolution. The condition of the peasant and the need for radical change that was advocated at the time can be easily perceived from Dessalegn Rahmato writing:

> How can the peasant change his condition? Will it be through better laws, clearer definition of tenure rights, or improved land registration and cadastral surveys? Can it be done by granting ownership right to tenants over government-owned land? Or will land reform, but of kind which does not disturb the equilibrium of the feudal system, provide the antidote?
>
> The peasant problem is too fundamental to be resolved with such facile measures. It is not the deficiencies of the system that creates rural misery, but the system itself. Peasant servitude and deprivation will not be eliminated so long as the land-less are under the economic subjection of the landlord. Only when the direct producers toil for no other but themselves will they be able to attain emancipation, and to raise their standard of living to a level consistent with human dignity. In this connection the slogan LAND TO THE TILLER is indeed subversive.[103]

The army, being better organized and having better gun power, took advantage of the situation and appointed itself as the agent of the people. A committee (junta) selected from all the army branches[104] was established to negotiate things with the emperor and to bring corrupt officials of the *ancient regime* to justice.[105] This committee (popularly known as Derg), a collection of junior officers, later on removed the Emperor from his throne in September 1974 and took power itself promising the election of a popular government in the future. The Derg established a "provisional military government." Accordingly, until 1987, the country was administrated by the Provisional Military Administration Council (PMAC).

Following its assumption of power, the Derg, started to take radical socio-economic reforms which had Marxist ethos.[106] In the following pages we shall see the highlights of the rural land and urban land proclamations which were enacted by the Derg in a bid to transfer all rural and urban land and urban extra houses to state ownership.

---

[103] Dessalegn-Rahmato 1970. Condition of the Ethiopian Peasantry. *Challenger,* X. Quoted in Shiferaw, supra note 41, p. 124.

[104] With the highest rank of a Major, the army representatives were delegated from the air force, police force, navy, and ground forces. The would be president (Mengistu Haile Mariam) himself was a Major, representing ground forces from the city of Harar.

[105] For detail see Andargachew, supra note 96.

[106] It was on 20 December 1974 that the Derg's first fundamental political and economic programme, 'Ethiopian Socialism', was issued. (Andargachew, Ibid, p. 86). The reforms were dealing with nationalizations of urban and rural land, financial institutions and heavy and light industries.

2.5.1 Nationalization of Rural Land

When the Derg revealed its ten-point program of "Ethiopian Socialism" on December 20 1974, it declared that "land would be owned by the people."[107] And the "people" appeared to be identified under point No. 7 which stated that "the right to own land shall be restricted to those who work on the land"[108] which means that land would be privatized. Nevertheless, when the much anticipated proclamation[109] lastly came out on March 4 1975, the Derg ruled out for public/state ownership of all rural land.

The main reasons for the nationalization of rural land from the previous owners/holders and its transfer to state ownership are envisaged in the preamble of the proclamation. Without the need to reproduce the whole preamble, we pinpoint the main essence as follows:

> Whereas, in countries like Ethiopia a person's right, honor, status, and standard of living is determined by his relation to land;... that several thousands gas has of land was grabbed by insignificant number of feudal lords while the masses live under serfdom;... that it is necessary to change the past injustices and lay a base upon which Ethiopians may live in equality, freedom and fraternity;...that development could be achieved through the abolition of exploitation of many by the few;...In order to increase productivity by making the tiller the owner of the fruits of his labour;...to provide work for all rural people;...it becomes necessary to distribute land and increase rural income and thereby laying the basis for the expansion of industry.

To implement this objective, Article 3 of the proclamation clearly declared that: "all rural lands shall be the collective property of the Ethiopian people," and it prohibits any person, business organization (company) or other organization from holding rural land in private ownership (Article 3.2 of Proc. 31/1975). By doing so, the law once and for all eliminated any private ownership of rural land, which had started to flourish in the southern part of the country, and it overnight abolished the age-old tenure system of the country in general. Further, the law denied any compensation for the loss of land and any forest and tree-crops thereon. On the other hand, it provided that fair compensation would be paid for movable properties and permanent works on the land (Article 3.3). Nonetheless, when it came to practice, the Derg paid no compensation at all to such properties across the country.

The proclamation, on the other hand, created free access to land to the many rural landless and tenants. Without discrimination of any kind, the law provided opportunity for any person, who was willing to cultivate, to get rural land sufficient for his maintenance (Article 4.1). The size of land to be allocated for a household was made to be, as far as possible, equal, and allowed for a maximum of 10 ha (Article 4.3). No person was allowed to use hired laborers to cultivate his land (except the weak, the sick, widows, and minors (Article 4.5).

---

[107] Andargachew, supra note 96, p. 99.

[108] Clapham, supra note 44, p. 45.

[109] Public Ownership of Rural Lands, Proclamation No. 31/1975. *Negarit Gazeta.* Year 34, No. 26. (Hereinafter cited as Proc. No. 31/1975).

Until land distribution was to be carried out, it was stated that all "tenants or hired laborer shall have possessory right over the land they till;" on the other hand, "a resident landowner who has leased out all his lands shall have the right to equally share to the land with his tenants" (Article 6.1). The proclamation also abolished any landlord-tenant relationship, and the tenant was made free from any rent, debt or any other obligation. Likewise, a landowner who gave his land as antichresis to his tenants would be free from payment of the debt (Article 6.3). All large-scale farms, held by private investments, were transferred to state ownership or cooperatives.

Since land became state/public property, it was also important to delimit the scope of rights to be given to individual peasants. In this case, it did not give much. Under a title "Prohibition of Transfer of Land," Article 5 of the proclamation declares:

> No person may by sale, exchange, succession, mortgage, antichresis, lease or otherwise transfer his holding to another; provided that upon the death of the holder the wife or husband or minor children of the deceased or where these are not present, any child of the deceased who has attained majority, shall have the right to use the land.

Thus, the proclamation completely prohibited any sale, mortgage, antichresis,[110] lease/rent, inheritance (outside of family), donation, or exchange of any sort that affects the land. It seems the government was cautious not to create controversy with the church and the northern land holders since the proclamation did not say anything about church lands, and provided separate provisions related to "communal lands", specifically *rist* lands. According to some studies, the total amount of land held by the church by the time was estimated to be 20 % of all arable land and 5 % of all the land in the country.[111] Concerning *rist* land, the proclamation under Article 19 provides "peasants in *rist* and *dessa* areas shall have possessory rights over the lands they presently till." It denies any claimant thereafter to come up with new claims. However, unlike the southern parts, in the north, since every plot of land was held by peasants, there was no need for the proclamation to come up with such different provision.

In any case, Articles 3 and 5 of the proclamation had restricted the rights of transfer of land very much and this had a devastating effect to all the previous land owners in the south or *rist* holders in the north. This proclamation was, therefore, received with mixed sentiments across the country. For tenant farmers and landless peasants, especially of the southern part of the country, the abolition of land ownership removed a major source of exploitation in one case, and provided guaranteed access to land in the other.[112] Peasants of the north who owned their

---

[110] According to the Ethiopian Civil Code (Articles 3041 ff and 3117 ff), antichresis is like a mortgage except that the former is created by contract. The main difference is that in case of antichresis the immovable (land or building) shall be temporarily delivered/transferred to the creditor, while in case of mortgage it has to stay in the hand of the debtor.

[111] Cohen, J. M. 1977. Rural and Urban Land Reform in Ethiopia. *Afri. L. Stud.*, 14, p. 14.

[112] Clapham, supra note 44, p. 47.

own *rist* land that gave them effective control over it were threatened by a measure which required their security and put them on equal basis with the landless.[113] The *rist* holders of the north who considered their right to the land as coming from their family and no one else, considered it as encroachment in their God given rights. According to some studies, in the Northern Province of Tigray, farmers out rightly refuted the law and a war ensued immediately.[114] Armed struggle was declared and carried out by supporters of the old regime and various student led movements against the Derg, the sole survivor being the present incumbent. Rebellious conflicts were also arisen in the other Northern provinces of Gonder and Wollo.[115]

The management and distribution of land was given to peasant associations (PA), which were formed to cover a minimum area of 800 ha (20 *gashas*) of land.[116] The functions of the peasant associations were mainly to redistribute land, maintain common assets, resolve land dispute conflicts, enable development activities taking place in their areas and implementing villagization programs.[117]

The system, in a way, looked like the Chinese model where land was owned by the state and collectives and every village collective was given the power to own, administer, and lease out land to individual peasants.[118] This fact is also observed by Dessalegn when he said: "the post reform agrarian policies were modeled in part on the experience of China and Vietnam."[119] Of course, in Ethiopia, it was not the peasant association that would give land by way of lease. The right was life time in that peasants were allowed to use it for life and even to pass it as an inheritance to their spouses and children. In the Chinese model peasants get the land on lease basis for 15 years (later on amended to 30 years) and the village collective should renew the contract after its expiry.

Assessment of the land reform carried out in the years that followed the proclamation has been made by many writers.[120] The general agreement can be summarized as follows in the work of Dessalegn Rahmato:

---

[113] Ibid.

[114] See generally for example Young, J. 1997. *Peasant Revolution in Ethiopia The Tigray People*'s Liberation Front, 1975–1991,New York, Cambridge University Press.; Aregawi-Berhe 2008. *A Political History of the Tigray People's Liberation Front (1975–1991): Revolt, Ideology and Mobilisation in Ethiopia,* Amsterdam, Amsterdam University, p. 71.

[115] See Dessalegn-Rahmato 2009a-a. Land and Agrarian Unrest in Wollo: From the Imperial Regime to the Derg. *In*: Dessalegn-Rahmato (ed.) *The Peasant and the State: Studies in Agrarian Change in Ethiopia 1950s–2000s (collection of articles by same author).* Addis Ababa: Addis Ababa university Press, pp. 111–182.

[116] Article 8 of Proc. 31/1975.

[117] See the detail under Article 10 of Proc. No. 31/1975.

[118] See for example, Ho, P., supra note 20, pp. 5–10.

[119] Dessalegn-Rahmato 1993. Agrarian Change and Agrarian Crisis: State and Peasantry in Post-Revolution Ethiopia. *Africa: Journal of the International African Institute,* 63, 36–55, p. 36.

[120] See for example Yeraswork-Admassie 2000. *Twenty Years to Nowhere: Property Rights, Land Management and Conservation in Ethiopia* Asmara, The Red Sea Press, Inc.

- Erroneous state policies (villagization, grain requisitioning, resettlement, agricultural, collectivization) which were not discussed with the people at grassroots level cost the country lots of energy and money.
- The peasant associations (PAs) which were given authority to redistribute land, maintain, common assets, resolve conflicts and enable development activities taking place in their areas were captured/hijacked by the state to do its 'political work', such as tax collection, maintaining order, channeling propaganda, requisition grain, and recruiting young men for the war.
- The land reform was successful in that it abolished the landlordism and tenantship in the country and created free access to land to all the landless, but it failed because (1) it defined land rights as usufructuary rather than private (2) the mandate given to the PA encouraged them to practice periodic land distribution, in consultation with local government agents, created tenure insecurity.
- By and large, it replaced the landlord with the state, providing the latter with direct and uncontrollable access to the peasantry. "In conclusion, the end product of the land reform was it failed where it succeeded."[121]

2.5.2 Nationalization of Urban Land and Extra Houses

2.5.2.1 Urbanization and Pattern of Urban Land Ownership

The second very important legislation enacted by the Derg was a proclamation that nationalized all urban lands and extra rentable houses.[122] Before giving the details about this proclamation, however, few words need to be said about the pattern of urbanization and urban land right before the revolution.

Urbanization in Ethiopia is a recent phenomenon because of the historical factors in the country. Many of the middle sized towns in Ethiopia were founded during the nineteenth century for political-military reasons.[123] According to Donald Crummey, three major institutions shaped Ethiopian towns during the 19th and 20th centuries: palace, market and church, and these institutions played three roles: political, economic and cultural.[124] The establishment of the current capital, Addis Ababa, in 1886, is the third in line following Axum and Gonder in the ancient and middle age Ethiopian history respectively. Throughout most of its history, Ethiopia remained a

[121] Dessalegn: 1993, supra note 119, pp. 36–40.

[122] Government Ownership of Urban Land and Extra Houses, Proclamation No. 47/1975. *Negarit Gazeta,* Year 34, No. 41. (Hereinafter cited as Proc. 47/1975).

[123] Markakis, supra note 39, p. 197.

[124] Bahru-Zewde 2008a. The City Center: A Shifting Concept in the History of Addis Ababa. *In*: Bahru-Zewde (ed.) *Society, State and History: Selected Essays.* Addis Ababa: Addis Ababa University Press, p. 486.

land of small villages and isolated homesteads.[125] The reason for the absence of large settlement of urban areas in Ethiopia for a long time, according to Richard Pankhurst, was the continuous move of the royal camp. Middle age royal court was composed of immense agglomerations of population which consisted of not only of courtiers and warriors, but also numerous non-combatants, among them wives, servants and slaves, armourers, tent-carriers, muleteers, priests, traders, prostitutes, beggars, and even a few children.[126] On the other hand, some argued that there was a little need for urbanization, since it contradicted the existing self-sufficient peasantry life style; urbanization by its nature needs to transfer more land away from agricultural production to urban settlement.[127] And yet, it can be concluded that modern Ethiopian urbanization flourished during the 20th century because of political stability (especially during the reign of Emperor Haile Sellassie I), and the modernization of the country. Most cities in the country flourished around some economic center such as railway, factory, or trade route.

Addis Ababa was established in 1886 by Emperor Menelik II and it is said that in the beginning it was a collection of camps where the royal camp was located in a tent at the center of the high ground. The imperial camp was surrounded by the Emperor's servants, and other nobility were granted land for their own and their followers to construct houses. Over time, because of the insecurity they felt, the lords and foreign embassies made a request to Menelik for some kind of security over their holdings. Accordingly, the emperor promulgated a decree[128] in 1907 that recognized private ownership of land, and allowed its free transfer through sale (Article 3). The decree also created land cadastre system which enabled the registration of every sale of land and the giving of land ownership certificates to owners (Articles 5, 10, 11, and 14). Further, it gave a guarantee against arbitrary confiscation of land by providing compensation in the event of land expropriation for public purpose activities (Articles 25 and 26). This gave property holders greater security and a stake in the fate of the city. Not only did the land charter become the most prized certificate of any urban household but it also contributed to activating the urban economy through sales and mortgages.[129]

A detailed study of earlier land tenure in the 17–18th century urban Gonder also shows that land was held in private hands and subjected to free sale and exchange.[130] Thus, urban land in Ethiopia, from the beginning, was held in private ownership. During the eve of the revolution, Addis Ababa was by far the biggest

---

[125] Pankhurst, R. 1990. *A Social History of Ethiopia,* Addis Ababa, Institute of Ethiopian Studies, Addis Ababa University, p. 275.

[126] Ibid.

[127] Molla-Mengistu 2009. The Ethiopian Urban Landholding System: An Assessment of the Governing Legal Regime. *In*: Muradu-Abdo (ed.) *Land Law and Policy in Ethiopia since 1991: Continuities and Changes.* Addis Ababa: Law Faculty, Addis Ababa University.

[128] See the full edict in Amharic in Mahteme-Selassie: 1970, supra note 55, pp. 166–171; or an English version in Pankhurst: 1966, supra note 29, pp. 156–158.

[129] Bahru-Zewde: 2008a, supra note 124, p. 490.

[130] For good explanation see Crummey: 2000, supra note 35.

city and center of economy and politics. The city grew fast, inhabiting a considerable population, which was estimated to be between sixty and one hundred thousand in 1910[131] to about 1.1 million during the revolution in 1974.[132] Other towns had insignificant population growth compared to the capital. For example, according to a 1970s estimate, out of the registered 268 towns, the eight biggest towns had a population of 25,000 each, while Addis Ababa at that time registered 800,000 inhabitants (one third of all urban inhabitants in the country).[133]

Much of the land in the city was controlled by insignificantly few elites. Pankhurst has provided the figures based on the first reliable survey of the city's 212 km^2 made in 1961 as follows:

> This survey showed that 58 % of the total area was owned by 1,768 large proprietors each with more than 10,000 m^2, or an average of 71,000 m^2 per owner, whereas 24,590 small proprietors owning less than 10,000 m^2 had only 7.4 % of the total, the average size of such plots being 150 m^2. 12.7 % of the land belonged to the Government and foreign embassies. A further 12 % belonged to the Church, while the remaining, 9.9 %…was a royal land.[134]

It means 58 % of the surveyed land was held by 6.7 % of the population. An estimate made 5 years later, in 1966, showed that 5 % of the population in Addis Ababa owned 95 % of the land in the city.[135] Almost all the elites who controlled rural and urban land ventured in the construction of rental houses, which was an attractive investment at that time.[136] This ranged all the way from the appalling hovels (slums) of the urban poor to elegant villas which found a ready market among diplomats and expatriate experts in a city that headquarters international organizations.[137] Land value rose alarmingly from 0.25 birr in the 1950s to 200–300 birr per m^2 in the 1970s (1 USD was about 2 birr).[138]

2.5.2.2 Nationalization of Urban Land and Extra Houses

As discussed above, when the Derg came to power, it first nationalized all rural lands and natural resources. Then upon the enactment of Proclamation 47/1975 it nationalized all urban lands and extra houses. The preamble of the Proclamation

---

[131] Pankhurst: 1966, supra note 29, p. 154.

[132] Lapiso-G-Delebo 1983 EC. *Ye Ethiopia Ye Gebar Sireat-na Jimir Capitalism: 1900–1966 (Ethiopian Gabar System and the Begining of Capitalism: 1908–1974),* Addis Ababa, p. 267.

[133] Markakis, supra note 39, pp. 198, 199. This was based on the second census of the city.

[134] Pankhurst: 1966, supra note 29, p. 154.

[135] Mesfin-Wolde-Mariam. Year. Problems of Urbanization. *In:* Proceeding of the Third International Conference of Ethiopian Studies, 1970 Addis Ababa. Institute of Ethiopian Studies, Haile Sellassie I University, supra note 111, p. 25.

[136] For example, during the late 1960s, 60 % of the occupied houses in Addis Ababa were rental ones. (Cohen, supra note 111, p. 25).

[137] Clapham, supra note 44, p. 50.

[138] 1978. Urban Land and Extra House: From Yesterday to Today (Amharic). Addis Ababa: Committee established for the Fourth Anniversary of the Revolution.

47/1975 that nationalized "all urban land and extra houses", justifies its nationalization of urban land on three main counts: to abolish the shortage of land and the soaring of prices caused by the concentration of land in the hands of a few feudal lords, aristocrats, high government officials and capitalists; to abolish the exploitation of the many by the few (through uncontrolled rent); and to abolish tax evasion. The proclamation also aimed to create credit access to the poor once they got the land and built their houses.[139]

Like its rural counterpart, Proclamation 47/1975 under Article 3(1) declares that as of the effective date of the proclamation, all urban lands should be property of the Government; and no person, family or organization was allowed to hold urban land in private ownership (Article 3.2). Besides, all extra houses, houses other than one residential house and another business house were nationalized (Article 13). Houses owned by minors were immediately nationalized (Article 15) unless his/her parents did not own their own residential house. It further declares that no person would be compensated for the loss of urban lands (Article 3.3) although the loss of houses through nationalization was said to be compensable (Article 18.1). However, in reality no compensation was paid for the nationalizations of houses.[140] But, for those persons whose livelihood was depended on rent, collected from the nationalized extra-houses, government allowed payment of pension allowance (Article 21).

Since all urban land became the property of the Government, it was prohibited to transfer urban land through sale, antichresis, mortgage, succession or otherwise (Article 4.1). As an exception, however, a widow/widower or children are given the right to inherit the land. Instead of ownership, urban residents were given lifetime use right (usually referred as *permit system*) to the urban land except that holders of the land were obliged to pay urban land rent (Article 9) and housing tax (Article 11.4). Also, those who used to live in private rental houses were allowed to continue possessing the houses, but made to continue paying a reduced rent to the state. It seems, the state once again replaced the urban landlords in controlling urban land and houses and exacting rent therefrom. Landless people were guaranteed to get not more than 500 m^2 of land to construct a single dwelling house (Article 5.1). People became full owners of the houses they built on the granted land, and thus, were allowed to transfer it by way of sale, succession or barter provided that the government would have pre-emption right in case of sale (Article 12.1).

In the same fashion as had been done with the rural land, in here as well, any relationship that existed between urban landlords and tenants was abolished, and the tenant was made free from payment of rent, debt or any other obligation arising from the relationship to the landlord (Article 6.1). Further, the law allowed any tenant without any dwelling house to possess or retain the land he used to rent before the enactment of the law (Article 7). Creditors who possessed buildings as

---

[139] Preamble of Proc. 47/1975.

[140] According to Andargachew, supra note 96, pp. 94, 95, the government had paid compensation only to foreign investors who lost their assets to the government. The assets were mainly factories, large-scale farms, banks and insurances.

security for a loan were denied any right of attachment to a house. The house was either to be returned to the debtor (if he has no other dwelling house) or to be nationalized by the state. The creditor was just expected to search other ways to collect his money (Article 17). There is no doubt that creditors who lent money on this basis must have lost their money.

Upon the effective date of the proclamation, all people were prohibited from renting out their houses and receiving any rent accruing therefrom (Article 20.1). The state was the only legitimate organ allowed to let properties and receive rent. The arrangement set in the proclamation was for the state to replace all former landlords and to receive rent from the lessees. Of course, the amount of rent was reduced, ranging from 15 to 50 %, depending on the value of the properties. For instance, houses, which were rented out for 25 birr, had a 50 % reduction in rent, while for those houses rented out for 300 birr the reduction was 15 % (Article 20.4)). The administration of houses which rented 100 birr and below was given to local cooperative societies (later on known as *Kebeles*), while the administration of those houses that rented above 100 birr per month was given to the Ministry of Public Works and Housing (later became Housing agency) (Article 20.5; Article 2.15).

The low rental charges, however, left little room for investment in the *Kebele* houses resulting in physical and structural deterioration owing to the lack of appropriate management and maintenance.[141] The idea is that people were encouraged to live in *Kebele* houses (because they were cheap) rather than constructing their own houses. Secondly, since all the rental revenue was transferred to central government, there was not much left for maintenance and construction by the *Kebeles*.[142] Further, new land provision for construction was highly restricted, halting the expansion of the city, which only led the inner city to be densely populated. Later, squatter settlements and illegal land transactions intensified, and this forced the Derg to adopt self-help housing cooperatives that helped to tackle the problem.[143]

[141] UN-HABITAT 2010. The Ethiopia Case of Condominium Housing: The Integrated Housing Development Programme. Nairobi: United Nations Human Settlements Programme.

[142] UN-HABITAT 2008. Ethiopia:Addis Ababa Urban Profile. Nairobi: United Nations Human Settlements Programme, p. 12.

[143] Feyera-Abdissa & Terefe-Degefa 2011. Urbanization and Changing Livelihoods: The Case of Farmers' Displacement in the Expansion of Addis Ababa. *In*: Teller, C. & Hailemariam, A. (eds.) *The Demographic Transition and Development in Africa: The Unique Case of Ethiopia.* London: Springer, p. 217.

2.6 The Current Land Tenure System

2.6.1 *Land Policy: Two Debates on Ownership of Land*

Immediately after the revolution and the assumption of power by the Derg and the subsequent land reforms conducted by it, various insurgent groups lifted arms against the Derg. The causes were multifarious, but they may be summed up into two. The earliest opposition was made by the landed nobilities of northern Ethiopia whose land was completely nationalized by the government. The second opposition had come mainly from contemporary university students, who believed that the revolution was betrayed by the Derg. This was because the Derg declared itself as the sole vanguard of the revolution and banned any form of political activity. And yet, there was no basic ideological difference between the Derg and the other student led opposition groups, as all of them claimed to believe in Socialism. One of the earliest student dominated armed groups in Ethiopia was the TPLF (Tigray People's Liberation Front) which during the late 1980s made a coalition with other groups from central (Amhara) and southern (Oromo) Ethiopia. This coalition became known as EPRDF (Ethiopian People's Revolutionary Democratic Front) which finally won the war and replaced the Derg in 1991. Since then, the EPRDF is the incumbent party in the Ethiopian politics.

The EPRDF conducted land reform activities during the struggle (1975–1991) in the area where it had effective control. The TPLF, a follower of Albanian type of Socialism and ardent enemy of the feudal nobilities who controlled large amount of land, carried out smooth land distribution in Tigray.[144] After the downfall of the Derg, in May 1991, the new Transitional Government disbanded all collectivization and villagization programs based on the consent of the people. Collective farms were privatized and the government stopped the grain requisition program, allowing peasants to sell their produce at market value. In December 1992, a new economic policy was adopted whereby the government declared that until a new constitution were in place, land would remain under state ownership.[145]

Judging from the process of the 'post-socialist transition' that had been carried out by the Transitional Government, and above all the free market economy type of policy that it embraced, many hoped that the new constitution would allow private ownership of land. However, when it finally came out in 1995, it decided to keep all rural and urban land under public ownership. According to the FDRE Constitution, all urban and rural land is the property of the state and the Ethiopian people.[146] Accordingly, sale, exchange and mortgage of land are prohibited. As one writer commented, "by inserting the land policy into the constitution, the current

[144] For full discussion see Aregawi-Berhe, supra note 114, pp. 285–290; Young, supra note 114.

[145] Tamirat-Layne 1991. Ethiopian Transitional Period Economic Policy. Addis Ababa: Office of Prime Minister.

[146] Constitution of the Federal Demecratic Republic of Ethiopia, Proclamation No. 1/1995. *Negarit Gazeta.* Year 1 No. 1. Article 40(3) (hereinafter FDRE Constitution.).

government has effectively eliminated the possibility of flexible application of policy."[147]

In many countries land ownership is not a constitutional issue, but in Ethiopia, because of its socio-economic importance, land ownership goes beyond being a mere policy matter. Rather, it is inserted in the Constitution and the issue of its ownership has become a settled subject. The argument forwarded by the ruling party for the continuation of land as public/state property rests mainly on two policy objectives: social equity and tenure security. The FDRE Constitution as well as other Federal and Regional Land Laws ensure the free access to agricultural land. The amount of land to be provided to peasant farmers, as far as possible, is made equal. Accordingly, the policy objective is to ensure equality of citizens in accessing the land. However, the weakness of this policy objective is that first, it does not address the urban land; Article 40 of the FDRE Constitution that deals with property talks only about rural land. Second, it is argued that since there is lack of arable land in the highlands of the country, equality of access to land is ensured through transfer of land from large holders to small holders and/or to new comers; the result being diminution of holding plots (0.5–1 ha). Social equality in Ethiopia is, thus, a costly one in that equality in privilege is tantamount to equality in poverty.[148]

Tenure security is the other policy objective and concern of the state. As mentioned above, the FRDE Constitution prohibits any sale and exchange of land. State ownership of land is considered to be the best mechanism to protect the peasants against market forces. In particular, it has been argued that private ownership of rural land would lead to massive eviction or migration of the farming population, as poor farmers would be forced to sell their plots to unscrupulous urban speculators, particularly during periods of hardship.[149] The justification is that for large-scale modern farms, there is an abundant idle arable land in the low lands; both for rain fed and irrigation farming. Most of the farmers, on the other hand, live in the highlands where there is scarcity of land but large amount of accumulated human power due to high population density. Allowing the farmer to sell land here, would lead either to displacing the farmers or converting them to tenants. In both ways, large amount of capital and labor will be wasted.[150] This argument of the government is criticized for lack of corroborative evidence. Some researches show otherwise. Some conclude that farmers would not sell their land

---

[147] Samuel-Gebreselassie 2006. Land, Land Policy and Smallholder Agriculture in Ethiopia: Options and Scenarios. *Future Agricultures Consortium meeting.* the Institute of Development Studies, p. 4.

[148] Dessalegn-Rahmato 2009b. An Assessment on the Ethiopian Agricultural Policy. *In*: Taye-Assefa (ed.) *Digest of Ethiopian National Policies, Strategies and Programmes (Amharic).* Addis Ababa: Forum for Social Studies and The European Union, p. 149.

[149] MOIPAD 2001. Federal Democratic Republic of Ethiopia Rural Development Policies, Strategies and Instruments (Amharic). Addis Ababa: Ministry of Information, Press and Audio-visual Department, pp. 67–90.

[150] Ibid.

wholly or partially if given the right to own their plots.[151] Another study, conducted by the World Bank, reveals that most farmers would rather rent their land during stressful periods compared with any other alternative, such as selling it.[152] The study concludes that the availability of formal land rental markets will serve as a caution to enable farmers to withstand unfavorable circumstances by temporarily renting their land rather than selling it.

The state ownership of land has been criticized by researchers and international donors who favor neo-liberal economic thinking. The usual argument forwarded by these people against the state/public ownership of land is one that focuses on lack of tenure security. For them, state ownership of land by default creates tenure insecurity since, they argue, the government may use land as political weapon by giving and taking it away as the case may be.[153] They argue that absence of tenure security for land users provides little or no incentive to improve land productivity through investment in long-term land improvement measures, increases transaction cost because of land dispute, and hinders the emergence of property market such as, credit availability/land mortgage.[154] However, the government rejects such fears as groundless; on the contrary, it claims that government provides better security as is now taken by regional governments. A good example is the land registration and certification processes which are being conducted in Tigray, Amhara, Oromiya, and the Southern regions which enable farmers to have a land certificate for their holdings. This gives protection and security to the holder.

The current practice of land registration and certification provides tenure security, according to a recent study made by the World Bank and others.[155] It is also believed that it brings "significant economic benefits" to users, mainly through rental as farmers feel secure when the agreement is registered.[156] Others, though, still do not

---

[151] See EEA/EEPRI 2002. A Research Report on Land Tenure and Agricultural Development in Ethiopia. Addis Ababa: Ethiopian Economic Association/Ethiopian Economic Policy Research Institute.

[152] Deininger, K. & Binswanger, H. 1999. The evolution of the World Bank's Land Policy: Principles, Experience, and Future Challenges. *In Research Observer*, Vol. 14. No. 2. Washington DC, World Bank. Cited Ibid.

[153] Tesfaye-Olika 2006. Ethiopia: Politics of Land Tenure Policies Under the Three Regimes, a Carrot and Stick Rulling Strategy in Ethiopian Politics. *In*: Tesfaye-Olika (ed.) *Ethiopia: Politics, Policy Making and Rural Development.* Addis Ababa: Department of Political & International Relations, Addis Ababa University, pp. 1–25.

[154] Dessalegn Rahmato: 2006, supra note 93, p. 3; EEA/EEPRI, supra note 151, p. 29.

[155] See Deininger, K., Daniel-Ayalew, Holden, S. & Zevenbergen, J. 2007. Rural Land Certification in Ethiopia: Process, Initial Impact, and Implications for Other African Countries. *World Bank Policy Research Working Paper 4218.* World Bank, p. 14; Palm, L. 2010. Quick and Cheap Mass Land Registration and computerisation in Ethiopia. *Facing the Challenges—Building the Capacity.* Sydney, Australia: FIG Congress, p. 10.

[156] Deininger, K., Ayalew, D. & Alemu, T. 2009. Impacts of Land Certification on Tenure Security, Investment, and Land Markets: Evidence from Ethiopia. *Environment for Development, Discussion Paper Series, EfD DP 09-11* [Online]. Available: http://siteresources.worldbank.org/NEWS/Resources/land_eegistration_in_ethiopia.pdf, p. 29.

have confidence on the land registration and certification process and conclude that the process has not brought about the feeling of tenure security. For example, Dessalegn argued that since the land laws do not avoid completely the possibilities of future land distribution and since government still possesses the power of taking land by way of expropriation, farmers could not feel secure on their holdings.[157]

In general, the debates seem to be based on ideological differences rather than empirical studies. The private versus state ownership of land by itself is not as such a decisive factor. What is important is whether or not there are adequate measures and regulations in place to guarantee tenure security, such as land certification, just compensation in the event of expropriation, long duration of rights, good governance, absence of corruption, and easy access of courts. In the following discussion we shall highlight the rights provided to land holders and judge from there the protections accorded to the individual land holders.

2.6.2 Governing Land Laws

Ethiopia is a Federal State constituting two special administrative cities (Addis Ababa and Dire Dawa) that are accountable to the Federal Government and nine other administrative national regional states, which are autonomous in the administrative affairs of their people. The powers and functions of the Federal and Regional Governments are provided in the FDRE Constitution. The power to "enact laws for the utilization and conservation of land and other natural resources, historical sites and objects" is provided, under the constitution, to the Federal Government.[158] Regional Governments are empowered "to administer land and other natural resources in accordance with Federal laws."[159] To this effect, the Federal Government enacted a "Land administration and Use Proclamation" (RLAUP) in 1997 (Proc. 87/1997), and then replaced it with the current legislation, proclamation No. 456/2005. Proclamation 456/2005 delegates regional states with the power to "enact rural land administration and land use law"[160] which is consistent with it (Proc. 456/2005) in order to implement the FDRE RLAUP at regional level. Besides, there are other legislations in Ethiopia related to land matters among which the Urban Land Lease proclamation (Proc. 711/2011) and the Expropriation Proclamation (Proc. 455/2005) are the main ones. Further, six of the regional states (Tigray, Amhara, Oromia,SNNPRS, Beni Shangul Gumz, and Afar) have adopted their own RLAUPs and Urban Lands Holding Lease Regulations in order to implement the Federal Land Proclamations.

---

[157] See Dessalegn-Rahmato 2009a–b. Land Registration and Tenure Security: A Critical Assessment. *In*: Dessalegn-Rahmato (ed.) *The Peasant and the State: Studies in Agrarian Change in Ethiopia 1950s–2000s*. Addis Ababa: Addis Ababa Univrsity Press.

[158] FDRE Constitution, Article 51(5).

[159] Id., Article 52(2)(d).

[160] Federal RLAUP, 456/2005, Article 17.

2.6.3 The Constitution

The FDRE Constitution under Article 40, that deals with "Right to property", provides details about property in general, and land ownership in particular. The Constitution under Article 40(1) guarantees for every Ethiopian to own "private property" with all its benefits. Private property includes "any tangible or intangible product which has value and is produced by the labor, creativity, enterprise or capital of an individual citizen" (Article 40.2).

Article 40(3) which is the relevant provision concerning land ownership in Ethiopia states that:

> The right to ownership of rural and urban land, as well as of all natural resources, is exclusively vested in the State and in the peoples of Ethiopia. Land is a common property of the Nations, Nationalities and Peoples of Ethiopia and shall not be subject to sale or to other means of exchange.

Regarding its means of acquisition, Sub-Article 4 states that Ethiopian peasants have the right to obtain land without payment and the protection against eviction from their possession. Likewise, concerning the pastoralists of the lowland areas, sub-Article 5 declares that Ethiopian pastoralists have the right to free land for grazing and cultivation as well as the right not to be displaced from their possession. Although the peasant is not entitled to private ownership rights to the land itself, he is guaranteed a "full right to the immovable property he builds and to the permanent improvements he brings about on the land by his labor or capital," and this right includes "the right to alienate, to bequeath, and, where the right of use expires, to remove his property, transfer his title, or claim compensation for it."[161] Thus, unlike the Derg era, peasants have the full right to their produce and can sell it at market value. Moreover, the Constitution guarantees peasants against arbitrary eviction by the state. The Constitution clearly says: "... the government may expropriate private property for public purposes subject to payment in advance of compensation commensurate to the value of the property."[162]

Concerning urban land, the Constitution said nothing about the acquisition and transfer of land by urban dwellers. Nevertheless, some interpret Article 40(6) that deals with "right of investors" to get land, as one that includes urban dwellers as well.[163] Article 40(6) of the constitution envisages that private investors may get land on the basis of payment arrangement. In other words, unlike peasant farmers and pastoralists, investors must pay a reasonable fee for the land they get from the state. Literally, an investor is a person who uses the land for business activities and his main objective is to reap profit. So, it is obvious that urban dwellers cannot be

---

[161] FDRE Constitution, Article 40(7).

[162] Id., Article 40(8).

[163] This line of argument was supported by the claims of government officials who argued that the source of urban land law is Article 40(6) of the Constitution. This was said by officials of the Addis Ababa Municipality and the ministers of the Urban Construction and Development following the passage of the controversial lease proclamation in October 2011.

categorized as investors. Noticing this problem, it seems, some regional Constitutions replace the word "investor" by another word "proprietor."[164] The effect of such change is that urban dwellers may be included in this definition, since the word proprietor may also include any person who owns a property.

The basic flow and a reason for controversy in the valuation and compensation of assets is that the disagreement between Article 40(3) that recognizes joint ownership of land by people and the state and Article 40(8) which gives compensation only to private property, fixtures on the land but not the land. The constitution seems to give a right to ownership of land on the one hand, and denies its benefits on the other.

2.6.4 Rural Land Laws

2.6.4.1 Access to Rural Land

Two years after the adoption of the FDRE Constitution, the Federal government enacted a Rural Land Administration and Use Proclamation (RLAUP) (Proc. 87/1997) that replaced the 1975 (Proc. 31/1975) rural land law. Proclamation 87/1997 was again itself repealed and replaced by the current RLAUP (Proc. 456/2005) in 2005. This proclamation follows the constitutional principle that creates free access to rural land. It declares that "peasant farmers and pastoralists engaged in agriculture for a living shall be given rural land free of charge."[165] A person, above the age of 18 years may claim land for agricultural activities, and women who want to engage in agriculture shall also have the right to get and use land.[166]

This principle of free access to rural land has also been reproduced in the regional rural land administration and use proclamations (hereafter Regional RLAUP).[167] The conditions attached to this right are, firstly, the person must want to engage in agricultural activities. In other words, agriculture must be his/her main means of livelihood or profession. Secondly, s/he must reside in the area where the agricultural land is located. Although this principle is not clearly seen in the Federal

---

[164] FDRE Constitution, Article 40(6).

[165] Federal RLAUP. Proc. 456/2005, Article 5(1).

[166] Id., Article 5(2), (3); See also Article 5(1) of Oromia Rural Land Law that says "Any resident of the region, aged 18 years and above, whose livelihood depends on agriculture and/or wants to live on, have the right to get rural land free of charge."

[167] See The Revised Tigray National Regional State Rural Land Administration and Use Proclamation, Proclamation No. 136/2007. *Tigray Negarit Gazeta.* Year 16 No. 1. Article 5(1) (hereinafter Tigray RLAUP); The Revised Amhara National Regional State Rural Land Administration and Use Proclamation, Proclamation No. 133/2006. *Zikre Hig.* Year 11, No. 18. Article 5 (2) (hereinafter Amhara RLAUP); Oromia Rural Land Use and Administration, Proclamation 130/2007. Article 5(1) (hereinafter Oromia RLAUP); The Southern Nations, Nationalities and Peoples Regional State Rural Land Administration and Utilization Proclamation, Proclamation 110/2007. *Debub Negarit Gazeta.* Year No. Article 5(1) (hereinafter SNNRS RLAUP).

RLAUP, Regional RLAUPs have clearly envisaged it.[168] Thus, residency and profession are the two important conditions to get rural land in Ethiopia. The reason seems that since there is shortage of agricultural land in rural areas, because of population pressure, it is not advisable to give land to those who live elsewhere (absentee owners) and those who earn income from other professions.

The criticisms raised against this rule are first, the principle of free access to rural land has, in practice, not been working for shortage of land in rural areas and because the laws prohibit redistribution of land.[169] Second, because of the residency requirement in the law, peasant farmers are locked in on their land instead of searching for additional income by staying in urban areas for longer periods. Thirdly, regional states may abuse "residency requirement" by misinterpreting it as "nativity requirement" and deny land to those who come from other regions. This is true, for example, in what happened in February 2012 when the authorities of the SNNPS evicted about 20,000 peasants from a place called Gura Farda forcefully, who had migrated from the northern part of the country (Amhara).[170] The peasants claimed that they lived from 2 to 20 years, and finally they were evicted because their case was labeled as "illegal settlement." The same incident was repeated in March 2013, when the Beni Shangul Gumz region evicted and expelled about 5,000 people because they were Amhara ethnic origin coming from Amhara Region.

2.6.4.2 Nature and Duration of Land Rights

Concerning the nature of right provided to the farmers, the Federal and Regional RLAUPs uphold the constitutional principle that denies private ownership to land. Rather, the RLAUPs provide farmers with a right termed as "holding right." The Federal RLAUP defines the term "holding right" as right of peasants and pastoralists "to use rural land for purposes of agriculture and natural resource development, lease and bequeath to members of his family or other lawful heirs, and includes the right to acquire property produced on his land thereon by his labour or capital and to sale, exchange and bequeath same" (Article 2.4). Similar definitions have also been adopted by the other regional RLAUPs. The general understanding today is that peasant farmers will have all the rights of an owner except sale and mortgage. They can use the land for agriculture production, have full ownership to the produce collected there from, have right to rent to fellow farmers (sharecropping), lease to investors, and inherit and donate (as a gift) to family members.

---

[168] See for example, the Amhara RLAUP that uses the phrase "any person residing in the region…" as a condition to get agricultural land (Articles 5(2), 6(1), 7(1)); The Tigray RLAUP uses similar words like "any resident of the region" (Article 5(1)).

[169] The Federal RLAUP simply says that upon the wish of the people land may be redistributed (Article 9); the Amhara RLAUP says, if 80 % of the people agree (Article 8); the Oromia RLAUP completely prohibits redistribution (Article 14).

[170] Daniel W. Ambaye, *Ethiopia Yemanat* (Whose land is the Land [Ethiopia]), News Paper, *Reporter Amharic*, March 28, 2012.

Peasants shall have such rights for lifetime and beyond, since they can donate and inherit it to others. It has been declared that "…rural land use right of peasant farmers, semi-pastoralists and pastoralists shall have no time limit."[171] In a way, this gives tenure security to the holder of the land as the right of using the land and the investments made thereon will not be threatened by time limitation. It must be noted that the longer the duration of rights of using land is the better in terms of ensuring tenure security.

The missing element in the Federal RLAUP is, though, the issue of pastoralist lands. The pastoralists are people who live in the lowlands of the country depending on animal husbandry. They do not have a plot of land like the highland farmers to settle on; they are always on the move in search of food and water for their animals. Now the point is that how could we define their right of grazing over vast territories of the lowland as holding right, a right that includes lease, rent and donation? The type of property regime dominating the areas is more of communal rather than private holding. The remedy would be for the lowland regions to come up with their own rural land laws that take into consideration the regional reality.

2.6.4.3 Means of Land Acquisition

There are different modalities through which a person may acquire land in Ethiopia. The Federal RLAUP recognizes the following ways for a person to get rural land:

a. Land Grant

As mentioned above, the constitution and the subsequent land laws have created a free access to rural land to whomsoever who wishes to engage in agricultural activities. Any person, who is 18 years and above has the right to get rural land free of charge. The government, through its different land administration apparatuses, is empowered to give land to those who are in need of it. Land grant may be made from unoccupied government lands, communal lands, land reserve (land left without heirs and claimed back by government, land claimed back by the state because the holder leaves the area permanently or neglect the land), and finally by conducting land distribution.[172] Land redistribution, as discussed above, has less appeal to land holders who are supposed to give consent for its distribution.

b. Bequeath

The second means of acquiring land is through inheritance or donation. Any person who is a member of peasant family may have the right to get rural land from his/her family through inheritance or donation (Article 5.2 of Proc. 456/2005). A family member is defined as "any person who permanently lives with holder of holding right sharing the livelihood of the latter" (Article 2.5). Unlike the family members who are recognized by the FDRE Revised Family Law (RFC) as those who are

[171] Federal RLAUP, Article 7(1); Amhara RLAUP, Article 5(3); Tigray RLAUP, Article 5(1), (b).

[172] See Federal RLAUP, Articles 5(2), (3) and 9(1); Amhara RLAUP, Article 7.

related by marriage, blood and adoption, the Federal RLAUP follows a slightly different path. As can be inferred from the above cited provision, a family member is one who "lives" with the peasant who holds the land and "shares" his "livelihood."

The requirements are basically two: residency and management. It means, first, the beneficiary must permanently live with the farmer under the same roof (residency element); and second, s/he must totally rely on the peasant farmer for her/his livelihood and has no other income of her/his own. S/he is under the control and administration of the farmer (management element). This means, the law does not specifically require marital or blood relations for a person to be considered as a family member. Hence, a laborer who has no alternative income of his own and lives with the farmer, without salary, under the same roof may be considered as family member and eligible for inheritance. The Amhara RLAUP even goes one step ahead by allowing inheritance of land by will to any farmer engaged in agriculture.[173]

By contrast, it is not possible to inherit or donate rural land to one's children who live elsewhere or are engaged in other professions. The rationale behind such rule seems that since land belongs to the state and the people and not a private one, it has to be transferred to those who are in need of it, irrespective of their blood relations. Yet, the FDRE RLAUP, except the possibility of passing one's land to family members, presumably through expressed testament (will), doesn't tell the situation of inheritance during intestate succession. The assumption is that in the absence of legitimate will left by the deceased landholder, the rules of the RLAUP and the Civil Code succession part would be applied. Looking into this problem, the Amhara (ANRS) and the Benishangul Gumz RLAUPs included provisions to settle the issue. Regulation 51/2007 of the ANRS, for example, under Article 11(7) puts the beneficiaries of intestate succession in the following priorities: minor children, if not, family members; children of full age who have no land of their own; children of full age who have their own landholding; parents. In order to be a legitimate beneficiary to the intestate succession, all the above people must show interest to engage in agricultural activities and reside in the area.

c. Lease

The third modality to acquire land is government land transfer to private investors through lease contract (Article 5(4)(a)). This is the base for the current *large-scale agricultural land transfer* practice carried out in the country. Ethiopia is one of the countries that attract the interest of investors and sovereign states from different countries. In the past two decades, millions of hectares of land have been transferred to many foreign and domestic investors ventured in the flowering industry, bio-fuel, sugar, cotton, palm oil, tea production etc. The Ethiopian government has a favorable investment policy that attracts foreign direct investment in such sectors. It has been claimed that so far about 3.5 million ha of land has been transferred to

[173] See Article 16(1) of ANRS RLAUP. Whether or not this contravenes with the Federal Rural Land Law is debatable.

both foreign and domestic investors, and the government has still a plan to transfer the same amount of land in the coming 5 years.[174] The government, on the other hand, puts the figure at about 2.6 million[175] (2.2 million given by regional states and 380,000 given by the Federal Government). However, recent press and other reports[176] about actual or proposed large farmland acquisition by big investors have raised serious concerns about the danger of neglecting local rights and other environmental concerns. They have also raised questions about the extent to which such transactions can provide long-term benefits to local populations and their contribution to poverty reduction and sustainable development.

2.6.4.4 Transfer of Land Use Rights

As already mentioned above, land rights could be transferred permanently through inheritance and donation. Besides, there are other modalities through which land use rights may be transferred temporarily to others. We can call them commercial land transactions, to differentiate them from inheritance and gift. To be specific, the law recognizes rent and lease as the two possible ways to transfer land use rights temporarily. Sale and mortgage are not yet allowed. The FDRE RLAUP provides a general provision that allows rent and lease the details of which shall be decided by regional rural land laws. It generally says that peasants and pastoralists can "lease to other farmers or investors land from their holding of a size sufficient for the intended development *in a manner that shall not displace them*, for a period of time *to be determined by rural land administration laws of regions* based on particular local conditions [emphasis added]" (Article 8.1). It means, the law gives the discretion of deciding on the duration of the lease period and the amount of land to be leased out to regional governments. Another point is that the law uses only the term "lease", and excludes the word "rent", whereas regional RLAUPs give different meanings to the two terms.[177]

Regional RLAUPs do not follow similar approach in the size of land to be leased out and the duration of the lease period. For instance, in Tigray, the peasant is

[174] Dessalegn-Rahmato 2011. Land to Investors: Large-Scale Land Transfer in Ethiopia. *FSS Policy Debate Series*. Addis Ababa: Forum for Social Studies, p. 5.; Daniel W. Ambaye Author. 2004 E.C. Sefafi ye Gibrina Investment le Ethiopia min Yifeyidal? (What is the Benefit of Large Scale Agricultural Investment for Ethiopia?). *Reporter*. Accessible at http://www.ethiopianreporter.com/old_ver/index.php?option=com_content&view=article&id=4934:2012-01-21-08-27-41&catid=303:commentary; See also an article published on Fortune News paper, http://www.addisfortune.com/Published%20On.htm.

[175] Interview with Ato Essayas Kebede, Director of the Agricultural Investment Directorate, Ministry of Agriculture, 2011.

[176] See for example, Horne, F. 2011. Understanding Land Investment Deals in Africa: Country Report Ethiopia. Oakland, USA: The Oakland Institute.

[177] For example in the Amhara and Oromia RLAUPs "rent" is understood as "transfer of land to fellow farmers for shorter period of time", while "lease" is defined as "transfer of land from farmers to investors or from government to investors for longer period of time.".

allowed to rent out up to 50 % of the size of his land for 20 years if the lessee uses modern technology, and 3 years if s/he uses traditional means of production (Article 6(1), (3) of Tigray RLAUP). In Amhara Region, renting land is allowed for a maximum of 25 years, although the size is not mentioned. There are practices in the region where farmers rented out the whole of their holdings to small scale investors. The argument for deviating from the Federal one (which says *in a manner that shall not displace them*) is one that depends on recognizing the rationality of the farmers; that farmers know better for themselves. The Oromia RLAUP follows the Tigray approach in terms of size and duration. The SNNPRS RLAUP follows a somewhat different approach. According to Article 8(1) of Proclamation No. 110/2007 of SNNPRS, the duration of land rented to a peasant by a peasant is 5 years, by a peasant to investor is 10 years, and by a peasant to those who cultivate perennial crops is up to 25 years.

Investors who rent land either from the government or peasant farmers have the right to mortgage their lease right as security to banks (Article 8(4) of Proc. 456/2005). Regional states have also reproduced this right in their respective proclamations. This implies that an investor may lease land from two sources: first from individual farmers, and second from the government. When we look the practice, it is the land which is rented from the government that is given as collateral to banks; not the one rented from peasant farmers. The reasons are firstly, the land rented from peasants is too small to pass it as mortgage, and secondly, the peasant may not agree that his land be given as collateral to banks.

Another recent development is that commercial investors who acquire land from clan chiefs in the lowland Afar Region complained that banks did not recognize the land deal and hence denied them loan by securing the land. In the nomadic areas of Afar and Somale Regions of Ethiopia, rural land is controlled and administered by clan chiefs rather than the state. Even though the Afar Region passed RLAUP and regulation, this law could not be implemented in the region because of the resistance it encountered from the clan chiefs.[178]

This is because the land tenure in the lowlands of Afar and Somalie Regions is customary in nature. The people live by moving from place to place in search of water and food for their cattle. They have strong attachment to their clan chiefs than the government. It is the clan chiefs who effectively administer land in the sense of granting land for housing, defining communal grazing lands and enforcing rights as well as resolving disputes. It is even alleged that government authorities require the permission and approval of clan chiefs to expropriate land, and compensation has to be directly paid to clan chiefs.[179]

But the Ethiopian legal system does not recognize the customary land tenure and land administration system operated in these areas. The existing RLAUP was

---

[178] *Ethiopian Reporter*, Amharic bi weekly, October 28, 2012.

[179] See for example Kabtamu, supra note 28, p. 128, 129. Kabtamu claims that government agencies, investors and others who want land in Somalie Region have to request to and negotiate with clan chiefs. Clan chiefs are also the ones who determine the amount of compensation and receive it in the name of the community.

enacted taking into consideration the highland sedentary life style which is governed by formal law. For this reason, any land negotiation and deal made with the clan chiefs is considered as informal and not acceptable by formal institutions, such as banks.

2.6.4.5 Termination of Land Rights

Rural land rights are not immune to government intervention. Hence, a farmer may be required by law to use his rights in some fashion than another. For instance, a farmer may not cultivate land having 30° slope, without putting terraces on the land (Article 13.4). Such restrictions are made for various reasons, such as environmental, equity, health and others. Violation of such obligations may render the loss of the land itself. Concerning the reasons of loss of the land rights, the proclamation does not as such give a coherent list. But, one may locate them in different parts of the proclamation. For instance, it is said that a holder of rural land "shall be obliged to use and protect his land. When the land gets damaged, the holder of the land shall lose his use right (Article 10.1).

In general, a review of the Federal as well as Regional RLAUPs reveals that the following may be considered as reasons for the loss or termination of rural land rights:

- Permanent employment of the farmer that brings him an average salary determined by government
- Engagement in professions other than agriculture and for which tax is paid
- Absence of a farmer from the locality without the knowledge of his whereabouts and without renting the land for more than 5 years
- Following the land for three consecutive years without sufficient reasons
- Failure to protect land from flood erosion
- Forfeiting land right upon written notification
- Voluntary transfer of land through gift
- Land distribution (the loss will be partial)
- Expropriation of land without replacement of another land.

2.6.5 Urban Land Law

2.6.5.1 Overview of Past Lease Proclamations

a. Proclamation 80/1993

It has been discussed that urban land was administered by proclamation 47/1975, which was adopted by the Derg in 1975. After the downfall of the Derg in 1991, the Transitional Government of Ethiopia (TGE) came up with a new urban land law. Unlike the permit system operational before it, the new urban land law follows a lease system. So, for the first time a lease system was introduced in Ethiopia as a mode of urban land holding when the new law was adopted in 1993.[180] Since the lease system was enacted before the adoption of the Constitution, and since the constitution does not explicitly say anything about urban land allocation, it can be argued that this proclamation was the base for the current urban land holding system, although its constitutionality is questionable.

The objectives of the proclamation, as indicated in its preamble, were summarized as follows: to create equitable distribution of land, to control the growth of city centers, to increase urban revenue to finance urban infrastructure, to expedite construction of urban houses to alleviate the existing shortage, to provide land utilization value[market value of urban land] which was not in existence, to ensure transparency in land transfer and avoid land speculation, to promote the economic development of urban centers through involvement of investors, and to ensure tenure security by providing land rights of longer durations.[181]

Compared to the permit system of the Derg era, a significant characteristic of this proclamation is that it allowed a free transfer of lease right in the form of sale, mortgage and contribution in Share Company (Article 10.1 of Proc. 80/1993). Yet, according to sub-3 of same Article, the "lessee may not, on transferring his right of lease, collect income which is higher than the rent of land he paid; nor may he mortgage such right at a value which is higher than the rent." Where the lessee collects or gains higher than what he actually paid as ground rent, he has the duty to pay back the difference to town administration (Article 10 0.4). The idea was that the increment in land value would be captured by the government rather than individuals.

b. Proclamation 272/2002

Proclamation 80/93 was repealed and replaced by the Revised Urban Land Lease Proclamation (Proc. 272/2002) in 2002.[182] The objectives of Proclamation No. 272/2002 were mainly two: to collect income from land lease in order to assure fair share from urban land wealth, and to transform the holding system (permit system of the Derg era) into a lease system.[183] Compared to its predecessor, the objectives of the revised proclamation 272/2002 were few.

Proclamation 272/2002 offers two methods to get access to urban land, unlike its predecessor which says nothing about the subject. Article 4(1.a) of the proclamation recognizes "auction" and "negotiation" as the two modalities to acquire urban land.

---

[180] Urban Lands Lease Holding Proclamation, Proclamation No. 80/1993. *Negarit Gazeta*. Year 53, No. 40.

[181] The Preamble of Proclamation 80/1993.

[182] Re-enactment of Urban Lands Lease Holding Proclamation, Proclamation No. 272/2002. *Negarit Gazeta*. Year 8, No. 19.

[183] Mesganaw-Kifelew 2009. The Current Urban Land Tenure System in Ethiopia. *In*: Muradu-Abdo (ed.) *Land Law and Policy in Ethiopia Since 1991: Continuities and Changes*. Addis Ababa: Ethiopian Business Law Series, Faculty of Law, Addis Ababa University, p. 171; Also, see Preamble of Proc. 272/2002.

Nevertheless, sub-Article (1)(b) of the same Article empowers regional cities to come up with additional means of land acquisition. Accordingly, besides the two systems mentioned above, the Addis Ababa City Government and other regions came up with three additional methods: namely, lot, assignment and award.[184] Like its predecessor, this proclamation also allows the free transfer of lease right (Article 13). But as a significant development, unlike proclamation 80/1993, the revised proclamation did not require the repayment of an enhanced land value gained by the leaseholder during transfer of the lease right.

2.6.5.2 Current Urban Land Lease Proclamation

a. Background, Justifications and Objectives of the Proclamation

Ten years after the adoption of Proclamation 272/2002, the Ethiopian government was reconsidering the revision and change of the lease proclamation on account of reasons discussed hereunder. Accordingly, the FDRE parliament adopted a new lease proclamation in October 2011.[185] The proclamation was one of the most contentious legislations ever proclaimed as it sparked intense public debates following its adoption, and public officials were forced to give explanations almost every day for more than 3 months without interruption.

The reasons offered by government officials for the revision of the existing lease proclamations are, in fact, reflected in what was later enshrined under Article 4 of the proclamation as "Fundamental Principles of Lease":

1. The right to use of urban land by lease shall be permitted in order to realize the common interest and development of the people.
2. The offer of lease tender and land delivery system shall adhere to the principles of transparency and accountability and thereby preventing corrupt practices and abuses to ensure impartiality in the process.
3. Tender shall reflect the prevailing transaction value of land.
4. The urban land delivery system shall give priority to the interests of the public and urban centers to ensure rapid urban development and equitable benefits of citizens and thereby ensure the sustainability of the country's development.

The first principle (Article 4.1) was represented, as we shall see soon, in different parts of the proclamation. The idea is that it should be the government, and by extension, the people, who should be benefiting from the lease system. One way to do this is by capturing the enhanced urban land value instead of allowing speculators to reap it. One of the arguments forwarded by government in the aftermath of the adoption of the proclamation was that speculators and urban brokers were the beneficiaries of the lease system. Urban speculators have been profiting by selling bare land (only lease right) without adding value to it. As noted above,

[184] Ibid., p. 173.

[185] FDRE Urban Lands Lease Holding Proclamation, Proclamation No. 721/2011. *Negarit Gazeta.* Year 18, No. 4.

Proclamation 272/2002, as opposed to Proclamation 80/1993, allowed free transfer of lease right with the full advantage of capturing the enhanced value of the leased plots. Proclamation 80/1993, on the contrary, required the lessee to pay back the difference in profit between what he paid as lease rent and the sale price. But, later on, when it was replaced by Proclamation 272/2002, this very provision was deleted. Because of this privilege allowed in Proclamation 272/2002, in the past 10 years, lessees and urban speculators were able to reap the benefit of enhanced urban land value, while the government was limited to insignificant tax premium. Government has been complaining that although it expected to generate adequate income for urban infrastructure from the lease system, it was somebody else who reaped that. For this reason, as we shall see below, the defunct rule of Proclamation 80/1993 that provides the enhanced value of urban land to government has been reinstalled in the new proclamation.

The other point addressed by Article 4(2), (3) is that urban municipalities became corrupt and inefficient in land delivery. Corruption, non transparency and injustice were reined in the system which created a safe haven for few urban speculators and brokers. The modalities of land delivery such as negotiation, award and lot were considered as non-transparent and sources of corruption. Lack of detailed rules in tender processes was also cited as another reason for corrupt behavior. Thus, the proclamation is also expected to be instrumental in efficient land transfer (Article 4(4)). It has been argued that demand for land in urban areas has been much greater than the supply of land made by the land authorities.

These principles are also encompassed in the objectives of the proclamation. The objectives of this new proclamation, as envisaged in the preamble, are two: to satisfy the growing urban land demand which resulted from the fast economic growth of the country; and to ensure good governance in the development of efficient land market and a transparent and accountable land administration system (Preamble of Proclamation 721/2011).

b. Application of Lease System and Fate of Old Possessions

Lease is the only means of land holding system in urban Ethiopia, and except for those lands which were acquired before the coming of lease system in 1993, it is prohibited to acquire land through modalities other than lease system (Article 5.1). However, as an exception, regional governments may identify urban centers to which this rule may not be applicable, although this may not be longer than 5 years (Article 5.4). In other words, as a matter of principle, lease shall be the cardinal tenure system for urban land holding, but in small towns where it is not yet possible to place leasehold system, other modalities of tenure system (perhaps permit system or rural holding system) may be used temporarily, for a maximum of 5 years.

What about old possessions? An "old possession" is "a plot of land legally acquired before the urban center entered into the leasehold system, or a land provided as compensation in kind to persons evicted from old possession" (Article 2.18). Thus, all land acquired and held during the imperial era, Derg era, and after that, outside lease system will be considered as old possession. Besides, replacement land given to owners whose land was expropriated may also be considered as old possession since the land was given without lease contract. Although it is difficult to put the exact figure, the number of old possessions in Addis Ababa, for example, may constitute half of the total properties in the city. So what will be the fate of such properties?

As a matter of principle, all land in urban areas shall henceforth be transferred into lease system (generally see Article 5). But, concerning old possessions, it is said that their fate will be decided by the Council of Ministers upon detailed study to be made in the future (Article 6.1). In other words, all "old possessions" will not be converted in mass at once to leasehold. The law, however, requires the conversion of old possessions into lease system in one of the following events:

- Where a property attached on an old possession is transferred to a third party through any modality other than inheritance (Article 6.3)
- Informal settlements that have been regularized pursuant to the regulations of regions and urban administrations (Article 6.4)
- Where an application to merge an old possession with a lease hold is permitted, (Article 6.6)

Property transfer in this case includes sale, exchange or donation, excepting inheritance. It must be noted that since land is not saleable, the subject matter of "transfer" is not the land itself but the immovable on the land, i.e. building. Hence, whenever a house rested on old possession is sold, exchanged, or donated, the new owner shall possess the land on lease basis. The other situation is the "regularization" of informally held possessions. Land may be held and construction of houses may be carried out without the permission of the urban land administration offices. In Addis Ababa and many other urban city centers, there are lots of houses constructed in such a way. The usual measure taken in such cases is demolition of the informal settlement. But, sometimes, urban centers or regional governments may pass a specific regulation to regularize, formally register, the informal settlements. If an informal settlement is now regularized, then the new possession arrangements must be changed to lease system.

The third case in which an old possession should be converted to lease system is where old possession is to be merged or amalgamated with leased land. It means the old possession and the leased land must have been bordering each other and now have changed into one property. What about amalgamation of two old possessions? The law does not say anything about it, and the assumption is that unless it is clearly required by the law, it is not mandatory to convert them to lease system. In relation to this, a directive of the Addis Ababa City Administration says: "where old possessions are to be merged, they will be administered according to old possession tenure."[186]

---

[186] Addis Ababa City Administration 2004, *Land Delivery Service Manual,* No. 12/2004 E.C, Article 18.2.4.

c. Effect of Lease

Transfer of land holding into lease system means that all land in urban areas, after being identified and registered by the municipality, shall be known as lease land, and the holder shall enter with the government a lease contract that, among others, includes lease period and lease price to be paid (Article 16). The lessee will then be given a "Lease Holding Certificate" that shows the name of lessee, land size, location, land use purpose, lease price, lease period and so on (Article 17). The important effect of converting a possession to leasehold is through the payment of a specified amount of ground rent to the government. In the event of the above three situations, the lessee will pay "lease benchmark price" (minimum lease price), which shall be set by every urban center, multiplied by the area of the land size (Article 6.7). The calculation of this "lease benchmark price" takes into "account the cost of infrastructural development, demolition cost as well as compensation to be paid to displaced persons in case of built up areas, and other relevant factors" (Article 2.11). Currently, the capital city adopted a new lease benchmark price for various locations of the city and "the new prices range from 1,686 birr per m^2 designated as central market places to 191 birr that are grouped as expansion (suburb) places in the city."[187] The initial payment will not be less than 10 % (Article 20.2) and the remaining will be paid over long period of time which will be decided in the contract. This is also true of land plots granted by "allotment" to those organs specified under Article 12. For others, the amount of payment shall be determined by the tender (auction) process.

When an old possession is converted to lease system, there is no guarantee that it will be maintained as it had been in the past. It means the land use (residential, business, building height etc.), land size, land shape, land rent/tax, initial lease payment, and so on shall be determined based on the current or existing rules (such as structural and local plans, land lease regulations, etc.)[188] This will, no doubt, cause a fluctuation in land size (large size of lands may be reduced and small plots may be enlarged) and the lessee will be compensated for any fixture on the land in case his land is reduced, and he is obliged to make lease payment for the addition in case his possession is enlarged (see Article 6.2 of Proc. 721/2011).

The other argument that can be inferred from this change is that this law will have an impact on the urban land market. The general idea is that the market price of urban land and housing will increase or decrease. For example, the price of urban real properties will be too much for the buyer (since he shall pay both the purchase price and the lease price) if sellers continue to demand the usual price; or it may be too small for the seller since the buyer by considering the lease price which he is supposed to pay, will make a smaller offer for the property. On the other hand, the

[187] See for example the news as published in a weekly news paper, *Capital*, of June 2012. Available: http://www.capitalethiopia.com/index.php?option=com_content&view=&id=1225:new-lease-tariff-for-addis&catid=35:capital&Itemid=27.

[188] See details under Article 6 of Urban Land Lease Regulation No. 49/2004 E.C of Addis Ababa City Administration; Article 7 of Model Urban Land Regulation of Ministry of Urban Development and Construction.

state will be in a safe position since its revenue will be increasing from every transaction and change made on the lease right.

Although it is not possible to conclude at this time, the early results on lease auction in the capital city show that land lease price has become very expensive. For example, in a land lease auction floated by the Addis Ababa City, on October 31, 2012, all the land found at the periphery of the city was sold at a price ranging from 10,000–14,000 birr per m^2. This shows an increase in three to fourfold.[189] As mentioned above, the initial bid price for these areas has been fixed as 191 birr per m^2.

d. Modalities of Land Acquisition

Tender

Previously, as mentioned above and stipulated by the federal and state lease laws, there were five modalities of urban land acquisition: auction, negotiation, assignment, award, and lot. Auction and negotiation were the two most important methods for cities to collect income from land lease transfers. In bigger cities, auction is still the most utilized method to transfer land from municipalities to investors. Land was also assigned to civic associations, charitable organizations, embassies, and international organizations. Award was the least utilized method of land transfer by urban land authorities to those who contribute extraordinary accomplishments. Lot or lottery was a mechanism by which urban land had been distributed to low and middle income citizens. This method was an extension to what had been exercised by the permit system during the Derg era.

Now, however, since most of the modalities are categorized as bad practices that opened the door for corruption, the government argued, the law recognizes only tender (auction) and allotment (land lease transfer without auction) as the two basic means of lease transfer from government to citizens (Article 7.2 of Proc. 721/2011). As a matter of principle, every land needed for residential, commercial (agriculture, industry, or service), and other purposes will be transferred by tender. Bidders will use the "lease benchmark price" as a base to offer their price, and the highest bidder will be identified based on the "bid price and the amount of advance payment he offers" (Article 11.5). To make it more transparent, accessible and free from corruption, the law allocates more detailed provisions (Articles 8–11) to the tender process.

Allotment

As exception, however, city municipalities may give land by allotment to selected bodies which have paramount importance to society. "Allotment" is defined in the proclamation as "a modality of land use right transfer applied for providing urban lands by lease to institutions that could not be accommodated by way of tender" (Article 2.10). Whether or not allotment requires payment of the minimum lease bench price is not known. But, at least, in some cases (such as replacement land

---

[189] This piece of news was published in the English weekly, *Capital,* Year 14, No. 726 of Nov 4, 2012.

given to expropriated person and land required for religious worship) it is not feasible to expect payment. What is clear is, though, those listed under Article 12 (3), (5) are expected to pay a lease bench mark price, as we shall see below. The following list includes entities or persons eligible to get land by allotment (Article 12 of the proclamation):

1. (a) office premises of budgetary government entities, (b) social service institutions run by government or charitable organizations, (c) places of worship, (d) public residential housing construction programs and government approved self-help housing constructions, (e) use of diplomatic missions and international organizations, (f) manufacturing industries, and (g) projects having special national significance and considered by the president of the region or the mayor of the city administration and referred to the cabinet (Article12.1).
   What is interesting among the list is "d". Under Article 12(1)(d) the beneficiaries are government condominium housing projects and "government approved self-help housing constructions." As discussed above, the land assignment to self-help construction is something that is maintained from the past. This is the same with the lot (lottery) type of land allocation that had been applied. This is the only provision that accommodates the cheaper and/or equitable land transfer to urban residents. The idea is that since low income group people may not be able to compete in bidding for urban plots with higher income groups, a special land allocation system that accommodates their interest is fair and realistic. As mentioned above, whether or not the beneficiaries under this list are required to pay lease bench mark price is not known. But the assumption is that, in the absence of such clear requirement, payment should not be expected.
2. In addition to what we have under (1) above, a person who is displaced from his house/land (an old possession or leased one) as a result of urban renewal (like in case of expropriation) shall get a replacement plot by allotment. Under the FDRE Expropriation proclamation, one of the components of a compensation package is provision of replacement land (Article 8(4)(a) of Proc. 455/2005) for the person to build his house, and it will not be logical to expect payment of lease price for such land.
3. A lawful tenant of government or *Kebele* owned residential house outside Addis Ababa shall be entitled to allotment of residential plot of land at benchmark lease price if displaced due to urban renewal program. In Addis Ababa, he is entitled to purchase of condominium housing unit (Article 12(3), (4)).

The criticism that one may raise against this modality of land acquisition is that it will defeat the very purpose of the proclamation, discouraging speculators. This is because it will be again the rich people who can afford to pay the highest lease bid price and sell it at profit in the future. The majority of the poor will be excluded from the system. For example, as already mentioned previously, in the land lease bid floated on the 31st of October 2012, residential land area whose benchmark (floor value) was fixed at 191 birr fetched exaggerated prices ranging from 10,000 to 14,000 birr per m^2.[190] The government tries to accommodate the interest of the poor and middle income citizens by providing condominium houses and other similar mechanisms. But the problem with such systems is that it is corrupt and inefficient. For example, the Addis Ababa City Administration that started condominium housing construction in 2004 said to be completed and transferred 97,000 houses (up to 2012) to residents, while around 350,000 people are still awaiting their chance.[191] This shows that the performance of the past 8 years in construction and distribution of housing was not satisfactory.

It seems rather that people opted for illegal land grab (informal settlement) in the absence of efficient and equitable land distribution. Recent study conducted by the Addis Ababa city reveals that after the passage of the lease proclamation, massive land grab has been made by landless urban residents in the expansion areas of the city. The Addis Ababa City Administration has demolished 7,000 houses and claimed back 393.3 ha of land from illegal settlers in the six sub-cities of Bole, Yeka, Nefas-Silk Lafto, Akaki Kaliti, Kolfe Keranio, and Gulele. In connection with the incident 23 *Woreda* officials have been removed from their positions and another 163 are under investigation.[192]

e. Transfer of Lease Right

Like any other property right, lease right is also freely transferable, although this time it is burdened with some restrictions. The new lease proclamation declares: "a lessee may transfer his leasehold right or use it as collateral or capital contribution to the extent of the lease amount already paid" (Article 24.1) In here, the phrase "to the extent of lease amount already paid" refers to the collateral and capital contribution, and partly, as we shall discuss below, to the sale of uncompleted constructions. Caution is necessary, though, in understanding its implication.

In the previous Proclamation No. 272/2002, there was no limit or restriction to such right. Lessees who had been transferring either the lease right (bare land) or lease right with construction (complete or incomplete) on it have been getting the full profit of the transfer without any restriction. Lots of urban speculators were said to be benefiting by capturing the full enhanced land value over the years and even abused it and became "rent collectors." In other words, it is said that the absolute freedom, introduced by the previous proclamation, has created the problem of "rent

---

[190] See the weekly *Capital,* Sunday, 4, October 2012, Year 14, No. 726. The paper expresses its worry that the poor would be excluded from future dealings of such nature because of this unheard type of prices offered.

[191] See for example a report made by the weekly English *The Reporter*, Saturday August 18, 2012.

[192] An official press explanation given by Ato Getachew Ambaye, City manager of Addis Ababa City, December, 2012. See details *Addis Fortune,* Sunday Dec 2, 2012, Vol. 12, No. 657. Available: http://addisfortune.net/s/an-unsettling-time-for-addis-abebas-newly-homeless/; *Ethiopian Reporter* (Amharic), Wednesday Dec 5, 2012, available: http://ethiopianreporter.com/news/293-news/8747-2012-12-05-06-21-18.html.

seeking" activities. This means that speculators were encouraged to transfer lease right only, without any construction made on it. This generally did benefit neither the economy nor the people, since its purpose was filling the pocket of few people rather than alleviating the housing shortage that exists in the country. The value of urban land was unreasonably inflated for no reason other than speculation and confusion. There were ample experiences which show that in recent years, in the capital as well as in regional cities and towns, land value (bare land) has been increasing twofold every year without any value added on it.

For this reason, the government has been complaining that speculators purchase and transfer land without adding value to it. Among others, even real estate companies were said to have been transferring bare land (lease right to the space only) without building the necessary construction over it. Because of this, in 2010, the city of Addis Ababa had reclaimed more than 1 million m^2 of land from real estate developers on the ground that they had been transferring land without adding value thereto.[193] To fight this practice, the new proclamation introduces four strategies that limit the free transfer of lease right. The government argues, of course, that they were made with the intention of curbing speculative activities and boosting the state revenue.

Barring repeated transfer

First, the proclamation prevents people who repeatedly transfer leasehold right, without completion of construction, in anticipation of speculative market benefit, from participation in a future bid (Article 24.7). This means, the city administration can prevent selected people, who are identified in selling lease right or unfinished properties repeatedly from participating in future auctions. The reason behind such restriction is to discourage speculators who are engaged in the sale and transfer of unfinished properties; instead, the government wants to encourage them to complete the constructions before selling, and thereby alleviate the housing problems. The proclamation does not tell as to how many times people are supposed to transfer unfinished property before they get banned. The FDRE Model Lease Regulation (Article 43.1) and Addis Ababa City Directive, however, provide a clue in this regard. According to Article 56(1) of the directive "if the person transfers unfinished properties three times within 3 years, he shall be barred from any future bidding in lease for 2 years".

Supervision of sale

Second, as per Article 24(2) of the proclamation, "If a lessee, with the exception of inheritance, wishes to transfer his leasehold right prior to commencement or half-completion of construction, he shall be required to follow transparent procedures of sale to be supervised by the appropriate body." Note that this requirement is not necessary for the sale and transfer of fully completed properties. The implication of this provision is understood only after reading the next sub Article of this provision.

---

193 Addis Fortune, weekly news paper, Vol. 11, No. 539.

The sub-Article points out that since the seller of the lease will not be entitled to the full profit of unfinished construction, it is necessary to involve a government agent to assess the value of construction and current land lease price.

Limitation on transfer of unfinished property

Third, transferring only leasehold right (bare land) or leasehold right with only half-completed construction gives no benefit at all to sellers. Previously, completed or not, lease holders used to reap the full benefit of enhanced land value during transfer of the lease right. Now, however, as a strategy to encourage completion of construction, to avoid rent seeking activities, and to rather capture the benefit by the state, the sale and transfer of half completed properties is not attractive. "Half completed construction" is defined under the proclamation (Article 2.16) differently for different types of constructions as follows:

(a) In the case of a villa, completion of foundation, columns and top beam;
(b) In the case of a multi-story building, completion of foundation and 50 % of the total number of floor slabs;
(c) In the case of a real estate development, completion of the construction phase referred to, as the case may be, in paragraph (a) or (b) of sub-Article (1) of this Article relating to the entire blocks.

What will happen if a lessee wants to transfer half completed construction or bare land? The first requirement, as already raised above is, to invite municipal agent to oversee the sale process. Besides, the amount of money collected by the lessee is limited to the following items. According to the law, a lessee who wishes to transfer his leasehold rights before commencement of construction or half-completed constructions will get first, the effected lease payment including interest thereon, calculated at bank deposit rate; second, the value of the already executed construction; and third, 5 % of the transfer lease value (Article 24.3). This 5 % relates to the difference between the lease purchase price paid and the sales price; in effect, it must be referred to the gain or profit made by the transfer.[194]

So far as the first two conditions are concerned, there is no problem in understanding the amount of lease price paid (plus the bank based interest rate), and the amount of money expended for the construction made. The difficulty lies in understanding the third point: how do we determine the *transfer lease value*? Are the lessee and the new beneficiary (e.g. buyer) supposed to deal in the open? What is the role of the municipality agent at this point? Details, similar in content, are provided in the Model Lease Regulation and the Addis Ababa City Administration Lease Regulation and Addis Ababa City Administration Lease Directive.

The Addis Ababa City Administration Lease Directive No. 11/2004 provides details as described below. As a matter of principle, it is the government, through

---

[194] Look to this type of argument in Mekasha-Abera 2012. *Ye Eethiopia Meseretawi ye Lease Hig Hasabochna Yemiasketlachew Chigroch (Fundamentals of the Ethiopian Lease Law and its Problems),* Addis Ababa, Far East Trading, p. 79. The writer say that "If the lease sales value is more than the lease price paid at the beginning by the seller, then the seller will be entitled to 5 % of the difference and the rest of it will go to government."

the supervisor mentioned above, that can decide the amount of transfer value (Article 51.1). The lease transfer value shall be the average value of the current/ market tender value of the locality and the lease value by which transfer was made to the current lessee (Article 51.2). The government supervisor will take the average price of the current lease price of the area and the actual lease price for which the lessee (now seller) got the land. In the absence of an offer by the buyer, this average value will be the binding transfer value (Article 51.4). If, on the other hand, the buyer makes an offer that is equal or less than the average value calculated above, then the transfer is acceptable (Article 51.3). When the average value is less than the previous lease price, then the relevant body may either take one of the better values (either the previous or the current one) as transfer value (Article 51.5) or put the lease land on auction [to get better price] (Article 51.6).[195]

To make it clearer, let's assume that Ms. A has bid 200 m^2 of land from the city municipality for 4,000 birr per m^2 (total 800,000 birr). Let us again assume that she has made a 10 % advance payment of 80,000 birr as lease price. Let's further assume that she constructed a foundation at a cost of 40,000 birr. Her total cost at this point amounts to 120,000 birr. For some reason, however, she now wants to sell the property after 1 year. The bank interest is 5 %.

A further assumption that is made is that the current lease value of land in a similar location is 5,000 birr per m^s and this sums up to a total value of 1,000,000 birr.

Decision (Average value is 900,000)

1. The buyer shall pay birr 900,000
2. The seller (lessee) will get the following:

    2.1. 80,000 birr (lease price paid)
    2.2. 4,000 (5 % of 80,000)
    2.3. 40,000 (construction cost)
    2.4. 5,000 (5 % of 100,000 birr profit (900,000–800,000)

3. Total = 129,000 (net Profit for seller = 9,000).
4. Government profit = 95,000 birr.

On the other hand, if the construction is completed or becomes more than half, then there is no limitation as to the value of the sale price. Hence, the whole purpose behind limiting the right to the transfer of half-completed properties seems to encourage owners to complete construction and thereby alleviating the housing shortage.

The flaw of this provision is that it will not stop the connivance that might be made between buyers and sellers. It means that it would not be possible to avoid an under table (internal) agreement that might be carried out between the two. Secondly, even if it is possible to control the connivance, people will shift radically from selling unfinished properties to finished ones. For instance, for residential

[195] Ibid. Articles 41 and 44 respectively.

houses, half completed construction refers to construction of foundation, columns and top beam. Thus, if one puts a roof to the house, then it is considered as a complete one. As compared to sale price, the difference in cost is indeed very small. In this way, speculators will shift to this new way of trading properties. Thirdly, constitutionally speaking, this practice is against the property rights of property holders. Once the government gets its money from the lease price during original transfer, why is it that it again insists on sharing the profit from the appreciation of land value? Of course, the justification is to encourage people to put a building on the land before they sell it, and to add value to their holdings, but, this should not be done by violating the constitutional right of property which, among others, gives the right to collect the increment in property value.

Mortgage of leasehold right

As stated above, leasehold right is subjected to any form of transaction including sale, lease/rent, inheritance, donation, mortgage, and as capital contribution to a company. But again, as mentioned previously, the right to mortgage is limited to the "*extent of lease amount already paid*" (Article 24.1). This "already paid lease amount" may be the initial down payment and the yearly installment, if the lease agreement was made before a year and more. Under Article 24(4) the proclamation further introduces, as a fourth strategy, the following:

> …where a lessee uses his leasehold right as collateral prior to commencement of construction, the collateral value may not exceed the balance of the lease down payment after considering possible deductions to be made pursuant to Sub-Article (3) of Article 22 of this Proclamation.

The deductions mentioned under Article 22(3) are "…7 % of the total lease price in addition to a lease amount that covers the period from the date he took possession of the land."

The contents of the above Articles may be summarized as follows:

- Lease right may be mortgaged to the extent of lease payment already made (that includes down payment and yearly installments).
- If the lease right is without any construction on it, the mortgage value will be equal to lease payment already made, minus 7 % penalty and unpaid yearly installments.

To further elaborate this provision, let us closely look into the different sub-Article s of Article 24 mentioned in this section. Based on Article 24(1), as a matter of principle, lease right may be used as collateral when borrowing from banks or creditors in general. But, the amount of money the lessee may borrow against mortgaging his lease right is restricted to the amount of money s/he has paid so far, as lease price. This lease price includes the *down payment* paid at first (e.g. 10 %) and the following yearly *installments*. In other words, the land cannot give the lease holder a value which he had not made on it; what one can get from the land is what he "sows" on it. This is a radical shift from the previous practice where banks used to give higher amount of value to location (to the land only).[196] Thus, for example, a person who had made a total of 100,000 birr lease payment may not borrow more than this amount by mortgaging his lease right. Of course, if there is a construction, banks may also consider the value/cost of such construction in their loan calculation. In other words, the market based location value which used to be given by banks during loan agreement (e.g. up to 4,000 birr per m^2 in *Piazza* and *Mercato*, prime locations in Addis Ababa, the capital city) will be reduced to a much smaller amount.[197]

The other point that is incorporated in relation to mortgaging of lease right is envisaged in Sub-Article 4, which declares that if the lessee used his right *as collateral prior to commencement of construction,* then the amount of loan will be a much lesser one. It is declared that, this time, from the loan to be extended, a reduction of 7 % of the total lease price agreed in the contract and the total lease price unpaid (if any) starting from the time the land was delivered to the lessee shall be made.

To support this with an example, assume the lessee has got the land for a total of birr 1.2 million. He made a down payment of 10 % (120,000 birr) and continued to pay for the next 3 years, an annual lease rent of 40,000 (total of 120,000) birr. So far the total lease price paid is birr 240,000. Suppose also that there is no construction activity made on the land. If he wants to mortgage the lease right, what he can get is only birr 223,200 (i.e. 93 % of the total lease price paid). What about if a construction of some value is made on the land? Then the calculation will be completely different. He will get the whole lease price paid, i.e. 240,000 birr. The above calculation is mandatory. Concerning the valuation of the construction, complete or incomplete, made on the land, the right is given to the lending banks to make the valuation.[198]

This rule will immediately cut down the amount of loan to an insignificant level. After the adoption of the proclamation, one of the stern complaints made on the proclamation was by the business community. Even if their properties (buildings) might be sold in the open for tens of millions for their location's sake, banks will not consider the market value of the property. The kind of valuation banks follow now is cost replacement; that is, construction value of the building only, which probably may be 10–20 % of the market value of the property. This means the difference between the sales value and the mortgage value of the property is extremely big, and this raises the question of sanity of the system.

---

[196] See for example Daniel-Weldegebriel-Ambaye 2009a. Land Valuation for Expropriation in Ethiopia: Valuation Methods and Adequacy of Compensation *7th FIG Regional Conference.* Hanoi, Vietnam, 19–22 October 2009 FIG (http://www.fig.net/pub/vietnam/papers/ts04c/ts04c_ambaye_3753.pdf). It is said that before the coming of this lease legislations, banks used to give location value in the capital up to 4,000 birr per m^2.

[197] See details for example Ibid., p. 30.

[198] See Article 59.3 of the Addis Ababa Lease Directive.

f. Formation and Termination of Lease Contract

Formation of contract

Any person permitted urban land lease holding in accordance with this Proclamation shall conclude a contract of lease with the appropriate body (Article 16.1). The lease contract shall include the construction start-up time, completion time, payment schedule, grace period, rights and obligations of the parties as well as other appropriate details (Article 16.2). The assumption is that the general provisions of contract law envisaged under the civil code will be applied here as well. Chief among the elements of a lease contract is the lease period. The lease proclamation has set different lease periods for residential and other activities. As in the case of the previous proclamation, 99 years has been set for residential purposes and 70 years for industry, 60 years for commerce, and 15 years for urban agriculture (Article 18).

Termination of contract

The proclamation introduces three situations that may lead to the termination of the lease contract (Article 25.1):

1. failure to use the land in accordance with Article 21(1), (violation of contract)
2. expropriation of the leased land, and
3. expiry and non-renewal of contract.

The proclamation confirms that except in the case of the above three situations, "no leasehold land right may be terminated and the lessee cleared from the land" (Article 26.3). A brief analysis of the three situations is given below.

Violation of contract: According to Article 21(1)(a) "A lessee shall use the land for the *prescribed purpose* within the *period of time* stated in the lease Contract" (emphasis added). The law is concerned about two things: that the land must be used for the intended purpose (land use issue), and that construction must be started within the agreed time (avoiding delay). This means, if the person fails to use the land for the purpose for which it was designated (e.g. constructing commercial building instead of residential, building a house contrary to the agreed plan, use the land for agriculture rather than industrial, etc.), then the city municipality may terminate the contract. Similarly, failure to commence or finish construction and commencement of the business (for which the land was provided) may also be another reason for terminating the contract.

The "land use" obligation is mandatory to follow since the permit of the lease was made by considering the master plan of the city. Of course, if the master plan accommodates/permits, the land use may be converted upon the application of the lessee and an approval by the concerned organ (Articles 21.2 and 3). It must be noted that one of the purposes of leasehold is to manage urban growth through the enforcement and implementation of urban land use regulations.[199] The effect of violating land use, as prescribed under Article 25(3) of Proclamation 721/2011, is retaking of the land and returning a paid-up land lease price, after deduction of costs and penalty.

The use of the land within the agreed time implies three things: commencement and completion of construction and use of land for the intended purpose. The first two have to do with the construction, while the third is concerned with the operational activities, such as starting the industry, business, agriculture, etc.

Any lessee must commence construction within the agreed time. This is not an innovation to this proclamation; it was also included in the previous proclamation. The difference is that, the current proclamation contains more harsh measures against those who contravene the lease contract. For example, if one fails to start construction on time, the land will be reclaimed by the city administration and some penalty or fee may be imposed on the lessee (Article 22).

Moreover, a lessee who got land by tender or allotment shall complete the construction according to the agreement. The law provides 24, 36 and 48 months to complete construction for small, medium and large scale construction activities respectively. Depending on the type of construction and regulation to be issued by each city administration, the period may be extended from 6 to 12 months. Where the lessee fails to complete construction within the agreed time, the contract shall be terminated and the land will be retaken by the city administration. The lessee is also obliged to remove any construction activity at his own cost from the land or else the city may transfer it by tender to another person or remove the property on the land and then claim the cost from the lessee (Article 23).

Expropriation: Article 21(1)(b) introduces taking of land for other public purpose activities (expropriation) as the second reason to terminate a lease contract. Unlike the above cases, the lease shall be compensated based on the relevant laws (Article 25.4). The details of expropriation of leasehold right are discussed below.

Expiry and Non-renewal of Contract: the "non-renewal of the lease period in accordance with Sub-Article (1) of Article 19" of the proclamation was given as a third ground to terminate a lease contract (Article 25.1.c). The lease period provided is different for different purposes. There is also difference between Addis Ababa and other cities/towns. In determining the maximum lease period of urban land lease agreement, the law classifies the cities into Addis Ababa and other urban centers. In both Addis Ababa and other urban centers, a maximum of 99 years is set for the use of land for residential housing, science and technology, research and study, government office, charitable organizations, and religious institution purposes. Besides, for all types of urban centers, the maximum period given for urban agriculture is 15 years (Article 18.1.a).

In the case of other land use purposes, in Addis Ababa, the duration given is 90 years for education, health, culture and sports, 70 years for industry, 60 years for

---

[199] One may also further study the contents of the FDRE Building Proclamation No. 624/2009 and FDRE Urban Planning Proclamation No. 574/2008 to see the land use regulations included.

commerce, and 60 years for others(Article 18.1.b). In other urban centers, a slightly higher period is arranged: 99 years for education, health, culture, sports, 80 years for industry, 70 years for commerce, and 70 years for others (Article 18.1.c).

What will happen after the expiry of the lease contract? The lease right may be renewed upon the application of the lessee, using the prevailing benchmark lease price of the time (Article 19). It seems the discretion of renewing the contract is given to the city administration; the city municipality may renew or refuse to renew the contract. Whether or not the city is required to give good reasons for not renewing the contract is not known. But, the reading of the FDRE Model Lease regulation gives a clue which may be used by city centers. Article 48(2) of the FDRE Model Lease Regulation provides three events in which the lease contract may not be renewed: change of structural plan, the need of the land for other public purposes, or the inability of change of the land to current land use purpose.

The effect of non-renewal of contract is that the land will be taken after the removal of any property erected on the land by the owner. There shall be no payment of compensation for any property loss caused to the owner. The municipality is empowered to "take over the land together with the property thereon without any payment where the lessee has failed to remove the property within the period" given (Article 25(5), (6)). The possible problem or criticism that may be forwarded against such provision is that it may create tenure insecurity and hysteria when the expiry date approaches.

g. Expropriation of Lease Right

Expropriation refers to taking of someone's immovable property for public purpose and upon payment of compensation. The details of the concept and nature of expropriation are discussed in following chapters, and it is sufficient to mention here that "the appropriate body shall have the power, where it is in the public interest, to clear and take over urban land upon payment of commensurate compensation, in advance, for the properties to be removed from the land" (Article 25.1). The two most important points one may gather from this provision are that land may be taken *for public purpose* activities and upon payment of *commensurate amount of compensation*. Urban center may take urban land and any property thereon, if the land is needed for public purpose activities. A good example, of *public purpose* in urban areas may be roads, private investments such as hotels, commercial and industrial buildings. During such takings, the government is required to pay *compensation* commensurate to the loss of property on the land. This includes the replacement cost of buildings of any sort on the land and the market value of any other fixtures such as trees and fruits. The valuation and assessment of such properties shall be made based on the Expropriation Proclamation (455/2005) and Regulation (135/2007). Besides the compensation that is made in terms of cash money for the properties found on the land, the person who lost the land will also be provided a "substitute plot of land within the urban center" (Article 25.2).

The first procedure in the process of expropriation is provision of clearance notice to the holder of the land. According to Article 27(1) of the lease proclamation, "the possessor of the land shall be served with a written clearing order stating the time the land has to be vacated, the amount of compensation to be paid and the size and locality of the substitute plot of land to be availed." And this notice should be served upon the possessor of the land in not less than 90 days before the appropriation of the land by the city administration. Any person who believes that his interest is infringed as a result of the notice has the right to submit a grievance within 15 days to the appropriate body (Article 28.1). This person may be the owner of the property who has grievance on the amount of compensation or another third party who may claim the ownership of the land. The appropriate body (most probably the administrative body itself) will give its decisions after considering the application and evidences (Article 28.3).

The Proclamation further provides an opportunity for the aggrieved person to make an appeal if he was not satisfied by the decision of the appropriate body. The appeal will be made to an appellate tribunal which shall "be established by regions or city administrations" (Article 30.1). Thus, this body is outside the hierarchy of regular courts and is rather affiliated to the administration, since its accountability is to the region or urban center (see Article 30.3). Its power seems restricted to "urban land clearing and compensation" cases and "decisions of the Tribunal, except relating to compensation, on issues of law and facts including claims for substitute land shall be final" (Article 29.3). So the only appealable issue to regular courts is the complaint on the inadequacy of compensation, which for many critics is strange since issue of law is always appealable to higher court far up to the cassation court itself.

2.7 Summary

This chapter described the land tenure system of Ethiopia from the perspective of three historical periods. This time span covers from early times up to the current period. The three historical periods represent three different regimes having three different ideologies. In feudal Ethiopia (before 1974), land had been controlled by the elite, in that although peasants of northern Ethiopia were allowed to have usufructuary right (*rist*) on their land, they were encumbered with different obligations. The peasants of the southern part of the country, on the other hand, were evicted from their land during the nineteenth century and became landless *gabbars,* servants to the northern settlers who took their land. The Derg, which replaced the imperial regime, came to power accompanied by famous slogan "Land to the Tiller" with the objective of distributing land to the tiller, and thereby made the peasant the owner of the land and any produce wherefrom. However, the first thing the Derg did was nationalizing all urban and rural lands and extra houses in urban areas, without payment of compensation. The government replaced the previous landlordism in all its forms and it became the sole renter and rent collector. The rural and urban land laws completely prohibited sale, mortgage, lease/rent, donation, and inheritance (except to spouse and children) of land. In spite of this, the measure had, at the beginning, got great support from the rural peasantry, especially of the southern regions of the country. However, because of erroneous policies of the government that followed thereafter, and the repeated land distribution activities that carried out, the motto "Land to the Tiller" was aborted.

In 1991, the Derg, a Marxists government, was toppled by the current incumbent party, and a Transitional Government was established until the adoption of a new Constitution in 1995. The new FDRE Constitution maintains land ownership of the Derg by putting ownership of the land under public and state hands. Currently, there are other land related legislations in the country dealing with urban and rural lands and natural resources. According to the FDRE Constitution, all urban and rural lands and natural resources belong to the state and the public.

The rural land laws provide peasants with lifetime rights (holding right) to the land. This land right includes use, lease/rent, donation and inheritance rights. Sale, exchange (barter) and mortgage are not allowed. The rights of lease/rent, donation and inheritance are allowed, but their usage is restricted for different reasons. The rural land laws also create (at least in principle) free access to rural land although because of land shortage and restriction on land distribution, this right has not been realized.

In urban areas, land can be held only through lease system. According to the newly adopted urban land leasehold proclamation, residents are allowed to get land only through auction. It is only under exceptional circumstances that land may be given by allotment (without auction). Compared to the previous lease proclamation, the new one highly restricts access to urban land. The Constitution stipulates that land belongs to the "people and the state", but there is no clue which shows that urban dwellers are as much owners of their land as their rural counterparts. Secondly, the different strategies included in the new proclamation restrict the free transfer of lease right. In the case of sale of unfinished properties, it is the government who shall take the profit. Land literally becomes valueless for mortgage purposes.

Chapter 3
Conceptualizing Expropriation

3.1 Introduction

Expropriation as a means of land acquisition is a recent phenomenon in the Ethiopian legal history. For the first time it was formally introduced by Emperor Menelik II when he enacted a land charter of the newly established city of Addis Ababa in 1908. There is no much historically known fact that indicates whether previous kings of Ethiopia used expropriation to take privately owned land for public purpose activities. Active public development engagements, such as road construction, dam building or establishing new towns which necessitate the acquisition of private lands always trigger the use of expropriation. Looking into the Ethiopian past, only few incidents in the history of the country show that emperors of different eras engaged in such activities. There is no known record from the first century of the Axumite era, the first civilization of the country, although a relatively good amount of historical fact is known from the seventeenth century of the Gondarine Era. And yet, historians or royal chroniclers of the time had either deliberately left mentioning about expropriation, or could have considered it as an issue not worth mentioning in their records. Therefore, it can be argued that expropriation is a relatively new legal concept of the twentieth century. Much development has been witnessed on the nature and use of expropriation with the economic and social changes and developments of the country. Specifically, the 1960s, the golden years on the legal system in the country, saw the codification of laws, among which the 1960 civil code was the most important. The Civil Code, unlike before, allocated a good number of provisions for the treatment of expropriation. However, this part of the civil code was suspended for 20 years following the demise of the imperial era in 1975 and the coming of the Derg to power. This was followed by a new era, and new genre of expropriation rules which were adopted in 2004 and then revised in 2005.

D.W. Ambaye, *Land Rights and Expropriation in Ethiopia*,
Springer Theses, DOI 10.1007/978-3-319-14639-3_3

Expropriation as a form of land acquisition has been a known concept of law in the Western world since time immemorial. Biblical stories of King Ahab and his subject Naboth were considered as the starting point in the history of expropriation. Similar stories were also narrated from the Greek and the Roman periods. With all their legal developments the Romans had not clearly raised it in their laws, although in reality it had been practiced since the state was engaged in the construction of roads, streets, aqueducts and public baths. The theory is that Roman governors must have used expropriation to build all those pubic woks.

Expropriation, in the name of "eminent domain" was christened by the Dutch jurist and philosopher Hugo Grotius and his followers Samuel von Pufendorf and Cornelius van Bynkershoek in their respective discourses. The concept of expropriation was also in practice in continental Europe and England for centuries. The Americans were also familiar with the concept and procedure of expropriation or eminent domain starting from their earliest colony in the western hemisphere.

Expropriation as a means of land acquisition by sovereign governments has been exercised as a matter of right but for and upon two fundamental reasons: for public purpose and upon payment of compensation for the property lost. These two provisos survived and strengthened in modern world legislations although there are still contentious debates on the expansive nature of public purpose and the fairness of compensation.

Modern day Ethiopia is depicted as a country in rapid economic development where massive construction of roads, building of hydropower and irrigation dams, renewal and redevelopment of urban centers, expansion of cities, transfer of large-scale rural agricultural land to investors, zoning of industrial lands etc. are being carried out. Millions of hectares of land have been taken from farmers and transferred to foreign and domestic agricultural investors. Thousands of blight houses that rested on hundreds of hectares of land in the city center of the capital, Addis Ababa, have been demolished to redevelop the areas. Thousands of farmers who used to live on the boarders of the many cities around the country have lost their land for the establishment of newly emerging towns or for the expansion of the existing ones. Although Ethiopia is one of the least developed countries in the world, the government has managed to carry out or has attracted investors to carry out lots of development activities for cheap land lease price since land is basically controlled and owned by the state. In other words, the fact that the state has become the sole owner of the land has relieved it from paying compensation for the land. As was raised in the first chapter, and will be reemphasized in the following chapters, land has no value to the individual holder in terms of sales value or compensation.

This chapter is designed to define the concept of expropriation in general and analyze its basic nature and justification. Besides, the philosophical and practical reasons for expropriation are discussed by reviewing major literatures in the area. The experience and reality of major legal systems from selected countries are also the subjects of this discussion.

3.2 Concept and Nature of Expropriation

Jurists and students of laws of many nations and many periods have devoted their efforts to the determination of the nature and characteristics of the power of expropriation or eminent domain. Knowledge of the meaning of expropriation, its origin, and the evolution of the power provides an insight into the present-day practical application of the law which a dogmatic exposition of apparently axiomatic principles could not possibly hope to achieve.[1]

Although the power may be simply and succinctly described, there is an inherent complexity which renders a simple definition difficult and possibly misleading. It has been hedged in by many exceptions, qualifications and limitations. It has been differentiated from other powers to which it bears a resemblance. Under the circumstances it becomes necessary to use the analytical approach. From such point of view, the nature of the power of expropriation may be broken down into its constituent elements.

3.2.1 Concept of Expropriation

Although there are many legal terminologies used by different legal systems that share the same name and transmit same meaning, Expropriation, on the other hand, assumes different names in different legal systems. While in the United States it is known by the name "Eminent Domain", in the United Kingdom and continental Europe it is termed as "Compulsory Purchase" and "Expropriation" respectively.[2] Ethiopia, being a follower of the continental legal system, uses the term "expropriation". Hence, throughout this paper we shall employ the word "expropriation" with due regard to the possibility of mentioning the other terminologies as well, whenever necessary.

The most authoritative legal dictionary, Black's Law Dictionary, defines eminent domain as "the power to take private property for public use by the state, municipalities, and private persons or corporation authorized to exercise functions of

---

[1] Nichols, P. 2007 (Sackman J. & et al. (eds)). *1 Nichols on Eminent Domain.* Matthew Bender & Company, Inc., 1.11.

[2] A court in Louisiana, a state in the USA that follows a Civil Law (continental) legal s system, once declared that *the term "expropriation" used in our statutes is practically synonymous with the term "eminent domain."* See (Tennessee Gas Transmission Co. v. Violet Trapping Co., 200 So. 2d 428 (1967); In Louisiana, taking land for public use by eminent domain is called by the name "expropriation." See WEST'S LAS C.C. 2626; Both FAO and FIG study reports used the three of them interchangeably (FAO 2008. Compulsory Acquisition of Land and Compensation. *FAO Land Tenure Studies 10.* Rome: Food and Agriculture Organization of the United Nations.; Viitanen, K., Falkenbach, H. & Nuuja, K. 2010. Compulsory Purchase and Compensation Recommendations for Good Practice. *FIG Policy Statement.* Helsinki International Federation of Surveyors.

public character."[3] An older legal dictionary, Bouvier, defines the term as "The superior right of property subsisting in sovereignty by which private property may in certain cases be taken or its use controlled for the public benefit, without regard to the wishes of the owner."[4] Eminent domain is also defined in Nichols as "the power of the sovereign to take property for 'public use' without the owner's consent."[5] In all the definitions, eminent domain or expropriation is described as the power of the sovereign state or agencies delegated by it to compulsorily take land for public use purposes. What is missing from the definitions is the "compensation" element. Actually, when we look into the definition of eminent domain in earlier decisions of American courts or State Constitutions, compensation as an essential constituent of its meaning had come later.[6] In some modern definitions of the terminology, the element of compensation is still left out. For example, FAO's definition of the term could be a good example: "Compulsory acquisition is the power of government to acquire private rights in land without the willing consent of its owner or occupant in order to benefit society."[7] It must be admitted, despite the logical accuracy of the foregoing definition and despite the fact that the payment of compensation is not an essential element of the *meaning* of eminent domain, that it is an essential element of the *valid exercise* of such power. The absence of an explicit provision requiring compensation for the taking of property should not be seen as evidence of a rejection of the compensation principle. On the contrary, compensation was a well established feature of takings by eminent domain in most countries, as we shall see in the next section.

In Ethiopia, the first systematic definition for the concept was given in the 1960s Ethiopian Civil Code. The Code, under Article 1460, provides:

> Expropriation proceedings are proceedings whereby the competent authorities compel an owner to surrender the ownership of an immovable required by such authorities for public purposes.[8]

---

[3] Black, H. C. 1991. Black's Law Dictionary. 6th ed. St. Paul, Minn.: West Group.

[4] Bouvier, J. 1984. Bouvier's Law Dictionary. 4th ed.: William S Hein & Co.

[5] Nichols, supra note 1, § 1.1.

[6] Id. § 1.11. Example in *Jones v. Walker, 13 F. Cas. 1059, 2 Paine 688 (Va. Cir. Ct. 1800)*, "eminent domain" is defined as: "The right of society, or of the sovereign, to dispose, in case of necessity, and for the public safety, of all the wealth contained in the state." Looking into the State Constitutions of the early States in the USA, one can observe that in their eminent domain clauses, "most state constitutions omitted any specific mention of a right to compensation." See Harrington, M. P. 2001. "Public Use" and the Original Understanding of the So-Called "Taking" Clause. *Hastings Law Review,* 53., p. 1276.; Kratovil, R. & Frank J. Harrison, J. 1954. Eminent Domain-Policy and Concept. *Cal. L. Rev.,* 42, 596–652, p. 596; Grant, J. A. C. 1930. The "Higher Law" Background of the Law of Eminent Domain. *Wis. L. Rev.,* 6, p. 70. According to Grant, only Vermont and Massachusetts required compensation during expropriation.

[7] FAO 2008. Compulsory Acquisition of Land and Compensation. *FAO Land Tenure Studies 10.* Rome: Food and Agriculture Organization of the United Nations. § 2.1.

[8] Article 1460 of the Civil Code.

In this definition, the idea of the taking of private land by the state or authorities without the consent of the owner for public purpose is clearly envisaged. The phrase "expropriation proceeding" is employed here instead of the word "expropriation" because of a translation error from the original French version.[9] It is said that the original French version has defined the term as follows: "expropriation is a procedure by which the administration obliges an owner to surrender to it the ownership of an immovable which it needs for the purpose of public utility."[10] And yet, like the above definitions, the rule noticeably fails to include the element of compensation in its definition.

Without undermining the above definition, the following one may be considered as a working definition in discussing the details, as it is more comprehensive. This definition elaborates the concept eminent domain as follows:

> …it is the right of the nation or state, or of those to whom the power has been lawfully delegated, to condemn private property for public use, and to appropriate the ownership and possession of such property without the owner's consent on paying the owner a due compensation to be ascertained according to law.[11]

This definition seems more complete, since it includes all the basic elements. First of all, expropriation or eminent domain is a right that is exercised by the state itself or its sub-branches such as municipality and other public or private companies and people legally authorized by the state/legislature. Sustainable development requires governments to provide public facilities and infrastructure that ensure safety and security, health and welfare, social and economic enhancement, and protection and restoration of the natural environment.[12] An early step in the process of providing such facilities and infrastructure is the acquisition of appropriate land. Government may use alternative land acquisition mechanisms such as purchase, to secure land for public purpose activities. But, it is impossible to rely totally on land market as individuals may create a holdout on the projects or the land required may involve the interest of more owners that warrants the exercise of expropriation power. As we shall see in the next section, the expropriation power is inherent in the state power.

The second element is that the state or the organs authorized to take such lands must follow some procedure. In the U.S., it is known as "condemnation proceeding" while in other countries, mainly European, it is referred to as an "expropriation procedure." The main idea is that the state must ensure due process of law before

---

9 Getachew-Desta. 1975. *Expropriation: Law and Practice*. Unpublished senior thesis at the Faculty of Law of Addis Ababa University. Addis Ababa, p. 6. The original draft of the Civil Code was prepared by the French Comparative Lawyer, René David, in French, and then translated to English and from that to Amharic. There are many translation errors throughout the code, Article 1460 being one of them.

10 Ibid.

11 Amendola, F. C. & et al. (eds.) 2006. Eminent Domain *Corpus Juris Secondum*. 29A C.J.S: Thomson West. § 2 (hereinafter C.J.S.).

12 FAO, supra note 7, p. 1.

appropriating the property. In the U.S., courts usually involve in the proceeding, and the process consists of two phases: proceedings that relate to the existence of "public use" that justifies the taking, and proceedings to set the amount of compensation to be paid for the property taken.[13] The state or an authorized organ shall first petition to court for appropriation of the property and the owner will be given the right to be heard and to negotiate on the amount of compensation, and finally, the court must approve of it. In other countries, expropriation procedure is either purely administrative procedure or a hybrid of the court and administrative decisions.[14] This procedure avoids arbitrary takings of land by the state without fair compensation.

The third point worth discussing is the issue of "public use." The doctrine of expropriation stands in opposition to the right of private property. Thus, expropriation requires to find the balance between the public need for land on the one hand, and the provision of land tenure security and the protection of private property rights on the other hand. In seeking this balance, expropriation principle includes the requirement of "public interest" as one limitation on the state power of expropriation. This limitation or requirement is known by different names in different countries, such as public use, public benefit, public good, public interest, public purpose or public welfare.[15] The idea is that, there may be exceptional times and places in which the very foundations of public welfare cannot be laid without requiring concessions from individuals to give up their private property in the interest of the common good.

The appropriation or taking, mentioned in the definition, is the fourth important aspect or stage in expropriation procedure. There are several types of appropriation which can occur through expropriation: total appropriation, partial appropriation, temporary appropriation, easement and right of way being the main ones. Under the Ethiopian Civil Code, the defunct expropriation rules show that expropriation may be used either to acquire or terminate rights *in rem* such as servitude, usufruct or lease.[16] Expropriation differs from such similar concepts like police power (termed in the USA) or regulations that limit the use right of the property due to health, public safety, etc., in that it involves the loss of the core constituent right of disposal. In the latter case, what the owner loses is some part of his use right over his property, while in the former case, he loses the entire or part of the property.

The fifth point embodied in the definition is the absence of consent on the part of the owner. The power of eminent domain/expropriation is a sovereign power of the state to take private land without the consent of the owner. What makes

---

[13] 2005b. West's Encyclopedia of American Law. *In*: Lehman, J. & et al. (eds.) *Eminent Domain.* Vol. 4, 2nd ed. San Francisco, London and Munich: Thomson Gale. (Hereinafter West Encyclopedia), p. 125.

[14] See details for example in Kitay, M. G. 1985. *Land Acquisition in Developing Countries: Policies and Procedures of the Public Sector,* Boston, Oelgeschlager, Gunn & Hain, Publishers, Inc.

[15] FAO, supra note 7, p. 10.

[16] See Ethiopian Civil Code, Articles 1460–1461.

expropriation different from other consensual types of land acquisition mechanisms is the complete absence of consent on the part of the property owner. It is true that many public and private organs do also collect land through purchase and similar transactions which are based on the willingness of the person. But, it may not be realistic to totally rely on the good will of the owner to get land for different reasons. The state, hence, resorts to such coercive proceedings for two main reasons: first, owners may create a holdout on the public development activities either by totally refusing the sale of the land at any given price or by requesting unrealistically higher prices for the sale of their properties; and second, public development projects which demand long and continuous land holdings involve the interest of many owners and it may be difficult to reach agreement with all owners. In both ways, owners try to impede the public welfare that could be attained by using their land.

The last principle included in the definition is the obligation of payment of fair compensation. This principle is the most important guarantee to individual owners on their lawful possessions. All major legal systems and constitutions include this concept as a guarantee to the owner and as a limitation to the power of government. The just compensation requirement demands that the state reimburse the owner for the value of the property interest taken and place the latter in as good a pecuniary position as if the property had not been taken. The assessment of compensation is extremely complicated, and different countries incorporate different valuation methods within their expropriation legislation to reach market value.[17] Nevertheless, the existence of compensation makes expropriation tolerable and differentiates it from other government actions, such as confiscation, nationalization, and eviction, in that these three are devoid of the state obligation to compensate for the taking.

3.2.2 Nature and Power of Expropriation

There are different theories on the nature of the eminent domain power. Matthew Harrington,[18] an American professor of law, identified and developed three theories based on the jurisprudence, legal systems, and court decisions of the continental/civil law and the common law legal systems. The first theory conceives eminent domain as "reserved right" of the sovereign; the second presumes eminent domain as "inherent right" of the state; and the third theory argues that eminent domain power emanates from "consent" of the governed.

[17] See generally Kitay, supra note 14.

[18] Harrington, cited supra note 6, pp. 1245–1301.

3.2.2.1 Reserved Right Theory

The "reserved rights" theory, as we shall discuss soon, was formulated by Hugo Grotius and his followers saying that the power of eminent domain was based upon the principle that the state had an original and absolute ownership of the whole property possessed by the individual members of it antecedent to their possession of it, and that their possession and enjoyment of it was derived from a grant by the sovereign and was consequently held subject to an implied reservation that it might be resumed, and that all individual rights to such property might be extinguished by a rightful exertion of this ultimate ownership by the state.[19] Pufendorf termed this power as "exercise of transcendental property" whereby the sovereign resumed possession pursuant to the tacit agreement implicit in the original grant that the property might be resumed to meet the necessities of the sovereign.[20]

According to this theory, a citizen's possession of property is subject to an implied reservation that the state might retake the property at any time for a public purpose.[21] In this view, an individual's ownership of property is limited to a mere possessory right, at least with respect to the government. The right to hold property is, therefore, subject to a tacit agreement between the citizen and the sovereign that the property might be reclaimed by the latter to meet public necessity, and the citizen holds his land with such awareness and cannot complain of injustice when it is lawfully exercised.

This theory was received and incorporated into the laws of continental system,[22] and many earlier courts in the U.S. accepted this theory in reasoning their decision.[23]

The consequence of such a reserved-rights theory is that it has the potential to deny compensation to the landowner and to eliminate the necessity of going through all the judicial procedures. The most clear objection to this theory had

---

[19] Nichols, cited supra note 1, at § 1.13.

[20] Ibid.

[21] Harrington, cited supra note 6, p. 1250.

[22] The General Civil Code of Louisiana (West LSA-C.C. Article 2626) that adopts an expropriation clause similar to the French, reasoned the rationale behind expropriation in a manner similar to what Grotius said: "The first law of society being that the general interest shall be preferred to that of individuals, every individual who possesses under the protection of the law, any particular property, is tacitly subjected to the obligation of yielding it to the community, wherever it becomes necessary for the general use." (Tennessee Gas Transmission Co. v. Violet Trapping Co., 200 So. 2d 428 (1967).

[23] For example, in Todd v. Austin, 34 Conn. 78, 88 (1867) the court says, "The right to take property for public use, or of eminent domain is a *reserved* right attached to every man's land, and paramount to his right of ownership, he holds his land subject to that right, and cannot complain of injustice when it is lawfully exercised." In another case, Beekman v. Saratoga R.R. Co., 3 Paige Ch. 45, 73 (N.Y. 1831), it is said: "Eminent domain represents the highest and most exact idea of property remaining in government, or in the aggregate body of the People in their sovereign capacity, giving a right to resume possession of property …whenever the public good requires it." (Both cases are cited at Harrington, cited supra note 6, at footnote 15).

come from latter American courts, for whom reservation of rights in the sovereign "sounds too much like feudalism."[24] The most obvious rebuttal to this theory is that it simply is not in accord with actual practice.[25] Unlike Europe or England, feudalism was totally unknown in America for it was established on equality of citizens and rights.[26] Accordingly, it is now generally considered that the power of eminent domain is not a property right, or an exercise by the state of an ultimate ownership in the soil, but that it is a power based upon the sovereignty of the state.[27] Historical precedents in America and England show no reservation of power in the hand of the sovereign. Even in continental Europe, in the Roman period there were evidences of compensation for the taking of private property.

3.2.2.2 Inherent Powers Theory

As shown above, the strongest objection to the reserved rights approach came from the American courts. Confronted with many theoretical problems, as well as because of the nature of the American federal structure, many courts in the United States eventually rejected the theory of reserved rights and came to view eminent domain simply as an inherent right of sovereignty.[28] The state's power to take land for public use came to be regarded as a power which inheres in the right of the state to govern the *polis*—which is to say, inherent in its "police power"—and was not dependent on any pre-existing property right.[29] According to this view, governments have the sovereign power to enact any regulation affecting persons or property located within their borders, subject to such limitations as might be imposed by their respective constitutions. By adopting this approach, the American courts equated the source of power for eminent domain to other similar powers of the state, such as police powers and the power to levy taxes, which are inherent powers founded in the primary duty of government to serve the common needs and advance the general welfare of the people. Currently, the principle of inherent power seems dominantly accepted everywhere. It is said that the power of eminent domain is an inherent attribute of sovereignty and exists even without constitutional

---

[24] Id., p. 1251.

[25] Stoebuck, W. B. 1972. A General Theory of Eminent Domain. *Washington Law Review,* 47, p. 558.

[26] Some of the founding fathers actually argued for the elimination of any allusion to feudalism in their property arrangement. They demanded an explicit recognition of private property rights that could not be taken by the government. For instance, Thomas Jefferson contended that all remnants of feudalism in regard to property should be eliminated. He vigorously pushed for allodial ownership wherein land owners would hold absolute dominion over their property. In other words, he contended that land holders should not be treated as stewards, with property ultimately controlled by the prerogative of the state (see Paul, cited infra note 63, p. 9).

[27] Nichols, cited supra note 1, at § 1.13.

[28] Harrington, cited supra note 6, p. 1251.

[29] Ibid.

recognition; therefore, constitutional provisions relating to eminent domain must be construed as limitations upon, rather than grants of such power.[30]

Such right or power antedates constitutions and legislative enactments, and exists independently of statutory or constitutional sanction or provision.[31] Thus, modern laws only try to recognize it and prescribe limits for its application. A reading of the expropriation laws of most countries reveals that they confirm the state's authority to confiscate private property, but impose two conditions on the exercise of such authority: the taking must be for a public use, and just compensation must be paid to the owner.[32]

3.2.2.3 Consent Theory

Although it seems the above two theories propagate two different ideas, in reality, the underlying principle is one and the same. Both inherent powers and reserved rights theories permit no real restraint on the sovereign's exercise of the power of eminent domain. A sovereign's eminent domain power is absolute and total. It is superior to all other property rights, and every owner of property holds his land subject to the right or power of eminent domain. The taking of property by a government's exercise of its power of eminent domain is not a government infringement of the property owner's fundamental right to own property, since the power of eminent domain is itself a constitutional right.

Hence, a third theory based on the consent of owners is developed. This theory is actually back to the English practice of middle-ages where the power of the sovereign (king) was restricted in favor of parliamentarian power. As shall be discussed in the history of expropriation in England, the power of expropriation was transferred to parliament as early as 1400.[33]

The theory of consent is best understood as being a function of the theory of consent inherent in the representative government. That is to say, the power to take property for public use resides in the legislature, and not the executive, because such takings require the consent of the owner and that consent can be given directly or through his legal representatives. In this respect, takings by eminent domain are on the same footing as takings through taxation. Just as the sovereign lacks the

[30] Comments 1948–1949. The Public Use Limitation on Eminent Domain: An Advance Requiem. *Yale L. J.*, 58, 599–614.

[31] C.J.S., cited supra note 11, at § 4.

[32] See for example Erasumes, G. M. 1990. *Compensation for Expropriation: Comparative study,* Oxford, Jason Reese in association with The UK National Committee of Comparative Law. (Published in two volumes, the book, edited by Erasmus, describes the nature, process and compensation during expropriation of different countries representing all continents and legal systems.

[33] See generally Reynolds, S. 2010. *Before Eminent Domain: Toward a History of Expropriation of Land for the Common Good,* Chapel Hill, The University of North Carolina Press.

power to levy taxes without consent of the legislature, so too does it lack the power to take property from a subject without similar consent.

In modern laws, (irrespective of the theoretical arguments that eminent domain power is reserved or inherent in the state, it is dormant until the legislature rouses it into activity by taking steps for the exercise of the power, declaring the objects to which, and the mode and agency through which, the power shall move.[34] The legislature, by adopting legislations to this effect, may delimit the powers of expropriation of the state. Hence, it can be said that the taking of property by government exercise of its power of eminent domain does not amount to an infringement of the property owner's fundamental right to own property, since the power of eminent domain is itself a constitutional right. Therefore, we can conclude that eminent domain or the power of expropriation is superior to all property rights, and every owner of property holds it subject to the right of eminent domain.

3.2.2.4 Principles of Expropriation

The United Nations Food and Agriculture Organization (FAO) has published guidelines for countries to follow during expropriation of land. We hereunder reproduce the principles of compulsory purchase and the problems that may created because of improper expropriation process.

According to the FAO guideline, when enacted their expropriation legislations, countries should consider the following principles[35]:

- Protection of due process and fair procedure: Rules that place reasonable constraints on the power of the government to compulsorily acquire land strengthen the confidence of people in the justice system, empower people to protect their land rights, and increase the perception of tenure security. Rules should provide for appropriate advance consultation, participatory planning and accessible mechanisms for appeals, and should limit the discretion of officials.
- Good governance: Agencies that compulsorily acquire land should be accountable for the good faith implementation of the legislation. Laws that are not observed by local officials undermine the legitimacy of compulsory acquisition. Good governance reduces the abuse of power and opportunities for corruption.
- Equivalent compensation: Claimants should be paid compensation which is no more or no less than the loss resulting from the compulsory acquisition of their land. Laws should ensure that affected owners and occupants receive equivalent compensation, whether in money or alternative land. Regulations should set out clear and consistent valuation bases for achieving this.

[34] Fletcher, W. M. 2011. Eminent Domain. *Fletcher Cyclopedia of the Law of Corporations*. 6A Fletcher Cyc. Corp. § 2905.

[35] FAO, supra note 7, p. 6.

The problems that may arise when compulsory acquisition is not done properly are[36]:

- Reduced tenure security: Policies and legislations that strengthen land rights of individuals and communities may be eroded through compulsory acquisition. People may believe they lack tenure security if the government can acquire rights in private land without following defined procedures, and/or without offering adequate compensation.
- Reduced investments in the economy: Insecure tenure, with the threat of the arbitrary loss of land and associated income, discourages domestic and foreign investment.
- Weakened land markets: Threats to tenure security discourage land transactions, reduce the acceptability of land as collateral, discourage people from investing or maintaining their property, and depress land values.
- Opportunities created for corruption and the abuse of power: The lack of protection and transparency can result in injustices which anger citizens and undermine the legitimacy of government.
- Delayed projects: Appeals against unfair procedures may hold up the acquisition of land, and thus block projects and increase costs.
- Inadequate compensation paid to owners and occupants: Financial awards may be inadequate to allow people to enjoy sustainable livelihoods after their land is acquired. People may feel that they are not compensation.

3.3 History of Expropriation

3.3.1 Ancient Greece and Rome

Looking into the early history of the power of expropriation, it seems that the origin and history of expropriation was lost in obscurity since there was no definitive legislation that clearly gives expropriation power to the ancient governments. This does not mean, however, that it was not in actuality practiced. As we shall see in a while, there are ample evidences that show its existence in the early and middle ages. In any case, the concept indisputably finds its roots in the natural law movement.[37] Despite its practical application, though, it was not until after the close of the middle ages that the taking of property for public use as a distinct branch of governmental power began to be discussed among jurists and philosophers.

---

[36] Id., p. 6–7.

[37] Lenhoff, A. 1942. Development of the Concept of Eminent Domain. *Columbia Law Review,* 42, p. 596.

To start with the Bible itself, some people ascribed the biblical story of King Ahab's seizure of Naboth's land as the first example of an act of expropriation.[38] According to the Bible,[39] Israel's King Ahab desired a vineyard owned by Naboth the Jezreelite to grow herbs on it. He offered Naboth his choice of either a new vineyard or "the worth of it in money." When Naboth refused to sell, Jezebel, Ahab's wife, conspired with others to put Naboth to death. The theory that this was the first act of expropriation was first put forth by Merlin de Douai, the nineteenth century French legal theorist.[40] Scholars, however, became skeptical as to the existence of the king's power of expropriation. They argue that if the king had the power of eminent domain, he would not have needed to kill Naboth to grab his vineyard land.[41]

In tracing the history of the power of expropriation in ancient Greece and Rome, we find only unsatisfactory allusions to the existence of such a principle. Looking first to Greece, we read in the Athenian Constitution of Aristotle about the reconciliation of the Athenians who were in exile and those who stayed in the city during the aftermath of the fall of the ten tyrants who were elected after the overthrow of the previous thirty tyrants.[42] An agreement was reached concerning the Athenians who wished to immigrate to the city of Eluesis and get property there upon payment of compensation that implicates an expropriation like practice:

> If any of the seceding party [Athenians] wished to take a house in Eleusis, the people would help them to obtain the consent of the owner; but if they could not come to terms, they should appoint three valuers on either side, and the owner should receive whatever price they should appoint.[43]

Susan Reynold provides two additional evidences from ancient Greece that may show the possible existence of expropriation practices: one is about a legislation concerning the valuation of noncitizens' property that might be wanted for building temples; and the other is, the laying of drains in private fields in Euboea, with payment to the landowner.[44]

When we come to the Roman expropriation practice, although Romans had detailed laws on private ownership of property, it is difficult to find one that shows whether expropriation was part of the formal Roman laws, for it was never formulated into legislation.[45] However, from the ownership right of the Romans, it can be said that the Roman owner had a general or residuary, rather than an unrestricted

---

[38] Stoebuck, supra note 25, p. 553.

[39] *Holy Bible*. King James Version, 1 Kings 21:1–16, pp. 315–316.

[40] Harrington, cited supra note 6, p. 1249.

[41] Ibid.; Stoebuck, cited supra note 25, p. 553; McNulty, W. D. 1912. Eminent Domain in Continental Europe. *The Yale Law Journal,* 21, 555–570, p. 555.

[42] Aristotle [Translated] 1984. *The Athenian Constitution,* London, Penguin Books. Chapters 36–38.

[43] Ibid., Chap. 39; Boynton, S. 1962. Components of Eminent Domain: an ancient tool for contemporary use. *South Carolina Law Review,* 15, p. 944; Reynolds, supra note 33, p. 15.

[44] Reynolds, supra note 33, p. 15.

[45] Stoebuck, cited supra note 25, p. 553.

right. So, when the need for public works made it necessary to take over land in private ownership, there was nothing inherent in the nature of ownership which could be urged against this course.[46] Scattered bits of evidence which have been studied by scholars also suggest that "there is a good deal of evidence to indicate that the Romans took private property to further a variety of public purposes."[47] In this regard a study conducted by Jones observes:

> It is impossible to believe that the construction of the Roman roads, extending in a straight line from one end of the Empire to the other, or of the Roman aqueducts, was at the mercy of the owners of the land through which they were to pass.[48]

Nathan Matthews, an American scholar, who researched the Roman Valuation systems, on his part concludes:

> Notwithstanding the paucity of surviving precedents for the expropriation of real estate, the general opinion seems to be that this function of government must have been freely exercised, particularly under the later (Roman) emperors, in aid of highways, municipal buildings and other public improvements.[49]

A further scrutiny on the subject also reveals some evidences of expropriation practices. For instance, the edict of Justinian, A.D 535, provides that church lands could be taken for such other purposes as the authorities might deem to be in the public interest upon condition that the religious bodies should receive other property of equal or greater value.[50] Where land was taken for the construction of a tower in Constantinople, the landowner was compensated by a right to live in the tower when built. Sometimes the compensation took the form of remission of taxes.[51] The Roman senate decreed in 11 B.C. that it should be lawful to take from the adjoining lands of individuals the materials needed for the repair of aqueduct, upon an estimate of the value or damages, to be made by good men.[52] And in the *Annals of Tacitus* we are told that, when a private house was injured by a public road or aqueduct, the Emperor Tiberius paid the damage on petition by the party to the senate.[53] All these instances, however, although striking, do not prove that the expropriation principle was recognized under the Roman law. The fact that the Roman law treated private property and citizens in high regard coupled with the absence of expropriation rules in the Institutes of Justinian and the Codes create considerable doubt on the existence and application of the practice.

---

[46] Jones, J. W. 1972. Expropriation in Roman Laws. *Law Quarter Review,* 45, p. 521.

[47] Meidinger, E. E. 1981. The "Public Uses" of Eminent Domain: History and Policy. *Envtl. L.,* 11, p. 8.

[48] Jones, supra note 46, p. 521.

[49] Matthews, N. 1920. The Valuation of Property in the Roman Law. *Harvard Law Review,* 34, pp. 253–254.

[50] Ibid., p. 254.

[51] Ibid.

[52] Nichols, supra note 1, at § 1.2; Also see Jones, cited supra note 46, p. 524.

[53] McNulty, supra note 41, p. 557.

3.3.2 The Civil Law of Continental Europe

With the decline and gradual fall of Rome, all trace of the power of eminent domain disappears for centuries, and during the medieval period, when the demand for public improvements was small and the rights of individuals little regarded, the power of eminent domain was neither considered nor discussed.[54] Although there was no clear and known philosophical or legal discourse on the subject up until the seventeen and eighteen centuries, the practice of expropriation seems, though, to have survived all these years. Susan Reynolds, who investigated the history of expropriation in Western Europe, complained that lack of "evidence before 1100 and absence of community solidarity"[55] during this age makes it difficult to trace the existence of expropriation until the early middle ages. An attempt has been made by her to piece together the scattered references from across Western Europe in order to establish the existence of expropriation. The general conclusion of her work is that expropriation in middle ages Europe was mild and was exercised by central authorities and sometimes by local lords for the "common good" of society, such as erection and construction of fortifications, river canals, city walls, and roads upon payment of compensation either in kind or in money.[56] The general belief was that individuals had no power to resist a royal power in taking property for a public work. This can be described in what an English Chancery decided in 1664 on a disputed case by remarking that "it should not be in the power of one or two willful persons to oppose a public good."[57]

The government's authority was thought to be emanating from its being lord of all the land and the people, which gave the government the right to take back what it granted before to the people. This is associated with the concept of "feudalism" which, according to the English Jurist, Blackstone, was a universally received type of governance throughout the Middle Ages' Europe. The fundamental maxim and nature of feudalism has been described by Blackstone as follows:

> The grand and fundamental maxim of all feudal tenure is that all lands were originally granted out by the sovereign, and are therefore holden, either mediately or immediately, of the crown.[58]

---

[54] Nichols, supra note 1, § 1.2.

[55] Reynolds, supra note 33, p. 17.

[56] For details see Ibid.

[57] Id., p. 45.

[58] Blackstone, W. 1825. *Commentaries on the Laws of England,* London, A. Strahan Law Printer. Book II, Chap IV, p. 39. The King was considered to be the owner of all the property and land within his kingdom. In order to defend the property, he permitted lesser persons such as nobles, knights, and other royalty to inhabit lands, subject to them paying rents or tithes to him. They in turn let others occupy lesser amount of property, again subject to tithes or rents being paid to them. This hierarchy extended all the way down to slaves or serfs. All of these individuals were permitted to use the land ultimately subject to the pleasure of the king [to take it back when necessary.] (see Schultz, infra note 181, p. 49).

This means, as a source of the land grant, the sovereign has a reserved power to claim back what it had granted earlier. In explaining the English feudal system, Blackstone also says elsewhere that, "the king is the universal lord and original proprietor of all the lands in his kingdom; and that no man do or can possess any part of it, but what has mediately or immediately been derived as a gift from him, to be held upon feudal services."[59]

Expropriation, in the name of "eminent domain", started to take definitive shape after Hugo Grotius' influential work, *On the Law of War and Peace*, where he "constructed an argument that derived and justified the right of expropriation clearly from the origin and nature of all property rights."[60] Like John Locke and Thomas Hobbes, who came after him, Grotius assumed in the "state of nature", where there had not been law and state, land was owned by the people in common.[61] He claimed, "by the law of nature, before property was introduced, everyone had a right to the use of whatever he found unoccupied."[62] Thus, mankind, as joint inheritors of one general patrimony, holds all things of this earth as their "common stock."

The next question raised by Grotius was how man moved from this common right of the earth and its riches to private ownership. For Grotius, private property is a result of occupation and subsequent recognition by the community. According to Grotius, in the primitive stage of mankind "man exercised a general right to seize for his own use or consumption whatever he needed, and it became unjust to deprive anyone of what he had once captured."[63] Thus, private property hinges on two factors- occupation and consent.[64] Since people could not continue to live in a state of anarchy, they had to enter into contract to establish a "civil society." Property becomes now a civil right. "The civil right is that which is derived from the civil power. The civil power is the sovereign power of the state. A state is a perfect body of free men, united together in order to enjoy common rights and

---

[59] Ibid., Blackstone, Book II, Chap. IV, p. 38.

[60] Reynolds, supra note 33, p. 94.

[61] The Social Contract theory advocated by Hugo Grotius, Thomas Hobbes and John Locke claimed that in the early days of mankind, which they called it "the State of Nature", there was absence of state and laws enacted by the state. In this stage of human society, the earth and all its wealth were given to the common use of mankind. On the evolution of private property, though, the three of them have different opinions. While for Grotius occupation of land and social recognition is the means to change property from common to private holdings, the mixture of labour to the common holdings was the sole reason for Locke. But, for Hobbes, only the creation and establishment of the Civil Society (Government and laws) was the source of creations of private properties. (see Hobbes, T. 1996 (J. C. A. Gaskin (ed.), originally published 1651,). *Leviathan,* New York, Oxford University Press.; Locke, J. 1980 (C.M. Macpherson (ed.), originally published 1690,). *Second Treatise of Civil Government* Cambridge, Hackett Publishing Company Inc.).

[62] Grotius, H. 1625 [orig.] *On the Law of War and Peace* A.C. Campbell translation, *De Jure Belli ac Pacis.* Book I, Chap. I, Sect. X.

[63] Paul, E. F. 1987. *Property Rights and Eminent Domain,* New Brunswick and London, Transaction Publishers, p. 197.

[64] Ibid.

advantages."[65] Since private property right is a result of the human will which transcends to the recognition of the state, the state becomes now powerful since it represents the interests of all people. By virtue of this superior power, the state keeps a residual power over citizens' private property to take it back when suffering extreme duress. Grotius, in his *Introduction to Dutch Law*, emphasized that "property was established by human communities," and by virtue of which "the whole community had, and has, a higher right over the goods of its members."[66]

In his second book, *On the Law of War and Peace*, Grotius shows the existence of two types of rights in the civil society: one, for the advantage of the individual, and the other superior, *eminens dominium*, a power that the sovereign has on the individuals and their property. In case of necessity, Grotius wrote, "the Sovereign has a greater right over the property of his subjects, where the public good is concerned, than the owners themselves have."[67] The taking of private property for common good is termed by Grotius as "eminent domain," which is otherwise known as expropriation. He argued that the state may take individual property by eminent domain "but to do this by the force of Eminent Dominion, there is required, in the first place, public utility; and next, that, if possible, compensation be made, to him who has lost what was his, at the common expense."[68] Elsewhere, on the eminent domain power of the state, he argues:

> The property of subjects is...under the eminent control of the state, that the state or the sovereign who represents it, can use that property, or destroy it, or alienate it, not only in cases of extreme necessity, which sometimes allow individuals the liberty of infringing upon the property of others, but on all occasions, where the public good is concerned, to which the original framers of society intended that private interests should give way. But when that is the case, it is to be observed, the state is bound to repair the losses of individuals, at the public expense, in aid of which the sufferers have contributed their due proportion.[69]

What is new in Grotius's writing is his contribution to the philosophical justification of source of eminent domain power: that the power is derived from the assumption that those who consented to join the civil society, by entering into the social contract, thereby intended that private claims should give way to those of "public utility." Precisely why such a presumption should be inherent in the social

---

[65] Grotius, supra note 62, Book I, Chap. I, Sect. XIV.

[66] Garnsey, P. 2007. *Thinking about Property From Antiquity to the Age of Revolution,* Cambridge, Cambridge University Press, pp. 217, 220; Reynolds, supra note 33, p. 95. Grotius follows the earlier natural law approach specially emphasized by Thomas Aquinas who says: "in extremes property rights are suspended, and everything reverts to common property, as in Gods original dispensation." The idea was that in case of extreme necessity a person may take another's property and this should not amount to theft. Grotius' main innovation was his extension of the claim of necessity from the safety of individuals to the safety of the states.

[67] Grotius cited supra note 62, Book I, Chap. I, Sect. VI.

[68] Id., Book II, Chap. XIX, Sect. VII.

[69] Id., Book III, Chap. XX, Sect. VII.

contract, Grotius did not say.[70] On the other hand, he maintains the traditional value given for private property and the fact that eminent domain can only be effected only if it is necessary for public purpose activities and upon compensating the property owner.

Samuel von Pufendorf, another natural lawyer and follower of Grotius, on his part argues that originally private property emanated from the grant of the ruler, and it is the ruler who determines what rights the people have over the property. The ruler has three rights over citizens' private property whether granted or acquired latter by the individual. The first has to do with the right to set rules regarding the "use of property in conformity with the interest of the state", "quality of their possession" and "method of transaction." The second right is pertaining to taxation, while the third right is concerned with the right of eminent domain. He elaborates:

> The third right is that of eminent domain, consisting in this, that when public necessity demands it, the property of any subject which are very urgently needed at the time, may be seized and used for public purposes, although they may be more valuable than the allotted share which he is supposed to give for the welfare of the republic. On this account, the excess value should, insofar as possible, be refunded to that citizen in question, either from the public funds, or a contribution of the other citizens.[71]

The important point that we may gather from Pufendorf's writing is the rational that he provided for compensation, that no one should be compelled to pay more than his fair share for public improvements, and if such a sacrifice is required, the burden should be redistributed to others so that those called upon to make excessive sacrifices can be recompensed.

The next step in the history of expropriation in continental Europe was to insert the principle of expropriation into their respective legislations and codes. Although they were short lived and rarely cited, there were some legislations in the seventeenth and eighteenth century Europe that recognized the principle of expropriation as a means of land acquisition for the common good of the people. For instance, in Germany the Bavarian *Landrecht* of 1616 refers to the taking of land for roads, and the *Codex Maximilianus* of 1756 says that no one could be compelled to sell property against his will unless the government needs it for the common good.[72] Legislation for Austria in 1784 ordered that where the public good required, those who held land that was needed for new roads had to give it up, either at a price to which they agreed or at one fixed by the government engineer.[73]

Finally, the inclusion of the expropriation principle in the 1789 French *Declaration of Rights of Man and of the Citizen*, the 1793 French Constitution and finally in the French Civil Code of 1803 were significant steps forward in defining the power of the state versus individual property right. The 1789 *Declaration of Rights*

---

[70] Paul, cited supra note 63, p. 75.

[71] Pufendorf, S. V. 1673. *De Officio Homines et Civis (On The Duty of Man and Citizen According to the Natural Law)*. Book II, Chap. XV.

[72] Reynolds cited supra note 33, p. 71.

[73] Id., p. 54.

of Man and of the Citizen under Article 17 says, "Property being an inviolable and sacred right, no man may be deprived of it, unless in cases where public necessity, legally recorded, clearly demands it, and on condition of just and prior compensation."[74] The 1793 French Constitution under Article 19 on its part provides: "No man may be deprived of the least portion of his property without his consent, unless it is when legally recorded public necessity demands it, and on condition of a just and prior compensation."[75] The French Civil Code, which then after served as a source for many countries around the world, carries this principle under article 545 as follows: "Nobody may be forced to cede his property unless for purpose of public interest, and against the prior payment of a just compensation." By the revolution of 1789, the state became no longer the holder of absolute power,[76] which was carried by the "eminent domain" phraseology argued by Grotius and his followers.

3.3.3 Historical Developments in the United Kingdom

The term "eminent domain" was a phrase not known to English law as it was understood in the United States. Even currently, it is known by the name "compulsory purchase." The doctrine, as expressed in England, was applied only in the exercise of the sovereign to enter lands for the defense of the realm.[77] English kings before the sixteenth century used to take private lands to build castles, fortifications, churches and the like. The scanty evidence gathered from this era shows that compensation used to be paid mainly in terms of land to land compensation.[78] However, the European conception of absolute power of the king on his subjects and their property was restricted in England after the adoption of the Magna Charta in 1215. This was because the Magna Charta prevented the king from applying such power to all types of rights. With regard to property rights, the Magna Charta declares: "no free man shall be… dispossessed… his freehold liberties… except by the lawful judgment of his peers, or by the law of the land."[79] This means, at least, the king could not expropriate private land without paying compensation.

This expropriation power of the sovereign was further curbed due to dominance of parliament over the king's power in the English politics. Unlike what was dictated by Grotius and others in continental Europe, in England, the supremacy of

74 Dwyer, P. G. & Mcphee, P. (eds.) 2002. *The French Revolution and Napoleon: A Source Book*, London: Routledge, p. 28.

75 Ibid., p. 94.

76 Picard, E. 1990. Expropriation in France. *In*: Erasmus, G. M. (ed.) *Compensation for Expropriation: A Comparative Study*. Oxford: St. Edmund Hall University of Oxford, p. 33.

77 Boynton: 1962, supra note 43, p. 946.

78 Reynolds, supra note 33, pp. 34–45.

79 2005a. West's Encyclopedia of American Law. *In*: Lehman, J. & Phelps, S. (eds.) *Foundations of the U.S Law: Magna Charta*. San Francisco: Thomson Gale. Chapter 39, p. 8.

the king was long refuted and replaced by parliamentary supremacy.[80] Blackstone himself sided with the parliament by refuting the inherent power of the Crown to take land for public purpose activities. Blackstone, in his Commentaries, after emphasizing the high regard of the law on private property and the impossibility of taking of private property against the will of the owner even for "general good" of society, as exception, declared:

> …it would be dangerous to allow any private man, or even any public tribunal, to be the judge of this common good, and to decide whether it be expedient or no. Besides, the public good is in nothing more essentially interested, than in the protection of every individual's private rights. In this and similar cases the legislature alone can, and indeed, frequently does, interpose, and compel the individual to acquiesce. But how does it interpose and compel? Not by absolutely stripping the subject of his property in an arbitrary manner, but by giving him a full indemnification and equivalent for the injury thereby sustained. And even this is an exertion of power which the legislature indulges with caution, and which nothing but the legislature can perform.[81]

Hence from as early as 1402, only Parliament was empowered with the authority to effect compulsory sale,[82] which in effect means the power of expropriation of land for public purpose was transferred to parliament.

However, there were two exceptions in which the king could exercise the power of expropriation. In these circumstances, the king had prerogative powers to act in the public interest and without making compensation for private property taken or destroyed. These conditions were when it was necessary to defend the realm or where he was thought to have some special property right.[83] Concerning national defense, the king, for example, in order to save and protect the realm against enemies or the sea could erect bulwarks and other fortifications on private land, tear down the houses in the suburbs of a city, or dig in private land for saltpeter to make gunfire, if necessary to wage war.[84] Necessity also justified the king in razing houses to prevent the spread of fire, or building walls or dikes to protect lands from imminent flooding.[85] Although in *Burmah Oil Co Ltd* v *Lord Advocate* (1964) the House of Lords decided that this war prerogative could not be exercised without paying compensation to expropriated owners, this decision was altered by the retrospective War Damage Act of 1965 denying such compensation.[86]

---

[80] Parliamentary supremacy triumphed in England after the defeat and execution of King Charles I in 1651. There was a protracted civil war (1642–1651) and struggle in England between supporters of the parliament and that of the Royalty to reduce the prerogatives of the king.

[81] Blackstone, supra note 58, Book I, Chap. I, p. 139.

[82] Harrington supra note 6, says "the first recorded exercise of the powers to expropriate property appears to have been a statute of 1402, in which parliament declared to be common highways, and authorized the inhabitants of the area to take gravel, trees, or loam for the repair of the structures along the way." p. 1260.

[83] Harrington supra notes 6, p. 1259.

[84] Ibid.

[85] Ibid.

[86] Green, B. D. 2009. *Compulsory Purchase and Compensation,* London, EG Books, p. 22.

Sometimes, the king was thought of as having exclusive right in some objects seized. Thus, the Crown had a right to all royal fish, abandoned shipwrecks, waifs (goods stolen and thrown away by a thief in his flight), wandering animals, and treasures unclaimed by owners.[87]

Unlike the king, Parliament had complete power of eminent domain to take private property upon payment of compensation. With the increase of urbanization and the expansion of sophisticated public facilities, during the period between the seventeenth and nineteenth centuries, Parliament issued a series of statutes condemning private lands for the construction of roads, bridges, drainage systems, naval bases, etc. In any case, it is said that the idea of a "power of eminent domain was well established in England by the time of the American Revolution, and the obligation to make compensation had become a necessary incident to the exercise of the power."[88] Today, the power of compulsory purchase is delegated by acts of Parliament to regional authorities to enable municipal and other corporations to take property for their use.

3.3.4 Brief History of Eminent Domain in the United States

As far as the necessity of eminent domain powers were concerned in the American colonies, the appropriation of property for public use was primarily limited to the establishment of roads, dams, or grist mills.[89] One can imagine the need for more roads in new settlement, totally unimproved lands, like the early colonies of the United States of America. From as early as 1639 the states of Massachusetts, New York, New Jersey and others started constructing town streets and roads by taking land from private owners or by allocating land for such purposes originally. Usually, men were selected by courts to assess the level of damage and the amount of compensation to be paid.[90] Next to roads, the most important object for the exercise of eminent domain during the colonial period was the erection and maintenance of mills. Statutes authorizing lands to be taken to enable the owner of a mill site to construct or maintain a dam in order to raise a head of water sufficient to operate a mill were in force in seven of the colonies prior to the Revolution.[91]

A review of the pre-constitutional period in the U.S. reveals two significant characteristics. First, property was usually expropriated without resort to litigation. Like the tradition in England, Americans repeatedly declared that the power to expropriate private property for a public purpose rested in the legislature alone.[92]

---

87 Id., pp. 1259–1260.

88 Meidinger, Cited supra note 47, p. 9; Nichols, supra note 1, at § 1.21.

89 Boynton: 1962, cited supra note 43, p. 947.

90 For details see Nichols, cited supra note 1, at § 1.22.

91 Ibid.

92 Harrington, cited supra note 6, p. 1247.

To this end, it is said that both the colonial and confederation governments made extensive use of the power to expropriate property for all manners of social and economic ends.[93] Second, the duty to compensate a deprived land owner was generally not recognized.[94] Yet, there are evidences that show that some states used to pay compensation. For example, in the Dutch colonies compensation was paid during expropriation of land.[95] Immediately before and after the adoption of the U.S. constitution, though, courts tried to scrutinize the legislative acts of expropriation by requiring the payment of compensation based on the principle of natural justice.[96] At the end of the American Revolution, although eminent domain as a legal form had begun to take shape, its exercise by governments or courts was not yet limited. In other words, there was no concept of public use in the statutes and court decisions at that time. Later, when the U.S. Constitution was adopted, the concept of eminent domain with its limitation of public use was incorporated into the Fifth Amendment.

When the Americans finally adopted their Constitution, the absolute and unlimited form of the power, which had been limited in England by the Magna Charta, was restricted even more by the United States Constitution's Fifth Amendment. The last clause of this amendment says: "…nor shall private property be taken for public use, without just compensation."[97] The eminent domain clause under the Fifth Amendment is not though as comprehensive as it should be. It does not contain particulars that clearly grant expropriation power or substantive limit on the power. Rather, what is "commonly thought to be a takings clause is in fact nothing more than a compensation clause."[98]

---

[93] Ibid., p. 1253.

[94] Alabama-Section 1976. Eminent Domain: A Survey of Alabama Law. *Alabama Law Review,* 28, p. 401.

[95] Meidinger, supra note 47, p. 13–16. He traced the earliest eminent domain law to the 1639 Massachusetts' statute which authorized county courts to condemn a private land for a highway.

[96] Id., see also Fisher, W. 1990. Ideology, Religion and the Constitutional Protection of Private Property: 1760–1860. *Emory Law Journal,* 65, 104. Especially the decision of Judge Kent justifying compensation on natural law principle was one that is usually cited by scholars. Most decisions, before the American civil war were relied on natural law principles (see Stoebuck, cited supra note 25, p. 555; Grant, supra note 6).

[97] The whole content of the Fifth Amendment of the U.S. Constitution goes as: "No person shall be held to answer for a capital, otherwise infamous crime, unless on a presentment or indictment of a Grand Jury, except in the land or naval forces, or in the Militia, when in actual service in time of War or public danger; nor shall any person be subject for the same offence to be twice put in jeopardy of life or limb; nor shall be compelled in any criminal case to be a witness against himself, nor be deprived of life, liberty, or property, without due process of law; nor shall private property be taken for public use, without just compensation.

[98] Harrington, supra note 6, p. 1248.

3.3.5 Historical Background of Expropriation in Ethiopia

In Ethiopia, the power to take land for public purpose did not become a matter of great concern until the early twentieth century. Until this point in history, Ethiopia remained relatively small and its need for public works rather limited. The country's economy was predominantly agriculture, and urbanization was totally unknown[99]; hence, there were fewer motives for the leaders of the time to take land for public works. Throughout most of its history, Middle Age Ethiopia remained a land of small villages and isolated homesteads.[100] Modern urbanization only started with the establishment of the present capital, Addis Ababa in 1886. Although modern road construction works started on a small scale and for military purpose earlier during the middle of the nineteenth century, it was intensified only after the establishment of the capital.[101]

3.3.5.1 Pre Constitutional Era

Turning into the Ethiopian history of property right vis-à-vis the power of the sovereign kings, it has been mentioned by different writers, national or foreign travelers, that the powers of the Ethiopian monarchs had been absolute over the people and their objects.[102] As already discussed in the preceding chapter, land had been controlled by the sovereign and distributed to the people and elites on, theoretically, some kind of condition, like paying tribute tax, or rendering manual or military service to the emperor, very similar to the Middle Ages of European feudalism. Therefore, we could assume that the emperors could take land that belonged to any person, at their pleasure, although this may not have happened frequently for two main reasons: first, up until the early twentieth century, there was no significant economic development in the country that warranted the taking of land for public construction activities; and second, the emperors who mostly relied on the teaching of the Christian morality would not resort to cruel measures of land

[99] This is true with due regard to the existence of two previous capitals of the realm, namely Axum (100 BC–800 AD) and Gonder (17–18th Century).

[100] Pankhurst: 1990, supra note 125 in Chap. 2, p. 275.

[101] As detailed by Richard Pankhurst, modern road building began during the reign of Emperor Tewodros II (1855–1868) with the intent of creating easy and rapid movement for his military and cannons. Assisted by foreigners he was able to link his capital, *Debre Tabor*, with three main routes to Goneder, Gojam and Gafat. To break Tewodros, the British had also resorted to road construction by starting from the sea. But quality and modern roads started to emerge with the establishment of Addis Ababa by Emperor Menelik II. The early half of the twentieth century was thus a time in Ethiopia which can be portrayed as a time of public works development and extensive use of expropriation. (see Pankhurst, R. 1968. *Economic History of Ethiopia 1800–1935,* Addis Ababa, Haile Sellassie I University Press, pp. 284–289).

[102] See details in supra footnote 30 of Chap. 2 of this dissertation.

confiscation unless the person commits serious crimes. Both of these assertions are backed by some evidences presented hereunder.

With regard to the powers of the monarchs and right to property held by the people, we have already established the kind of property rights in Ethiopia in Chap. 2. In the northern part of the country a relatively secured land right, *rist* right that provided the holder all rights except sale used to be practiced. In the southern parts of the country, which was annexed to the empire during the late nineteenth century, land was generally held in private by individuals, by the Church or by the state, and was freely transferable. Although there is ample evidence on the nature and type of land holding rights over a long period in Ethiopia, expropriation is mentioned very rarely. We find some allusions here and there that might give us a clue on the existence and practice of expropriation; and yet, it is not conclusive to say that it existed in full practice until the enactment of the 1908 Addis Ababa Land Charter, which we shall discuss soon.

According to the evidence that is found, it is said that King Lalibella of the *Zagwe* Dynasty (early thirteenth century)[103] had made payments to the land he used to construct his well known churches. The hagiographer of the King compliments him for paying for the land on which he built his churches. "He attributes this to the king's special sense of piety and saintliness and asks a rhetorical question to demonstrate the traditional power of the monarch in the distribution of land: 'who would have forbidden the king if he had decided to take the land' (without compensation)?"[104] As James Bruce, the eighteenth century Scottish traveler to Ethiopia, underlined, although the monarch had this absolute right over the land and the subjects in respect of taking, it "makes no violent use of its power in that respect."[105]

Another evidence that is associated with Christian morality, is the rule that was incorporated to the fifteenth century law of the country, *Fiteha Negest* (The Laws of the Kings). There is a provision inserted in the *Fiteha Negest* that was influenced by the Biblical story of King Ahab: "Do not take wealth of any one by violence, and do not buy from him by force; neither openly nor by trick, in order not to be afflicted by God in this world and in the future…"[106] Of course, this rule by itself is not as such telling about expropriation, but what is important is the message that it incorporates. The message here is that nobody (a person or a king) should take the property of another person by violence (such as theft and robbery) or buy by force (such as compulsory purchase). One may argue that this provision does not give the power of expropriation to the sovereign for it clearly forbids the taking of land

[103] The *Zagwe* dynasty ruled the country from approximately 1137–1270. Zagwe means in the ancient Geez language "that of the Agew" in reference to the Agew People that constituted its ruling class. King Lalibella (later Saint Lalibella) is the most celebrated king of this dynasty who built eleven rock-hewn monolithic churches from blocks of solid rock to be known as "New Jerusalem." The Churches of Lalibella are now in the list of the UNESCO World Heritage sites.

[104] Taddesse-Tamrat, supra note 33 in Chap. 2, p. 98.

[105] Paul and Clapham, supra note 30 in Chap. 2, p. 290.

[106] Id., p. 293; see also Fitha Negest, supra note 59 in Chap. 2, Article 1544.

without the consent of the owner. But, the implication is that in the event of pressing public necessity, the king would have no choice but to expropriate the land, and to rectify this wrong (transgressing of the *Fiteha Negest*), he would make a recompense in kind or in cash to those who lost their property.

When Emperor Fasiladas (1632–1667) established the medieval capital city of Gonder, he must have taken lots of land from farmers, or he must have built it on barren hilltops. There are extensive records that show the free transaction of land in the Gonderine period.[107] In other words, land was held in private hands during that period. But, there is nothing important that is said about the expropriation of land in that era. Yet, we can assume that the later monarchs must have taken land either by purchase or expropriation from private owners for the construction of churches, royal castles, streets and market places during the subsequent century and half, following the establishment of the city by Fasiladas.

As already discussed previously, the church was a holder of large tracts of land property in all the history of Ethiopia. Emperors of different eras made the grants to churches and monasteries so that the latter would be supported from the income. However, sometimes, this smooth relationship between the church and the palace encountered difficulties, which resulted in the expropriation of church lands. For example, as a result of the clash he had with the Church on religious matters, Emperor *Susneyos* (1607–1632) is said to have seized a substantial part of land belonging to the monastery of *Debre Bizen.*[108] In a later period, extensive land which caused tension was expropriated by *Ras Michael Sehul* of Tigre. According to James Bruce's records, as a result of the friction that Michael had with the Church authorities, a royal proclamation was issued at Gonder in 1771 ordering that "all lands and villages, which are new, or have been given to the Abuna by the king, shall revert to the king's own use, and be subject to the government, or the Cantiba [mayor] of *Dembea*, or such officers as the king shall after appoint in the provinces where they are situated."[109] In both cases, church land was taken or reverted to the kings' hands without compensation. Besides, there is no evidence that shows that the land was taken for the common good of society; rather it was taken because of power struggle between the monarchs and the Church.

We find a similar story, in a later age, when Emperor Tewodros II (1855–1868) wanted to reform the land tenure and the Church itself. Among others, he ventured to reduce much of the Church's land and transfer it to landless tenants[110] and to his

[107] For example see Crummey: 2000, supra note 35 in Chap. 2, p. 183.

[108] Pankhurst: 1990, supra note 125 in Chap. 2, p. 33.

[109] Bruce, J. 1790. *Travels to Discover the Source of the Nile in the Years 1768, 1769, 1770, 1771, 1772 & 1773,* Edinburgh, R G. G. J. and J. Robinson, Paternoster-Row. Vol. 4, Book 7, Chap. 3: 78.

[110] Tewodros passed a proclamation in 1856 which seems to institute property in *Shoa*. It decreed that land should belong to those whose fathers had already held it as fiefs and that persons without any such claim should look to the Emperor as their father (Pankhurst: 1968, supra note 101, p. 142).

soldiers who used to live by plundering and raiding peasants.[111] The Emperor was complaining on the multitude of Church land as compared to his own which was intended to be allotted to the soldiers. The clergy resisted the Emperor's plans but as the contemporary missionary, Henry Blanc said, "Theodore could not tolerate any power in the state but his own. He had fought hard to be the supreme ruler of Abyssinia … and when he thought the occasion favorable to do away entirely with his power and influence, he confiscated all the Church lands and revenues."[112] His ultimate aim was to transfer the Church land to landless peasants and soldiers for better use, as salary, and to make it more productive.[113] Although his attempt was not successful,[114] this, at least, may be taken as a good example of expropriation, because the establishment of modern salaried military (defense) could be considered as an act done in the interest of the public.

The sovereign's right in respect to the land in *Shoa* (central Ethiopia) was also similar, if not greater than that of the northern Ethiopia. In a similar fashion as noted above, it has been said that in *Shoa* "all the best portion of the soil pertain to his Majesty, and all the life as well as the property of every subject is at his sole and absolute disposal."[115] And yet, some evidence from this part of Ethiopia shows that expropriation to meet royal needs seems to have been accompanied by the provision of alternative land for the dispossessed. Richard Pankhurst, citing a contemporary English traveler of the time, Charles Johnston, relates that when *Sahel Sellasssie,* King of *Shoa* (1813–1847) erected his palace at *Ankobar,* many people had been evicted from their land so that their land could be used for the palace construction. The Englishman was greatly interested in the matter and made careful

111 Caulk, R. A. 1978. Armies as Predators: Soldiers and Peasants in Ethiopia c. 1850–1935. *The International Journal of African Historical Studies,* 11, 457–493. For centuries soldiers used to get food from peasants either by force or through voluntary provision.

112 Blanc, H. 2007 (Original 1868). *A Narrative of Captivity in Abyssinia: With Some Account of the Late Emperor Theodore, His Country and People,* Harvard, Harvard University.p, 150; See also Pankhurst: 1968, supra note 101, p. 143. All Church land was confiscated and the number of priests was limited to five to seven. The Emperor disliked monks and above all *dabtaras,* complaining that they "wore turbans on their heads and neither fought nor paid taxes", preferring to "live in cities with prostitutes and other people's wives." (Ibid.).

113 Pankhurst: 1966, supra note 29 in Chap. 2, p. 95; Crummey, D. 1969. Tewodros as Reformer and Modernizer *The Journal of African History,* 10, 457–469. Crummey argued (at p. 468) that Church lands were making no real contribution to the national economy since the larger part of them were uncultivated, partly through the indolence of the clergy, partly through the disincentive which they gave to any peasants who might want to till them by means of high taxes.

114 With a clash that he had with Great Britain, the Emperor shot himself before the English put hand on him. And the opposition from the priesthood contributed significantly to his fall for they were prime movers and instigators of various regional rebellion rose against him. The rebellions debilitated his power which created an opportunity for the British to win him easily. After the death of Tewodros, leaders of different regions and by and large the succeeding Emperor, Yohannes IV, declared at once the restoration of Church lands to their former owners. (Pankhurst: 1968, supra note 101, p. 143).

115 Harris, C. 1844. *The Highlands of Ethiopia,* London, Longman, Brown, Green, and Longmans. Vol. 3, p. 33.

investigation about the fate of the peasants. He particularly wanted to know whether "any injustice had marked this course." His informants all agreed that ample compensation had been given by the king to the peasants.[116]

Ethiopia witnessed considerable amount of road construction after Emperor Menelik II came to the throne in 1889. Many and impressive amount of roads were constructed in the city of Addis Ababa during his reign.[117] Another important accomplishment of his period was the construction of a 781 km railway from Djibouti to Addis Ababa and the establishment of new towns along the new railroad. In 1894, the railway company was established and the Emperor was asked to "grant to the company a continuous stretch of territory along the entire length of the line."[118] The amount of land, according to Section Eleven of the concession contract, was to be 1,000 m in width. But, a 1908 revised contract under Section Four indicates that the land would be 1,000 m from Djibouti to Dire Dawa, 200 m from Dire Dawa to Awash, and 50 m from Awash to Addis Ababa.[119] This shows the amount of land given decreased as the line came from the lowland desert to the highland populous areas of the country.

Although there is information on the sale and purchase of land in those newly established towns, such as Dire Dawa, whether the land utilized for the railways construction was acquired through purchase or expropriation is not known. Nevertheless, the assumption is that since the eastern part of the country on which most of the rails were rested was a desert and was inhabited by the *Afar* nomads, the land might not have been purchased or expropriated. But, in towns and in the central highland plateaus, where the land was populated, there is no doubt that the Emperor must have expropriated land for such purpose. Yet, there is no available information whether or not compensation was paid at that time.

Nonetheless, there is relevant information from the same period that seems to enlighten us on the tradition of the time concerning expropriation procedures and compensation. This interesting story was told by Rober Skinner, the head of American Mission in Ethiopia during the Menelik II era. He noted that in 1903, a year before the road between *Dire Dawa* and *Harar* was projected, it was necessary to take the land required for the construction of the road. The local Oromos who lost their land waited upon the governor, Ras Mekonnen,[120] and complained saying that

---

[116] Pankhurst: 1968, supra note 101, p. 140; See also Pankhurst: 1966, supra note 26 in Chap. 2, p. 81.

[117] For details see Pankhurst, R. 1961. Menelik and the Foundation of Addis Ababa. *The Journal of African History,* 2, 103–117.

[118] Id., p. 168.

[119] See the whole 1893 and 1908 railroad construction concessions as reproduced in Mahteme-Sellassie: 1970, supra note 55 in Chap. 2, p. 440–449. The original agreement dictates that the first phase was to be built from Djibouti to Harer, and the second from Harar to *Enteto.*

[120] Ras Mekonnen was a cousin of the Emperor and a father of Teferi Mekonnon, the future Emperor Haile Sellassie. He was a trusted General and Governor of the eastern city of Harar and the surrounding Somali areas. *Ras* means literally "head" and it was the highest military title given by that time.

their farms would be ruined and as a result they could not accept a price offered for their land. Surprised, the Ras asked, "But it is fair price, is it not?" and the peasants answered: "It is not the price we complain of, most gracious lord; we don't want our farms destroyed." The Ras thereupon ordered them out of his presence, saying, that there was but one Governor of Harar, and that he alone would say what might or might not be done. The road was constructed…and when it was all over, the Ras called the peasants before him, and telling them that he had been compelled to exert his authority in order to demonstrate his supremacy, he was now prepared voluntary to pay them twice the value of their property, thus showing them that their Governor could be generous as well as just.[121]

This story is interesting in the sense that the concept of expropriation is fully explained by it. Road construction is a work considered as a public good in expropriation. We also see the absence of consent on the part of the peasants to surrender their land; it was rather compulsorily taken. We even see the compensation paid to the farmers in lieu of their lost land. The other important assumption that we may gather from it is that there was the tradition of payment of compensation in the event of expropriation. The Governor of *Harar* was a trusted General and a close counsel of the Emperor, and hence what he had done at that time must be based on the examples of tradition or the acts of the Emperor himself. Taking into consideration the fact that both the railroad and the gravel road were constructed at the same period, and the fact that both cousins (the Emperor and the Governor) shared the same principles and beliefs, we can safely conclude that land owners who lost their property to the construction of the Ethio-Djubouti railroad must have got compensation.

To strengthen this point one may also look into the historical developments of the time concerning property rights, all of which reinforce the above assertion, that the King must have been paying compensation. Emperor Menelik II was a modern leader who not only allowed the introduction of modern technology, but also established a cabinet of ministers to run the state. The Emperor in consultation with his ministers passed a series of edicts, among others, concerning land property. For example, his royal chronicler tells us that in January 1891, Menelik, after consulting the *Fitha Negest,* passed an edict concerning land found in *Shoa* (from *Wayt* to *Awash*). It shortly says that "no *rist* land shall be expropriated from the owner irrespective of his crimes; let his cattle be taken as penalty".[122] A general decree containing similar intention was adopted by Menelik's council of ministers in 1908, which said that "…no one should be evicted from his *rist* land except those escapee killers and state treasonous."[123] Menelik's daughter, Empress Zewditu, had also passed similar edict in 1928 which guarantees protection of *Rist* land. "The edict

[121] Pankhurst: 1966, cited supra note 26 in Chap. 2, p. 169; Pankhurst: 1968, supra note 101, p. 289.

[122] Tsehafe-Tezaz-Gebre-Sellasie 1959 (EC). *Tarik Zemen ze Dagmawi Menelik Nuguse Negest Ityopia (History of the Lives and Times of Menelik II King of Kings of Ethiopia),* Addis Ababa, Artistic Ltd, p. 179.

[123] Id., pp. 334–336.

gave legal confirmation to the ownership right of all *rist*-holders, guaranteeing against expropriation for whatever crimes committed."[124] These series of edicts solidify the principle and commitment of Emperor Menelik and his descendants to protect and guarantee private ownership of land in Ethiopia.

Menelik's final commitment to the protection of private property came in 1908 when he decreed the Addis Ababa City Land Charter that affirmed, once again, the protection given to private ownership of urban lands. It is in this charter, for the first time, that we find the principle of expropriation clearly set as an independent principle. Articles 25 and 27 of this legislation[125] are of particular significance to the topic under discussion:

> Article 25. For the safety and security of the city, private owners might be compelled to sell their land together with a house, if any, to the government. The amount of compensation payable shall be determined by government experts.
> Article 27. If there is building on the land, the government shall pay the amount agreed upon or should give an equivalent thing.

The Charter brilliantly included all the necessary elements of expropriation: that land and any building on it might be compulsorily taken by government, that this was to be done where it deemed necessary in the interest of public, that the owner would be compensated based on the assessment of experts, and that the compensation would be made either in money or in kind. The Charter was influenced by the French Civil Code (Code Napoleon) since the last clause of the charter referred us to "Code Napoleon in the event this edict is not sufficiently covering other different issues." In any case, what we gather from the reading of the expropriation provision of this decree is that expropriation procedure had to be done by the city municipality itself. Courts were unlikely to be involved either in deciding the existence of "public purpose" or fairness of compensation since nothing has been said about them. In the event of compensation assessment, "government experts" would be used to assess the value of the land and the house thereon, if any. These experts were most likely urban engineers from the city municipality.

3.3.5.2 Constitutional Era

What was started by Menelik, to safeguard private property, had been continued by his successors, mainly, by Emperor Haile Sellassie I, and "the crowning act in the process of reinforcing the security of *rist*-holders was the 1931 Constitution."[126]

---

[124] Bahru-Zewde 2008b. Economic Origins of the Absolutist State in Ethiopia (1916–1935). *In*: Zewde, B. (ed.) *Society, State and History: Selected Essays*. Addis Ababa: Addis Ababa University Press, p. 105.

[125] The 1908 Minelik's Addis Ababa Charter, as reproduced in Mahteme-Sellassie: 1970, supra note 55 in Chap. 2, p. 170; with slight difference in translation, see also Pankhurst: 1966, supra note 29 in Chap. 2, p. 158.

[126] Bahru-Zewde: 2008b, supra note 124, p. 106.

For the first time in the history of the country, a written constitution was adopted in 1931 which, among others, included protection accorded to private property. Concerning expropriation, one provision (Article 27) was dedicated in the constitution to allow the sovereign to take land in case of public necessity. Although unpublished with the Constitution itself, a supplement was added, of which Chap. 8 is of paramount importance. Chapter 8 of the supplement of the constitution contains three Articles (Articles 74–76) guaranteeing the inviolability of the property of the Emperor and the royal family, the princes, territorial governors and other Ethiopian citizens by banning, except in the event of ascertained public utility, expropriation of land as form of punishment for crime[127]:

> Article 27
> Except in cases of public necessity determined by the law, no one shall have the right to deprive an Ethiopian subject of any movable or landed property which he owns
> Article 74
> It is determined by law that land and property hitherto in the hands of the Emperor and of members of the Imperial family, and all lands which they may acquire in future by purchase like any ordinary citizens shall, subject to the observance of the established regulations concerning land, be confirmed to them and shall be heritable to their descendants
> Article 75
> It is determined by law that similarly princes and territorial governors and all other Ethiopian citizens, who commit any sort of crime, shall be punished according to the provisions of the law, but landed property which they have hitherto held, or which they may acquire in future by purchase, shall not be confiscated.
> Article 76
> Nevertheless, if it is necessary for the Government to construct on another person's land installations for the public welfare, such as forts, roads, markets, churches, schools, hospitals, townships or any work of this kind, it is determined by law that if the Deliberative Chambers have declared it necessary, the land owner shall be given a fair price as determined by law, or, subject to the landowner's consent, he shall receive some other similar compensation, and he shall be compelled to surrender the property; but except in a case of this kind where the public welfare is involved, a person's land may not be taken from him with a view to benefiting an individual.

The main provision (Article 27) is brief and cannot tell whether or not it includes compensation. But the supplementary provision (Article 76) details and describes the former. Thus, where public welfare (purpose) requires, a privately owned land may be taken by government upon the declaration of parliament to that effect and payment of compensation as fixed by a different law. What is interesting is that the Constitution, although written in the image of the Japanese Meji Constitution, incorporates in its expropriation declaration an English type of requirement when it demands parliamentarian approval of the project before expropriating the land. The other important characteristic of this rule is that expropriation would not be made with the sole purpose of benefiting another individual. This rule by and large

---

[127] The 1931 Ethiopian Constitution as reproduced in Paul and Clapham, cited supra note 30 in Chap. 2, pp. 326–336; see also Mahteme-Sellassie: 1970, cited supra note 55 in Chap. 2, p. 771, 789; also it is found on some web pages, such as http://www.worldstatesmen.org/Ethiopia_1931.txt.

restricts the absolute prerogative of the sovereign powers of the king as well as territorial governors in interfering in the private holding or ownerships of individual citizens.

Although the constitution presumes that a different subsidiary legislation would be enacted pertaining expropriation, this had not come to light during the lifetime of the constitution. Nevertheless, we have other decrees which incidentally mentioned it, such as the 1933 "Land Lease to Foreigners Decree" which under Article 8 reflects the principle enshrined in the constitution:

> The Government shall have the right to take any land deemed necessary for market, churches, fortifications, railways, or other similar services upon payment of due compensation.[128]

Significant developments have been occurring in Ethiopia following the Italian occupation of Ethiopia around the Second World War. During its occupational period of Ethiopia from 1936–1941, Italy invested much in infrastructure construction of the country. The Italians constructed thousands of kilometers of roads, bridges, urban streets, town halls, government and court buildings in Ethiopia within the 5 years of their occupation. They had also a plan, the execution of which had actually been started, to settle Italian farmers in Ethiopia. To this end, land was expropriated from private individuals in urban and rural areas to implement the Italian colonial policy. In spite of its scantiness, there are evidences that the colonialists used to pay compensation, although not adequate. The Ethiopians were paid much less than the market value for their land. In Addis Ababa, for example, between 1937 and 1938, property worth about ten million Italian Lire was confiscated for colonization and new urban planning, but less than two million Lire was paid by way of compensation.[129]

On the contrary, it seems, the Italians profited by selling land, which was expropriated from the local people. In Addis Ababa, for example, land taken from Ethiopians was parceled out into small plots and sold at between 15 and 60 % higher than the price of compensation.[130] Large tracts of rural farm lands occupied by the Ethiopian state and private farmers were also confiscated to settle Italian farmers. The precise scale of such confiscations is not easy to establish. Yet, cases suggest that the Italians, at an early stage, did not hesitate to take any land thought essential for the viability of settler farms. By the end of 1939 land given in this way to the settlers totaled 186,000 ha, not including lands made public domain but not yet allocated.[131]

After the expulsion of the Italian forces from Ethiopia in 1941, the Imperial regime of Haile Sellassie resumed office, and the old laws were restituted. The Italians neither declared nor left any legislation concerning land in Ethiopia. The

---

[128] Pankhurst: 1966, supra note 26 in Chap. 2, p. 208.

[129] Larebo, H. M. 1994. *The Building of an Empire: Italian Land Policy in Ethiopia 1935–1941*, Oxford, Clarendon Press, p. 245.

[130] Ibid.

[131] Ibid.

1931 Ethiopian Constitution rather had been operating for the next decade and half without any change. Then it was revised in 1955 and a new rule replaced the previous expropriation provisions, although it was not as articulate as the former ones. And yet, it puts the expropriation provision in one Article with enough information:

> Article 44
> Everyone has the right, within the limits of the law, to own and dispose of property. No one may be deprived of his property except upon a finding by ministerial order issues pursuant to the requirements of a special expropriation law enacted … and except upon payment of just compensation determined in the absence of agreement, by judicial procedures established by law…[132]

A detailed scrutiny of the rule reveals that unlike the 1931 Constitution, the revised one follows an American type of procedure by involving courts in the expropriation proceeding. The constitution anticipated the passage of detail expropriation proclamation in the future that would put all the procedures of expropriation among others, presumably, the public interest aspect. But concerning compensation, the assumption of the constitution seems that an agreement would be arrived on the amount between the condemning ministerial authority and the landowner; otherwise compensation would be determined by court of law.

3.3.5.3 The 1960 Ethiopian Civil Code

The above quoted constitutional principle, "*everyone has the right, within the limits of the law, to own and dispose of property*," was reproduced in detail in the 1960 Ethiopian Civil Code.[133] The Civil Code allocated a substantial part of its section to property law in general and expropriation in particular.[134] The Civil Code was drafted by the French Comparative Lawyer, *René David*, and one can see the major influence of the French Civil Code on the Ethiopian property law and by extension on the expropriation provisions. Like the Roman law tradition of continental Europe,[135] "ownership" is defined under the Ethiopian Civil Code as "the widest right that may be had on a corporeal thing," and "such right may neither be divided nor restricted except in accordance with the law."[136] In the Roman law tradition,

---

[132] The Revised 1955 Constitution of Empire of Ethiopia: http://www.angelfire.com/ny/ethiocrown/Constitution.html.

[133] Ethiopian Civil Code.

[134] Of the Civil Code, Book III, Titles VI–X are allocated for property. In particular, under Title IX, Articles 1460–1488 are dedicated to expropriation.

[135] Article 544 of French Civil Code reads: "Ownership is the right to enjoy and dispose of things in the most absolute manner provided that they are not used in a way prohibited by statute or regulations." The Code is available at http://195.83.177.9/upl/pdf/code_22.pdf.

[136] Article 1204(1), (2) of Ethiopian Civil Code.

ownership is conceived as absolute[137] except that it may be sometimes restricted where it is provided so by law. Expropriation is one example of those restrictions or interferences on ownership right.

Although we shall see the detail of the content later on, in here, we will discuss briefly the main elements of expropriation as incorporated in the Civil Code. The Code recognizes "alignment" and "expropriation" as the two methods of land acquisition. Expropriation is used for the "creation of new roads and streets"[138] while alignment proceeding serves to "widen or straighten existing roads or streets."[139] As already pointed out above, expropriation has not been properly defined in the code; what is defined is "expropriation proceeding." The purposes of expropriation are generally gathered from two different provisions of the law. They are to "acquire land for public purposes,"[140] and to "acquiring or extinguishing a rights of usufruct, servitude or other rights *in rem*"[141] and to "terminate" any "prior lease contract"[142] on the immovable. Before resorting to the expropriation proceeding, the competent authority shall first declare the intended project is for public purpose and notify the owner of the land thereof; and where a public discussion appears to be necessary, the condemning authority shall consult the public before declaration of public purpose.[143] What constitutes public purpose has not been clearly envisaged in a manner such as what we saw above under the 1931 Ethiopian Constitution. But, the code gives a clue by saying that expropriation may be used "to enable the public to benefit by the increase in the value of land arising from works done in the public interest."[144] What we can assume is that roads and streets may increase the value of adjacent properties and this is what the law intends to say. On the other hand, expropriation proceeding may not be used for the sole purpose of obtaining financial benefits.[145] Concerning compensation, it has been said under Article 1474 that "the amount of compensation or the value of the land that may be given to replace the expropriated land shall be equal to the amount of the actual damage caused by expropriation;" and this compensation shall be one "which is assessed by the committee on the day when it makes its decision."

---

[137] In the Roman law tradition ownership right is conceived as absolute. Although difficult to define, it connotes, among others, that ownership is the greatest right that a person can have in property, that it is inherently unrestricted and that it is the only right of its kind, that there is no lesser form of ownership. For details see Simpson, S. R. 1961. Towards a Definition of "Absolute Ownership": II. *Journal of African Law,* 5, 145–151, Birks, P. 1985. The Roman Law Concept of Dominium and the Idea of Absolute Ownership. *Acta Juridica,* 28, 1–37; Pierre, B. 1997. Classification of Property and Conceptions of Ownership in Civil and Common Law. *Revue Generale De Droit,* 28, 235–274.

[138] Ethiopian Civil Code, Article 1450(1).

[139] Id. Article 1450(2).

[140] Id. Article 1460.

[141] Id. Article 1461(1).

[142] Id. Article 1461(2).

[143] See Articles 1463–1465.

[144] Id. Article 1464(2).

[145] Id. Article 1464(1).

The Civil Code expropriation provisions were partially suspended following the demise of the Imperial regime and the assumption of power by the Marxist Military Junta, Derg. As already detailed in Chap. 2, the Derg nationalized all rural and urban lands and urban extra houses and abolished private ownership of land. The very idea of sanctity of private property and the need to use expropriation under exceptional cases of "public interest" was defeated by the very nationalization act of the military government. What makes nationalization different from expropriation is that the former is devoid of any compensation.

Rather, without mentioning the status of the civil code expropriation rules, the Derg inserted its own expropriation rules in its rural and urban land proclamations as follows:

Proclamation 31/1975 (Rural land proclamation)

Article 17: Power of Expropriation

(1) The Government may use land belonging to peasant associations for public purposes such as schools, hospitals, roads, offices, military bases and agricultural projects.
(2) The Government shall make good such damage as it may cause the peasant association by decision to expropriate the holding.

Proclamation 47/1975 (Urban land Proclamation)

Article 8: Power of Taking and Expropriation

1. Where a person, family or organization fails to utilize his or its urban land within the period to be specified by the Ministry, the Ministry may take back such land and put it to appropriate use.
2. The ministry shall, by giving compensation in kind, expropriate for public purpose urban land held by person, family or an organization.

Article 19: Expropriation of Houses
The Government may, by paying compensation, expropriate for public purpose an urban house held by any person, family or organization.

What is clear is that in the event of expropriation of urban and rural land the compensation is to be made in kind, that is land to land. Since land was owned by the state, it is obvious, that the location of replacement land was little concern. It means, since land had no value, a change in location would not bring about a change in compensation amount.

Concerning expropriation of urban houses, proclamation 47/1975 declares that compensation would be paid. However, it does not bother to show the modality of property assessment. Whether it should be valued based on market value of the property or as cost replacement is not known. But in the absence of such detail rules, the assumption is that courts would use the civil code as reference.

The military government was removed from power in 1991, and after some years a new expropriation proclamation was introduced in 2004 (Proc. 401/2004). This proclamation was brief that contains only sixteen provisions. Most of its contents were included in the current expropriation proclamation (Proc. 455/2005) that replaces it.

3.4 The Justification for Expropriation

How can expropriation be reconciled with the institution of private property? In any country that claims as having democratic constitution, private property rights are protected from any outside interference, including that of the government itself. Moreover, private property is protected by international conventions to which countries become signatory.[146] One of the important rights of ownership of property is the right of "exclusion" that gives the owner the right not to be interfered with. The exclusion right is a right *in rem* that can be claimed against the whole world. If this is the case, how can expropriation be justified by including it in the constitution or property law as another principle? It is clear that expropriation is a restriction imposed on the property rights of an individual for the sake of common good of society. Common good is a certain general or specific condition that benefits all or most of the members of society. Thus, in the private property versus expropriation discourse, the conflicting interests are that of the individual and the society, and apparently, individual interest cedes to the interest of society. In justifying the social interest over that of the individual, four types of theories are present below.

3.4.1 Economic Justifications

3.4.1.1 Holdout Problems and the Concept of Public Goods

Efficient land use and holdout problems are often raised as fundamental economic reasons to exercise expropriation power of the state. The inherent power of the state's eminent domain power can be explained by what economists call market failure. Market failure is a concept within economic theory which occurs when the allocation of goods and services by a free market is not efficient. In simple terms, the market may not always allocate scarce resources efficiently in a way that achieves the highest total social welfare. The solution to market failure is the intervention of the state in allocation and supply of the goods. More specifically, a property assignment is mentioned as one of the possible intervention areas by the state to solve the market failure. Although there are many reasons for market failure, Gravelle and Rees argue that more fundamentally, the underlying cause of market failure is often a problem of property right. According to them, "A market is an institution in which individuals or firms exchange not just commodities, but the *rights* to use them in particular ways for particular amounts of time. [...] Markets

[146] For example the United Nations Universal Declaration of Human Right (Article 17), African Charter on Human and Peoples' Rights (Article 14), and Protocol No. 1 of the European Convention for the Protection of Human Rights and Fundamental Freedoms are some of the conventions which provide protection to private property.

are institutions which organize the *exchange of control* of commodities, where the nature of the control is defined by the *property rights* attached to the commodities."[147] The general idea is that since property right provides individual owners the monopoly of exclusion and transfer over their property, they may affect the efficiency of the market by methods such as holdout.

In other words, the market is imperfect because it fails to provide the needed goods. If we associate this to the issue at hand, land is chiefly acquired from the market through voluntary or consensual transactions, such as purchase, lease, easement/servitude and so on. In most cases, voluntary transaction of land is cheaper than forced transaction and in fact about eighty percent of federal land acquisitions in the United States use the market.[148] But, this may not work always for sometimes individual owners of land may either create a holdout or completely refuse to transfer their land voluntarily, and this consequently increases the transaction cost.[149] As Merrill noted, market mechanisms do not always yield optimal land assembly when very large tracts are needed.[150] Some large-scale projects require the assembly of several contiguous parcels of land whose ownership is dispersed. For instance, pipeline, railways, highways, urban redevelopment projects need large amount of contagious land. The problem facing providers in these cases is that, if a large number of landowners know about the intended purchase ahead of time, they will all want to be the last individual to sell in order to be in a monopoly position and extract the highest possible price. Such strategic behavior on the part of sellers would result in expected transactions costs for the buyer being so high that s/he gives up the effort and the potentially welfare enhancing development is never undertaken.[151] Thus, economists generally suggest that in order to break the

[147] Gravelle, H. & Rees, R. 2004. *Microeconomics,* Essex, Prentice Hall, p. 314.

[148] Munzer, S. R. 1990. *A Theory of Property,* New York, Cambridge University Press, p. 423.

[149] Transaction costs are costs associated with the transfer of the land such as costs paid to brokers, formation and enforcement of contracts, negotiation, notary, registration and so on.

[150] Merrill, T. W. 1987. The Economics of Public Use. *Cornell Law Review,* 72, 61–116, p. 77.

[151] Benson, B. L. & Brown, M. 2010. Eminent Domain for Private Use: Is it Justified by Market Failure or an example of Government Failure? *In*: Benson, B. L. (ed.) *Property Rights: Eminent Domain and Regulatory Takings Re-Examined.* New York: The Independent Institute, p. 150. (As quoted by the writers, the eminent law and economist, Richard Posner elaborates the problem: "An economic reason for eminent domain, although one applicable to its use by railroads and other right-of-way companies rather than by government, is that it is necessary to prevent monopoly. Once the railroad or pipeline has begun to build its line, the cost of abandoning it for an alternative route becomes very high. Knowing this, people owning land in the path of the advancing line will be tempted to hold out for a very high price—a price in excess of the actual opportunity cost of the land. The high cost of acquiring land will, by increasing the costs of right-of-way companies, induce them to raise the prices of their services; the higher prices will induce some consumers to shift to substitute services; the companies will therefore have a smaller output; and as a result the companies will need, and will purchase, less land than they would have purchased at prices equal to (or slightly above) the opportunity costs of the land. Furthermore, higher land prices will give the companies an incentive to substitute other inputs for some of the land that they would ordinarily purchase. As a result of these factors land that would have been more valuable to the right-of-way company than to its present owners remain in its existing, less valuable uses, and this is efficient.".

strategic bargaining (holdout) problems and thereby to ensure public welfare through the construction and implementations of public works, the state is justified to intervene by using its expropriation power.

Applying this theory to the Ethiopian scenario, where there is limited land market especially that of sale, market based land acquisition methods will not offer the necessary land required for any project activity. This means, since land sale and purchase is completely prohibited, expropriation of land from users or lessees is left as the only alternative to collect and transfer land necessary for public or private projects determined as beneficiary to society.

3.4.1.2 Efficiency

Concepts of "Value"

Another justification for expropriation is the need to ensure the efficiency of land use. Efficiency means the most productive use of resources to satisfy competing material wants.[152] Hence a plot of land may be expropriated if the diversion of its use can bring about higher benefit to society. For example, land currently used for agriculture may be expropriated and converted to urban residential houses; or a blight urban center may be changed to vibrant commercial district by expropriating the land and demolishing the old residential houses. In each of these cases we may assume that society is acting rationally in the sense that the new conditions of resource employment will produce a greater amount of welfare in society than the old one did. One effect of the decision to reallocate resources would be to redistribute welfare among the members of society. The economic benefit is assumed to be higher enough to put the old and new owners in better offs.[153]

When economists talk about efficiency in relation to resources, they mean an allocation of resources in which value is maximized. However, it is necessary to look further at what counts as value-maximization.

In economics, 'value' is an ambiguous term, but for present purposes 'value' can be taken to mean how much someone is prepared to pay for something, or, if they have it already, how much they would demand to part with it. In assessing value for these purposes, economists do not look at the amount that someone can afford to pay for something. What matters is how much they would pay if they had the money. Also, it is necessary to bear in mind that value, when used in this sense, can be dramatically different from utility, or happiness in the utilitarian sense. Posner illustrates the difference using the following example:

---

[152] Kalbro, T. 2000. Compulsory Purchase and Restrictions on Land Use: Principles of Compensation in Swedish Law. *Property Development and Compulsory Purchase.* Stockholm: Royal Institute of Technology (KTH), p. 126.

[153] This is similar to what economists called *Pareto Efficiency,* which explains that efficiency is obtained when a distribution strategy exists where one party's situation cannot be improved without making another party's situation worse.

> Suppose that pituitary extract is in very scarce supply relative to the demand and is therefore very expensive. A poor family has a child who will be a dwarf if he does not get some of the extract, but the family cannot afford the price and could not even if they could borrow against the child's future earnings as a person of normal height; for the present value of those earnings net of consumption is less than the price of the extract. A rich family has a child, who will grow to normal height, but the extract will add a few inches more, and his parents decide to buy it for him. In the sense of value used in this book, the pituitary extract is more valuable to the rich than to the poor family, because value is measured by willingness to pay; but the extract would confer greater happiness in the hands of the poor family than in the hands of the rich one.
> As this example shows, the term efficiency, when used … to denote that allocation of resources in which value is maximized, has limitations as an ethical criterion of social decision-making—although perhaps not serious ones, as such examples are very rare.[154]

Pareto Efficiency

Strictly speaking, value is maximized when the allocation of resources cannot be bettered, in the sense that it would be impossible to transfer or reallocate the resources in such a way as to make anyone better off without also making at least one other individual worse off. This strict notion of efficiency is called Pareto efficiency (after the nineteenth-century Italian economist and social scientist Vilfredo Pareto), sometimes Pareto superiority or optimality. Pareto efficiency is not a very useful concept, in particular when assessing whether a transaction is efficient, because while voluntary transactions can be expected to make all the parties to the transaction better off (if not, they would not have entered into it) they nearly always make someone somewhere worse off to some degree (if only by altering the market price of the resource).[155]

Kaldor-Hicks Efficiency

For the reason given above, economists more usually use a modified concept of efficiency, termed Kaldor-Hicks efficiency. A transaction is efficient in the Kaldor-Hicks sense if it makes someone better off, provided that it does not make someone else worse off by a greater amount.[156] Or in other words, "A change is an improvement by the Kaldor-Hicks criterion if the gainers value their gains more highly than the losers their losses."[157] Any transaction that produces a net increase

---

[154] Posner, R. 2002. *Economic Analysis of Law,* New York, Aspen Publishers, pp. 11–12.

[155] Clarke and Kohler, supra note 13 in Chap. 2, p. 49.

[156] Ibid.

[157] Mathis, K. 2009. *Efficiency Instead of Justice? Searching for the Philosophical Foundations of the Economic Analysis of Law*, Springer, p. 39.

in value (lumping all affected persons together and balancing their total losses against their total gains) is therefore Kaldor-Hicks efficient.

Again, it is important to appreciate that efficiency in this sense has nothing to do with fairness or justice in distribution. A transaction cannot be Kaldor-Hicks efficient unless it leaves the net gainers with a gain that is great enough to compensate the net losers, but no compensation need actually be made. The outcome will remain efficient even if the gainers pocket all the gain and leave the losers worse off. If the transaction in question did involve all losers being fully compensated, and still left the gainers with a net gain, it would be Pareto efficient. Because of this, Kaldor-Hicks efficiency is sometimes called potential Pareto efficiency. For these two reasons, therefore, because value-maximization is not the same as happiness or utility-maximization, and because efficiency requires only that there is a net gain in value or wealth, and not that the gain is fairly or justly distributed, most people would not use economic efficiency as the sole criterion for judging the efficacy of property rules. It is, however, a criterion, and an important one. An inefficient allocation of resources may be justifiable on the basis that it produces socially or morally desirable ends, but it does require justification.

Critics of the efficiency/economic theory have reservations, though. For one, allowing the government expropriation power instead of other mechanisms such as purchase is against the inalienable property right of owners.[158] This type of argument obviously comes from the proponents of natural law (naturalist) view of property right. Secondly, the economic assumption that says the use of eminent domain provides a comparative advantage over the free market in assembling contagious parcels of land held by different owners "is dubious."[159] Quoted in Paul, Munch, in her study of Chicago assembly of land parcels for urban renewal concluded that neither the assembly was efficient (because of delay in land transfer) nor the compensation paid was fair.[160] Finally, even economists themselves share the fear that the efficiency and holdout justification may embolden the government and broaden its eminent domain power to the extent that it harms private property rights.[161]

3.4.2 Natural Right Theories

A natural right theory generally asserts the existence of some rights (life, liberty and property) preceding the state and its laws. Natural rights are the rights that all men possess, by virtue of their nature as humans. According to the teaching developed primarily by Hobbes and Locke, there are many natural rights, but all of them are

[158] See generally Paul, supra note 63, especially pp. 254, 255.

[159] Id., p. 257.

[160] Ibid.; see also Munch, P. 1976. An Economic Analysis of Eminent Domain. *Journal of Political Economy,* 84, 473.

[161] See generally Benson, B. L. (ed.) 2010. *Property Rights: Eminent Domain and Regulatory Takings Re-Examined,* New York: Palgrave Macmillan.

inferences from one original right, the right that each man has to preserve his life. All other natural rights, like the right to liberty and the right to property, are necessary inferences from the right of self-preservation, or are conceived as implicit in the exercise of that primary right. But, even within the naturalist philosophers, there is divergence on the inalienability of property rights. While Locke and his followers conceive property right as an inalienable natural right, others refute its inalienability nature. Those led by Thomas Hobbes and David Hume argue that property right is a result of a civil society (and sometimes a pre-social institution) and it could be restricted by the state as it sees it fit. In this section we shall look into the first type of theorists (naturalist theory) while the second type of theory which we call as Social Contract theory, will be discussed in the section that follows.

3.4.2.1 John Locke

John Locke, a seventeenth century British philosopher, hypothesizes property as the fruit of human labor. In his philosophy we find no evidence that shows whether the state is empowered with expropriation power in the interest of the community. To summarize his theory, Locke contended that private property rights were natural rights tenable independently of government and law. Like Grotius he agreed that the earth and all its riches were given to the common use of mankind.[162] But, in the state of nature, "every man has a 'property' in his own 'person'. The 'labor' of his body and the 'work' of his hands we may say are properly his."[163] And by mixing his labor to the common property, the man in the state of nature, could appropriate private ownership.[164] Hence, whatever fruit one gathers from a tree, fish one fetches from the river or deer one kills in the jungle, will be his private property. The reason why labor gives ownership right is that because, he argued, labor puts the difference of value on everything. About ninety nine per cent of the value of the land or other things that are useful to us can be attributed to the work we have done.[165] But, eventually it becomes clear that the state of nature could not provide adequate protection to property, and hence, men agree to enter into social contract to create a civil society/government.

Thus, the sole reason for which men enter into commonwealth and establishing government was to protect their property,[166] which, according to Locke, includes one's life, liberty and estate. No government could claim its citizen's allegiance should it transgress this most sacred of all men's natural law privileges. According to Paul, Locke departs from Grotius and others in his understanding of property as natural right. Locke holds modern view of natural right that understands "natural

[162] Locke, J. 1986 [original 1690]. *The Second Treatise on Civil Government*. New York, Prometheus Books. § 24, p. 19.

[163] Id., § 26, p. 20.

[164] Ibid.

[165] Id., § 27 and § 40, pp. 20 and 26 respectively.

[166] Id., § 138, p. 77.

right" as "entitlement to things that men hold by virtue of their nature, combined with their acts." Grotius held a classical notion of natural rights as meaning simply "something that is right or good by its conformity to reason."[167] Hence, Locke's natural right view is very strict in that it gives little room for social or political interference.

Locke wanted to protect property rights from political interference,[168] and that is why he clearly declares that the government could not take private property without the consent of the owner:

> …the supreme power cannot take from any man any part of his property without his consent. For I have truly no property in that which another can by right take from me when he pleases against my consent…the prince or senate…may have power to make laws for the regulating of property between the subjects one among another, yet can never have a power to take to themselves the whole, or any part of the subjects' property, without their own consent.[169]

Locke even goes to the extent that government may not levy and collect tax from the people without their consent or that of their representatives at parliament.[170] In other words, unless the people by majority vote or using their representatives (the legislator) agree to such a measure, the executive body may not unilaterally impose tax obligation on the people. What makes Locke's argument peculiar is that he does not leave a room for the government to take property even for the "common good", as accepted by Grotius and other philosophers.

This line of argument is also shared even by some modern writers such as Robert Nozick and Ellen F. Paul. Paul, who shares Locke's natural rightness of property, admonishes any action of eminent domain that is done without the consent of the owner. She agrees that it is true that eminent domain may be justified on pragmatic or utilitarian grounds, but not upon property right theories: "it is terribly important that pragmatic considerations of efficiency and the like cannot touch fundamental rights … [for] the right to property stands on higher moral ground than consideration of efficiency."[171] She exemplified the violation of property right by eminent domain to the crucification of an innocent person in order to deter future crimes by potential criminals. Hence, government which is established to protect "preexisting rights" may not expropriate someone's property short of extreme exigencies of war where it is forced to take property in order to protect the lives of persons and properties (even in that case they must be compensated.) If government wants to build socially implicated constructions, Paul argues, "then it should purchase the land necessary for these installations on the open market just like any other private buyer. Anything else would violate individual's right to private property."[172]

---

[167] Paul, supra note 63, p. 198.

[168] Garnsey, supra note 66, p. 143.

[169] Locke, supra note 150, pp. 77, 78.

[170] Id., p. 79.

[171] Paul, supra note 63, p. 255.

[172] Ibid.

Robert Nozick, a twentieth century philosopher, also argues for a "minimal state" with "night-watchman" limited functions of "protecting all citizens against violence, theft and fraud and enforcement of contracts and so on."[173] No state is empowered with more powers; in particular, the state is not justified in distributing wealth or other resources in order to achieve some favored share-out. Private property without limit is justified as far it follows the procedure that he set out as follows[174]:

1. A person who acquires a holding in accordance with the principle of justice in acquisition is entitled to that holding. (This means, if one mixes his labor and held previously un-held objects, he is legitimate owner).
2. A person who acquires a holding in accordance with the principle of justice in transfer, from someone entitled to the holding, is entitled to the holding. (This means, when an owner in step one voluntarily transfers to another person, the transferee is also an owner.)
3. No one is entitled to a holding except by (repeated) application of 1 and 2.

Nozick notices the danger of his three steps argument of accumulation of wealth in the hands of few. Moreover, Nozick's state is powerless in respect of distribution of wealth to ensure justice. But, he argues that it should be the "invisible hand" of free market economy that should play that role of distribution rather than a powerful government. Now, what we can gather from both the "minimal state" and the absence of involuntary transfer of property rights is that the state is not justified in expropriating private properties.

The possible criticism that can be raised against all the above positions is that it is not practically feasible to rely on the consent of the owner to accomplish some public development activity. Unless we fully accept Nozick's "minimal government" that is not supposed to carry out any development activity, a limited government as we know today is a contradiction in terms. If we differ from the idea of "minimal state" or limited government and rather choose a strong state that plays wider roles in development (especially in developing countries), how is the state supposed to do that with having absolutely no right to the property of its citizens? Looking into this impasse, Richard Epstein commented that, "the categorical command that property shall not be taken without consent must be rewritten to provide the property may be taken upon provision of just compensation [since] the prohibition against taking private property could mean to prevent the government from discharging the very mission that justifies its existence."[175]

And still, without rewriting it (as Epstein says), we can also argue that although Locke left out the state power of expropriation or the superior right of society over individual interests, by implication, he gives the power to enact expropriation

[173] Nozick, R. 1974. *Anarchy, State, and Utopia,* Oxford, Blackwell, p. 26.

[174] Id., p. 151.

[175] Epstein, R. A. 1985. *Takings, Private Property and the Power of Eminent Domain,* Cambridge, Harvard University Press, pp. 15–16.

legislations to the representatives of the people at parliament, as in the case of the tax collection. Locke's argument seems to focus on the arbitrary taking or confiscation of private property by a government without compensation rather than expropriation of property for the common interest of the people and upon payment of fair compensation.

This line of argument seems also acceptable to Blackstone, who in all manners follows Locke's argument except the issue at hand. Like Locke, Blackstone emphasizes the importance of property saying that "There is nothing which so generally strikes the imagination and engages the affections of mankind," and "... it would be dangerous to allow any private man, or even any public tribunal, to be the judge of this common good, and to decide whether it be expedient or no." Rather, "the legislature alone can, and indeed frequently does, interpose, and compel the individual to acquiesce."[176]

3.4.3 *Social Contract Theories*

The idea of the social contract theories discussed here focuses on the issue that whatsoever the origin of property (natural law as in Locke) or others, the right to property is restricted by a social contract made between the people and the government, by which men are agreed to pass part of their liberties to the government. This argument goes to the extent that property rights will be restricted by the government for the sake of social good. Thomas Hobbes, the seventeenth century natural law philosopher, argued that the state of nature is a state of anarchy where every person is an enemy to everyone else. According to Hobbes, in the state of nature, people are absolutely free to do whatever they wish against whosoever they wish. While absolutely free to do whatever they wish, people live, however, in constant fear. The only security for men is their strength. In the absence of conception of right and wrong, there is no just or unjust action and hence no reliance, or assurance for standing expectations. To get out of this, people enter into social contract. The price for order is the surrender of liberty and property to an absolute sovereign.[177]

The following philosophers are categorized under this section.

3.4.3.1 Hume

David Hume, an eighteenth century British philosopher who follows Hobbes's argument also rejected the natural right of property advocated by Locke, and rather

---

[176] See Blackstone, as discussed in Sect. 3.3.2.

[177] See generally Hobbes, T. 1996 (J. C. A. Gaskin (ed.), originally published 1651). *Leviathan*, New York, Oxford University Press.

set out the view that there is no property, or property right, until civil society has been established. As opposed to Locke, Hume claimed that "Justice is not a natural virtue, and property is not a natural institution, for both have their origins in human convention."[178] This means that people simply came to accept, over time, some relationships, including what was considered to be just and fair. Property rights, for Hume, arise out of natural possession of objects. At some point the rules of justice come to respect our possession of property.

3.4.3.2 Grotius

As already discussed thoroughly in this chapter (Sect. 3.3.2), Hugo Grotius was responsible for coining the term "eminent domain" and he was also the one who tried to justify expropriation of private property for public good. For Grotius, property in its first invention was an act of human will, created by expressed agreement as in 'division' or tacitly as in case of 'occupation', and it becomes a breach of the law of nature for one man to seize the property of another.[179] But, Grotius has also added that since private ownership originated, after all, from the social recognition and acceptance, it is imminent that the property might be taken back during extreme necessity by society or the state that represents it.[180] Expropriation is well justified in Grotius teachings, since society will prevail over private property rights which emanated from the consent of the majority.

3.4.3.3 Jean J. Rousseau

In contradiction to Locke's and Blackstone's strict protection of private property, Rousseau is a critic of the institution of private property. As quoted in Schultz, Rousseau, in his *Discourse on Inequality*, criticized Locke especially on the issue of labor as source of ownership and rather described property as source of conflict and inequality:

> THE first man who, having enclosed a piece of ground, got the idea of saying 'This is mine', and found people simple enough to believe him, was the real founder of civil society. From how many crimes, wars and murders, from how many horrors and misfortunes might not any one have saved mankind, by pulling up the stakes, or filling up the ditch, and crying to his fellows, 'Beware of listening to this impostor; you are undone if you once forget that the fruits of the earth belong to us all, and the earth itself to nobody.'[181]

Elsewhere in the same book, Rousseau declares the inappropriateness of labor as a reason to claim not only the fruit of the land but also the land itself: "No matter if they said: it is I who built this wall; I earned this plot by my labor. Who sets the

---

[178] Garnsey, supra note 66, p. 155.

[179] Paul, supra note 63, p. 197.

[180] For details on Grotius see supra Sect. 3.3.2, where history of expropriation in the Civil Law tradition is discussed.

[181] Schultz, D. 2009. *Evicted! Property Rights and Eminent Domain in America*, Praeger, p. 18.

boundaries for you, they could be answered; and by virtue of what do you claim to being paid at our expense for labor we did not impose on you?... regardless of how they painted their usurpations, they remained just that, usurpations. No one had invited them to build walls, mark out plots and expend labour on them."[182]

The above quoted arguments by Rousseau focus on the origin of private property. Yet, he believes that the creation of private property was inevitable since the production of the land requires its distribution. He says that occupation would be the basis for property arrangement, but that right is recognized only on certain conditions: that the land is not yet taken; that only so much land be held as is necessary for subsistence; and that the land be worked.[183]

Now, once after being held in private hands, the status he gave to private property is, though, lesser as compared to the social interest. The claims that property rights are "sacred," "absolute," and "inviolate" in Locke or Blackstone's arguments were always such that they could be trumped by important social purposes. Rousseau envisages this idea in his second book, *The Social Contract,* as follows:

> In whatever manner the acquisition of ownership is carried out, the right that each individual has over his property is always subordinate to the right that the community has over everyone; otherwise, the social bond would be lacking in firmness and the exercise of sovereignty would lack true power.[184]

3.4.4 Utilitarianism

Beyond the arguments of natural right theories, there are other theories or claims about the origin or justification of property rights. A theory of moral philosophy called utilitarianism arose in Britain in the nineteenth century and included chiefly such thinkers as Jeremy Bentham and John Stuart Mill. The core of utilitarianism is that the ideas of justice, or what is right and wrong, are based upon maximizing utility that is producing the greatest good for the greater number of individuals. In defining utility Bentham says:

> By the principle of utility is meant that principle which approves or disapproves of every action whatsoever, according to the tendency it appears to have to augment or diminish the happiness of the party whose interest is in question … [and] … A measure of government may be said to be conformable to or dictated by the principle of utility, when in like manner the tendency which it has to augment the happiness of the community is greater than any which it has to diminish it.[185]

---

[182] Garnsey, supra note 66, p. 146, 147.

[183] Id., p. 165.

[184] Rousseau, J. J. 1762 [translated by Christopher Betts-1994). *The Social Contract,* Oxford, Oxford University Press, p. 62.

[185] Bentham, J. 2000 (Original 1781). *An Introduction to the Principles of Morals and Legislation*, London, Batoche Books, Kitchener, p. 14 and 15.

Although Bentham defines "utility" in terms of happiness, later utilitarians understand it differently, for example, as pleasure, happiness, welfare, and preference satisfaction.[186] For the sake of convenience, we will use the word "welfare" in this discussion. Utilitarianism is a version of consequentialism that claims "the moral rectitude of an action is a function of its expected consequences."[187] This means, actions or rules for action are not judged as right or wrong on their own account, but by reference to the consequences or effects they cause on the majority of the people.

Now, the question is how utilitarians would view expropriation, a government action that trumps individual property rights in the interest of society in general. In other words, how does a utilitarian balances individual and social interests? Private property is created in as far as it gives maximum utility to society. Bentham defines property as "a basis of expectations;"[188] the expectation deriving certain advantages from a thing which we are said to possess, in consequence of the relation in which we stand towards it. Accordingly, the utility of people is enhanced by securing people's expectations in relation to their possessions. However, this utilitarian theory also means that if in some situations limiting property rights could also yield a greater social good, then they could be limited. It is a utilitarian theory of property right that may also underscore the justification of eminent domain and the taking of private property away from one person and giving it to another for economic development reasons.[189]

In discussing utilitarianism's position in respect to expropriation, what is not clear is the limitation of state expropriation power. It is clear that utilitarians choose, first, the interest of the majority as compared to that of the individual, and expropriation is a perfect example that shows this scenario. It is argued that utilitarianism is not friendly to the idea that individuals have any absolute right, as claimed by Locke for instance. Bentham was said to be suspicious of all these natural rights; he could see no reason why the good of individual should trump the greater good of many others.[190] Although justice is supposed to protect individual human beings against being sacrificed for any societal greater good, this focus on individuals is something utilitarians typically have had difficulty grasping. That individuals should have any claim against the greater good of society simply doesn't make sense to Bentham hence his dismissal of "natural right."[191]

At this stage, here, we can raise two criticisms in a bid to show the problems of utilitarianism in addressing expropriation. One criticism is that utilitarianism is not concerned with how welfare is distributed: its concern is with the maximization of

[186] Munzer, supra note 148, p. 191.

[187] Simmonds, N. E. 2008. *Central Issues in Jurisprudence: Justice, Law and Rights,* London, Sweet & Maxwell and Thomson Reuters, p. 18.

[188] Munzer, supra note 148, p. 195.

[189] Schultz, supra note 181, p. 23.

[190] Fleischacker, S. 2004. *A Short History of Distributive Justice,* Massachusetts, Harvard University Press, p. 103.

[191] Id., p. 108.

welfare, with how much there is in total. As Nigel Simmonds, a writer on legal jurisprudence, exemplified, if a utilitarian is asked to choose between two societies in which one prefers an equal distribution of welfare and another prefers gross inequality, he will regard as morally preferable that society in which the sum total of welfare is higher.[192] Suppose that in state X property is equally distributed (10, 10, 10, 10, 10), the sum total of which is 50 and in state Y, where the property arrangement is very unfair (2, 2, 2, 2, 95,) in which the sum total is 103. Being concerned about maximization of welfare, a utilitarian will prefer the property distribution of State Y to State X. The implication is that utilitarianism may advocate policies that would make many people or individuals worse off.[193] This implication is against the principle of expropriation which is supposed to bring about a higher welfare to the public.

The second criticism has to do with the disregard of the individual by utilitarians. Quoted by one writer, the legal philosopher Hart had once said, "Utilitarianism does not take the *distinction between people as individuals* seriously and is thus incapable of guaranteeing their *basic rights*."[194] The idea is that utilitarians are ready to make small sacrifices to get large gains, by trading-off the welfare of some against the welfares of others. The person/s who make the sacrifice and those who get the benefit are two different groups or persons. In this respect, it is argued that utilitarianism fails to see individuals as legitimate right bearers. Examining utilitarianism from expropriation point of view, although compensation is supposed to be paid at all times for those who cede their land to the common good, there is this potential of denying compensation if paying will diminish the welfare of the majority.

A third criticism is one raised by John Rawls, a contemporary philosopher, which says that utilitarianism makes the mistake of defining the "right" in terms of the "good."[195] This means, utilitarianism does focus on the goodness (whether it maximizes welfare) of outcome instead of the ethical rightness of the means. In other words, for utilitarians, the end justifies the means.

3.4.5 Theory of Justice

3.4.5.1 Distributive Justice

Justice is said to be existing "when a person receives that to which he or she is entitled"[196] based on relevant characteristics that justifies her or his entitlement.

---

[192] Simmonds, supra note 174, p. 29.

[193] Id., p. 30.

[194] Mathis, supra note 157, p. 111.

[195] Rawls, J. 1999. *A Theory of Justice,* Massachusetts, The Belknap Press of Harvard University Press, p. 26.

[196] Buchanan, A. & Mathieu, D. 1986. Philosophy and Justice. *In:* Cohen, R. L. (ed.) *Justice.* New York and London: Plenum Press, p. 11.

And distributive justice has to do with distributing benefits and burdens within society in "just" and "fair" manner.[197] Distributive justice is needed because of competing and conflicting interests in a resource scarce world. In other words, had there been abundant resource, and people were satisfied with what they got, there would have been no need for the application of justice. In allocation and distribution of benefits and burdens, the most important formal rule of justice is "treatment of equals equally and unequals unequally."[198] Of course, since this formal rule doesn't tell the basic characteristics to discriminate or comparatively measure the entitlement of the people, philosophers further developed factors which are called "material principles of justice." For example, Rescher suggested seven common material principles of distributive justice applicable: equality, need, ability, effort, productivity, public utility, and supply and demand.[199] What is missing from the above discussion is, though, the underlining basic moral philosophy that justifies distribution of benefits and burdens. What makes it right to treat people equally? Why do we need to follow justice? Attempts to answer such questions were delivered through different philosophical justifications, some of which shall be discussed hereunder.

3.4.5.2 Justice as Fairness

John Rawls, a famous twentieth century philosopher, developed a theory of justice which is completely different from utilitarianism. While utilitarianism is based on teleological moral theory, Rawls' justice as fairness is deontological in nature. Rawls' effort was to establish not the whole justice system but the justice of the "basic structure" of society. The basic structure is the basic framework of institutions that distribute the benefits and burdens of social life and thereby fundamentally change peoples' life and prospects.

Although it is true that in a liberal democracy ideas and principles are diverse, Rawls argued, it is possible to develop principles of justice which are based on fairness that may get the approval of society. According to Rawls, rational and self-interested individuals with the task of developing the principles of justice will be chosen and put in a "veil of ignorance" so that they would be ignorant of their identity, interest, ability, morality and so on. This is to be done in a bid to ensure

---

197 Cook, K. S. & Hegtvedt, K. A. 1983. Distributive Justice, Equity and Equality. *Annual Review of Sociology* 9, p. 218.

198 Buchanan and Mathieu, cited supra note 196, p. 15. This famous rule is actually ascribed to Aristotle. In allocating shares between people Aristotle says "shares will be [divided]in the same ratio to one another as the person; for if the persons are not equal, they will not have equal shares; and it is when equals … are assigned unequal shares, or people who are not equal, [get]equal shares, that quarrels and complains breakout." See Urmson, J. 1998. *Aristotle's Ethics*, Blackwells Publishers, Oxford. Book V.

199 Rescher, N. 1966. *Distributive Justice: A Constructive Critique of the Utilitarian Theory of Distribution,* Indianapolis, In: Bob Merrill, pp. 73–83.

impartiality and to avoid conflict of interest. The people in the veil of ignorance, although they are ignorant of their interest and other parameters, they at least want, like any rational person, to have some basic things which Rawls called "basic goods". These include liberties, opportunities and income and wealth.

Rawls, hence, argues that in the "original position" the people in the "veil of ignorance" will develop the following two principles of justice[200]:

1. Each person is entitled to the most extensive system of basic liberties that is compatible with a similar system for everyone else;
2. Social and Economic inequalities are just only when:
   a. they work to the advantage of the least advantaged people in society (the difference principle);
   b. they are attached to offices and positions that are open to all under circumstances of fair equality of opportunity.

These principles are subject to certain priority rules. One is the primacy of the first principle over the second; liberty can be restricted only for the sake of liberty, not for social or economic advantages. Essential among these basic liberties are political liberty such as vote, freedom of speech and assembly, freedom of thought, personal freedom, right to hold personal property (not including all other types of property such as means of production.). The liberties cannot be compromised for any reason except in the case of protecting another liberty. They cannot be encroached even for a greater economic advantage of the person himself or society in general. The second rule is that fair equality of opportunity to offices and positions (b) takes priority over the difference principle (a).

The "difference principle" that justifies inequalities of economic incomes is of a paramount importance for our argument here. Social and economic inequalities are justified in the original position, if they are thought to be advantageous to the least well off. The idea is that this arrangement is better to the least advantageous as compared to the strict equality principle. Those with higher economic and social status must show some reason by benefiting the lower income group. Surprisingly, this argument is found to be relevant today like no other time.[201] Assume that a manager and workers in a company are paid equally (50:50) and the production level is 100. The company changes the manager and brings in another one. Within a year the new manager registered a success by making the company profitable. He

---

[200] Rawls, supra note 195, p. 53.

[201] In his recent article, the Economics Nobel Laureate, *Joseph E. Stiglitz, argues* that currently in the US defenders of America's inequality argue that the poor and those in the middle shouldn't complain. While they may be getting a smaller share of the pie than they did in the past, the pie is growing so much, thanks to the contributions of the rich and superrich, that the size of their slice is actually larger. Indeed, America grew far faster in the decades after World War II, when it was growing together, than it has since 1980, when it began growing apart (see http://www.thereporterethiopia.com/Business-and-Economy/the-price-of-inequality.html).

increased production from 100 to 300. The company, as a result, increases his salary to 150 and that of the workers to 100. Now, according to Rawls, this difference in income is justified, because the least well of (workers) are in a better position. In other words, had the manager been paid equal with the workers, then income would have fallen, and the workers would have found themselves in more precarious position.

3.4.5.3 Where Does Expropriation Fall?

Although it lacks clarity, one can argue that property is represented in both the first and the second principles of justice. The right to own private property is one of the basic liberties of people and it actually is included under the first principle.[202] What is not clear is whether this rule requires equal distribution in *amount* or in *right.* What seems logical is, though, that it is not the amount but the right itself that matters, the right to own property. In this regard, Dworkin, a contemporary legal philosopher, classifies the equality principle as "equal treatment" and "treated as equals."[203] In this case, while the first requires equal distribution or allocation of resources, the latter ensures the existence of equality principle so that people can exercise it. In other words, justice does not require equal welfare or equal degree of success in the realization of life plan, but only equalization of what is needed to produce welfare and success. The second problem with the first principle is that whether land is included in the first principle of "personal property" is not clear. He clearly says that "means of production" is not to be included in the first principle, and hence no such strict protection. Now the question is whether land is "personal" property or not.

The amount and distribution of property must be governed by the second principle. Unless other factors are in play, the difference principle requires that property be distributed equally unless unequal holdings maximally benefit the least advantaged. If other factors are in play, holdings would be less, or more, nearly equal depending on whether these other factors respectively offset or exacerbate the effect on lifetime expectations. It is not clear whether the rules of expropriation should fall under the first or the second principle. But, we can deduce that the first principle forbids the arbitrary taking or confiscation of property without compensation even if that brings about greater welfare to society. In other words, as far as expropriation measure is corrected through payment of fair compensation, expropriation is not prohibited under the first principle. The question is whether it is possible to differ from making fair compensation under the second principle. For example, in case of takings, the value of property may be substantially affected without getting any compensation for it. Frank Michelman, Harvard Law Professor, made analysis of this scenario using utility and Rawlian theories and this is shown below.

---

[202] Rawls, supra note 195, p. 54.

[203] Dworkin, R. 1977. *Taking Rights Seriously,* Harvard, Harvard University Press, p. 227.

3.4.5.4 Takings and the Michelman Solution

In property law discussions, what becomes contentious these days is "takings", the uncompensated government action or regulation that diminishes property value. The government using its "police power" may pass regulations on health, safety, security or environmental accounts that restrict one's right to exercise property rights and thereby making the property economically unviable. And the dilemma that is shared by many countries is "how to deal with the shifts in land values inevitably caused by land use regulation?"[204] For instance, government may install high voltage electric grids on the neighborhood; new airstrip may be built on the area that creates great disturbance; a new heritage law may be passed to prohibit owners from making any change on their properties; a regulation may be passed to prohibit mining for environmental reasons and miners need to stop extracting; the military may take one's land during distress temporarily, etc. Some of the regulations reduce the value of the property while others completely destroy the use or income generated from the property. These actions may be compensable or not based on the legislations of countries.

In a bid to give its philosophical base, Michelman has employed utilitarian and Rawlian methods to determine the compensability and non compensability of regulatory actions of the state.[205] By invoking utilitarian considerations, Michelman hoped to arrive at a solution that took efficiency into account, and John Rawls's fairness criteria were employed to satisfy the ethical institutions.[206]

Since utilitarianism is concerned only with the maximum utility gained across the board, it does not care about the individual and thereby making it difficult to employ it to decide on compensation issues. As a result, Michelman inserted the idea of "efficiency" to the equation. The concept of efficiency is an "ethical maximization, implying the goodness of increasing some quantity to the limit of possibility."[207] Employing the Pareto rule, he puts efficiency rule in superior position in terms of individual property rights protection: "a change in resource use which can improve the situations of some people without damaging the situations of any is desirable."[208]

By combining both efficiency and utility, he argues that society could not afford to pay compensation for every kind of injury caused as a result of government regulations.[209] Making compensation for every loss would impoverish society and

[204] Alterman, R. 2011. Regulatory Takings and the Role of Comparative Research. *In*: Alterman, R. (ed.) *Takings International: A Comparative Perspective on Land Use Regulations and Compensation Rights.* Chicago: American Bar Association, p. 3.

[205] Michelman, F. I. 1966. Property, Utility, and Fairness: Comments on the Ethical Foundations of "Just Compensation" Law. *Harv. L. Rev.*, 80.

[206] Paul, supra note 63, p. 142.

[207] Michelman, supra note 205, p. 1175.

[208] Id., p. 1176.

[209] Id., p. 1181.

no profitable project can be launched. And yet, there are others which deserve compensation; so, the point is how to differentiate the two.

In pursuing this strategy, Michelman defines three terms: "Demoralization Cost", "Settlement Cost", and "Efficiency Gain." Roughly speaking "Demoralization costs", (D), are the disutilities to uncompensated losers and sympathizers and the lost future production from impaired incentives or social unrest if no compensation was paid. "Settlement costs", (S), are chiefly administrative costs, operating compensation programs in a bid to avoid demoralization costs. "Efficiency gains", (E), are the excess of gains produced by a government action over the losses inflicted by it.

By assessing benefits and costs of the action and the benefits and costs of making compensation, Michelman reached at two public policy conclusion:

a. If the cost of demoralization and settlement both exceed the efficiency gain of the government action, then the action is unjustifiable and should be rejected. In other words, if $D > S > E$ or $S > D > E$ the action should be forfeited.
b. If the efficiency gain exceeds the costs of either the costs of demoralization or settlement, then compensation should be paid, i.e. $E > D > S$ or $D > E > S$. On the contrary, the government should not pay compensation if settlement costs exceeded demoralization costs. It is not worthwhile to compensate if the costs of administering payments are higher than the demoralization to be avoided. Hence, if $E > S > D$ or $S > E > D$ no compensation.

3.4.5.5 Principles of Justice

Besides the utilitarian-efficiency method, Michelman also invokes quasi Rawlian standard of fairness to evaluate the compensability or otherwise of regulatory takings. When we come to compensation issue, as Michelman notes, since they are not directly related to compensation issues it is hard to decide on compensation issues of regulatory takings. Yet, he argued, it is possible to apply the principle of justice to compensation issues by analogy. His idea is summarised as in the following two points[210]:

1. equal liberty principle forbids all efficiency motivated social undertakings, which have the prima facie effect of impairing "liberties" unequally, unless corrective measures (compensation payment) are employed to equalize the impact
2. based on the second principle of justice, a departure from the full compensation rule may be possible if it could be shown that some other rule should be expected to work out best for each person affected by the social measure that raises issues of compensation.

Michelman presented two alternatives of compensation rule: more stringent or less stringent compensation rules. If we follow the more stringent compensation

[210] Id., p. 1221.

rule, it could be costly and efficient projects that could, in the long run, benefit the loser may be abandoned. On the other hand, if we apply the less stringent compensation rule, the person may sustain the whole loss which could have been averted. It is obvious these alternatives do not give answer to the compensability or non compensability of government regulations, and hence he formulated another rule which of course is based on the above two alternative rules:

> A decision not to compensate is not unfair as long as the disappointed claimant ought to be able to appreciate how such decisions might fit into a consistent practice which holds forth a lesser long-run risk to people like him than any consistent practice which is naturally suggested by the opposite decision.[211]

There are two points worth discussing related to this rule. Firstly, unlike the case in utilitarianism, the question of fairness does not bother with individual's psychology of loss of benefit, but with the arbitrariness of the action. What is unjust or unfair is not the non compensability of the action, but its arbitrariness. If the individual understands that the action taken is consistent with other similar actions, then he will not feel it, but if the action is unwarranted and arbitrary, then he will resent it. Secondly, as far as the action taken now brings about greater benefit to society and the victim, in the long run, the non compensability of today's action is not unfair.

By way of conclusion, Michelman claimed that both the utilitarian and Rawlsian formulations would lead to pretty much the same answers in most cases; both rules turn upon the same factors: the disproportionate of the harm a measure inflicts on individuals and the likelihood that those harmed would be able to extract balancing concessions. Only to the extent that people are not as far-sighted as the Rawlsian fairness model assumes, would the two standards diverge, and the utilitarian rule would allow a greater likelihood of compensation to those demoralized individuals, unwilling to wait a while for their equilibrating rewards. For judges who might be a bit overwhelmed by all this philosophizing, Michelman, in the end, distilled out the cash value of his principle. Compensation is due only when:

1. A physical occupation occurs, or
2. An owner experiences the nearly total destruction of some previously crystallized value that did not originate under clearly speculative or hazardous conditions.

3.5 Sources and Justification of Expropriation Power in Ethiopia

As already repeatedly mentioned, in Ethiopia, land is not subject of sale and exchange. This means, individual people are relied on the state to acquire land. In the traditional feudal Ethiopia, the power of the kings was absolute, as discussed

[211] Id., p. 1223.

above, and the theory was that all land property rights emanated from the benevolent gift of the king, which once again confirm the reserved right of the sovereign.

The source of expropriation practice in today's Ethiopia is Article 40(8) of the FDRE Constitution which provides:

> Without prejudice to the right to private property, the government may expropriate private property for public purposes subject to payment in advance of compensation commensurate to the value of the property.

As noted under Sect. 2.6.3, private property in Ethiopia signifies all properties (tangible and intangible) except the land itself. Land belongs to the common ownership of the people and the state. Hence, what the Constitution considers as the subject of expropriation is other erections, buildings, plants and so on, which are created by the labor, enterprise or capital of the owner. The theoretical assumption behind this conclusion is that, since land belongs to the state/public, there is no need of expropriating it; it is just being returned to the owner who is not required to pay compensation for it. This, of course, shall be explored in detail in the next chapters, and it is suffice to mention here that the Constitution does not implicate the payment of compensation for the land itself; what the constitution guarantees is payment of compensation for the loss of private property.

Since the Federal government is empowered in the FDRE Constitution with the enactment of laws related to the "utilization and conservation of land and natural resources" (Article 51.5) and to administer it on behalf of society (Article 89.5), the Federal Parliament passed an Expropriation Proclamation (Proc. 455/2005) that governs the taking of private property for public purpose activities. To further implement this proclamation, the Federal Council of Ministers has also adopted a Compensation and Valuation Regulation No. 135/2007 after 2 years. Most regional governments (except Addis Ababa and Amhara) use the above two legislations to expropriate private prosperities. In case of Addis Ababa and Amhara they further enacted detailed Directives and manuals.[212]

The justification for expropriation in today's Ethiopia is envisaged in the preamble of the expropriation proclamation. The preamble of the present expropriation legislation (Proclamation No. 455/2005) justifies expropriation on the fact that:

> urban centers of the country have, from time to time, been growing and the number of urban dwellers has been increasing and thereby land redevelopment for the construction of dwelling houses, infrastructure, investment and other services has become necessary in accordance with their respective plans as well as preparation and provision of land for development works in rural areas has become necessary.

Thus, the reason is one and simple, that expropriation is necessary because land is needed for development activities carried out in both urban and rural areas. Group or social interest is clearly visible in the country. The incumbent party's governing

---

[212] In Ethiopia the hierarchy of laws is put as follows: Constitution (passed by people), Proclamation (passed by parliament), Regulation (passed by council of ministers), Directive (passed by specific minister), Manuals (passed by specific department).

principle is known as "Revolutionary Democracy" that allows heavy state led economy and superior rights of society over individual persons. It seems, the utilitarian principle best describes the socio-economic principle in the country, and as we shall see in Chap. 5, every activity that is believed to bring about socio-economic advantage to society, is considered as public purpose and land is easily expropriated for such activities.

3.6 Conclusions

In this chapter a review of different thoughts has been made concerning the justification of expropriation. The main thrust in the investigation is whether or not private property interest has been viewed as superior right over public interest. Except the natural rights view, in all the other cases, expropriation is justified based on the superior nature of public interest. Public interest has been given priority over the interest of the individual in respect of land rights. Even in the case of natural right advocators, it cannot be said that they are completely against public development which after all will also benefit the individual. Rather, the argument seems that the power of expropriation should be based on the consent of owners or their legal representatives, in this case, the parliament. And it seems, today, in many countries, parliament/congress has the power to pass laws concerning expropriation.

In Ethiopia, clear legislative history of expropriation practice began in the 1908 Addis Ababa Land Charter and since then it shows impressive development. In a country that had little regard for private property, the inclusion of expropriation provisions that demand payment of compensation by the state was a remarkable development. Expropriation practice reached its apogee with the codification of the western inspired civil code of 1960 that allocates significant amount of provisions for expropriation. With the coming of the Derg, the expropriation provisions were suspended, and it is only recently that new sets of rules were adopted. Today, expropriation is used extensively in order to satisfy the need of the vast economic development activities in the country. Taking into consideration the massive economic development activities coupled with the "Revolutionary Democracy" principle, which is biased in favor of "group rights", the rights of individual property right is no doubt less protected.

Chapter 4
Expropriation Procedure

4.1 Introduction

Expropriation procedure, also known as condemnation, is the process of implementing the taking of private property under expropriation power. Although it is said that the government has an inherent right to take private land by way of expropriation, due process of law requires following some procedural steps. In other words, to follow the procedure is in accord with some legal right or requirement of justice. A discussion on expropriation procedure must consider and investigate the authorities which are involved with the taking and the mandatory procedures they follow. Therefore, this chapter discusses the institutions that have roles in the expropriation process and the procedural steps that must be fulfilled during expropriation in Ethiopia. Some of the steps that should be followed before appropriating the land are: public discussion, serving notice, taking inventory and assessing value of property and effecting payment of compensation. In discussing the Ethiopian case, the institutional setup of some countries is also reviewed to have a clear picture of the trend and the place of the Ethiopian system.

4.2 Expropriation Power

4.2.1 Brief Overview of Foreign Practice

After studying the practice of different countries, Kitay in his valuable book, *Land Acquisition in Developing Countries,* differentiates the allocation of expropriation power into two: horizontal allocation and vertical allocation.[1] In the horizontal allocation, the expropriation authority may be given to the legislator, executive or

[1] Kitay, supra note 15 in Chap. 3, p. 57.

D.W. Ambaye, *Land Rights and Expropriation in Ethiopia*,
Springer Theses, DOI 10.1007/978-3-319-14639-3_4

judiciary, while in the vertical one it may be allocated to federal or state governments or their departments and other quasi-government organs, such as, utility and power companies. Of course, the amount of involvement of these organs (horizontal or vertical) differs from country to country.

While the right or power of eminent domain is inherent in the state, it is also dormant until the legislature rouses it into activity by taking steps for the exercise of the power, declaring the objects to which, and the mode and agency through which the power shall move.[2] In transforming this right or power from a potential one into an active one, the legislature may proceed directly and appropriate the required property by legislative act, or it may proceed indirectly by delegating its right or power to take such property to its chosen agent. In most countries, the legislatures use the second method and allocate power to the executive and judiciary. The basic idea is that in horizontal allocation of authority, the legislature sets out expropriation legislation that determines the public purpose for which land may be expropriated, the procedures which should be followed, and the roles of different organs of the executive branch and that of the judiciary. For example, in the USA what constitutes a public use, although in the first instance a legislative question, is in the last analysis a question of Constitutional Law to be determined by the courts.[3] Concerning the powers of the executive and the courts, Kitay elaborates, the executive decides when a project is of public interest, designates the property to be expropriated, and appoints an expert to evaluate the property. Then, a judicial proceeding resolves any dispute over the public purpose and amount of compensation.[4] The vertical power allocation focuses, on the allocation of power within the executive branch itself; whether a certain project amounts as public purpose and whether land is needed to be expropriated may be decided starting from top by a president or minister to local municipality, as the case may be. In many countries, property valuation is the task of the executive branch; it may be carried out either by panel of external valuators or by staff experts within the executive organ. But, in other countries, the court involves in the valuation process.[5]

Therefore, the trend seems that expropriation may be either purely administrative that excludes the court, or a judiciary in nature, or a hybrid of the two. As we shall see, the Ethiopian expropriation procedure is totally administrative in nature. Likewise, in some countries, such as Singapore, expropriation procedure is purely administrative in nature. Starting from declaration up to compensation and appropriation of land, the procedure is decided by the administrative (executive) body.[6] Yet, in others, the whole expropriation process falls under the jurisdiction of courts. For instance, in Nicaragua, both the designation of the property for the project and

---

2 Fletcher Cyclopedia, supra note 34 in Chap. 3.

3 Nichols, P. 1940. The Meaning of Public Use in the Law of Eminent Domain *B.U. L. Rev.*, 20, 615, p. 615.

4 Kitay, supra note 15 in Chap. 3, p. 57.

5 Id., p. 58–59.

6 Id., p. 61.

the valuation are the responsibilities of the judiciary.[7] But, in most countries, the process involves both the administration and courts. For example, in Peru, the first stage is administrative and results in the declaration of public purpose, the designation of the particular parcel to be expropriated, and an initial appraisal of its value. The second stage is a judicial one, wherein the court approves the valuation result and provides an order for land transfer.[8]

4.2.2 Expropriation Power in Ethiopia

4.2.2.1 Who May Decide Expropriation

In Ethiopia, like in any other country, the role of the legislature is to enact expropriation legislation that determines the powers and roles of different actors. To this effect, the legislature enacted the current expropriation proclamation in 2005.[9] Article 3 of this Expropriation Proclamation is the relevant provision in Ethiopia to identify the appropriate authority that is empowered with expropriation power. The provision under the title "Power to Expropriate Landholding" declares:

> A woreda or an urban administration shall, upon payment in advance of compensation in accordance with this Proclamation, have the power to expropriate rural or urban landholdings for public purpose where it believes that it should be used for a better development project to be carried out by public entities, private investors, cooperative societies or other organs, or where such expropriation has been decided by the appropriate higher regional or federal government organ for the same purpose.

A *wereda* (district) and urban administration (municipality) are both the administrative organs that are responsible for the administration of rural and urban land respectively. They are empowered with the expropriation of land, after following other steps that shall be discussed hereunder. If the *woreda* or municipality believes that the project for which land is requested will serve the society, it just can expropriate the needed land. In other words, they have the power to determine the nature of the public purpose of the project by themselves. Secondly, the *woreda* or the urban administration designate the necessary land, setup a valuation committee to assess the property thereon, issue notice, effect compensation and finally take delivery of the land and transfer same to the project owner, the details of which will follow. Most of the time, this is done when the project involves small-scale investments, socially bounded developments (school, health center, religious and cultural sites) and so on, except in big cities like Addis Ababa, of course.

---

[7] Ibid.

[8] Id., p. 60.

[9] FDRE Expropriation of Landholdings for Public Purposes and Payment of Compensation Proclamation, Proclamation No. 455/2005. *Negarit Gazeta.* Year 11, No. 43. (Hereafter cited as Federal Expropriation Proclamation or Proclamation 455/2005).

The other possibility that is envisaged in the provision is that expropriation may be decided *by a higher regional or federal government organ*. From the observation conducted by the researcher, in various areas, starting from urban upgrading to big private investments, decisions and orders usually come from above, and the *woreda* or urban administrations just execute the orders by performing the above process (designate the land, value property, provide notice, pay compensation and takeover of the land). Therefore, the role of the *higher organ* is limited to approving the project and deciding its public purpose nature; the other steps are carried out by the lower administrative organs (*woreda* and municipality.). When it is said a *higher organ,* depending on each case, it could be the prime minister, a particular minister, a regional governor, or a bureau in a region. At federal level, the Ministry of Agriculture, Ministry of Trade, Investment Agency, Ministry of Construction and Urban Development, and Ministry of Mining are the most notable ministries that give expropriation decisions and request the relevant *woreda* or municipality to proceed with the land transfer.

4.2.2.2 Who Can Initiate Expropriation

Initiation means requesting land or the expropriation of land for public purpose activities. In this regard, the proclamation identifies the organ that may initiate expropriation as an "implementing agency." Implementing agency, according to Article 2(7) of the proclamation, is defined as "a government agency or public enterprise undertaking or causing to be undertaken development works with its own force or through contractors." This "implementing agency" is required to prepare detailed plan before a year and pay compensation to landholders when the time comes (Article 5). But, the definition seems narrow for it excludes other organs; what is included in the definition is only the government: government as a public body and government as business enterprise. This argument may also be strengthened when we see the contents of Article 3. From the outset, it is envisaged under Article 3 that the projects may be carried out *by public entities, private investors, cooperative societies or other organs*. It seems the definition given to the implementing agency is mistaken since it makes the proclamation to contradict with itself; on the one hand, it allows all these organs to get land by expropriation and on the other, it excludes them from benefiting from it. Therefore, it must be understood that the initiator may be one of the following: government administrative body, government business enterprise, private investors, cooperative societies, local community, charitable organizations, diplomatic missions, Micro and Small-Scale Enterprises (MSEs), etc.

In any case, assuming the proclamation includes all of the above as initiators (which is also the practice), what is expected from the initiator of the expropriation procedure? As stated under Article 5 of the Expropriation Proclamation, the first thing expected from it is to:

prepare detail data pertaining to the land needed for its works and send same, at least one year before the commencement of the works, to the organs empowered to expropriate land in accordance with this Proclamation and obtain permission from them (Article 5.1).

To elaborate this provision, in practice, the detailed data or plan has to be submitted with an application for land access. The plan, usually known as 'project plan', needs to indicate the type of project work to be carried out, financial statements, social benefits, environmental impact assessment, and the time frame within which to finalize the work. This application may be made either to the *woreda* or municipality or to one of the higher organs which have the power to decide. For example, investors who want to engage in large-scale agriculture (more than 5,000 ha) must apply to the Federal Ministry of Agriculture, and those who want to engage in mining should apply to the Ministry of Mining. Those investors who wish to engage in manufacturing apply to the Ministry of Trade or Investment Agency. The idea is that an affiliated ministry that issues the license is in a better position to understand and judge the public purpose nature of the project. Once the applicant gets approval, his application will be re-directed to the respective *woreda* or municipality which is supposed to give the necessary land. The *woreda* or municipality may not need the detail of the 'project plan'; they rather need a "land plan" that shows the land size, location, and a map of the area.[10]

If the project work is of a small-scale, such as a hotel or small scale agricultural investment, both the 'project plan' and 'land plan' may be submitted to the concerned *woreda* or urban administration.

Sometimes, it may be a government agency, such as Ministry of Water and Natural Resources, which is responsible for both the expropriation decision and the implementation of the project. For example, in the Amhara Region, the Ministry has acquired land in various areas by expropriation for the construction of dams, and in all cases the *woreda* got only an order to expropriate (value properties, and transfer land) a specific land area.[11]

Still, another possibility is that the project may be initiated by the local community itself. Usually, local community may want to build schools or health centers, or may demand a specific land for cultural or religious purposes. In such a case, it will be the *woreda* or municipality that may also even prepare the plan for the society.

The second obligation of the implementing agency, the initiator, is the payment of compensation (Article 5.2). The idea is that as a beneficiary of the land expropriation, the implementing agency should also bear the payment of compensation. However, in some cases, government or community may be encumbered with the compensation obligation. For example, in case of urban expansion, it is the

---

[10] See for example: Addis Ababa Valuation and Compensation of Replacement Land and Housing *Directive No. 3/2010*. Addis Ababa City Council. Article 3(1) (hereinafter cited as Addis Ababa Valuation Directive); Amhara Valuation and Compensation Directive. *Directive 5/2011*. ANRS Regional Council. Article 10(3) (hereafter cited as Amhara Valuation Directive).

[11] Interview made with Ato Mihret Dagnew, Senior Valuation Expert at Amhara BoEPLAU, January 8, 2012, Bahir Dar.

government that pays compensation to peasant landholders. Sometimes, in order to encourage investment, the government may give land for free in selected areas and the investor is not expected to pay compensation. The usual trend in urban areas is that a city municipality prepares land and puts it in its land bank in order to transfer it by auction.

4.3 Procedural Steps in Expropriation

The Expropriation Proclamation has not given clear procedural steps that should be followed by the administrative authorities in the event of land expropriation. Therefore, we have to construct one from the reading of the different provisions of the Expropriation Proclamations and the directives. The proclamation, however, provides one clear step concerning the issuance of notice of expropriation order:

> where a woreda or an urban administration decides to expropriate a landholding …it shall notify the landholder, in writing, indicating the time when the land has to be vacated and the amount of compensation to be paid.[12]

This provision by itself does not tell about the other activities that should be fulfilled and the priority levels existing among them. One clue that we find here is that notice would be issued after the completion of valuation, since the notice is supposed to mention the amount of compensation. In any case, using this very provision and others, we shall hereunder provide the basic steps.

4.3.1 Making Inquiries

Once the application for land and the accompanying "business plan" and "land plan" are made to the relevant authority, the latter must at least make the following inquiries:

4.3.1.1 Ensuring Eligibility

Ensuring that the applicant who requests the expropriation is a legally permitted person or organ is the first thing to be made. This is to say that it must be certain that the applicant is one of the eligible organs mentioned under Article 3(1). For example, an expropriation request for personal use, such as building ones house on the land, may not be accepted, for individuals other than investors are not mentioned in the law.

---

[12] Proc. 455/2005, Article 4(1).

4.3.1.2 Approving Public Purpose

The *woreda* or urban administration or another higher body that decides about expropriation must approve the public purpose aspect of the project. The proclamation may not help much in this respect since it is general, as we shall see in the next chapter. But, regions came up with lists of projects considered as public purpose activities. Besides, the land requested should not be related to protected or forbidden areas, such as natural, cultural and historical reserved areas, national parks, and natural forests.[13]

4.3.1.3 Weighing Pros and Cons

An expropriation act has both positive and negative side; while someone is benefiting, another may be adversely affected. Although it is possible in principle and legally permissible to expropriate, the public benefit thought to be gained may be insignificant compared to the inconveniences caused as a result of the action. In some countries, it is stated in their law that expropriation shall not be used if the inconvenience for private individuals outweighs the public advantage.[14] Similarly, the Federation of International Surveyors' (FIG) guideline on compulsory purchase dictates that compulsory purchase should not be opted if other routes of land acquisition methods can be pursued.[15] This has happened in the Amhara Region in one place.[16] Weighing the pros and cons, hence, helps the body to reach a rational decision.

4.3.2 Public Discussion

Whenever the administration decides on expropriation, the *woreda* or municipality calls a public meeting to explain the purpose. Public discussion should not be understood as a "notice" for the latter will be another stage. Public discussion is a

---

[13] See for example Amhara, Valuation Directive, supra note 154 in Chap. 2, Article 8.

[14] Kalbro, supra note 152 in Chap. 3, p. 34; See also a similar Finish experience in Viitanen, K. 2002. Just Compensation in Expropriation. *FIG XXII International Congress.* Washington, D.C. USA: International Federation of Surveyor, p. 3.

[15] Viitanen, K., Falkenbach, H. & Nuuja, K. 2010. Compulsory Purchase and Compensation Recommendations for Good Practice. *FIG Policy Statement.* Helsinki International Federation of Surveyors, p. 9.

[16] Ato Assefa Bezabih is a law practitioner in the City of Goder, 120 km north of Bahir Dar. The Municipality of the small town of Gorgora, on the north tip of Lake *Tana*, had provided him with 15,000 m^2 of land for recreation purpose. Later on the town's people complained because they used that place for grazing purpose, and the municipality changed its mind and has now started negotiation with Ato Assefa to give him another plot of land.

procedure actually practiced by all regions and cities, although it is not mentioned in the Federal Expropriation Proclamation. Public discussion is also a proposed and actually practiced procedure in many countries.[17] Public discussion provides an opportunity for people to learn more about the project, to receive answers to their questions about the process and the procedures and to voice their concerns. Open public discussion enables the government to appreciate the concern of the people and to create smooth environment for the project's undertaking. If the public is not clear about its benefit and the compensation packages before the commencement of the project, conflict may arise. Taking this into consideration, the Ethiopian government gives more focus to this stage as compared to others. From the interviews conducted with officials and affected farmers, it has been learned that in Amhara Region as well as in Addis Ababa, the government usually sends higher government officials to discuss with the affected people.[18] Sometimes, though, the officials simply exaggerate the benefits to be accrued to society, and this causes frustration when the expectation was not met. This has been observed, for example, in the field visit made in Rib Irrigation Dam Project in the Amhara region, where farmers who lost their land complained that what was promised to them by the officials during the public discussion did not materialize. Further people moved from the Arada, Basha Wolde Chilot and Sheraton expansion areas, confirmed the same frustration. They claimed that officials at the beginning have promised them that they would be given a place (condominium houses) on the same site, not at the periphery.

The purpose of public discussion should be to try to persuade the public to accept the project and cede its land peacefully. From good governance and security perspectives as well, it enables government to hear concerns of the public in a bid to give answers and to avoid tensions. Otherwise, it cannot be considered as a democratic meeting, wherein the people are supposed to accept or reject the project. Expropriation by its nature does not demand the consent of the owner, and demanding consent of owners will be a contradiction in terms.

Under exceptional circumstances, though, the *woreda* may need approval of the community before it begins a project. Such peculiar situation happens when the development work is supposed to be made by the community for its own use, like rural health centers, roads, or schools. In this respect, the Amhara RLAUP declares that "where the land expropriation activity is directly related with the development of the surrounding society, the case shall be submitted to the *kebele* people for discussion and obtain a majority vote thereof, before it is decided by the *woreda* branch office of the Authority to expropriate land for public service."[19] The wisdom of inserting this procedure is that if the society understands and agrees, first, there

[17] For example, after studying many practices, FAO's (FAO supra note 7 in Chap. 2, p. 21) guideline on Compulsory Purchase, puts public meeting as important stage in expropriation process.

[18] Group discussion made at Rib Dam Project area with farmers, October, 14, 2012; Interview with Ato Daniel, head of Valuation and Compensation Division at Arada sub-City of Addis Ababa City, October 31, 2012, Addis Ababa.

[19] Amhara RLAUP, Article 28(2).

will be little resistance to obtain the needed land and fund. Secondly, there is the possibility of compensation being paid by the community itself. This occurs when a local community agrees to give part of the community land as compensation to those who cede their land for the project development. A good example in this case is the rural roads construction in Amhara Region where government connects rural *kebeles*. The gravel roads pass through farm lands and the Regional Rural Roads Authority does not pay compensation, since the farmers are supposed to be compensated by the rural society.[20] The respective *kebeles* or *woreda* administrations give them land compensation, either from the land bank or from community lands. The point is that the community agrees first on the construction of roads and thereby to absorb those who lost their land for the construction of the roads. Its practicability shall be discussed in Chap. 6.

Public discussion may also be considered as a better way of informing the society about the project; instead of written notice, affected people will be notified through actual discussion.

In Addis Ababa, the city administration uses the public meeting as opportunity to elect representatives of the people who would deal with the government on behalf of the community throughout the process. The representatives participate especially during inventory of properties (measurement of land and building, counting of plants and other assets). Further, they will aid the experts in identifying properties and owners and protecting any abuse and falsification of data by owners.[21] For example, the representatives of the displaced people in the Basha Wolde Chilot No. 2 site are twelve, representing government tenants, *kebele* tenants, and private owners.[22] It seems the representatives are useful more to the government than to the people. In the research site, the houses were not properly registered and informal settlement (expanding without permit) was rife. Owners, therefore, tend to claim more than what is entitled to them and the committee serves as a watch-man to the government. It is also the government that pays them allowance for their services.

4.3.3 Inventory of Assets

A critical stage in an expropriation process in Ethiopia is one that involves the inventory and counting of assets. This has to do with the identification and designation of the land to be expropriated and the counting of assets thereon. Identification of land means locating the land on a map and certifying the owner thereof;

[20] Interview with Ato Mebit Admass, Deputy General Manager of ANRS Rural Roads Authority, January 2, 2013.

[21] See Addis Ababa Valuation Directive, Articles 4–5.

[22] Interview made with Ato Dereje Gebrie and Samson Mekonnen, representatives of the tenants in government houses, October 30, 2012, Addis Ababa.

whereas designation of the land means measuring and determining the land area necessary for the project. Besides identifying and designating the land, the assets on the land such as, buildings, plants and other fixtures must also be counted for assessment purpose. The law requires the *woreda* or municipality to setup a "valuation committee"[23] to carry out the valuation activity, and in principle, it is this committee that is supposed to go to the area and measure and count the assets. But, practically speaking, since the committee lacks the expertise in land measurement and map reading, it is another team (inventory committee) that performs this task. In Amhara region, the valuation directive provides the possibility of the valuation committee being accompanied and assisted by a "land administration and use committee", experts from land administration office, during its inventory phase (Article 12.1). But, in others, the practice seems different. For example, in the Tulu Kapi Gold Mining case,[24] the *woreda* conducted the inventory using the GIS experts and other people working in the *woreda* land administration desk as team, independent of the valuation committee. This means, the valuation committee is not necessarily the one that takes the inventory of land and assets. In Addis Ababa, the people who collect data about the land, houses and other fixtures on the land are surveyors, and the valuators are engineers and accountants.[25] The inventory committee needs to see and check the legitimacy of owners (of houses) and holders (of lands) by checking ownership or holding certificates and in the absence of which other evidences.[26] During the inventory of land and assets, the presence of owners/holders and representatives of *kebele* administration is mandatory. Further, after following and looking into the counting and measurements, owners and *kebele* representatives are required to sign to prove its accuracy.[27] In Addis Ababa, besides the presence of owners and *kebele* representatives, the law requires the committee to keep a video record of the whole inventory process.[28] All these requirements are in a bid to avoid latter contentions about non counted assets and unmeasured land and houses.

---

[23] Proc. 455/2005, Article 10.

[24] The Tulu Kapi Gold Mining is owned by a British mining company called NYOTA Mining. This gold mining is found in western Wolega Zone of Oromia Regional State. The researcher closely followed the valuation process and participated in the joint meeting of the company and the regional and federal government authorities held during September 22–25, 2012 concerning valuation and resettlement programs and procedures. See details in Chap. 1, Sect. 1.2.1.4c.

[25] Interview with Ato Mikias Goitom, Property Valuator at Yeka Sub-city, Addis Ababa, November 1, 2012; Interview with Ato Daniel, supra note 18.

[26] In rural areas where land certificate is not yet issued, the committee uses tax receipts or testimonies of kebele committees. In Urban areas where the land and houses are not certified, the committee looks into satellite and GIS data taken in 1996. All houses built before that period were regularized even though they were informal.

[27] Amhara Valuation Directive, Articles 10(6) and 12(1). In Amhara Region the "land administration and use committee" that helps the inventory will also sign; Addis Ababa Valuation Directive, Article 12(1); same practice also in Oromia Region (Ato Teshome, infra note 29.).

[28] Articles 9, 12 of Addis Ababa Compensation Directive.

A possible problem that may arise is who would be responsible in case some error or fraud is created? For example, in one case (Horo Gudru area) where the land had to be expropriated for the Ethiopian Electric Power Corporation, the number of coffee trees reported by the inventory committee was totally fictitious.[29] The inventory committee is not recognized under the law; it is created because of its indispensability in the process. It seems, in the absence of clear mandate by law to this committee, the valuation committee must ensure the accuracy of the data, at least by making some random tests, or else it would be responsible for any fraud or error in compensation. The other safe way out is, to create and empower the inventory committee by law.

4.3.4 Valuation of Properties

Once data about owners, land, and property on it is collected and refined, it will be given to the valuation committee. As mentioned above, the committee will be designated by the *woreda* or municipality and members must have some relevant expertise or knowledge. The number of the committee members should not be more than five, and they will perform their task discreetly and report their findings to the *woreda*. The committee will use relevant information that helps it to estimate the value of the properties. When the information is available in the hands of other offices, it may demand it from them. For example, productivity of land or market value of crops and trees may be acquired from the *woreda* agriculture office or trade and industry office.

In rural areas, there is no guarantee to have permanent valuation committee. The reason why a committee is to be formed every time a property is expropriated is because there are no expert valuators in the country. A typical valuation committee in a rural area is, hence, constituted of representatives from *kebele* (administrative), local agricultural office, local elder, land administration expert and other relevant bodies. In urban areas, the municipality usually employs permanent staff as valuators. The interviews conducted in Bahir Dar and Addis Ababa cities show that the valuators have one of the following qualifications: economics, accounting, law, geography or engineering.

4.3.5 Notification

Notice, as stated above, is one of the procedural requirements explicitly dictated in the proclamation. Notice has to be made in "writing, indicating the time when the

---

[29] Interview with Ato Teshome, Senior Valuation Expert at the Oromia BEPLAU, September 25, 2012, Nekemt. It is alleged that 16 million non-existed coffee trees were reported.

land has to be vacated and the amount of compensation to be paid." Thus, in theory, notice must contain every information about the amount of land to be taken (all or part), the time frame within which the holder is expected to move, and most importantly, the amount of compensation the implementing agency is ready to pay. This means, notice is something that comes after the valuation of the property and that is why we said that it is not the same thing as public discussion.

According to Article 4 of the expropriation proclamation, the period of notification, the time between the service of notice and clearance of land, should be determined by each region, provided that it is not less than 90 days (Article 4.2). If the land is a rural land with no crop on it, the time may be lowered to 30 days (Article 4.4). In any case, even though regions may come up with more days to give notice, the holder of land "shall hand over the land…90 days from the date of payment of compensation" (Article 4.3). In Addis Ababa, this date is lowered to 45 days after one receives compensation money and 30 days after one gets replacement house (Article 27.1 Addis Ababa Valuation Directive.).

This means, the number of days given in the notice may be more than 90 days and, for that matter, a specific date may not be mentioned. But, what is necessary is that the timing must be long enough to enable the owner to make complaints or an appeal, if necessary. It must also be noted that there are two time gaps in the process: a time gap between the service of notice and payment of compensation on the one hand, and a time gap between payment of compensation and handing over of the land on the other. The law requires that 90 days be given in each case. But, this simple intention of the law seems to be either misunderstood by the law makers of the subsidiary laws, or intentionally violated, because, what we find in the subsidiary federal as well as regional laws is the first spirit of the proclamation.

Additionally, in practice, written notice is not given to each and every household. What has been told to and seen by the researcher was that the result of the compensation is posted on notice board (in cities), and told to farmers in offices in rural areas. In almost all places visited such as Addis Ababa and the Rib dam project, and all the people interviewed by the writer, people did not receive any written notice.

Another problem that was exhibited during the investigation was the absence of cut-off date in the proclamation. Cut-off date is the date beyond which any improvement on the land is no longer possible. The idea is, once property is measured and counted for valuation purpose, the owner should not make additional improvements such as, planting trees and constructing buildings that increase the value of the property. Unless owners are stopped at some point from making such increments, the valuation process would become an endless process. Surprisingly enough, there is no clear provision in the proclamation to this effect, and what is provided is confusing one.

Under the expropriation proclamation, as shown above, what is mentioned is only the notice date that is 90 days before complete surrender of land. Further, Regulation No. 135/2007 under Article 19 elaborates on the subject by stating,

"There shall be no payment of compensation with respect of any construction or improvement of a building, any crops sown, perennial crops planted or any permanent improvement on land, where such activity is done after the possessor of the land *is served with the expropriation order*" [emphasis added.] What then is "expropriation order"? The reading of Article 4(3) of the proclamation reveals that "expropriation order" is the same thing as "notice." This means, the cut-off date introduced by the regulation is the date of service of notice. But, I have already argued above that notice is issued after the completion of inventory and valuation processes. So, this means, there is nothing in the proclamation or the regulation that stops the owner from making additional investments, even after valuation of assets had been completed. Now, the question is whether the land holder should be allowed to make unnecessary and speculative investments that would create additional costs to the investor and make the process unstoppable? Such a situation happened in the Tulu Kapi Gold Mining area in the Oromia Region when farmers continued planting coffee seedlings after the completion of inventory of assets. When they were told not to do so, they challenged the company claiming there was no legal ground to stop them.[30]

It seems, by anticipating a similar problem, the Amhara Region adopted a workable solution in its valuation directive stating that any person whose land is to be expropriated may not carry out any construction or improvement on the land that affects the inventory made for compensation purpose (Article 10.7 of Amhara Valuation Directive). In other words, the directive introduces a cut-off date other than the notice date. This date is the date on which the inventory of assets for assessment purpose is completed. Another cut-off date is introduced by the Amhara Urban Land Valuation Directive as the date of the public discussion (Article 3.3). Any additional expansion or improvement on the land will not be considered for assessment and compensation. The Oromia region, being late in adopting its own valuation and compensation directive, faces a challenge of the above nature.

One question that may be raised in association with these rules is whether it is possible for regional states to come up with different cut-off dates other than what is introduced by the regulation as the notice day? Under the Expropriation Proclamation (Article 14.2), Regional states are empowered to "issue directives necessary for the proper implementation of this Proclamation and regulations." Since considering the date of notice as cut-off date does not give sense and rather contradicts the law itself, it is logical and reasonable for regions to come up with some workable date. For all practical purposes, the date of completion of inventory seems reasonable as opposed to the date of public discussion. It may take years to finish inventory of assets after the first date of public discussion, and it is unreasonable to stop land owners from benefiting for so long without any compensation thereto.

---

[30] Tulu Kapi, supra note 24.

4.3.6 Payment of Compensation, Appeal and Appropriation of Land

As shown under above (Sect. 4.2), unlike some other countries where the issue of compensation is decided by courts, in Ethiopia, compensation is decided by the land administration body. Once the valuation committee finalizes its assessment, it reports the results to the *woreda* and the latter communicates this to the affected people and to the implementing agency. Mostly, the information is communicated through displaying on notice board, in urban areas, and in person in rural areas.

If the owner or holder has a grievance on the amount of the compensation, s/he may petition to the administrative "compensation grievance hearing committee" established within the *woreda* or municipality.[31] The Compensation grievance hearing committee, after investigating the matter may either affirm the amount or order re-evaluation of assets. If the person is dissatisfied with the decision of the grievance hearing committee, he may appeal to "regular appellate court or municipal appellate court within 30 days from the date of the decision."[32] Most of the complaints and appeals made in urban areas are associated either with the *improper measurement* of land or *non-consideration* of property for compensation.[33] Improper measurement has to do with errors made by surveyors when they measure the land area. The errors are attributable to faulty and backward measurement equipments, and indeed when the complaint hearing committee orders the re-measurement of lands, the results are mostly different from the first.[34] The refusal or non consideration of property for compensation by the inventory committee is another reason for complaints. The usual reason for refusal of the inventory committee is because either the owner has no legitimate document that shows his right, or the building made is on land outside his holding, or the building cannot be marked on satellite map taken some years back (1996 in Addis Ababa). Generally, it means, the person is an informal settler (one who builds on state land) or even if he is formal, he adds building or fence illegally or without permit.[35] Most people are not encouraged to go to regular courts challenging the amount of compensation (see details in Chaps. 5 and 6.).

As already stated above, the minimum period given for notice is 90 days. If he does not make a successful appeal within that period, then the holder will be assumed as if he has agreed on the amount and "…shall hand over the land to the *woreda* or urban administration within 90 days from the date of payment of

---

[31] Article 11(2) Proclamation 445/2005. All the subsidiary legislations in Regions also adopt similar procedures.

[32] Id., Article 11(4).

[33] Interview made with Ato Birhanu Andualem, Judge at Bahir Dar City Municipal Court, November 22, 2012, Bahir Dar.

[34] Interviews made with Ato Daniel, supra note 15; Ato Mikias supra note 25, Ato Addisu Begashaw, Civil Engineer and Valuator at Bahir Dar City, October 15, 2012, Bahir Dar.

[35] Ibid.

compensation or, if he refuses to receive the payment, from the date of deposit of the compensation in a blocked bank account in the name of the *woreda* or urban administration as may be appropriate" (Article 4.3 of Expropriation proc.) If the holder of the land still refuses to hand over the land, then the urban and *woreda* administration may request police assistance (Article 4.5).

Compensation must be paid in advance (before people moved from their land and houses), and it can be effected either by the *woreda*/municipality or by the implementing agency itself (Article 5.2 cum. 13.1 of Expropriation proclamation). If the implementing agency is a public body (administrative or enterprise), then, usually, it is the *woreda* that pays the compensation after the money is transferred to its account. On the other hand, if the implementing agency is a private one, then, mostly, it is this body that pays the compensation directly, but in some areas (such as Oromia), the *woreda* pays once the money is put in its account by the private investor.

One discrepancy that I detected is that the requirement of advance payment of compensation is not properly observed. All the interviewees in Rib Dam Project, in the Amhara region, explained that compensation was paid a year after they were removed from their land, and even in that case it was not paid at one lump sum but in different installments.

4.4 Resettlement Program

A workable definition about the meaning of resettlement and rehabilitation program is necessary before continuing the discussion. "Resettlement" means to settle or cause to settle displaced people in a new or different place, while "Rehabilitation" is restoring the community to its former state, way of life, capacity, or income level.[36] Resettlement program, in our context, is understood as a support provided to people who are physically displaced from their land as a result of expropriation decision. Although countries may adopt different packages of assistance in their laws, the World Bank lists the following as essential ones: transportation, food, shelter, and social services that are provided to affected people during their relocation. Assistance may also include cash allowances that compensate affected people for the inconvenience associated with resettlement and defray the expenses of a transition to a new locale, such as moving expenses and lost work days.[37]

Whether or not resettlement and rehabilitation program is a mandatory phase in the expropriation process in Ethiopia is not clear. Government organs that expropriate land do not consider the program as obligatory, since it is not clearly envisaged in the expropriation proclamation apart from one general provision in the

[36] See for example, Oxford Advanced Learner's Dictionary.

[37] IFC. 2002. *Handbook for Preparing a Resettlement Action Plan*, International Finance corporation, a member of World Bank Group, p. X.

Constitution. Thus, resettlement and rehabilitation for the displaced becomes all the more difficult in the absence of state level policy and legislative mechanisms. Nonetheless, some projects, funded by the World Bank, such as, irrigation dams, hydro electric powers, and big road projects do carry out resettlement and rehabilitation programs after the expropriation of land.[38] This is because the World Bank puts it as an important prerequisite when it lends money to the government[39] or finances private investments which are considered as sound investments by the Bank.[40]

The nature and existence of resettlement program in Ethiopia can be inferred from what is envisaged in the FDRE Constitution, Article 44, as follows:

> All persons who have been displaced or whose livelihoods have been adversely affected as a result of State programmes have the right to commensurate monetary or alternative means of compensation, including relocation with adequate State assistance.

Now, the question is whether this provision applies during expropriation as well? Does *displacement of people as a result of state program* also refer to expropriation? What makes us uncertain about this provision is that all expropriations are not necessarily related to *state programs*; expropriation may also be made for private programs/investments. In other words, if a certain land is transferred to a private investor, neither the investor nor the government is duty bound to resettle or pay the cost of resettlement for the people, except the usual compensation, of course.

What seems to us is, though, this principle of rehabilitation applies in selected displacement/expropriation cases, where the government moves people, *en masse*, from one place for a certain huge program that affects the livelihood of many people. In such cases, payment of compensation may not be enough for the people are numerous in number and the effect of the damage is too big to ignore. In such

---

[38] See, for example, many Resettlement Action Plans (RAP) of various World Bank or African Development Bank funded projects of the Ethiopian Electric Power Corporation (EEPCo), Ethiopian Roads Authority (ERA), and Ethiopian Ministry of Water and Energy posted on the web.

[39] The World Bank adopted an Operational Manual, of which, OD 4.30 has to do with "Involuntary Resettlement." (See IFC, supra note 37, pp. 67–75). The directive on "involuntary resettlement" describes the Bank's policy and procedures on involuntary resettlement, as well as the conditions that borrowers are expected to meet in operations involving involuntary resettlement. The purpose is, in short, to reduce the damage caused to the people by restoring their livelihood and by creating an opportunities to make them sharing from the project. The OD 4.30 is also available: http://web.worldbank.org/WBSITE/EXTERNAL/PROJECTS/EXTPOLICIES/EXTOPMANUAL/0,,contentMDK:20066696~menuPK:4564185~pagePK:64709096~piPK:64709108~theSitePK:502184,00.html.

[40] The International Finance Corporation (IFC) is World Bank Group's private sector investment arm, and it adopts a policy that requires private investors in which the Bank has an interest to develop first a Resettlement Action Plan (RAP) before they start moving the people. The RAP is supposed to specify the procedures the company would follow and the actions it will take to properly resettle and compensate affected people and communities. See IFC 2012. *Policy and Performance Standards on Environmental and Social Sustainability* International Finance Corporation, World Bank Group.

cases, the government, besides payment of compensation, may prepare a program to resettle them and help them to regain their capacity. Resettlement program is different from the regular compensation in that on top of the compensation, the people would be assisted to resettle in one area and to rehabilitate.

Good examples in this case are the villagization programs carried out by the Federal Government in cooperation with the lowland regions of Gambella, Beni Shangul Gumz and Somalie Regions. The Federal Government wanted to delineate potential large-scale agricultural land in these regions. Since local people live sparsely over vast territory of land, the government gathered and settled them in certain localities so as to clear the land for investment purposes and at the same time to provide them with basic amenities like electricity, water and health services.

Besides, in some projects which are public in nature and big in size, the government conducts both resettlement and rehabilitation programs. For example, currently large tracts of land are being expropriated from farmers to build sugar and fertilizer factories, to put dams, and to construct highways and railways. Because of the largeness of the number of people displaced from the expropriated area, the government usually prepares some resettlement program provided land is available in the area. This means, the people displaced from their original land will be resettled in another land where the government provides them with basic infrastructure and amenities. This is besides to the full compensation that they shall be entitled under the expropriation proclamation.[41]

The next logical question is whether the constitutional principle applies in ordinary/small scale expropriation cases as well? To understand the resettlement and rehabilitation program during expropriation, one needs to read what is provided in the expropriation proclamation itself. Under the expropriation proclamation, it is declared that "With respect to the implementation of the proclamation, *woreda* and urban administration shall have the responsibilities and duties to…provide them [the displaced people] with rehabilitation support to the extent possible."[42]

One important point inferred from the reading is that the law imposes a duty of rehabilitation program only, not resettlement. Resettlement presupposes the preparation of host land to settle the people in one place, with all the necessary services. Lack of excess arable land in rural areas seems to discourage the government from pursuing resettlement program as a mandatory strategy. As investigated in Chap. 6, one of the possible compensation modalities is provision of land-to-land compensation in the event of expropriation. The land available may not be big enough to accommodate all displaced people. Rather the strategy is to insert and assimilate one or few farmers in one locality and disperse the others in other places. There is no need of complete resettlement programs.

---

[41] A good example in this case is the Ethiopian Sugar Development Agency. The Agency is currently building ten sugar factories around the countries. It also expropriates thousands of hectares of land for sugarcane plantation. Because of the sheer number of the people displaced from each area, it is conducting the resettlement and rehabilitation programs that include provision of alternative land, construction of roads, health centers, water systems and so on.

[42] Article 13(1) of Expropriation Proclamation.

The other point gathered from the reading of this provision is that the proclamation requires the woreda and urban administration to "do their best" in providing the rehabilitation support. This means, rehabilitation support is provided to the displaced people provided that the woreda or municipality has the ability and capacity to do so. In reality, except for the usual compensation package, since woredas and municipalities lack separate budgets for this purpose, rehabilitation assistances are not given to expropriated people.[43] One of the noted problems, for example, with regard to farmers is that they squander out the money they got as compensation for lack of entrepreneurial skills.[44] So far, there is no clear practice on part of *woreda* or urban centers that helps farmers in investing their money.[45]

But in a World Bank financed private and public projects, there are attempts to carry out resettlement and rehabilitation programs. Especially, the private sector seems more eager to fulfill this obligation as compared to the public sector. For example, Nyota Gold and Allana Potash[46] are currently undertaking studies to move the displaced people to one place (host land) where the companies intend to build the people houses and infrastructure. Besides, there are plans to assist farmers to regain their livelihood through different programs such as developing their entrepreneurial skills, making their land more productive, and giving jobs in their companies. The companies are relatively strict, because of the commitment they have entered with the IFC.[47]

---

[43] Interview made with Ato Mihret Dagnew, supra note 11.

[44] Daniel W. Ambaye, supra note 196 in Chap. 2, p. 22.

[45] Mikias, supra note 25; Also Group Discussion made with Fasil Simeneh, Addissu Begashaw and Begiziew Tsehayu, Property Valuators at Bahir Dar City Municipality, October 15, 2012, Bahir Dar.

[46] Concerning Allana Potash a brief introduction is made in Chap. 1, Sect. 1.2.1.4c. It is A Canadian Mining Company currently about to start extracting potash from the Dallol area of the Afar Regional State. The Dallo area is known for its hostile temperature and hot magma. The Afar Region is a desert area inhabited by the Afar Nomads. See details about Nyota (supra note 35).

[47] Both Nyota and Allana have a World Bank interest, and they are required to follow the IFC resettlement program. The IFC *Handbook on Resettlement Action Pl*an (IFC, supra note 37, p. 28), provides the list of activities that a project owner company should follow during resettlement of involuntary displacement: Inform affected people of their options and rights concerning resettlement; Provide technically and economically feasible options for resettlement based on consultation with affected people and assessment of resettlement alternatives; Whether physical relocation is required or not, provide affected people with prompt and effective compensation at full replacement value for loss of assets due to project activities; Where physical relocation is necessary, provide assistance with relocation expenses (moving allowances, transportation, special assistance and health care for vulnerable groups); Where physical relocation is necessary, provide temporary housing, permanent housing sites, and resources (in cash or in kind) for the construction of permanent housing—inclusive of all fees, taxes, customary tributes, and utility hookup charges—or, as required, agricultural sites for which a combination of productive potential, locational advantages, and other factors are at least equivalent to the advantages of the old site; Provide affected people with transitional financial support (such as short-term employment, subsistence support, or salary maintenance); and Where necessary, provide affected people with development assistance in addition to compensation for lost assets described above such as land preparation, agricultural inputs, and credit facilities and for training and employment opportunities.

In the public sector, although there might be successful projects that carry out resettlement programs as per the requirements of the World Bank's Operation Manual,[48] what we witnessed in the case study in Rib Irrigation Dam Project was to the contrary. When the farmers were displaced from Rib Irrigation dam Project area, it was not possible to resettle them in one place for lack of excess land in the woreda. The alternative proposal made by the consultant and approved by authorities was "restoring the livelihood of the project-affected people through other non-agricultural income generating activities, such as bee keeping, small-scale irrigation (through partnership with those who own land at the bank of rivers and through buying water pumps), cattle fattening and dairy farming."[49] However, to this day, not a single project profile on these proposed ideas has been developed. All of the compensation beneficiaries have spent their entire life on agriculture and they do not have any idea as to how they are going to invest their money on another productive venture. Except very few individuals who had already bought houses, majorities still kept their cash compensation in banks. This is one important issue that needs to be addressed before the money is squandered and the people degenerate into life-long problem.

4.5 Conclusion

Expropriation procedure is an important aspect of land taking that explains the important phases within the expropriation process. It starts with the planning and public meeting and passes through valuation, notice and compensation processes. Following of these steps is mandatory, and is also important to safeguard the interest and rights of the displaced people. Looking into the Ethiopian procedure reveals the conspicuous absence of courts in the process. The involvement of courts in the process is minimal in that most cases do not even reach the courts. The other characteristic of the Ethiopian expropriation procedure is that 'notice' is required to be served after completion of valuation. But in reality, notice is not given to project affected people through written document. The law also fails to address the need for cutoff date; it is only subsidiary laws that have no uniformity which try to incorporate it. The other problem discussed in this chapter is the ambiguous powers of the valuation committee. It is confused and mixed with another committee, a.k.a. "inventory committee." Most importantly, the requirement of resettlement and rehabilitation program during expropriation event lacks clarity. Apart from a confusing provision in the Constitution, there is no specific legal basis nor a systematic policy and measures in place for resettlement of displaced farmers. In other words, whether the government is required to resettle and provide rehabilitative assistance to those people who are displaced as a result of expropriation procedure is not clear. The practice is mixed and uncertain.

[48] See OD 4.30, supra note 39.

[49] Beza, supra note 31.

Chapter 5
Public Purpose

5.1 Introduction

Although expropriation may fall in one of the three theories of reserved right, inherent power, or consent, as discussed in Chap. 3, its exercise is restricted by two important limitations: public purpose requirement and payment of compensation. The first limitation of the government's power of expropriation is discussed in this chapter. Public purpose, as discussed in Chap. 3, is also known by different names such as public use, public advantage, public welfare, public benefit, or public interest. This is true, though, with due regard to varying connotations that might be given by different countries. For example, for a long time the big debate in the United States has been whether the constitutionally recognized terminology "public use" can be synonymous to terms such as "public advantage", "public utility", or "public purpose"? On the contrary, in other countries we see no contention of such nature on the use of the terminologies. Yet, the basic tenet behind these and similar terminologies is that private land may not be taken by expropriation for purposes other than benefiting society; it is only the interest of society that can prevail over that of the individual. Therefore, expropriation can only be used to acquire property for public, not for private use.

Historically, although obscure and not well defined, the idea was expressed in the writings of the Civil Law jurists. Grotius, Pufendorf and others had all argued against the unjustified use of power, but were in disagreement as to exactly what limitations should be applied against the government.[1] As already discussed in Chap. 3, it was also being used by European rulers well before the coming of Grotius. The second and third sections of this chapter discuss the nature of public use and the debate following its expansion, especially in the United States, while the fourth section focuses on the Ethiopian scenario.

---

[1] Berger, L. 1977. The Public Use Requirement in Eminent Domain. *Or. L. Rev.*, 57. p. 204; Harrington, supra note 6 in Chap. 3, p. 1247.

D.W. Ambaye, *Land Rights and Expropriation in Ethiopia*,
Springer Theses, DOI 10.1007/978-3-319-14639-3_5

5.2 Conceptualizing Public Purpose

5.2.1 Public Purpose Defined

A looking into different countries' legislations reveals that the concept of public purpose is given different names. For example, in the USA it is known as "public use", in Europe it is generally known as "public interest" and in Ethiopia it is called "public purpose."[2] Yet, although the scope may be different, all of them have the same objective. Hence, in this chapter we may use them interchangeably.

Many argue that it is difficult to give specific or general definition to the terminology itself, or to determine what degree of public good will meet the requirement of a "public use/public interest" for the exercise of the power of eminent domain.[3] This is because, in every case, it is a question of public policy, the determination of which is dependent upon the facts and circumstances.[4] In other words, the meaning of the term is flexible and is not confined to what may constitute a public use at any given time; the term seems to be applied in the light of what the legislature seeks to accomplish and what it may properly consider to be a public use at a particular time.

The public purpose/interest is akin to the statements of ultimate ends that characterize political philosophy, varying from Plato's concern with the moral development of citizens as the purpose of the city-state, to Hobbes's emphasis on order, Locke's protection of natural rights, and the utilitarian's assertion of the greatest good for the greatest number.[5] The public interest can be visualized as a continuum that represents the values, aspirations, and objectives of the community or polity.[6] The concept of public interest holds the ultimate ethical or economic justification for the demands that the state makes on the individual. The high value placed upon freedom and justice calls for the readiness of the citizen to make sacrifices if necessary and to share responsibility for sustaining the values of the polity.[7]

The significant characteristic of public purpose/interest is that it is an elastic concept which does not have fixed and absolute objective; public responsibilities regarded as being in the public interest in one setting may not be so regarded in a different context. For this reason, it makes of greater utility in the quest for a supporting consensus as social changes occur and efforts at accommodation are made. From property right perspective, it can be said that public purpose serves as a

---

[2] See the U.S. Constitution Fifth Amendment; Article 1 of Protocol No. 1 of European Human Right Treaty; and the FDRE Constitution respectively.

[3] C.J.S., supra note 11 in Chap. 3, Section 29.

[4] Id.

[5] Herring, P. 1968. Public Interest. *In*: Sills, D. L. (ed.) *International Encyclopedia of the Social Sciences.* USA: The Macmillan Company & The Free Press. pp. 170–175.

[6] Ibid.

[7] Ibid.

parameter for the state to take private property for some social good and it usually "...has for its objective the promotion of the public health, safety, morals, general welfare, security, prosperity, and contentment of all the inhabitants or residents within a given political division."[8] From property right perspective again, another significant characteristic of the concept of the public purpose is that private property taken from individual 'A' may not be transferred to individual 'B' for personal use only. The transfer must assume some form of benefit accrue to society as whole or part of it. Thus, public purpose shall be determined by establishing an equitable balance between the social interest on the one hand, and that of the individuals' on the other.

The state is not provided with absolute expropriation power to take private property, even upon payment of fair compensation. The public use/purpose requirement demands that individual property may be taken only if that serves society at large, not an individual. One may question, at this point, the soundness of the requirement from efficiency perspective-that if we allow the state to freely transfer properties among and between individuals, that will save time and reduce transaction cost. But, the problem is that it may open a door for abuse of power in the long run, since people will try to influence the state to decide in their favor.[9] Further, the very freedom given to the state will deprive the owners of property their security of tenure and the protection accorded to private property.

5.2.2 *Nature of Activity that Qualifies as "Public Purpose"*

One may equate "public purpose" to those areas of activities which are known as "pubic goods." "Public goods" are goods and services made in the interest of society in general. In Ethiopia, they are generally known as "public services."[10] Public goods are goods which are provided by the state at no cost to individuals. Public goods entail no marginal cost for an additional individual to enjoy, and rather it costs a great deal to exclude an individual from enjoying, they are non excludable.[11] Thus the important characteristic of a public good is its indivisibility and or non-exclusivity. The main criterion of indivisibility or non-exclusivity is that the good in question should be available to all members of the society (or a section thereof) irrespective of their willingness or ability to pay for it.[12] A classical

---

[8] Black's Law Dictionary.

[9] Epstein, supra note 175 in Chap. 3, p. 165.

[10] Article 3207 of the Ethiopian Civil Code states: "Any activity which a public community has decided to perform for the reason that it has deemed it to be necessary in the general interest and considered that private initiative was inadequate for carrying it out shall constitute a public service."

[11] Stiglitz, J. E. & Driffill, J. 2000. *Economics,* New York and London, W. W. Norton & Company. p. 124.

[12] Bhatia, H. L. 2003. *Public Finance,* Mumbai, Vikas Publishing House Pvt Ltd. pp. 3–4.

example in this case is defense. Once the state ensures defense, every citizen will benefit from it. An additional person to the number of citizens will not cause the state an additional marginal cost, and it is difficult to exclude this individual from being protected by the defense system. Defense is considered as pure public good.

Besides, there are other "impure public goods" such as roads, streets, airports and parks which usually are provided by the state, but in reality which may also be operated by private individuals. These goods are public because of the nature of the benefit they provide-that they are universally available to all. They differ from the pure (defense) public goods in that their use and enjoyment is based on the willingness of the person; a citizen is protected by the military whether he likes it or not, but highways and parks furnish benefits that the individual citizen is able to refuse if he wants to. Highways and parks are also illustrative of cases where the marginal cost of servicing additional individuals is in practice always positive.[13] Private toll roads and parks are easily organized, so public parks and toll roads could be made private if the government chose to abandon them. The property in these cases is public only because the government chooses to provide the service.[14]

But, to consider "public purpose" as equivalent to "public goods" would be too narrow to accomplish the entire social activities. This means there are also other types of activities that must be considered as public purpose because of the service they render to the society. In such cases, of course, the non-exclusivity rule may not work as individuals may be required to make some form of payment for the service. On the other hand, as far as individuals make the required payment, they have the right not to be excluded from getting the service or benefit. Such services may be handled by the state or private individuals, as the case may be. If it is to be handled by private companies, as the case is in many countries, there is no need for continued government ownership of the property after expropriation. As part of a unified transaction, the property taken can immediately be conveyed to private parties subject to the appropriate common carrier restrictions.[15] A good example, in this case, is telecom or rail way services which are universally considered as public services, and the public as a matter of right can have access to them as far as they pay the minimum fixed payment. The companies are required to offer their services on non discriminatory basis to all clients at a legally fixed or reasonably acceptable price.[16]

The other area of interest, which is also contentious, is where land is taken and transferred to private organs. The question is whether the "public purpose" requirement is satisfied by showing that the taking creates some indirect benefits in

---

[13] Epstein, supra note 175 in Chap. 3, p. 167.

[14] Ibid.

[15] Id., p. 168.

[16] See, for example, Article 3224 of the Ethiopian Civil Code where it is dictated that neither the Administrative authorities nor the company that gets concession agreement to run public service activities (such as railway) shall put measures discriminating between the users and destroy the equality of treatment of the latter.

which the entire public shares.[17] Land has been expropriated and transferred to private individuals for purposes such as building hotels, mills, housing and other investments which give incidental or indirect benefits to the general public. In the following sections an attempt is made to look into the experience of some countries.

5.3 The Debate on the Scope of the Term in the USA and Europe

5.3.1 Narrower and Broader Views of the Concept

In the United States, the courts' notion of what exactly constitutes a public use has been changed and shifted along with their perception of when the exercise of eminent domain is appropriate. In the late eighteenth and early nineteenth centuries, for instance, there were only few situations in which the use of eminent domain was deemed necessary, including rights of way and easements.[18] In such limited circumstances, the public benefit flowing from natural resource or infrastructure development was held to satisfy the public use requirement. By the mid-nineteenth century, however, courts began to define "public use" as "use by the public."[19] This view reflected the concern that an expansive definition of public use would justify the taking of private property for any purpose. This narrower interpretation of the public use requirement, which proved to be difficult to administer and impractical in its application, was short-lived. Indeed, by the late nineteenth and early twentieth centuries, the modern demands of industry, transportation, mining, and agriculture led the U.S. Supreme Court to embrace the broader and more encompassing definition of public use as "public purpose."[20]

As already mentioned above, the terminology used in the United States is "public use," and regarding its meaning there are two kinds of views: narrow and broader views. Based on its narrow view, for example, Lewis, a scholar in eminent domain, has defined "public use" as follows:

> ... the employment or application of the thing by the public. Public use means the same as use by the public, and this, it seems is the construction the words should receive in the constitutional provision in question.[21]

This definition was also shared by some courts which interpreted the term "public use" strictly. Fearful of the fact that a broader view will provide the

---

[17] Epstein, supra note 175 in Chap. 3, p. 168.

[18] See generally Nichols, P., supra note 3 in Chap. 4.

[19] Haddad, N. W. 2006. Public Use or Private Benefit? The Post-Kelo Intersection of Religious Land Use and the Public Use Doctrine. *Fordham L. Rev.*, 75, 1105. p. 1111.

[20] Ibid.

[21] Lewis, Eminent Domain. Section 258 as quoted in Comments 1956. What Use is a Public Use in Eminent Domain? *St. Louis U. L. J*, 4, 316. p. 517.

government unlimited access into the right of private property, these courts adopted the narrower view that defines "public use" as "use by the public." A typical example of the narrower view was one held by a Californian Supreme Court in 1908, where the court put its position as follows:

> There can be no question as to the position of our Supreme Court upon this question. It has consistently held that "public use" means "use by the public," and that to make a use public, a duty must devolve on the person or corporation holding property appropriated by right of eminent domain to furnish the public with the use intended, and the public must be entitled, as of right, to use or enjoy the property taken.[22]

Thus, under this view, it is essential to constitute a public use that the general public has the right to a definite and fixed use of the property appropriated, not as a mere matter of favor or by permission of the owner, but as a matter of right. If the special benefit to be derived from the land sought to be expropriated is wholly for private persons, the use is a private one, and is not categorized as a public use merely for the fact that the public has a theoretical right to use it, or that the public will receive an indirect or prospective benefit from it.

A distinction was drawn between a purpose beneficial to the public and a purpose in which the public had a "right of use." As emphasized by a later New York Court, "The indirect contribution to the prosperity of the entire community resulting from activities from which only some individuals would profit was not sufficient to justify the exercise of eminent domain. It was necessary that the public possess a 'right' to use the facility or service for which the property was desired."[23]

However, with more public engagement and economic development, especially after the American Revolution, it is said, the "broader view dominated the courts,"[24] and today it has become the most held view in the U.S. Supreme Court.[25] Most courts became liberal in construing "public use" freely, holding that it is synonymous with "public purpose," "public benefit," "public utility," "public advantage," or "public convenience", by which they follow the broader view of the terminology.[26] The gist of the broader view is that it is not necessary that there be actual physical use by the public or the government. Anything which tends to enlarge the resources, increase the industrial energies, and promote the productive power of any considerable number of the inhabitants of a section of the state manifestly contributes to the general welfare and the prosperity of the whole community constitutes a public use.[27] Thus, public uses are not limited to matters of mere business necessity and ordinary convenience, but may extend to matters of public health, safety, recreation, and enjoyment; besides, it includes the field of

---

[22] Berger, supra note 1, p. 210; See also *36 Cal. App. 556, 178.* p. 153.

[23] Comments 1948–1949, supra note 30 in Chap. 3, p. 603.

[24] Berger, supra note 1, p. 205.

[25] Crabtree, S. 1983. Public Use in Eminent Domain: Are There Limits After Oakland Raiders and Poletown? *Cal. W. L. Rev.*, 20, 82. p. 86.

[26] C.J.S., supra note 11 in Chap. 3, Section 29.

[27] Berger, supra note 1, p. 213.

public welfare or public necessity or the prosperity of the community. The taking of property for aesthetic purposes may be also considered as taking for public use.

5.3.2 Recent Developments in the USA

Modern court decisions in the U.S. show that the court relies on the decision of the administration or Congress. Three modern decisions of the U.S. court explain the positions of courts held today. The first one is the *Berman v. Parker*[28] case, where the Supreme Court upheld in 1954 a redevelopment plan as being a public use. The case was that the government wanted to condemn land that involved a blighted area of Washington, D.C. in which over half of the housing for the area's 5,000 inhabitants was beyond repair, and was a threat to public health and safety. An owner of a department store located in the blighted area challenged the condemnation as an invalid public use on two grounds: first, his property was commercial and not residential or slum housing, and second, his property was being condemned for sale to a private agency for redevelopment. A unanimous Court upheld the condemnation act on the ground of avoiding the evils of blight that are "injurious to the public health, safety, morals and welfare"[29] which amounts to police power of the state, since the state has the duty to protect its citizens. "The public end may be as well or better served through an agency of private enterprise than through a department of government-or so the Congress might conclude."[30]

The second land mark case was the *Hawaii Housing Authority v. Midkiff,*[31] where in 1984 Hawaii used its eminent domain power to acquire lots owned by large landowners, and then transferred the lots to the tenants living on them or to other non landowners. Land control by few elites helped to promote social inequality and generated social unrest. By redistributing the property, the problems attributed to the land oligopoly and deficiencies in the real estate market could be corrected and a majority of the public would tangibly and directly benefit from the legislation. Importantly, because the scheme was a rational attempt to remedy a social evil, or correct a public harm, the Court held that it qualified as a public use.[32]

---

[28] 348 U.S. 26 (1954) *Berman* is often cited to support the proposition that the elimination of blight alone is sufficient to qualify as a public use and thereby to eliminate the speared of all evils that comes with blight.

[29] Id., p. 31.

[30] Id., p. 33–34.

[31] 467 U.S. 229 (1984). It aimed to reduce the concentration of land ownership in the hands of landlords by providing for the condemnation of privately held land and transferring ownership of the condemned land to existing lessees. The Court upheld the Act, finding that the elimination of the harms associated with land oligopolies served a valid public purpose.

[32] Mikkelsen, S. D. 2006. Eminent Domain after Kelo v. City Of New London: Compensating for the Supreme Court's Refusal to Enforce the Fifth Amendment. *Duke Journal of Constitutional Law & Public Policy Sidbar* 2, 11. p. 16.

In both the above cases, the Court rejected the argument that the takings were made for private purpose only. Instead, it is said, the Court equated "public use" and "public interest," and held that the government has virtually unfettered discretion to exercise its power of eminent domain to advance any conceivable public purpose,[33] and this sets an apparently nonrestrictive and subjective standard for future cases challenging the Public Use Clause.[34]

This line of argument reached its climax in 2005 when the U.S. Supreme Court approved the taking of private land by eminent domain from private owners to be used for other forms of private use. In *Kelo v. City of New London,*[35] after approving an integrated development plan designed to revitalize its ailing economy, the city of New London, Connecticut purchased most of the property earmarked for the project from willing sellers, but initiated condemnation proceedings when Kelo and the other owners of the rest of the property refused to sell. Kelo and et al. brought an action against the city claiming, inter alia, that the taking of their non-blight properties would violate the "public use" restriction in the Fifth Amendment's Takings Clause.[36] The question was whether transferring non-blight homes to another individual for economic purposes was justified as public use. The company that wanted the land had planned to transform the area into modern residential and commercial centers, malls, and parking areas. The city hoped that the project would bring economic development to the city through employment and tax payment.[37]

The Court, in five to four vote, held that the general benefits a community enjoyed from *economic growth* qualified such redevelopment plans as a permissible "public use" under the Takings Clause of the Fifth Amendment.[38] While the Court noted that "the sovereign may not take the property of *A* for the sole purpose of transferring to another private party *B* … it is equally clear that a State may transfer property from one private party to another if future 'use by the public' is the purpose of the taking."[39] What makes this decision similar to the *Berman* case is that the Court found that economic development constituted a valid public purpose and specifically rejected the proposition that the property to be condemned must be blighted in order to invoke eminent domain for economic development purposes.

Justice O'Connor, writing for four dissenting justices, viewed the decision with alarm. If economic development, without more, is a sufficient rationale for eminent domain takings, she wrote, then all properties are at risk of condemnation. All that

---

[33] Garnett, N. S. 2003. The Public-Use Question as a Takings Problem. *Geo. Wash. L. Rev.,* 71, 934. p. 940.

[34] Jones, S. D. 2006. That Land Is Your Land, This Land Is My Land … Until the Local Government Can Turn It for a Profit: A Critical Analysis of Kelo v. City of New London. *BYU Journal of Public Law,* 20, 139. p. 149.

[35] 545 U.S. 469 (2005).

[36] Ibid.

[37] Id., p. 473.

[38] Id, p. 484.

[39] Mikkelsen, supra note 32, p. 14.

is needed is a plausible argument that someone other than the current owner will put the property to a more valuable use.[40]

The Supreme Court further granted great deference to legislatures in determining which priority of the public justifies the use of eminent domain.[41] In other words, states were at liberty to come up with different legislations to strengthen their own property rights if they were dissatisfied with the decision. And what had been seen in the following years was indeed a massive political and legislative backlash against the *Kelo* decision. In a massive reaction to the *Kelo* decision, within 2 years, over 40 states enacted post-*Kelo* reform legislation to curb eminent domain use for economic reasons.[42]

5.3.3 Public Purpose in Europe

Although every European country has its own expropriation legislation that deals with the issue of public purpose, the unifying and binding principle for member countries is, though, Article 1 of Protocol No. 1 of the European Convention for the Protection of Human Rights and Fundamental Freedoms:[43]

> Every natural or legal person is entitled to the peaceful enjoyment of his possessions. No one shall be deprived of his possessions except in the public interest and subject to the conditions provided for by law and by the general principles of international law.
> The preceding provisions shall not, however, in any way impair the right of a State to enforce such laws as it deems necessary to control the use of property in accordance with the general interest or to secure the payment of taxes or other contributions or penalties.

The countries, of course, draw and adopt similar provisions in their respective constitutions and property laws. One can easily perceives that while the first paragraph deals with the expropriation power of the state, the second has to do with its police/regulatory power.[44] The basic idea behind the first paragraph is that private property may not be taken by expropriation except when it is found to be necessary for "public interest." So, the key term used in Europe is "public interest" rather than "public use" which signifies that in Europe the state expropriation right is wider than in the United States. Although it is not possible to look into the practice of all

[40] Merrill and Smith, supra note 2 in Chap. 2, p. 244.

[41] Mikkelsen, supra note 32, p. 17.

[42] Somin, I. 2010. The Limits of Backlash: Assessing the Political Response to Kelo. *In*: Benson, B. L. (ed.) *Property Rights: Eminent Domain and Regulatory Takings Re-Examined* New York: Palgrave Macmillan, p. 101; see also the detail assessment of these legislation in Dana, D. A. 2007. The Law and Expressive Meaning of Condemning the Poor After *Kelo*. *Nw. U. L. Rev*, 101, 365.

[43] Council-of-Europe 1952. Protocol No. 1 to the Convention for the Protection of Human Rights and Fundamental Freedoms. Paris.

[44] See also the European Court's decision on *Sporrong and Lönnroth* v *Sweden* (1982) as quoted in Green, supra note 86 in Chap. 3, p. 532. The court adopts the same interpretation.

countries, an overview of some and the decisions of the European Court of Human Right is discussed here.

In Sweden the public interest requirement has not been challenged when the land was required by public bodies. These days, however, because most of the public entities are privatized, the issue of public interest has become into focus. In any case, public interest is now interpreted loosely as some project "important" to community.[45]

In France, originally, the concept of "public interest" was understood restrictively and land expropriation had been used only to the construction of important public works, but not to social or aesthetic purposes, or rational urbanism.[46] A long series of statutes, though, expanded the scope of expropriation, and finally the 1953 Urban and Residential statute, among others, permits expropriation for the purpose of private housing, which illustrates the consideration of private interests as public ones.[47] Today, in France, the concept of public interest has become wider and it is no longer essential that the objective should be within the public domain (road, bridge or school). It is not even asked whether the taking promotes some public service, any broadly useful purpose is considered sufficient.[48] Accordingly, land may be taken by expropriation for end-use as the private property of a public person, even though it serves no direct public use, nor promote any public service.[49]

Concerning the interpretation of the "public interest" requirement of the European Convention mentioned above, it is said that "in cases involving the transfer of property from one private person to another, the Court of Human Rights allows States to frame the purpose of a taking so broadly that it is difficult to imagine how a redistribution would serve a public interest in some way."[50] The Court of Human Rights has also stated that economic policy may justify the transfer of property amongst private persons. For example, the Court has found that "the public interest in managing the economy justifies consolidations of private agricultural land, majority buy-out rules in company law, and compulsory debt adjustment programs."[51] The court has not given details on the relation between personal economic benefits and "public interest." Instead, it seems, it was enough for the court if the State believes that the interference with property would have a positive impact on the economy.[52] But, unlike in the United States, in Europe, the issue of land

---

[45] Kalbro, T. 2003. Private Compulsory Purchase and the Public Interest. *In*: Kalbro, T. (ed.) *Urban Land Management: Papers on Property Development and Compulsory Purchase*. Stockholm: KTH, pp. 51–53.

[46] Aubry and Rau, supra note 1 in Chap. 2, p. 192.

[47] Ibid.

[48] Ibid.

[49] Picard, supra note 76 in Chap. 3, p. 43.

[50] Allen, T. 2008. Control Over the Use and Abuse of Eminent Domain in England: A Comparative View. *In*: Malloy, R. P. (ed.) *Private Property, Community Development, and Eminent Domain*. Hampshire: Ashgate Publishing Limited, p. 78.

[51] Ibid.

[52] Id., p. 80.

expropriation for private use has not been encountered with strong resistance owing to better compensation packages provided to property owners.[53]

The common characteristics of both the U.S. Courts and the European Court of Human Rights seem that first, the courts tend to accept what is dictated by the legislator or the administration as public purpose, and second, they prefer to give deference to the legislator to come up with alternative legislative guidelines instead of putting restrictive guidelines by themselves, which the legislators fail to do so. The point is that unless the courts serve society as "the guardians of the guardian", by restricting the expanded use of the "public purpose" in expropriation, the private property right of individuals is at a great risk. As the legal philosopher Roscoe Pound once said, "...the chief danger to property has not been from the covetous neighbor nor from the habitual thief. It has been from the acquisitive and confiscatory activities of rulers. The will to power, the temptation to exercise power simply because one has it, has led rulers to arbitrary interferences with liberty of the person. Covetousness has led them to arbitrary seizures of property. Both have joined to bring about arbitrary interferences with liberty of using property."[54]

5.4 Public Purpose Limitation in Ethiopia

5.4.1 The Constitution

Public purpose as a limitation on the expropriation power of the sovereign state is well recognized in the current Ethiopian Constitution. As already mentioned (Sect. 3.5), Article 40(8) of the FDRE Constitution permits the expropriation of private property provided that the taking would be for "public purpose" activities:

> Without prejudice to the right to private property, the government may expropriate private property for public purposes subject to payment in advance of compensation commensurate to the value of the property.

The Constitution neither defines the term "public purpose" nor does it indicate the activities that might constitute as "public purpose" activities. The terminology is, of course, similar to what has been used in the Ethiopian Civil Code, Article 1460 that defines the term expropriation.[55] A reading of another limb of Article 40

---

[53] For example in England, in addition to fair market value, owners are also provided with "loss payment" of 10 % for residential houses and 7.5 % for business. (See Id. p. 84). In Sweden, an additional 25 % of the market value is paid to meet the expectation of the person who lost his land (see Swedish legislation infra note 55 in Chap. 6).

[54] Pound, R. 1939. The Law of Property and Recent Juristic Thought. *A.B.A.J.*, 25, 993–998. p. 995.

[55] Article 1460: Expropriation proceedings are proceedings whereby the competent authorities compel an owner to surrender the ownership of an immovable required by such authorities for public purposes.

Table 5.1 The use of "Public Purpose" terminologies by different legislations

Legislation's name	Legislation's no.	Article	Terminology used
FDRE constitution	1/1995	40(1)	Public interest (*Yehizb Tiqim*)
		40(8)	Public purpose (*Yehizb Tiqim*)
Expropriation proclamation	455/2005	2(5), 3(1)	Public purpose (*Yehizb Tiqim*)
Investment proclamation	769/2012	25(1)	Public interest (*Yehizb Tiqim*)
Urban land lease proclamation	721/2011	26(1)	Public interest (*Yehizb Tiqim*)
FDRE RLAUP	456/2005	7(3)	Public use (*Yehizb Tiqim*)
Mining proclamation	678/2010	53(1)	Public purpose
Civil code	165/1960	1460	Public purpose (*Yehizib Tiqim*)
		1463	Public utility (*Yehizb Agelgilot*)
		1464	Public interest (*Yehizb Agelgilot*)
Amhara RLAUP	133/2006	2(18), 11(1)	Public interest (*Yehizb Agelgilot*
		28 Title	Public use (*Yehizb Agelgilot*)
		2(15), 5(8), 28(1), (2), (4)	Public service (*Yehizb Agelgilot*)
Oromia RLAUP	130/2007	6(10), (11)	Public use (*Yehizib Tiqim*)

Source Different Ethiopian land related legislations

(1) of the Constitution reveals also that the term "public interest" is used a little bit wider than what "public purpose" purports to represent, although the Amharic meaning given for both of them is the same (see Table 5.1). Article 40(1) of the FDRE Constitution states:

> Every Ethiopian citizen has the right to the ownership of private property. Unless prescribed otherwise by law on account of public interest, this right shall include the right to acquire, to use and, in a manner compatible with the rights of other citizens, to dispose of such property by sale or bequest or to transfer it otherwise (emphasis added).

One can easily notice that this provision puts a general restriction on the use and enjoyment as well as disposition of private property "on account of public interest." As mentioned in Chap. 2, the use and enjoyment of private property may be restricted by the state for different reasons such as public health, public safety, environmental concern, or urban aesthetics. The restriction in such cases may not necessitate the physical taking of the property; rather the use and enjoyment may be restricted by pieces of regulations. This power of the government is best explained by what is known as the "police power" of the state rather than expropriation. The "police power", as it is termed in the USA, is an "inherent power of the government to make all laws necessary and proper to preserve the public security, order, health, morality and justice."[56] Hence, all restrictions imposed by urban planning laws on owners of real property concerning the building height, typology, construction and demolition, for example, fall under the police power of the government. Similarly,

[56] Black's Law Dictionary.

all restrictions imposed on the use of alcohol, drug, and fire safety measures are examples of governmental concern for public health and safety. The implication is that "public interest" in this provision of the Constitution is used to justify all restrictions imposed on private properties including expropriation. For this reason, it seems, Article 40(8) of the Constitution that deals with the expropriation aspect employs a different terminology, "public purpose" instead of "public interest" to indicate the wider and comprehensive nature of the second terminology. In other words, under the FDRE constitution, "public interest" has a wider application than "public purpose."

Some literatures also differentiate between the two concepts. In one literature, it says that the meaning of "public interest" is close to public concern in general, while "public purpose" is narrow in its scope and limited to the projects for the use of the public, under the law of expropriation.[57]

Yet, when one looks into the other subsidiary Ethiopian land related legislations, one may notice two facts: first, the two terminologies are used as synonyms, and second, there is no uniformity in the usage of the terminologies. Table 5.1 shows, for instance, the usage of the terminology in different legislations. We have supplemented their corresponding Amharic terms as indicated in the legislations. But, in the opinion of this writer, even the Amharic terms do not exactly explain the English ones. For example, the Amharic term "*Yehizb Tiqim*" denotes "public use" instead of "public purpose." And the term "*Yehizb Agelgilot*" means "public service" rather than "public interest." The term "public purpose" can better be explained by the Amharic term "*Yehizb Alama*," and the term "public interest" as "*Yehizb Filagot*". What we see, rather, is the use of the Amharic terms "*Yehizb Tiqim*" as referring to all the terms "public purpose", "public use", and "public interest." Whether the intention of the legislator was to use the narrower or broader application of the term cannot be known only by looking at these contradictory terminologies; one needs to contextually read other parts of the Expropriation Proclamation. In any case, the contradictory and inconsistent terminologies used in the different legislations (at least in the active existing ones) are the results of poor draftsmanship of the legislator.

5.4.2 The Federal Expropriation Proclamation

In his comparative study of land acquisition mechanisms made in different countries, Kitay states that in legislations, public purpose doctrines are expressed in two basic ways.[58]

---

[57] Awotash-Alemu. 2003. *The Impact of Expropriation on Investment: the Case of Ethiopia.* Unpublished Senior thesis, Law Faculty, Addis Ababa University. p. 32.

[58] Kitay, supra note 14 in Chap. 3, p. 40.

A. General guidelines, which state merely that expropriation requires a public purpose, or other similar words. This kind of expression leaves a great amount of discretion to the executive power/government and to the courts. Whenever the government wishes to take a land for a certain purpose, it can justify it on the general principle of public purpose.
B. List provisions that explicitly identify the purposes for which land may be taken. In this regard, most laws specify schools, health centers, government offices, roads, military installations, utilities and so on as activities that benefit the public. The list may be illustrative or exhaustive, as the case may be. If the list is of the latter kind, purposes not appearing on the list may not form the basis for expropriation of land. Neither the government nor the courts can add items to the list other than the ones expressly provided.

The above classification is, of course, with due regard to the possibility of employing a third different mechanism as used by some countries, where it may be possible to use a hybrid of the two approaches. In any case, when we look into the Ethiopian system, an investigation of the FDRE Expropriation Proclamation shows that the approach used is the first one. The previous repealed Expropriation Proclamation, Proclamation No. 401 of 2004, on the other hand, listed the kinds of projects that constituted public purpose. For example, power generating plants, highways, airports, dams, railways, fuel depots, water and sewerage facilities, telephone and electrical works and other related activities were listed as public purpose activities.[59] The Amhara RLAUP on its part adopts the third modality that includes a partial list as well as a general clause.[60]

The current 2005 Federal Expropriation proclamation defines "public purpose" as:

> …the use of land defined as such by the decision of the appropriate body in conformity with urban structure plan or development plan in order to ensure the interest of the people to acquire direct or indirect benefits from the use of the land and to consolidate sustainable socio-economic development[61] (emphasis added.)

As already discussed in the preceding chapter, the appropriate body that decides the public purpose aspect of a project is either the rural *woreda* administration or the urban municipality or a relevant higher federal or regional authority. This means, as far as these government organs believe that the project will bring some form of public benefit, land may be expropriated from private holders or urban lessees. Furthermore, Article 3(1) emphasizes that the appropriate body may expropriate land "for public purpose where it believes that it should be used for a

[59] Appropriation of Land for Government Works and Payment of Compensation for Property Proclamation, Proclamation 401/2004. *Negarit Gazeta.* Year 10, No. 42. Article 2(2).

[60] Article 2(15) of Amhara RLAUP defines "Public Service" as "a service given to the public directly or indirectly, such as government office, school, health service, market service, road, religious institutions, military camps, and the likes, and includes activities assumed important to the development of people by the Regional Government and to be implemented on the rural land."

[61] Article 2(5) of Proclamation 455/2005.

better development project to be carried out by public entities, private investors, cooperative societies or other organs…" [Italics added.]. Here the law envisages two important things: first, *better development* or a better use of the land may amount as public purpose, and second, the user may be a public body, private person or others. One may question the nature of the parameter the "appropriate body" should use in approving the expropriation procedure. In other words, what objectives or standards should "the appropriate body" use to determine the public purpose nature of the project? How does it decide whether the use of the land will be *better* if transferred to others? The reading of the above provision (Article 2(5)), reveals the following parameters.

5.4.2.1 Urban Structural Plan and National Development Plan

One clear parameter that we may infer from the reading of the provision cited above is that the expropriation decision should be in "conformity with urban structure plan or development plan." This means, any taking that aids the implementation of "urban structural plan" or the government's "development plan" may amount to public purpose. One may of course question, at this juncture, the meaning and nature of these plans. Accordingly, a brief explanation is due hereunder.

a. Urban Structure Plan

Urban structural plan is defined in the current Urban Planning Proclamation as

> ... a legally binding plan along with its explanatory texts formulated and drawn at the level of an entire urban boundary that sets out the basic requirements regarding physical development the fulfillment of which could produce a coherent urban development in social, economic and spatial spheres.[62]

Urban structural plan can be prepared by each and respective urban center anticipating 10 years future development of the urban center.[63] An urban structural plan must, at least, indicate the following aspects of the urban plan[64]:

(a) the magnitude and direction of growth of the urban center;
(b) principal land use classes;
(c) housing development;
(d) the layout and organization of major physical and social infrastructure;
(e) urban redevelopment intervention areas of the urban center;
(f) environmental aspects; and
(g) industry zone.

[62] FDRE Urban Planning Proclamation, Proclmation No. 574/2008. *Negarit Gazeta.* Year 14, No. 29, Article 9(1).

[63] Id., Articles 12 and 14.

[64] Id., Article 9(2).

It is witnessed in present day Ethiopia that, for example, in urban centers land may be expropriated to implement the urban structural plan. Thus, the blight part of the capital is being demolished to replace it with modern high-rise buildings; houses are demolished to widen roads; farm lands are being expropriated to construct condominium houses, and so on. As we shall see soon, if the structural plan requires a specific type of building on a given site, an owner is forced either to construct such type of building or cede the land to others who have the ability to do so.

b. National Economic Development Plan

The second type of plan mentioned above is "development plan." Although this term lacks clarity, it must be referring to the "national medium-term development plan" of the country. This national development plan is a 5 year development plan that encompasses all urban and rural development programs. Since 2002, Ethiopia has witnessed three 5-year national development plans, the current one being the "Growth and Transformation Plan" (GTP) that is to be implemented from 2010/2011–2014/2015.[65] The GTP is the guiding economic and social development program of the government. The current development plan aspires to attain very ambitious objectives within the plan's period. Starting from laying infrastructure and boosting the economy to improving the education, health and justice system of the country, it aims to fulfill the Millennium Development Goals (MDG) by the end of the plan's period.[66]

The GTP document lists down seven pillars[67] of the program with detailed explanation. Four of the pillars which have close effect on land expropriation are briefly described as follows:

1. Sustaining rapid and equitable economic growth: Ethiopian economy has been growing rapidly in the past and the government intends to maintain this growth by focusing on agriculture and industry. An ambitious plan is in place to open and expand textile, leather, cement, sugar, fertilizer, mining, energy, metal and engineering industries. At this moment, for example, ten sugar factories are under construction and the plan is to use 200,000 ha of land for sugarcane plantation.[68]
2. Maintaining agriculture as major source of economic growth: agriculture has been the backbone of the country's economy, and it will continue to play the leading role within the plan's period as well. For this reason, besides helping farmers to make intensive production on their farm, there is a plan to transfer

[65] In 2002 the Ethiopian government passed a 2002/2003–2004/2005 medium term development program/plan called "Sustainable Development and Poverty Reduction Program" (SDPRP). Then it adopted another 2005/2006–2009/2010 plan called "Plan for Accelerated and Sustained Development to End Poverty" (PASDEP).

[66] MOFED 2010. Federal Democratic Republic of Ethiopia Growth and Transformation Plan (GTP): 2010/2011–2014/2015. Addis Ababa: Ministry of Finance and Economic Development. p. 22.

[67] Ibid.

[68] Id., p. 59.

3.3 million hectares of land to foreign and domestic private commercial-farm investors.[69] This is in addition to the 2.8 million hectares of land that was already transferred, as discussed in Sect. 2.6.4.3.
3. Create conditions for the industry to play key role in the economy: to accelerate the industrial development in the country, favorable conditions in terms of tax holidays and provision of necessary land will be made to investors. Further, the government will provide special assistance to Micro and Small-Scale Manufacturing Enterprises (MSEs). As we shall see in due course, the MSEs already received large size of urban land to establish and expand their businesses in the capital as well as in other parts of the country. The 5 years' plan is to provide the MSEs 15,000 ha of land, mostly in urban centers.[70]
4. Enhancing expansion and quality of infrastructure development: the construction and maintenance of infrastructure such as roads, power and water supply will continue. The road network will be expanded not only by the construction of new highways but also by networking all rural *kebeles* to the main roads. Railway lines connecting different parts of the country will be developed. To encourage urban growth, all necessary infrastructure and housing demands will be met. From transportation perspective, the program shows that within the plan's period, 18,000 km asphalt roads, 71,000 km rural gravel roads, 2,395 km railway, and 34 km light weight urban rail will be constructed. In the energy sector, more than 8,000 MW (equivalent to 8 big nuclear reactors) will be produced, which is a big boost to the current 2,000 MW. Urban infrastructure will be improved by the construction and production of 150,000 houses in the capital only. About 101,000 houses will also be constructed in sugar development areas. Most of these works are now under way, and there is a good chance that they might be completed on time.[71]

The point is that all such activities will be immediately considered as public purpose activities, and land required for such projects will be immediately granted. The appropriate body, which is supposed to approve the expropriation, will, thus, use both the "urban structure plan" and the GTP (or similar future plans) as guiding principles to consider the public purpose nature of a project.

5.4.2.2 Acquiring Direct or Indirect Benefit

A particular project may give direct access or an indirect benefit to society. Direct and indirect benefits may be acquired either by "the use of the land" or through the consolidation of "sustainable socio-economic development."

Direct benefit could be something similar to what has been termed as "use by the public", as was already discussed in the American definition above. This means, the

[69] Id., p. 49.
[70] Id., p. 58.
[71] Id., pp. 68–70.

public will directly benefit by having an indiscriminate actual use of the facility such as schools, hospitals, roads, parks or hotels. From the outset, such projects are designed mainly with the intention of benefiting society.

In Ethiopia, where the State is the main player in the economy and the sole provider of all the infrastructures, the purpose of building such projects is nothing but benefiting society. The state has been instrumental in construction and provision of all the basic amenities and social services. In fact, the Ethiopian government has been praised for its pro-poor infrastructure investment which, according to one report, consumes 10 % of its GDP, the highest in Sub-Saharan Africa.[72] The current government's economic philosophy is known as "developmental state" where the state plays the role of "regulatory orientation and the developmental orientation." Chalmer Johnson's description of "developmental state" best describes the economic philosophy in Ethiopia:

> The developmental state is one that is determined to influence the direction and pace of economic development by directly intervening in the development process, rather than relying on the uncoordinated influence of market forces to allocate economic resources.[73]

The state, thus, plays the two roles of a regulator and a business man, and creates in effect two parallel economies, the state and private. For this reason, most of the developmental (economic or social) projects planned in the GTP are being carried out by the state.

Apart from those facilities which may directly be accessible by the public, there are also other projects which the public is thought to benefit from them indirectly (by consolidating sustainable socio-economic development). A good example in this case, and which is also contestable, is the land provided for private investments. All types of private investments are encouraged by the government, among others, by the provision of land for free. As we already discussed above (Sect. 2.6.5.2), the manufacturing sector is, for example, an area of investment where investors get urban land by allotment (without auction.) The existing investment law requires government organs to identify and prepare land for investment.[74] In the 2011/2012 fiscal year only, the FDRE Ministry of Trade and Industry received about 5,130 ha of land from different cities for industrial zone to be transferred to different companies in due course.[75] This is in a bid to reduce the bureaucratic delay investors

[72] The Awakening of a sleeping giant, *African Review*, December 14, 2012, available: http://www.africareview.com/Special-Reports/The-awakening-of-a-sleeping-giant/-/979182/1643668/-/sn8vxlz/-/index.html#commentsAnchor.

[73] Johnson, C. 1999. The Developmental State: Odyssey of a Concept. *In*: Woo-Cumings, M. (ed.) *The Developmental State*. New York: Cornell University Press, pp. 37–40.

[74] FDRE Investment Proclamation, Proclmation No. 769/2012. *Negarit Gazeta*. Year 18, No. 63, 31.

[75] This news was published in many news outlets including the webpage of the Ethiopian Embassy to the European Union: http://ethiopiaembassy.eu/ethiopia-allocates-5130-hectares-for-industrial-zones/; also see Addis Fortune of December 25, 2012, available: http://addisfortune.net/s/the-first-ethiopian-industrial-zone-to-be-ready-for-south-korean-investors-in-january/.

have been facing in acquiring land for investment. In regional states, too, rural and urban land administration organs prepare potential land (in their land bank) suitable for investment. The investments range from manufacturing to agriculture and service sectors. Hence, land is being expropriated from farmers and city dwellers in order to transfer it to manufacturing industries, horticulture farms, hotels, and private housing programs. Similarly, there is a recent move by the Ministry of Agriculture to establish "agriculture economic zones" in selected parts of the country with the intention of identifying, demarcating and making accessible land for agricultural investment.[76]

The usual reasons given for considering such private investments as public purpose are because they create jobs, increase tax revenue of the state, generate foreign currency (important for Ethiopia), create transfer of technology (especially from foreign investments), and improve the local infrastructure.[77]

5.4.3 Existing Practices

Today in Ethiopia, land rights are being expropriated both in urban and rural areas of the country. In urban centers, land is expropriated from within the city or from its periphery, whereas in rural areas, private farming plots and common lands of the people are subjected to expropriation. If we take Addis Ababa city as an example, extensive land has been expropriated from the city center and its periphery. Much of the city center is slum, and indeed according to the UN Habitat' report, 40 % of the total housing stock of the city needs replacement.[78] On practical level, the city's plan shows that out of the total 54,000 ha of the city's built area, 14,765 ha of land is considered as slum destined to be renewed.[79] Accordingly, large part of the city center is under demolition for urban renewal and upgrading purposes.

At this juncture, to avoid confusion, it is important to define the terms *urban redevelopment*, *urban renewal* and *urban upgrading*. These terminologies are adequately defined in the FDRE Urban Planning Proclamation as follows:

Urban redevelopment is a generic term which is understood as an undertaking that encompasses:

> …urban renewal, upgrading and land reallocation with the view to alleviating urban problems, improving living standards and bringing about urban dynamism and efficient land utilization.[80]

[76] Published in the Reporter (Amharic), Dec. 26, 2012, vol. 18, No. 17, available: http://www.ethiopianreporter.com/news/293-news/8979-2012-12-26-06-21-45.html; Addis Fortune, Vol. 13, No. 661, http://addisfortune.net/s/new-agency-likely-to-administer-land-for-agricultural-investment/.

[77] See for example, the Preamble and Article 5 of the Investment Proclamation, supra note 74.

[78] UN-Habitat, supra note 142 in Chap. 2, p. 12.

[79] Interview with Ato Adem, supra note 30 in Chap. 1.

[80] FDRE Urban Planning Proclamation, supra note 59 in Chap. 6, Article 40(1).

Table 5.2 Amount of land collected and transferred in Addis Ababa City

Year	Total land collected in ha	Total land transferred in ha
2008/2009	1,252	Not known
2009/2010	1,314	584
2010/2011	Not known	909
2011/2012	1,632	1,611

Source Addis Ababa City year books and Addis Ababa City land bank

And urban renewal is defined as:

> ...an undertaking aimed at improving the living and working environment in an urban center through fully or partly removing dilapidated, blighted or derelict structures in an urban center.[81]

On the other hand, urban upgrading focuses on:

> ...the improvement of the living and working environment of slum areas by maintaining and partially removing of structures and through the provision of infrastructures and amenities.[82]

So, unlike urban renewal that requires the demolition and removal of slum areas, urban upgrading prefers to treat the urban area as it is. It tries to improve the living conditions of residents by the provision of utility services, opening up and maintenance of roads, and sometimes by the removal of certain buildings, if necessary. Hence, it strives to improve not only the physical environment but also the socio-economic status of the residents without displacing them from the area. This means, the extent of expropriation in the case of urban upgrading is minimal.

As shown in Table 5.2 above, every year, the city collects large amount of land into its land bank and develops or grants out to other developers more than half of what it had collected. In 2012/2013 fiscal year only, the city has started to redevelop 108 ha of land (56 ha "Aroge Kera", 40 ha Legehar and 12 ha around African Union) of which the large part is for renewal purpose.

Out of the land acquired and transferred in 2011/2012, 743 ha of land was used for construction of housing, 480 ha for industry, 73.3 for MSEs, and 21.7 is set to be transferred by lease. All these hectares of land were acquired in the expansion area, by expropriating surrounding farm lands. Further, a total of 314 ha of land was acquired from within the city center of which 58.37 is used for private investment, such as hotels and company buildings, and 255.63 ha of land is used for public offices, embassies, and other NGOs.[83]

---

[81] Id., Article 41.

[82] Id., Article 43.

[83] AACA 2012. *Addis Abbeba: Ye2003 Ametawi Metsihaf* (Addis Ababa: 2011/12 Year Book). Addis Ababa: Addis Ababa City Administration Communication Affaira Bureau.

The Addis Ababa City Roads Authority (AACRA) on its part has been engaging in the construction and maintenance of roads. In 2011/2012 fiscal year, it claimed that it demolished and removed 1,907 houses, 959 fences, 469 telecom poles, 440 electric poles, and 234 km of water pumps, for which it totally paid 152.2 million birr in compensation.[84] The current roads coverage of the city is 13 %, which the Authority plans to increase to 20 % by 2020.[85]

The Ethiopian Railway Corporation displaced 2,700 owners in Adama City of the Oromia Region[86] and requires unknown amount of land in the capital city to put 34 km light weight rail and to set up train stations.

In all the above cases, the common element is that expropriation is the only means to acquire land for it is illegal either to buy or exchange land in Ethiopia.

Elsewhere, in the other parts of the country as well, almost all urban land or the land in the periphery is being taken from private holders to cope with the pressure of rapid urbanization. For example, the city of Bahir Dar, the seat of the Amhara Region, is said to have developed and expanded five to six times of its original size within the past 10 years.[87] Its population, according to the 1994 census, was 96,000, while today it has surged up to more than 300,000 residents. This pattern has also been noted elsewhere in the country.[88] Urban planners create and revise master plans which need large amounts of land for their implementation. As a consequence, municipalities expropriate land from farmers who live around towns and cities.

5.4.4 The Question of Private Use as Public Purpose in Ethiopia

It has been stated that there are two approaches concerning the scope of public purpose: narrow and broad approaches based on the possibility of transferring land from one individual for the use of another individual. This section examines situation of transfer of land to private users in Ethiopia.

---

84 Rights of Way Claims 10pc of AACRA's Budget Last Year, *Addis Fortune*, Aug. 5, 2012, vol. 13, No. 640, http://www.addisfortune.com/Vol_13_No_640_Archive_Rights of Way Claims 10pc of AACRA's Budget Last Year.htm; Also see: http://www.ethiopianreporter.com/news/293-news/7357———157———.htm.

85 Ibid.

86 Reporter May, 12, 2012 http://www.ethiopianreporter.com/news/293-news/6340-2012-05-16-06-34-47.html.

87 Interview made with Ato Addisu Begashaw, supra note 34 in Chap. 4.

88 See the data of the Central Statistics Agency that shows the tenfold population increase in some major cities.

5.4.4.1 The Wisdom or Otherwise of Following the Broader Approach

The question that may be raised here is the extent of exercise of expropriation power when the land needed is for private use. To what extent should the government be allowed to use its expropriation power in taking private land right just to transfer it to another individual? As already mentioned, the existing expropriation proclamation has put a general clause that perceives public purpose as activity that gives "direct or indirect benefit" to the public. Besides, the clues which are supposed to serve as directions to identify projects that give "direct and indirect benefits" are very wide in nature. As mentioned above, the "urban structure plan" and the "development plan" that create "direct" public use or consolidate the "socio-economic development" are to be used to identify whether a certain proposed project qualifies as public purpose. There is no doubt that these unqualified standards provide the state a very wide discretion to condemn a property by expropriation.

The usual complaint raised by people who lost their land by expropriation is, among others, the fact that the property was transferred for private use. Of course, the Expropriation Proclamation, under Article 3(1) allows even private investors to benefit as far as they can use the land for *better development* activities. It has to be noted that what the law permits is the transfer of land for "private investors", and not "private persons". The idea is that the private investor could create some jobs, pay higher taxes and perhaps bring in hard currencies (if s/he is exporter.) But, even in that case, should the transfer of land from one individual to another individual for pure economic reasons be allowed? This is the very essence of the *Kelo* case that infuriated the general public in the USA. The Ethiopian Civil Code under Article 1464 specifically prohibits the expropriation of land for the purpose of solely obtaining financial benefit. But, at the moment, this provision has no relevance, for it is replaced by another provision of the current expropriation proclamation and is thereby null and void. Yet the wisdom incorporated in the Code shows that the Code gives better protection than the present law. The Civil Code represents Western inspired law and inevitably reflects those countries' strong sentiment toward private property. These days, however, the protection for private property accorded by the Code as well as the Constitution has not sustained its novelty in Ethiopia.

One may argue that Ethiopia needs huge investment (domestic and foreign) in order to maintain the fast economic growth witnessed in the past decade. For this reason, the laws should create easy access to land so that private investors may get land easily and cheaply. This means, the government should not be deterred by laws and procedures, such as the expropriation law, that hinder its progressive development programs.

The counter argument is, though, that this should not be made at the huge expense of individual property owners. Governments should be generous and kind enough to listen to the pains and sufferings of their citizens. The Ethiopian government usually praises and takes as a model the Chinese economic development.

But, the Chinese are now regretting the gross human and property right violations they made in the past in the name of development.[89]

Another possible argument in favor of the unlimited expropriation power of the government is that Ethiopia is not the only country where such type of power is granted to the state. As we already mentioned above, in most European laws as well, the public purpose/interest doctrine is too broad to allow the expropriation of private land for the primary benefit of another individual.

But, the problem is we do not have the same economic environment in Ethiopia as in Europe. The assumption taken in the developed countries is that the individual will be well-off at the end of the day, for they have good compensation systems. In Ethiopia, taking land from a farmer means leaving the farmer without an alternative livelihood. Furthermore, the property market in developed countries ensures that the compensated owner is able to purchase another comparable property. That is not the case in Ethiopia, where arable farm land is not subject to sale, and particularly scarce for those who wish to rent.

5.4.4.2 Some Examples of Expropriations for Private Use

Let us consider the following examples of expropriation. In the Amhara region, 5–10 km outside Bahir Dar City, farmers lost their land to horticulture investors.[90] What had been done was that when investors applied for land to produce fruits and exportable flowers, the government expropriated part of the fertile land and transferred same to those investors. In the Oromia region, as well, there are several cases of such nature. But, in the Oromia region, besides expropriation, there is another land acquisition mechanism for the investor namely, rent/lease. In this system, besides the land they acquire from government, investors usually rent land from farmers for fixed period of time and upon payment of fixed or progressive amount of rent.[91] Farmers may also benefit from working in the company as laborers. There are similar arrangements in the Amhara Region as well where urban investors rent land from farmers to grow *Chat* vegetation.[92] It is also a common practice in urban centers where investors purchase plots of land with houses over

---

[89] Forced evictions (Expropriations) are particularly common in rural areas of China, and are a major source of unrest and public protest (http://www.economist.com/node/4462719). By some estimates, up to 65 % of the 180,000 annual "mass incidents" in China stem from grievances over forced evictions (http://blogs.cfr.org/asia/2012/02/07/a-land-grab-epidemic-chinas-wonderful-world-of-wukans/). Citizens who resist or protest the evictions have reportedly been subjected to harassment, beatings, or detention.

[90] About 100 ha of land was given around Bahir Dar city in 2007/2008, which is still idle.

[91] Interview with Ato Teshome, Oromia Region, supra note 29 in Chap. 4.

[92] *Chat* is a mild narcotic leaf widely used in East African countries and in Yemen. Although it is not illegal to chew *Chat* in Ethiopia, it is nonetheless considered as immoral and government does not encourage growers, among others, by giving land for such kind of investment. For this reason, *Chat* growers rely on land rent that is contracted with farmers.

them and change such place to hotels or shops, whenever the plan allows. Now, the question is shouldn't we use expropriation as a last resort to acquire land?

Sheraton Addis[93] is the biggest hotel in Ethiopia in terms of size and quality. It was opened before a decade and located in Arada and Kirkos sub-cities. In fact, it is exactly found besides to the Basha Wolde Chilot area. In 2009 Sheraton requested the Addis Ababa city for more space to expand its business, and accordingly, it received 42 ha (420,000 m^2) of land. The land was acquired by expropriating all the surrounding land held by kebele tenants and private owners. The singularity of this case is related to its sheer land size expropriated and transferred. In order to benefit one company, more than a thousand households were displaced.

In one case,[94] an owner of a hotel wished to purchase a neighboring land (small residential house) to use it as parking lot. He offered the owner 300,000 birr for the house but the owner refused to sell her property. The hotel owner, afterwards, applied for expropriation of the neighboring land in order to expand his parking lots. Accordingly, the respective urban land administration started expropriation process and acquired the land for the hotel owner upon payment of 60,000 birr, one fifth of the previously offered price.

Kuriftu Hotel and Spa is a luxury hotel found in Bahir Dar City along the bank of Lake Tana, the largest highland lake in Ethiopia. The owner received the land on negotiation basis for a very cheap lease price. The place used to be a public park accessible to the urban community. Paradoxically, after its completion, the hotel became inaccessible to almost all the public. The owner introduced a new working procedure whereby only members who pay expensive membership fee are allowed its service. Non members may get access but up on payment of exorbitant fee, which in effect excludes ordinary members of the community. One may argue that this is against the very intention of expropriating that very land for public purpose to give direct and non-discriminatory access and service to the public.

In the *Rib* Irrigation Dam construction area, almost all the interviewee farmers (90 % of 45 interviewees) who lost their land to the construction of the reservoir dam objected to the public purpose nature of the project. This is because the water collected in the dam will harvest other farmers' land as the command area is located in *Fogera woreda,* 35 km far from the *Rib kebele* (the reservoir area.) When they were asked whether they believed that the dam would benefit society, one elderly person retorted:

> What is a public benefit that does not benefit us? We are the bystanders while the users are the people of Fogera.

[93] http://www.sheratonaddis.con.

[94] The story was related to the researcher by Ato Yalew Abate, former head of the ANRS Urban Works and Development Bureau in May 2011.

In another irrigation dam construction in *Koga*, in Amhara Region, the practice was to absorb the displaced people in the community who had been holding the command land. It means, those who lost their land to the reservoir were given land from the command (irrigable) land.[95] A land redistribution or readjustment of the command area was made so that those displaced farmers could get land. Unfortunately, this was not practiced in Rib. The government was reluctant to follow a similar approach in the Rib irrigation project perhaps because of the long distance between the reservoir and the command areas.[96]

5.4.5 The Role of Courts

The role of courts in determining the public purpose nature of a project or its subsequent revision is not clear. What is clear, so far, is that courts have the mandate to hear grievances concerning the amount of compensation.[97] In practice, as well, courts are entertaining grievances related to denial of compensation. But, the law says nothing about the involvement or role of courts in determining or revising the public purpose decision. As already mentioned in Sect. 5.2.2.1, the power to decide about the public purpose nature of a project is exclusively vested in the administrative/executive organ (*woreda* or urban administration or other higher administrative body.) Whether courts can hear cases that challenge the administrative decision on the public purpose nature is not clear since the law neither grants nor prohibits them from exercising such power. Yet, with the possibility of arguing otherwise, one may assert the existence of this power based on the following arguments.

In Ethiopia, at Federal as well as State levels, all "judicial powers are vested in the courts."[98] Judicial power, according to Black's Law Dictionary, is "A power involving exercise of judgment and discretion in determination of questions of right in specific cases affecting interests of persons or property…"[99] It means courts have the power to hear and give decisions on justiciable matters. And justiciable matter is a "matter appropriate for court review."[100] Expropriation affects one's property right, and any dispute associated with the loss of property right is clearly a justiciable matter qualified for court review. Expropriation, unless carried out properly, is an intrusion and a violation to one's property right, and if people believe the

[95] See the full discussion of the case in Daniel W. Ambaye, supra note 196 in Chap. 2, p. 27.

[96] Interview made with Ato Sintayehu Dires, head of Land Administration Work Flow, ANRS Bureau of Environmental Protection Land Administration and Use (BoEPLAU), December 26, 2012.

[97] See Article 11 of the Expropriation Proclamation No. 455/2005; Article 40 of Amhara Compensation Directive.

[98] FDRE Constitution, Article 79(1).

[99] Black's Law Dictionary.

[100] Ibid.

expropriation decision would not be for public purpose, they must be allowed to take their case to court of law.

The other argument is that in most cases, when the legislator does not want judicial review of an administrative decision, it clearly prohibits courts' involvement by affirming the administrative decision as final one. For example, in Tax, Labour, Pension, Lease etc. proclamations, the law encourages grievances to be settled by decisions of administrative tribunals whose decisions are final ones. It is argued that such type of an approach takes away courts' power. In any case, since we do not find this kind of provision in the current expropriation proclamation, it must be construed as if courts are allowed to review administrative decisions concerning public purpose.

Further, the Ethiopian Civil Procedure Code declares that the high court will have exclusive jurisdiction over "expropriation and collective exploitation property."[101] This rule is now partly revised in that the "exclusive" right of the High Court is given to a different hierarchy of courts based on the amount of money the case claims. This means, based on the amount of money the expropriation case involves, a case may be heard either by the high court or lower courts in hierarchy (*woreda* courts in regions or first instance courts at Federal level.) In other words, regular courts still have the jurisdiction to hear and entertain expropriation cases for there is nothing that repeals the rule under the Civil Procedure Code.

In spite of the above arguments, a systematic search by the researcher for cases challenging the public purpose nature of a project yielded to very few cases.[102] It appears to be that people do not challenge the very decision of the government on the development or investment activities; people rather focus on the compensation package to be provided. Interviews in Rib dam project area and Addis Ababa reveal that people do not dare challenging the government decision for different reasons: first, there is a fear of one being labeled as anti-development by political cadres and *kebele* officials, and second, most people still believe on the omnipotence of the state power which is summed up in the traditional saying "*Semay Aytares, Negus Aykeses*", neither the sky can be ploughed nor the king be sued. People suspect that suing the state and blocking its decisions would end up in nothing fruitful-that it is not possible to win the state in such matters for the judges are neither free nor courageous.

---

[101] Ethiopian Civil Procedure Code. *Negarit Gazeta-Extraordinary.* Decree No. 52/1965, Year 25, No. 3. Article 15(2), (e).

[102] One ideal case is the case of Tsegaye Meseret et al. v. Federal Roads Authority in which 79 plaintiffs challenged an expropriation of their land by the defendant on two counts: absence of public purpose and denial of compensation. The defendant expropriated 130,777 m^2 of land in order to expand its drivers training center. Plaintiffs complained that it was not amount to public purpose. But the courts simply rejected it because the decision was approved by the Ministry of Urban Works and Development. Even the Cassation Court, the highest appellate court, did not try to investigate whether it could be done through other ways, whether it was really necessary, whether it was more important compared to the displacement of 79 people and so on (See Federal Supreme Court Cassation Division, Cass. File No. 50810, October 2010).

5.5 Conclusion

The Ethiopian Constitution, as a principle, puts public purpose as a limitation on the government's action to expropriate private holdings. The reason behind this is to provide a minimum protection to be accorded to land holders. Yet, this principle is substantially eroded by the Federal Expropriation Proclamation which allows expropriation of land for "...direct and indirect..." benefit of the public.

The scope of application of public purpose in Ethiopia is hence a broader one, where it seems impossible to limit the expropriation power of the state. The definition by itself is neither clear enough to guide the decision makers nor consistent in its use of terminologies. The broader use of the term "public purpose" allows the government to employ its expropriation power without limit for whatever purposes it wishes. Rural and urban land is extensively taken for a variety of activities, including for commercial private use. As Justice O'Connor summed up (in her minority view in Kelo decision, Sect. 5.3.2 above) all property owners in Ethiopia, especially those who live in the city center and the verge of it are under perpetual threat of expropriation. Even those land holders in transition zone (between center and periphery) are, in principle, under the risk of losing their land, because someone with better economic means may claim their land for "better use" of it.

Worse, the role of courts in interpretation and restricting the administrative decision of public purpose is not known. The silence of the law may be interpreted in some quarters and by some courts as if courts are denied such power. In current Ethiopia where the independence of courts is not encouraging, the tendency will be that they may not "dare" to restrict the government from its decision of expropriation. Of course, lack of jurisprudence and precedents could also be other reasons for courts not to have clear stand on the subject.

Chapter 6
Valuation and Compensation During Expropriation

6.1 Introduction

Expropriation is a forced sale and is distinguished from confiscation in that the owner will be compensated for the property taken. Besides the requirement of public purpose, payment of compensation is the second, but equally important, limitation on the government's power of expropriation. This is a fact generally found in all legal systems of the world, whether private property is respected or not. This means, even in countries like China and Ethiopia, where the private ownership of land is not yet allowed, payment of compensation for the holder of rights on the property is recognized by law.

In this chapter two important concepts/processes of expropriation are addressed. The first one is valuation of property during expropriation, while the second one is compensation. Valuation is the means or the process to determine the amount of compensation and hence both have close relationship.

6.2 Valuation

6.2.1 Defining Valuation

Valuation is the process of determining the current worth of an asset, mostly real property. The terms valuation and appraisal are mostly used interchangeably, but in reality they have differences. Appraisal is the judgment, assessment and quantification of the real property. Valuation is required when a definitive value is needed, while appraisal is intended only as a guide to pricing. For this reason, appraisal is

D.W. Ambaye, *Land Rights and Expropriation in Ethiopia*,
Springer Theses, DOI 10.1007/978-3-319-14639-3_6

defined as the "preparation of an estimate or opinion of *value* of some object or thing."[1] Appraisals are estimated by knowledge of the local market recent sale prices and should only ever be used as estimates of price. They are not definitive and have no legal standing. On the other hand, value is defined as the "worth, usefulness, or utility of an object to someone for some purpose."[2] Although the usual type of value to be estimated in appraisal assignment is market value, there are other purposes as well such as taxation, mortgage and investment.[3]

6.2.2 Valuation Approaches

There are three common methods used to determine value of the property being appraised. These are the sales comparison approach, the income capitalization approach, and the cost approach. It is the task of the appraiser to choose one or a combination of two or all to get the value of a real property. A brief definition and analysis is given about the nature and purpose of each of the above mentioned valuation methods.

6.2.2.1 Sales Comparison Approach

Sales comparison approach is a valuation technique in which the value of the real property is determined by comparing the property recently sold in the "market" to the land being appraised. Comparable sales approach is the most common method of land valuation which relies on market information to value the property.[4] The underlying concept is that a recent sale from a willing seller to a willing buyer of a property (the comparable property) can best reflect the value of a similar land (the subject property) in the vicinity. This method models the behavior of the market by comparing the subject property under valuation with similar property or properties that have recently been sold, or for which offers to purchase have been made. It assumes that a rational and prudent buyer will not pay more for the comparable property, while a seller in the same situation will not accept less for the same property. The sales price finally reached reflects the equilibrium of supply and demand for properties in a given market.[5] Therefore, if the subject property under valuation were offered for sale in the same market about the same time, the transaction would be completed at approximately the same price.

---

[1] Betts, R. M. & Ely, S. J. 2008. *Basic Real Estate Appraisal: Principles and Procedures,* New York, Thomson South-Western, p. 2.

[2] Ibid.

[3] Id., p. 51.

[4] Id.

[5] Wyatt, P. 2005. *Property Valuation in an Economic Context,* Oxford, Wiley-Blackwell, p. 128.

6.2.2.2 Income Capitalization Approach

An alternative to the comparative sales approach, typically used in situations where markets are relatively inactive, is called the income (or capitalization of income) approach. It is most applicable to agricultural land and investment properties. In this approach, an appraiser analyzes a property's capacity to generate future benefits and capitalizes the income into an indication of present value. In other words, the value of the land derived from this approach is the estimated present value of future benefits, including streams of incomes during the lifetime of the property and proceeds from the sale of the property.

This valuation approach derives land or building value by dividing annual net income from the property by an estimated capitalization rate. Under the income approach, valuation of a property is accomplished through capitalization. Capitalization is the division of a present income by an appropriate capitalization rate to derive the value of the income stream.[6]

6.2.2.3 Cost Approach

The cost approach is the valuation technique in which appraisers add property value to the depreciated value of improvements so as to determine the value of the subject property. In this approach, the value of a property is derived by adding the estimated value of the land to the current cost of constructing a reproduction or replacement for the improvement and then subtracting the amount of depreciation.[7] There would also be allowances made for depreciation that shall be reduced from the total value. The appraiser would base the appraisal on what it would cost to replace the existing facilities.[8]

The replacement cost approach for structures in a typical developed country setting of active markets is based on the theory that the market value of an improved parcel can be estimated as the sum of the land value and the depreciated value of the improvements. In other words, this approach is based on the assumption that cost equals value. The reliability of the cost method depends on the validity of the assumption that cost and value are equal; however, there are many circumstances where such an assumption is not justified.

To appraise a property, using cost approach, appraisals require information on cost of land, cost of building (improvement), and cost of depreciation. The cost method valuation is based on the cost of building less depreciation plus the site value. The approach recognizes the value of the site for a particular use. But if there

---

[6] UNECE 1996. *Land Administration Guidlines,* Geneva, United Nations Economic Commission for Europe, p. 38.

[7] Appraisal-Institute 2001. *The Apprisal of Real Estate,* Chicago, Apprisal Institute, p. 63.

[8] Sayce, S., Smith, J., Cooper, R. & Rowland, P. V. 2006. *Real Estate Appraisal: From Value to Worth,* Oxford, Blackwell Publishing, p. 16.

is no market for land, then it is the cost of the building that is taken into account. This produces a value for a new building; older building costs will require an adjustment to represent depreciation (the wearing out of the building fabric) and obsolescence (the inability of older building to facilitate optimum performance, as expected by current standards of design and technology and the present-day economics of location and use).[9]

The cost approach begins with the determination of site value. Once site value has been determined, the next step is to determine the cost estimate. Costs consist of all expenditures necessary to complete construction of a house or other building, which is called replacement cost. Replacement cost of new improvements means "Estimated Cost as though New". The cost approach views the value of the building at its cost of reconstruction as new on date of value. Because the structure subject to valuation may have been built many years ago, it is often difficult to determine the costs incurred when the structure was built. Thus, estimation of costs is often based on two different bases—"replacement cost" or "reproduction cost." "Replacement cost" refers to the estimated cost to construct, at current prices as of the effective appraisal date, a substitute for the building being appraised using modern materials and current standards, design, and layout. "Reproduction cost", on the other hand, refers to the estimated cost to construct, at current prices as of the effective date of the appraisal, an exact duplicate or replica of the building being appraised, using the same materials, construction standards, design, layout, and quality of workmanship and embodying all the deficiencies, super adequacies, and obsolescence of the subject building.[10]

Total cost of all improvements is the sum of direct costs, indirect costs and entrepreneurial services. Direct costs are general expenditures required for labor and materials used for construction of building improvements whereas indirect costs are expenditures of items other than materials and labor that are necessary for construction but are not typically part of the construction activity. These indirect items can be architectural and engineering fees, appraisal, consulting, or legal fees during construction, and national or regional taxes during construction and administrative expenses. When estimating the current cost to replace a property by reference to the current prices of a property's labor and material components, it may be appropriate to add amounts for entrepreneurial services and other costs that would typically be incurred in bringing the property to a finished state.[11]

By way of conclusion, the best valuation is achieved when there is sufficient information to apply all three approaches. But the simple technique of averaging the value indication arrived at by the three approaches is not acceptable. An appraiser

---

[9] Issac, D. 2012. *Property Valuation Principles,* New York, Palgrave, p. 64.

[10] Ventolo, W. L. & Williams, M. R. 2001. *Fundamentals of Real Estate Appraisal*, Chicago, Dearborn Financial Publication, Kahr, J. & Thomsett, M. 2005. *Real Estate Market Valuation and Analysis*, New Jersey, John Wiley & Sons, p. 153.

[11] Wyatt, supra note 5.

must reconcile a value conclusion from the three approaches by considering the strengths and weakness of each and by judging the reliability of the individual approach in appraising the particular property.

6.3 Compensation

6.3.1 Nature and Justification

Compensation is defined as "full indemnity or remuneration for the loss or damage sustained by the owner of the property taken or injured for the public use."[12] The compensation requirement under the law demands that the expropriator reimburses the expropriated for the property interest taken and places the latter in as good a pecuniary position as if the property had not been taken.[13] The owner must be made whole but is not entitled to more. The ideal solution is to leave the owner in a position of indifference between the taking and retention of the property. Compensation may be made either in terms of substitution of the lost property or the financial equivalence of same. Although the first could be an ideal mode of compensation, practical realities make it impossible to practice. The common practice is, therefore, to pay the financial equivalence of the lost property. As already mentioned in relation to the valuation techniques, it is "the property and not the cost of it that is safeguarded by the state."[14] In other words, it is the value of the property, not its cost, which determines the amount of compensation to be paid.

The reason for payment of compensation is justified on socio-political and economic, theories. Compensation is a means to keep the balance of social justice. It protects the rights of the politically under-represented groups,[15] requiring the government to bear the inconveniences resulting from expropriation. Hence, it is argued that no single individual should bear the costs of government projects that are intended to be for the common good.[16] There is no strong reason to single out one individual and compel him to shoulder the entire burden for the benefit of the society at large. This also serves as a protection against arbitrary and unauthorized actions of the legislature or the executive branches of the government. As Joseph Sax has argued, a compensation guarantee serves as a check on self-interested acts of public authorities.[17] Another scholar also reflects:

---

[12] C.J.S., supra note 11 of Chap. 3.

[13] This position was held first by a USA Court (in Olson v. United States) and became an accepted principle in almost all countries. See details in Epstein, supra note 170 of Chap. 3, p. 182.

[14] Ibid.

[15] Ndjovu, C. E. 2003. *Compulsory Purchase in Tanzania: Bulldozing Property Rights.* Ph.D. Thesis, Kungl Tekniska Hogskolan, C.E. (2003), p. 21.

[16] Epstein, R. A. 1993. *Bargaining With The State,* New Jersey, Princeton University Press, p. 6.

[17] Sax, J. 1964. Takings and the Police Power. *Yale Law Journal,* 74, 36

> It is not by accident that provisions for compensation are found in the basic laws of some countries, rather than left to the will of the legislature or executive but to protect private property from an arbitrary taking of those groups.[18]

Economically speaking, if the government is forced to pay for what it acquires, this could discourage it from making unwise and foolish decisions.[19] It will always strive to make rational economic decisions that will bring beneficial development to all parties. In addition to this, the law has to give reasonable protection to the expectations of those who have relied on it. Should the law deny this protection and fail to protect property, owners might not be willing to take risks and invest on their properties, for the benefit may be reaped by others. Neither would banks be willing to lend money for such risky business.

6.3.2 Theories of Compensation

As stated above, there is no doubt that compensation must be paid during expropriation. However, with regard to the manner of valuation and extent of amount of compensation, legislations follow especially two principles: indemnity and taker's gain principles. To shed some light on these principles, an analysis of both contradicting theories is proper.

6.3.2.1 Indemnity Principle

Under the indemnity principle, which is also called "owner's loss" theory, the owner is entitled to be put in as good a pecuniary position as he would have been if his property had not been taken.[20] This principle is predominant in most western countries, though there are slight variations. It assumes that a "dispossessed owner would go out into the market and purchase with his compensation money a property roughly similar to that which had been acquired, any incidental loss or expense being met from the proceeds of the disturbance claims."[21]

In the United States, court decisions show that the compensation to be paid to the owner is not measured by the value of the land to the property taker.[22] In France, as in the USA, compensation does not reflect what the taker has gained, but rather, what the owner has lost. Moreover, its purpose is to compensate for the taking and

---

[18] Marcus, P. 1942. The Taking and Destruction of Property under a Defense and War Program. *Cornell Law Quarterly,* 27, p. 508.

[19] Ndjovu, supra note 15, p. 21.

[20] Kratovil and Harrison, supra note 6 Chap. 3, p. 615.

[21] Ndjovu, supra note 15, p. 20.

[22] McCormick, C. T. 1932. The Measure of Compensation in Eminent Domain. *Minn. L. Rev.,* 17. No. 5, p. 465.

not to directly pay the cost of equivalent reinstatement.[23] In France, therefore, in addition to the market value of the deprived property, loss of rent, trading loss, moving expenses, dismissal benefits, severance damages, and the like are also coverable, although the taker gets nothing from it. Similarly, in Sweden, the land owner and other parties affected by an expropriation are compensated on the basis of their loss; the gain made by the expropriator does not affect the award.[24] The only exception is during forced re-allotment, in which the owner may, in addition to the compensation for the injury of property, be awarded a *share of profit*[25] the lost property may give to the future owner. If the compensation does not fully cover the economic injury to the property owner, compensation shall also be paid for "other damages,"[26] which, in this case, refer to removal costs and business losses.

In England, in addition to the full compensation of the land acquired, the expropriating organ is also obliged to pay "compensation for disturbance of interest and compensation for severance and injurious affection."[27] Severance occurs when the physical taking of the part of a parcel of land depreciates the value of the remaining land. Injurious affection applies to the depreciation in the value of the remaining land caused by the construction of and use of the works for which the part was taken. Hence, to put the owner of the expropriated property in the same economic position, these laws consider, during the course of valuation, the loss of the property owner. Whether the expropriating organ gets much or little benefit from the taking does not matter.

6.3.2.2 Taker's Gain

The taker's gain theory holds that "the government should pay only for what it gets."[28] This argument stems from the fear that to allow compensation for such items, as disturbance of a business on the land or other similar remote damages would drain the purse of the government or other beneficiaries for that matter. It is said that although it may make the owner whole, if paid, compensation for consequential damages, such as the future loss of profits, expenses of moving fixtures and personal property, the loss of goodwill that inheres in the location, should not be paid.[29] This is because when the government or other expropriating organ takes

---

[23] Picard, supra note 76 of Chap. 3, p. 57.

[24] Bjerken, T. 1990. Expropriation in Sweden. *In:* Erasmus, G. M. (ed.) *Compensation for Expropriation: A Comparative Study.* Oxford: St. Edmund Hall University of Oxford, p. 129.

[25] Kalbro, supra note 44 of Chap. 5, p. 59.

[26] Kalbro, supra note 152 of Chap. 3, p. 34.

[27] Moore, V. 1990. Compulsory Purchase in the United Kingdom *In*: Erasmus, G. M. (ed.) *Compensation for Expropriation: A Comparative Study.* Oxford: National Committee of Comparative Law. Vol. I, p. 6.

[28] Kratovil and Harrison, supra note 6 of Chap. 3, p. 615.

[29] Ibid.

only the land, having no use for any business operated thereon, it should pay only for what it gets, which is, of course, the market value of the land.

A case in point is the Chinese compensation principle enshrined under Article 47 of the 1986 (as amended in 2004) Chinese Land Administration Law (LAL).[30] Paragraph 1 of Article 47 clearly states, "Land expropriated shall be compensated for on the basis of its original purpose of use." Indeed, the details of the compensation for expropriation of arable land show that the farmer receives no market value for the loss of land. Rather a lump sum of money calculated at 6–10 years annual production is provides besides other minor payments.[31]

The right to and extent of compensation amount is not mentioned in the Chinese Constitution.[32] The basic rational for using this principle in the PRC is that land is a collective property of the people, and individual persons are provided with "use right" for fixed period of time. So when the state expropriates land, what is taking is not private property, but use right. Or in other words, it is not expropriating but "resuming."[33] Therefore, "the compensation in the expropriation of land is not for ownership but for land use rights, and paying that compensation is based on the national policy."[34]

Both arguments try to answer the modalities of and elements that should be included in assessments of compensation. Today, with the emphasis given to properties around the world, the indemnity principle is prevailing.

6.3.3 Notions of "Market Value" and "Just" or "Fair" Compensation

Most laws (constitutions or other minor legislations) which allow expropriation of private property usually attach the requirement of the payment of compensation.

---

[30] The People's Republic of China Land Administration Law. Available at: http://www.npc.gov.cn/englishnpc/Law/2007-12/12/content_1383939.htm.

[31] See details infra, under Sect. 6.5.3.3.

[32] Bin, Z. X. 2002. Compensation System in the People's Republic of China. *In*: Kotaka, T. & Callies, D. L. (eds.) *Taking Land: Compulsory Purchase and Regulation in Asian-Pacific Countries*. Honolulu: University of Hawai'i Press, p. 93.

[33] Land expropriation refers to the case in which the government does not have ownership of the land. For example, the land occupant has the freehold interest in the land, and the government needs to acquire ownership of the land through a compulsory acquisition process. This kind of 'land acquisition' is also known as a 'compulsory purchase'. Compulsory 'land resumption' refers to the case in which the government, not the land occupants, has the ownership of the land. For example, the occupants only have a leasehold interest in the land. Through the compulsory acquisition process, the government acquires the user rights and gets back the land it originally owns. This kind of compulsory land acquisition is known as 'land resumption' (Chan, N. 2003. Land Acquisition Compensation in China – Problems & Answers. *International Real Estate Review*, 6., p. 138.).

[34] Id., p. 95.

Depending on the legislation of each country, it may be termed as compensation, fair compensation, just compensation, reasonable compensation, adequate compensation or any other, like ‘commensurate compensation’ in Ethiopia.

In most Western countries[35] and, as shown in Kitay, in most developing countries,[36] the fundamental principle that guides valuations under expropriation laws is the payment of *fair market price* or *market value*. In other words, *market value* is generally taken as a test for the existence of just compensation.

Market value, as defined in *Appraisal of Real Estate*, is:

> The most probable price, as of a specified date, in cash, or in terms equivalent to cash, or in other precisely revealed terms, for which the specified property rights should sell after reasonable exposure in a competitive market under all conditions requisite to a fair sale, with the buyer and seller each acting prudently, knowledgeably, and for self-interest, and assuming that neither is under undue duress.[37]

The reason why market value is favored by courts or legislators is that because it is believed that the amount of compensation is believed to cover the damage sustained by the owners. The amount of compensation will enable owners to go to the market and fetch similar/identical property for the same price. The former owner should neither suffer a detriment nor reap a windfall profit.

Under the indemnity principle, the measure of compensation where all of a person’s land is taken is the *market value* of the property as of the time of the taking. Where only a part of the land is taken, however, the compensation measure may be either of the following:

- Fair market value of the portion taken plus damages to the part not taken less any special benefits to the land not taken. This is the “value plus damages” rule.
- The measure may also be the difference between the market value of the entire tract before the taking and the market value of the remainder after the taking. This is the “before and after” rule.[38]

In the United States, especially in its courts, market value has further been classified into two concepts. As stated earlier, the market value of land is the amount that the property would be reasonably worth on the market in a cash sale to a willing buyer if offered for sale by a prudent and willing seller. This is called the “willing buyer-willing seller” test.[39] The buyer would not pay more than the value of his expectation from the use of the land. The other approach is that market value signifies that the price offered must be what a reasonable buyer would pay for

---

[35] The term “just compensation” in the USA Constitution is understood by courts as “fair market value” (Paul, supra note 63 of Chap. 3, p. 81); the same conclusion is held in Europe as observed from the decisions of European Court of Human Right (Allen, T. 2007. Compensation for Property Under the European Convention of Human Rights. *Michigan Journal of International Law,* 28, 287–335, p. 288).

[36] Kitay, supra note 14 of Chap. 3, p. 50.

[37] Appraisal Institute, supra note 7, p. 22.

[38] Wright, R. R. & Gitelman, M. 2000. *Land Use in a Nutshell* Minnosota West Groups, p. 157.

[39] Id., p. 158.

the highest and best use of the land. This is "the highest and best use" rule.[40] The idea is that if the highest and best use of the land is, for example, for urban housing, the valuation must be based on the value of urban housing development even if the land is currently undeveloped. Thus, if farm land on the borders of a city is to be valued, the fact that it could be profitably subdivided into lots is relevant.[41] This means, high compensation must be paid. Today, in the United States, the fair market value of the land for its highest and best available use is said to be the standard measure of compensation.[42]

6.3.4 *Import of Qualifying Adjectives*

The other point worth discussing in relation to compensation is whether or not the absence or presence of words like "just", "fair" or "commensurate" can cause any substantive change in the concept of compensation itself. Can the word "compensation" fully stand on itself, without additional words like "fair" or "just"? As already mentioned, the term "compensation" is generally understood as the "full monetary equivalent of the property taken" and its purpose is to leave the owner unharmed to the maximum extent possible from government action. On the basis of this, some argue that since the idea of compensation itself implies a full and complete recompense, the word "just" apparently was added in order to emphasize the equality required of the exchange.[43] It seems, thus, the words "just," "fair," etc. are mere technical words having no legal significance. Quoting a prominent lawyer in the area under discussion, Roger M. Sullivan said: "these words are merely epithets rather than qualifications and add nothing to meaning."[44] Hence, different adjectives added to the word compensation are there only to give more emphasis rather than having separate legal significance. In the same way, the addition of words such as appropriate or commensurate in Ethiopian laws would not change the meaning of compensation as it is understood elsewhere.

---

40 Ibid.

41 McCormick, supra note 22, p. 462.

42 Id., p. 461; Paul, supra note 63 of Chap. 3, p. 81; Kratovil and Harrison, supra note 6 of Chap. 3, p. 616.

43 Alabama Section, supra note 94 of Chap. 3, p. 418.

44 Sullivan, R. M. 1990. Eminent Domain in the United States: An Overview of Federal Condemnation Proceedings *In*: Erasmus, G. M. (ed.) *Compensation for Expropriation: A Comparative Study*. Oxford: St. Edmund Hall University of Oxford. Vol. I, p. 166.

6.3.5 *Fairness and Objectivity of Market Value*

Researchers always question whether market value is really the fair and objective measure to determine compensation for expropriation.[45] Although market value is taken as the most probable price that reflects the loss, it nevertheless is not an ideal one that gives full compensation to the losers of the property. The central difficulty of the market value formula for compensation is that it denies any compensation for real but subjective values.[46] Kalbro calls these subjective values as "individual values" or "reservation prices."[47] A reservation price is defined as, "the lowest price at which a property owner would sale the property without the threat of expropriation."[48] Reservation prices are, in short, those prices an owner would put for non-monetary values he has on the property, such as sentimental attachment, family history, and similar personal values. Further, the purpose of the expropriation may also be another factor that alters the reservation value. It is argued that if people believe that the purpose is for social and public benefit, they tend to agree for lower compensation. On the contrary, if the land required is for private operators, such as Telecom Company, owners demand higher compensation amounts.[49] In general, since these sentiments have no monetary values, they are not considered during valuation. It is important to note that the market value for a given property can only be *assessed* or estimated, not calculated or exactly determined. Had the owner been allowed to fix the price, s/he would have added the subjective or personal price on top of the market value. For this reason, it is said that market value does not give full compensation.[50]

To tackle these problems, Epstein proposed fixing the amount of compensation somewhere between the market value and the reservation price of the owner.[51] But since this approach still creates ambiguity about the amount, the same writer provided another solution. He proposed a bonus increase over the market value.[52] This proposal is now adapted by some countries that have included it in their legislations. The mechanism is to increase a percentage over the market value assessed by the valuator. For example, for many years now, a 10 % bonus is allowed in England to those who lost their property by compulsory purchase.[53] In addition to the fair market value for the property, home owners get 10 % of the value of the home

---

[45] Norell, L. 2008. Is the Market Value a Fair and Objective Measure for Determining Compensation for Compulsory Purchase. *Land Reform.* Rome: FAO, p. 26.

[46] Epstein, supra note 175 of Chap. 3, p. 183.

[47] Kalbro, supra note 44 of Chap. 5, p. 59.

[48] Norell, supra note 45, p. 21.

[49] Kalbro, supra note 44 of Chap. 5, p. 60.

[50] Norell, supra note 45, p. 21; Kalbro, supra note 44 of Chap. 5, p. 59, 60.

[51] Epstein, supra note 175 of Chap. 3, p. 183.

[52] Ibid.

[53] Id., p. 184; Comments 1958. Eminent Domain Valuations in an Age of Redevelopment: Incidental Losses. *Yale Law Journal,* 67, p. 66.

subject to a minimum of £4,000 and a maximum of £40,000; for businesses, the amount is 7.5 % up to a maximum of £75,000.[54] A recent legislation in Sweden as well allows for a 25 % increase to the market value.[55] The percentage increase over the market price will enable owners to acquire the lost property and regain part of the reserved price.

A slightly different but discriminatory approach concerning the increase on the market value is also proposed by Kalbro and Epstein. This approach proposes that instead of increasing the reserved price across the board, it is possible to impose the increase only in the case of private uses. If the expropriation is made for the interest of the public, the owner will be satisfied by the compensation of the market value, but if it is made for private economic gains, then an increase, in the form of profit sharing, can be made.[56]

6.4 Valuation and Compensation in Ethiopia

The valuation process, whereby compensation is fixed according to law, is generally the most difficult, time consuming, and litigated part of the expropriation process.[57] A proper valuation process is the most important step for the land owner as that is the means to reach a just compensation. In Ethiopia, most of the complaints and litigations related to expropriation are related to the inadequacy of compensation and the irregularities followed during the valuation process. Before looking into such cases, it is proper first to deal with the valuation methods applied and the compensable interests considered.

6.4.1 The Compensation Principle

The compensation principle in Ethiopia is not clear. But one thing to say is that it does not fit to the indemnity principle which gives an equal or equivalent amount of compensation to the loss sustained by the owner of the expropriated property.

The defunct Ethiopian Civil Code Section on expropriation has provided something that looks like an indemnity principle. Article 1474(1) of the Code says that the amount of compensation or the value of the land that may be given to replace the expropriated land shall be "equal to the amount of the actual damage caused by expropriation." Yet this does not cover the potential damages, such as

---

[54] Allen: 2008, supra note 49 of Chap. 5, p. 84; see also the British Land Compensation Act of 1973, ss 29–30, 33.

[55] An Amendment to the Swedish Expropriation Act, SFS 2010:832, July 2010.

[56] Kalbro, supra note 84 of Chap. 5, p. 60; Epstein, supra note 175 of Chap. 3, p. 184.

[57] Kitay, supra note 14 of Chap. 3, p. 50.

future highest and best use of land values.[58] The Civil Code interests only on actual and real damages caused when the land was expropriated.

The current FDRE Constitution under Sub-Article 8 of Article 40 provides for advance payment of "commensurate" amount of compensation to the loss of private properties. But the constitution does not recognize land as a private property. What is considered as private property in the constitution is any other property planted or erected on the land by the skill, labor or capital of the person (Sub-Article 1). Therefore, the objects of compensation under the present legal regime are buildings, plants and other similar things, save the ground or land itself. This means the compensation valuation does not consider, among others, the value of location, and this significantly reduces the amount of compensation payable to the owner. Rather in my opinion the principle followed in today's Ethiopia is the "taker's gain" principle which stresses that the compensation paid must consider the original or undeveloped purpose of use of the land rather than its futuristic potential.

As shall be discussed in detail in this chapter, this fallacy is created because of the conflicting sub-articles of Article 40 of the FDRE Constitution. The constitution on the one hand creates the joint ownership of land by the people and the state, but on the other it denies the holder a market based compensation for the land in the event of expropriation.

6.4.2 Valuation Method

As already discussed, there are three common valuation methods: the sales comparison approach, the income capitalization approach and the cost approach. The choice of valuation method will depend upon the purpose of valuation, type of interest being appraised, type of property, physical and other features of the property, availability of relevant data, and government regulations. This section investigates whether they all are and can be applied in Ethiopia.

The valuation method followed in Ethiopia for the purpose of estimating the amount of compensation is the "cost approach."[59] In this approach, value is estimated as what it would cost to replace the structure. There are two methods of estimating this: the *reproduction cost* (cost of duplicating the subject property's structure completely) and the *replacement cost* (cost of building a similar structure, but using modern construction methods and materials). When estimating building costs, the appraiser can either use replacement costs or reproduction costs. Although there is no clear cut standard in selecting reproduction or replacement costs, the replacement cost is the approach required in Ethiopian laws. This is inferred from the reading of Article 7(2) of the Expropriation Proclamation which states:

[58] The indemnity theory pays, among others, the loss of future highest and best use of the land.

[59] See Article 7(2) of the FDRE Expropriation Proclamation.

> The amount of compensation for property situated on the expropriated land shall be determined on the basis of replacement cost of the property.

The proclamation left the details of the valuation formula to be developed by the Council of Ministers. Accordingly, the Council of Ministers passed a regulation (No. 135/2007) that provided details on the method of assessing different interests affected by the expropriation. Assessors are required to follow the legal provisions in estimating the replacement costs of each property on the land.

Structure or building can be valued by applying either comparable sales approach or income capitalization or cost approach. The sale comparison is the main method for determining the value of single-family homes. If the structures are primarily for investment or income-producing purposes, the income approach is sometimes used. But, if market data is insufficient and property does not generate income, the preferred valuation method for structures is usually the replacement cost method. However, in Ethiopia the laws clearly stipulate that regardless of the type of property expropriated, the amount of compensation shall be determined only on the basis of replacement cost of the property.[60] This implies that unlike appraisers elsewhere, who are at liberty to follow one or more valuation methods, in Ethiopia, the replacement cost approach is the only method to be adhered.

Comparative sales approach or income capitalization are unknown by property appraisers in Ethiopia. This may be ascribed to the fact that property valuation process for compensation purpose only requires estimation of costs of structure or building. Estimating value of the land or site is not needed. Land is state and public property and has no value to the holder. It is an obvious fact that the cost replacement approach cannot give a market value for every type of property.

The economic interpretation of the above provision implies that replacement cost approach estimates the present cost of building a structure that is same or similar to the existing structure under assessment, with a subtraction of accrued depreciation from the total present cost of the substituted structure. Property valuators reduce depreciation allowance after finding the cost of a new building of similar nature. However, there is no provision in the Expropriation Proclamation that indicates how accrued depreciation could be estimated. Moreover, the proclamation does not explicitly put the fate of value of salvage materials from the destroyed structure: whether or not it should be deducted when this approach is used for structures.

Although the reason for the exclusion of the other methods for valuation is not known, we discuss hereunder the problems appraisers might encounter if they try to apply income or comparative sales approach. In order for an appraiser to apply the sales approach, s/he needs to know market prices of sufficient number of properties comparable to the one being valued. The value of a subject is determined by using recent sales of similar properties. Because no two properties are exactly alike, the sales prices of the comparable properties must be adjusted up or down for each of the differences between the subject property and the comparable properties.

---

[60] See generally Article 7 of the FDRE Expropriation Proclamation and FDRE Compensation Regulation No. 135/2007.

Therefore, this approach also needs some common variable that can be used to standardize the price of comparable properties. It is also important to note that when comparing different properties, not only must the differences in the properties, such as the actual structures, its ages, and conditions be compared and accounted for, but also what property rights are being transferred or were transferred in the comparable properties, and also any differences in encumbrances must be considered. In general, sales comparison method is easier to use whenever there is recent sales transaction of similar properties carried out in the locality. The appraiser would also be provided with full and updated data on the history of the property, the types of rights and encumbrances the owner has over the property.

In Ethiopia, the value of property cannot be estimated by looking at how much the market prices are "similar" or "comparable". Absence of modern real property registration and cadastre, non-transparency of the real property market system, and absence of systematically organized data makes the work difficult for the appraisers. In other words, appraisers could not get all necessary data from the market that is important for application of sale comparison approach. Therefore, what we need first is to lay modern real property registration and cadastral system that keeps and disseminates all data concerning transaction, price, property history, etc.

When we examine the income approach, it assumes that every property has an intrinsic value that can be estimated, based upon its characteristics in terms of cash flows, growth and risk. The attempts to estimate intrinsic value requires far more inputs and information than other valuation approaches. To use income capitalization, one needs to estimate the life of the property, the cash flows during the lifetime of the property, and the discount rate to apply to these cash flows to get present value. These inputs and information are not only abstract and difficult to estimate, but can also be manipulated by the savvy analyst to provide the conclusion he or she wants. Therefore, the income capitalization approach works best for investors who have a long time horizon, allowing the market time to correct its valuation mistakes and for price to revert to "true" value or are capable of providing the catalyst needed to move price to value. The income capitalization approach also works best for properties the cash flows of which are estimated with some reliability for future periods, and where a proxy for risk that can be used to obtain discount rates is available.

Unfortunately, there is no "easy way" of applying income capitalization approach in Ethiopia. On the one hand, this approach is limited because the income estimates capabilities of investors are weak; cash flow cannot be estimated with some reliability for future periods. This means there are uncertainties about the amount of income that one may generate in the years to come. On the other hand, sales data is not available to extract or confirm capitalization rates, and buyers consider other issues more than the property's income potential. Since the land has no value (no location value), it is difficult to conclude that the income generated is solely coming from the building only.

6.4.3 Assessors

The other issue related to valuation is the qualification and expertise of professional assessors. Existing experience shows that professionals who practice valuation are largely ignorant of basic approaches of valuation, have no special training and have not even gone through short courses or trainings on property valuation. This has caused difficultly in adopting other alternative approaches to valuation. Because of the lack of education as well as the former property right system (especially the fact that private property had little value during the Marxist era), professional real property valuators are unknown in the country. Even today, 20 years after the fall of the Marxist regime, there is no sign of their existence.

The reality on the ground demonstrates that valuations are suffering as current gaps in the system have led to inadequacy of compensation, corruption,[61] and accelerating number of cases reporting of appeals in courts.[62] This implies that there should be a mechanism by which fair property valuation can be carried out in order to balance the public and private interests.

As a matter of fact, valuation may be "carried out by certified private or public institutions or individual consultants on the basis of valuation formula adopted at the national level."[63] But the capacity is not yet created, and "until the Ministry of Federal Affairs, in consultation with the appropriate federal and regional government organs, ascertains the creation of the required capacity to take valuation of property … such valuation shall be carried out by committees to be established" by respective rural woreda or urban administrations.[64]

As already mentioned in the previous chapters, the rural woreda administration or the urban municipal administration is empowered with the expropriation of land for public purposes. Therefore, like in the other stages, it is empowered to coordinate the valuation process as well. The idea is that if there are expert valuators in the market, the administration may hire them. Currently, however, the rural and urban administrations simply use locally available experts or elders. In rural areas, the woreda is expected to establish a committee of five people who have relevant knowledge.[65] The woreda administrator appoints the chairman of the committee. Usually, the committee consists of one local elder, a representative of the local land administration office, a representative of agricultural office, a representative of trade

---

[61] The Ethiopia ethic and Anti corruption Commission has in its study declared that the valuation system during expropriation is "exposed to awkward system and vulnerable to corruption." See details at: http://www.ethpress.gov.et/herald/index.php/herald/news/1104-land-exploration-compensation-problematic-commission.

[62] Interview with Ato Yeneneh Simegn, Supreme Court President of Amhara Region; Interview with Ato Almaw Wole, Federal Supreme Court Judge; Interview with Ato Birhanu, supra note 33 of Chap. 4. All judges confirmed that there are increasing number of expropriation cases, most of which are related to inadequacy of compensation.

[63] Federal Expropriation Proclamation, Article 9(1).

[64] Id., Article 9(2) cum. 10(1), (2).

[65] Id., Article 10(1).

and industry office and another person selected by the woreda.[66] The local elder assists the committee in identifying plots and owners; the representatives from agriculture and the trade office are knowledgeable in local market value of crops, trees and building materials; and the representative from land administration office provides data about plots and owners. The proclamation delegates regional governments to come up with the details of the powers and responsibilities of the valuation committee. Today, concerning rural land, only the Amhara region has adopted a detailed directive[67] dealing with valuation process and the responsibilities of the woreda and the valuation committee. The directive provides the roles and responsibilities of the committee as follows.

The responsibilities of the woreda are to[68]:

- Set up a valuation committee that is constituted of 5 people with relevant knowledge in land measurement, counting, valuation;
- Assign chairman and secretary of the committee;
- Determine time and place of valuation work;
- Ensure that proper documentation is being taken by the committee;
- Follow that compensation is paid, replacement land is given, etc. to the expropriated person
- Inform land holders, neighbors, and kebele officials to attend inventory and measurement events;
- Approve the compensation amount assessed by the committee and inform same to implementing agencies and paying organs;
- Serves notice to the affected people;
- Etc.

The responsibilities of the Valuation Committee[69] are to:

- Explain the purpose of valuation to property holders;
- Record and take inventory of land use, size, and productivity level; identity of land holders and their legal right on the land; improvement on the land such as house, fence, terrace, water well, trees, crops etc. in the presence of the holder and neighboring people as well as representative of the local woreda land administration desk officer;
- Ensure the presence of land holders and neighbors during land measurement and inventory of assets;
- Make all members of committee and owners of assets sign on the inventory documented
- Present the outcome of the inventory to the public for approval;
- Get necessary data on productivity of previous years from relevant sector offices;

---

[66] Interview with Ato Mihret and Ato Teshome, supra note 11 and 29 of Chap. 4 respectively.

[67] Amhara Valuation Directive.

[68] Id., Article 33.

[69] Id., Article 32.

- Analyze and calculate the amount of compensation without revealing it to anyone;
- Finalize the valuation and send the result with all the necessary document and minutes to the woreda administration.

6.5 Compensable Interests and Determination of Compensation

6.5.1 Compensable Interests

In this section the terminology “compensable interests” refers to those property rights which are affected by expropriation and thus qualify for compensation. The key legal provisions in this discussion are Articles 7 and 8 of the Expropriation Proclamation and a large part of the Compensation Regulation No. 135/2007. A general reading of the Proclamation and the Regulation reveals that the following interests are compensable.

- A property situated on the land
- Permanent improvements to the land
- Loss of land
- Relocation of property
- Lost income, in case of temporary loss of land

To further elaborate these interests, we divide them into three groups: loss of private property, loss of landholding, and relocation of properties incurred for transportation and erection. In this section, their nature will be examined and in the next, their manner of estimation shall be addressed.

6.5.1.1 Private Properties (Properties and Improvements on and to the Land)

As discussed earlier (Sect. 2.6.3), the FDRE Constitution recognizes all properties situated on the land as private properties. And according to Article 7(1) of the Expropriation Proclamation, “A landholder whose holding has been expropriated shall be entitled to payment of compensation for his property situated on the land and for permanent improvements he made to such land.” While *property situated on the land* refers to building, structure or plants of any kind that have value, *improvement to the land* refers to any work made on the land that increases the value, productivity, or fertility of the land.[70]

[70] These definitions are given based on the type and nature of properties mentioned in the Expropriation Proclamation (455/2005), Federal Compensation Regulation (135/2007), Addis Ababa Valuation Directive, and the Amhara Valuation Directive.

In urban areas, *properties situated on the land* include buildings (residential, commercial, and industrial), fence, utility lines, religious buildings, burial structures, tree plants, and other structures. In rural areas, residential houses, farm houses, storage houses, livestock sheds and shelters, fence, trees, crops and grass are considered as properties situated on the land. This can be inferred from the readings of the Compensation Regulation 135/2007 and the Amhara Compensation Directive.

When one looks into *improvements to the land,* based on the above definition, facilities (water and sewerage, streets etc.) and area beautification may be considered as improvements to the land in the case of urban areas. In rural areas, land terracing, clearance and leveling works, irrigation canals and ducts, and water wells and reservoirs are examples of improvements to the land which cost the holder for their construction.

6.5.1.2 Land

The other property interest subject to compensation is the loss of the land itself. This is especially visible during the loss of rural land. The Expropriation Proclamation orders, under Article 8, that "displacement compensation" should be paid in the event of complete loss of the farm land by way of expropriation. This means that in the absence of replacement land in the locality, the holder of the land shall receive *displacement compensation*. The question one may raise here is the nature of displacement compensation; is it compensation in its proper sense? Or whether it is a kind of rehabilitation support? Determining its nature helps us to judge later the fairness of the compensation provided for the complete loss of the landholding.

One may wrongly conceive the *displacement compensation* as compensation similar to those which are paid for the loss of private properties. But I differ from this conception for the reasons discussed below.

As already discussed earlier (Sect. 2.6.3), the Ethiopian Constitution recognizes any property on the land as private property but not the land itself. Owners of property on the land are guaranteed with *commensurate* compensation to the loss of their private property in the event of expropriation.[71] The Constitution doesn't say anything about the loss of land. In other words, government is not supposed to pay commensurate compensation for loss of land. Besides, "compensation" is defined in the Expropriation Proclamation as "payment to be made in cash or in kind or in both to a person for his property situated on his expropriated landholding" (Article 2.1). Further, Article 7(1) of the same proclamation adds *improvement to the land* (besides the property on the land) as interests subject to commensurate compensation.

So, what is really the subject of commensurate compensation is the private property (property situated on the land and improvement to the land) and not the land. As shall be discussed in the section that follows, the modality of

[71] FDRE Constitution, Article 40(8).

compensation for complete loss of rural land is "replacement of land" or "displacement compensation", a monetary compensation equivalent to 10 years income. It can be easily inferred from the name that what is given to the peasant for loss of land is not compensation for lost private property (for land cannot be owned privately), but a compensation to assist a displaced person to rehabilitate against the loss of the perpetual use rights of land in another type of life style. Although the 10 years' value of produce has no basic justification, at least it is believed that such amount of money would be enough to enable the farmer to start a new way of life.

6.5.1.3 Relocation Properties

The Compensation Regulation allows the payment of relocation compensation, a compensation paid in association with the cost incurred for removing, transferring, transporting and installing one's property. There are three things which fall under this category: utilities,[72] relocated properties[73] and graves.[74] To avoid confusion, relocation of a house means the salvages of the demolished house and the furniture. In some cases, the house could be reinstalled if it can continue its service as before. For example, in the case of Allan Potash,[75] which is currently operating in the Afar region, the company has paid compensation for reinstallation of homes. The people living in the expropriated mining area were pastoralists who live in simple movable sheds. What was expected from the company was, therefore, to cover the cost of moving and reinstalling these temporary homes at the replacement land.

6.5.2 Determination of Compensation in Urban Areas

In determining the amount of compensation, there are different techniques and methods applied. Besides, there are differences in the compensation packages concerning the expropriation of urban and rural land. Therefore, for the sake of clarity and in order to avoid confusion, in this section the determination of compensation for urban areas is examined while in the next section the case of the rural land shall be investigated. Finally a third section is added to discuss the modality of compensation in peri-urban areas, an area considered neither as urban nor a rural one.

The kinds of properties found in urban areas are buildings (houses and fences), utilities, graveyards, and plants (trees, permanent plants, crops, and grass).[76]

[72] Federal Compensation Regulation, Article 3.2.b.

[73] Id., Article 10.

[74] Id., Article 12.

[75] Allana, supra note 46 of Chap. 4.

[76] Look the Addis Ababa Valuation Directive, Article 16 which lists down the types of compensable properties.

Generally, it is said that the amount of compensation for property situated on the land should be determined on the basis of replacement cost.[77] However, for those unique properties which cannot be replaced, such as trees, crops and grass, the valuation regulation provides a onetime market value prices. Compensation for permanent improvement to the land are calculated based on the amount of capital and cost for labor expended.[78]

If an urban resident loses a house by way of expropriation, at least s/he shall get the following six types of compensations:

A. Cost of construction (material + labor),
B. Compensation for improvements to the land,
C. Compensation for plants,
D. Replacement land,
E. One year's house rent, and
F. Cost of relocation.

For the sake of convenience, the above list is classified and discussed in three parts. In order to avoid redundancy, compensation for plants is examined in the sub-section that deals with the *rural compensation.*

6.5.2.1 Cost of Construction and Permanent Improvements

The Federal Compensation Regulation (135/2007) under Article 3(1) states that "the compensation for a building shall be determined on the basis of the current cost per square meter or unit for constructing a comparable building." Similar principle also applies for estimating a fence (Article 4). If part of a building is demolished and renders the remaining part useless for the purpose it was intended, or the owner wishes to surrender the rest of the land, then compensation shall be paid for the whole property (Article 3.3). If, however, the owner prefers to keep the remaining part, compensation will be paid only for the demolished portion (Article 3.4). No compensation shall be paid for the part of land taken; it only applies for the building. In other words, there is no "severance compensation", compensation payable for the depreciation in value of a retained land caused as a result of a loss of a part of the land.

In estimating the compensation of buildings, appraisers should consider the building/house itself, floor tiles of the compound, septic tank and other structures attached to the land (Article 3.2.a). Besides, the appraisers are required to estimate cost for demolishing, lifting, reconstructing, installing and connecting utility lines of the building (Article 3.2.b).

In calculating cost of construction and improvements, valuators are required to consider two basic components: *current cost of construction materials* and *labor.*

[77] Article 7(2) of Federal Expropriation Proclamation.

[78] Id., Article 7(4).

Neither the proclamation nor the regulation mentions whether depreciation allowance should be reduced from the cost of the new building to replace. However, in practice valuators deduct depreciation allowance when they estimate the construction cost of a building.

The practice is that a central price index is prepared by the city administration (in Addis Ababa) or Urban Works and Development Bureau (in regional states). This price index that shows the current price of construction materials and labor cost is then distributed to each sub-city (in Addis Ababa) and town (in regions). The problem identified during our investigation was that the price index has not been updated frequently, in spite of increases in material prices and workmen's wages. The prices were supposed to be updated every 6 months, but the indexes we found in Addis Ababa were in place for more than 2 years without being updated. The last price index updated was in 2010,[79] though inflation at the time was galloping at a double digit rate.[80] This makes the amount of compensation calculated unfair because the failure to update such lists makes their significance to the valuation process questionable.

The other controversial issue is the reduction of the depreciation allowance. The practice is that appraisers first estimate the construction cost of a new building. Then they reduce depreciation allowance based on the age of the house. Since most of the houses in the city center (in our study area in Addis Ababa) were old and made of mud, the amount of compensation paid was not enough to construct replacement buildings. The master plan does not either allow the construction of houses from mud or similar sub-standard materials. So, even though the compensation paid is for low-standard houses, people are required to build standard quality houses. Of all those I interviewed, none was satisfied by the amount of compensation.[81] The reason is very simple; it does not even cover half of the construction cost of a similar asset.[82] For this reason, as shall be discussed, people in urban areas mostly prefer condominium houses to replacement of land, although the latter is more valuable to them.

One may ask what is wrong with the reduction of depreciation allowance since that is part of the *replacement cost* valuation method. It is true that in the *replacement cost* valuation method discussed earlier, one of the stages is subtracting

[79] Interview made with Ato Daniel and Ato Mikias, supra note 18 and 25 of Chap. 4 respectively.

[80] According to the Ethiopian Central Statics Agency (CSA) and the Ethiopian Government assessments, irrespective of the impressive economic developments exhibited in the past several years, inflation still remains as the biggest challenge for policy makers. Inflation for food was reached 44 % in 2011 while it is reduced to 32 in 2013.

[81] This conclusion was drawn from the group discussions made in Addis Ababa, the Basha Wolde Chilot displaced and in Bahir Dar city the Abay River Bank people.

[82] This sentiment is also shared by the valuators themselves. The people, as a matter of fact, do not oppose the development work, what they oppose is the insufficiency of the compensation. What are they supposed to do with half or quarter of the compensation money necessary to build the house (Interviews made with Ato Daniel, Ato Mikias, supra note 18 and 25 of Chap. 4 respectively).

depreciation allowance from the total estimated amount, i.e. construction cost and the land value. But the difference between this approach and the one used in Ethiopia is that in Ethiopia valuators do not add the value of the land. In fact, replacement land is given in Ethiopia. But since the land has no value, location is not considered during valuation. On the contrary, during sale of a house, location is considered and owners get very good price (market price) for their buildings.[83] The sales price enables owners to buy similar properties in a similar location. The compensation packages do not give a replacement house or land (in location).

The other discrepancy between the law and the practice is that the law requires the payment of utility connection. This means, since customers are required to pay connection fees, it is only rational to include this fee as compensation during the valuation process. But in some areas, the municipality rather retains (if it pays the compensation) or receives (if another organ pays the compensation) the utility connection compensation. Such was the case, for example, in Bahir Dar City in which the Regional Government expropriated land to build modern conference hall and an office for the regional governor and council. People who were displaced from the area alleged that they did not receive the utility connection compensation; it was rather the municipality that received it claiming that it was it, in the first place, that laid the connection for free.[84]

6.5.2.2 Replacement Land and Displacement Compensation (Rent)

One of the elements in the compensation package for a displaced urban resident is the provision of replacement land to construct a house. Besides, a 1 year's house rent is provided as displacement compensation.[85] The assumption is that until they finish constructing their houses, the displaced people would stay in rental houses. In calculating the amount of rent, the Addis Ababa City Valuation Directive considers two factors: amount of compensation paid and the land size the displaced person possessed. The method of calculation is provided in Table 6.1. Although it does not reflect the market price of the rental market, the amount of rent being provided is considered as fair by many.[86] If people choose condominium houses and the

[83] A very good example to describe this situation is to look into the property market. In a typical English news paper (Addis Fortune or Capital-the two large weekly English newspapers) one can find advertisements for sale of houses, such as this one "HOUSE FOR SALE. ADDRESS: BOLE. PRICE 4 MILLION. HOUSE TO BE DEMOLISHED." It means the house is old and probably made of mud and wood, and a person who pays 4 million is expected to put better house on the land. Therefore, the buyer is paying 4 million not for the old and would be demolished house, but for the location or the land. This is the market and it works perfectly okay. But, assume this land is being expropriated by the municipality. The owner will get at most one to four hundred thousand (one tenth) of the market price.

[84] Interview with Ato Gashaw Mitiku, representative of the residents, Feburuary, 2013, Bahir Dar.

[85] Article 8(4)(a) of Expropriation Proclamation.

[86] Interviews made with displaced people as well as the experts in the municipality.

Table 6.1 The modality of rent calculation in Addis Ababa City

Grade	Compensation range in birr	Rent/m^2 in birr	Example of land size in m^2	Annual rent	Total payment
Grade 1	Below 80,000	20	200	20 × 200 × 12	48,000
Grade 2	80,001–275,000	40	300	40 × 300 × 12	144,000
Grade 3	275,001–500,000	60	375	60 × 375 × 12	270,000
Grade 4	Above 500,001	80	400	80 × 400 × 12	384,000

Source The Addis Ababa valuation directive

condominiums are not prepared within a year, the government continues paying rents. On the other hand, those who got replacement land will not get an extension of rent payment even if they could not finish constructing the houses.

Concerning the size and location of the replacement land, the laws give discretion to regional governments and urban administrations to determine thereupon.[87] Accordingly, the city of Addis Ababa has included a detailed procedure in its Valuation Directive.[88] The Directive also provides the modality of determination of land sizes. This modality is shown in Annex A.

As a matter of principle, displaced people are offered with three alternatives of replacement land: a replacement land at the original site, a replacement land in the expansion zone, and a condominium house.

A replacement land at the original site is given when a replacement land is available in the expropriated area. This happens when a large area is expropriated for an urban redevelopment project. Part of the land is usually reserved for housing constructions of higher standard. A replacement land in the expansion zone is one found in the periphery of the city. A condominium house is a third alternative whereby people prefer a finished condominium unit instead of land and compensation for construction.

Most poor people do opt for this third alternative since they lack money to carry out the construction. As already emphasized, the compensation money is not usually enough to construct a building of similar nature. Those people who have some money or get support from their relatives choose the replacement land in the expansion areas. Those who have enough money go for the first choice, because they could afford to construct larger buildings in accordance with the master plan.

To corroborate this with evidence, let us see one of our case studies in Addis Ababa city. Arada sub-city, in Addis Ababa, has cleared and acquired 25 ha of land in the Arat Killo area for redevelopment purpose. The project is known as Basha Wolde Chilot number 2. The total number of people displaced from this project area was 1553.[89] Among these, only 520 were owners while the rest were tenants of

---

[87] See Ibid; Article 14 of Compensation Regulation.

[88] See Articles 20–23 of the Addis Ababa Valuation Directive.

[89] Information gathered from the records of Arada Sub-city Land Development, Bank and Urban Renewal Office.

government/*kebele* houses. Among the 520 owners, 148 preferred condominium houses, 290 owners chose replacement land in the expansion zone, and 70 people got land at the redevelopment/expropriated site. And among the 70 owners who were given land at the redevelopment site, 27 were commercial buildings. In general, of the total number of people displaced from the study area, about a thousand people have been moved to condominium houses.

This shows that only few people prefer their old place at the center, because they have the money to construct expensive buildings according to the city's plan. Poor people preferred condominium houses. Even in that case, since the compensation money could not cover the cost of the condominium houses, they had to add extra money from their savings.

The amount of compensation paid in the study area, ranges between 3,909 and 348,581 birr. On the other hand, the price of one studio condominium house is 51,800. The law says that at any time, the compensation money should not be less than an amount that can buy a single studio house.[90] So, all those people whose houses were valued below this amount were offered 51,800 birr or a studio house. Those who got more than 51,000 birr could either get the money or a condominium house depending on their choice. For instance, a one bedroom condo costs about 136,000 and a person who wants to get that must add to the compensation money s/he was given to buy the condo house.

Selected interviews[91] conducted with the people who chose to receive land at the expansion zone show that most of them have not still constructed the houses for various reasons, such as unavailability of utility services and inadequacy of funds. But in the meantime, the compensation money they were given has been spent on other things. Further, during the discussion, they revealed that their original plan was to sell the land and to buy smaller houses inside the city. But, as discussed in the Chap. 2, the new lease proclamation makes the sale of a bare land useless.

The other complaint associated with the replacement of land is the location aspect. Displaced people are not compensated for the location of the place they were in. This has two consequences: firstly, since location has no value, displaced people do not get market value for their properties; and secondly, they are not compensated for additional cost they incurred as a result of change in location. Both points are elaborated as follows.

As already discussed, the location or land is not considered during the estimation of compensation. The modality of redressing this loss is, though, made through land to land compensation. Although there seems to be no harm in this type of redress, in reality, it does not make the compensation full. As in the Basha Wolde Chilot and

---

[90] Article 7(3) of the Expropriation Proclamation; Article 16.1.2 of the Addis Ababa Valuation Directive.

[91] Group discussion made at the Jemo site with group of displaced people. The women specially complained that unlike their former residence area in the city center, they could not operate in the new settlement any small business. The people displaced from the study area are dispersed into different locations of the expansion areas of the city such as Jemo, Summit, Bole-Ayat and Gofa Camp. All these areas are on average 16 km far from the study areas, their former homes.

Table 6.2 Lease and sales land values in birr in Addis Ababa City

S.N	Zone	Initial lease price in birr/m^2	Upfront paid market prices in birr/m^2	Auction lease prices in birr/m^2	Compensation for land in birr/m^2
1	Central market	894–1,686	8,000–10,000	20,000–25,000	–
2	Transitional	555–1,035	5,000–7,500	14,000–20,000	–
3	Expansion	191–355	3,000–5,000	5,000–14,000	18

Source Addis Ababa City lease price directive (See *Capital* news release, supra note 7 of Chap. 3), Access Real Estate data (Access Real Estate is one of the leading real estate companies that acquired land through purchase from private owners from around the city and its data can reflect the market price of the properties), and auction prices in 2012/13 (See for example *Addis Fortune*, May 12, 2013, Vol. 13, No. 680; *Ethiopian* (Amharic) news reports of Sunday May 12, 2013)

other similar cases around the country, most urban displaced people are given replacement land at the peripheral area. The value of properties at peripherals is smaller than in the city centers from where the people have been moved. It is a clear fact that home sales at the center bring higher value as compared to the periphery, because of the location. Had property owners been allowed to sell their prosperities, they could have collected three to tenfold higher price as shown in Table 6.2.

The other side of the story is that it is the state that reaps the highest profit from land expropriation and its subsequent transfer by lease to developers and investors. As can be seen from the above table, the Addis Ababa City administration, for example, expropriates land from farmers by paying displacement compensation calculated at 18 birr/m^2 and subdivides and transfers it by leases to private residents for an average of 8,000 birr. Assuming farmers have an average land size of 1 ha (10,000 m^2) one can imagine the size of profit that is collected by the government, while leaving the farmer with insignificant amount of compensation.

The same thing happened to the Basha Wolde Chilot residents as well. For example, one resident,[92] who was interviewed in Jemo condominium site (16 km far from Basha Wolde), had a house in Basha Wolde Chilot area that was rested on 400 m^2 of land. He received around half a million birr as compensation for the house and an opportunity to buy a condominium (instead of land replacement). His old residential place at Basha Wolde Chiolot was transferred by lease to a high-rise building developer for 24,000 birr/m^2. This means, by paying half a million to the owner, the municipality collects 9.6 million birr. The point is that it is unfair beyond any proportion to leave the displaced people with compensation which is not enough to replace what they had, while the state takes away an exaggerated profit.

It is true that the state has its own role in the value addition of an area through provision of infrastructure, but by and large, it is the residents themselves who contribute a lot for the increase. Especially in areas, such as new and un-serviced

[92] Interview with Mamo Hailemariam, owner and displaced from Basha Wolde.

ones, infrastructure usually comes years after residents moved to it. If this is the case, it would be unjust to completely deny them a share of the profit.

The second point raised in relation to land location aspect is that people are not compensated for the costs they incur as a result of the change in location. Except those who get land at the redevelopment site, all the others have to move to the periphery, whether they chose condos or replacement land. In the study area, most of the subjects had been either working in the city center or operating small business in their homes. When they moved to the new homes in the periphery, the people (mostly women) who used to do small home based business lost their income. The new settlement has little demand for their products. This is also what exactly happened in another case in Bahir Dar City. The people were displaced from the city (the bank of river Abay-Blue Nile) for the construction of the conference hall and the governor's office. The women in that neighborhood used to process lentil, peas and beans for the local grain stores. The moment they were moved to the city's outskirt, the storeowners gave the processing business to other people who live nearer to the city. As a result, the displaced women were forced to rent their houses to others and come back to the city again by paying higher rents.[93]

The location caused not only the loss of incomes, as in the above case, but also an additional burden on those who work in the city center. In their former residential areas, people were close to public services and work places. Now, however, they have to travel longer distances to go to their workplaces and to access public services, such as market places and government offices. This means, again, additional expenses for transportation. One respondent accurately described the situation saying, "I used to walk 500 m from my home to work, while now I have to commute 32 km every day."[94] In short, it can be said that the expropriation resulted not only in physical displacement of the people but also in unrecompensed economic displacement.[95]

Another problem is that displaced people are not guaranteed to get equal size of replacement land. For example, even if it is too much to bring in here for analysis, it is enough to summarize that in Addis Ababa, as illustrated in Annex A, the size of the replacement land that is given in the redevelopment area (center) is reduced by half, while the land given at the expansion areas is almost equal to the expropriated one.

Last but not least, business entities are not compensated for business loss or trading loss that is caused as a result of the expropriation. The Expropriation proclamation has clearly stipulated that compensation modality applied for residential

---

[93] Interview with Ato Gashaw, supra note 84.

[94] Ato Abebe Negash, during group discussion in Jemo Condo site, January 22, 2013. Jemo and the other sites are located on average 16 km far from Basha Wolde (Arat Killo) area.

[95] Economic displacement may cause together with physical displacement or without it. For example, if an expropriation takes farm lands without affecting the residential houses, economic displacement is said to be occurred without physical displacement, see for example the description in IFC document, supra note 37 of Chap. 4.

houses shall, *mutatis mutandis*, apply for business houses as well.[96] In practice the only difference is that owners of business may be given replacement land on preferential basis.[97] The replacement land is one found in central location.

6.5.2.3 Cost of Relocation

Relocation compensation refers to the cost of demolition, transferring and installing the property from the expropriated land to another replacement land.[98] As mentioned above, these properties are utilities, household furniture, salvaged things and graves. In all cases the law requires the payment of estimated costs of labor and material for the demolition, transporting and installing the utility, the house or the grave.

6.5.3 Determination of Compensation in Rural Areas

Peasants who lose land by expropriation receive the following compensations: compensation for property on the land, compensation for improvement to the land, replacement land, or (in the absence of replacement land) displacement compensation.

Similar to the urban area, the types of properties found in rural areas are building structures, plants, improvements to the land and the land itself. These are examined in three main divisions as follows.

6.5.3.1 Compensation for Structures and Improvements

The modality of assessing compensation for rural buildings and structures is similar to what has been discussed above in relation to urban constructions. The only difference is that in rural areas the constructions and structures are smaller in scale and different in nature. Rural houses are mostly made of mud and wood and besides, farmers also keep crop depots, animal sheds and fences.

Permanent improvements to rural land include clearing and leveling of an uncultivated land, digging of a water well, constructing terraces, building irrigation canals, preparing water harvesting reservoirs, and other structures that protect

---

[96] Expropriation Proclamation, Article 8(5).

[97] Ato Daniel, supra note 18 of Chap. 4.

[98] See Article 13.5 of Federal Compensation Regulation.

the land from further damages and erosions. In both cases, the basic elements considered during assessment of compensation are the current cost of material and labor expended.[99]

6.5.3.2 Plants

In considering the compensation for plants grown on the land, the law recognizes the following as compensable types of plants: annual crops, perennial crops, trees and grass.[100]

a. Annual Crops

Compensation for annual crops grown on expropriated land is assessed based on the type, amount and current market price of the crop which would have been collected from the land. As an alternative, the owner of a ripe crop is given the opportunity to collect the grain from the land.[101] This happens if the crop is ready for immediate harvest. The usual complaint raised by farmers is that the price fixed for crops is not updated as frequently as it should be. Crop prices should be updated at least annually, but in some places it remains without being updated for 2 years and more.[102]

The other problem identified during our investigation is that the prices of crops fixed by urban and rural administrations are different. Since the urban and rural areas are administered by two different organs, different prices are set for the same crop of same locality. The implication is that farmers of the same locality who lost an equal amount of land may be awarded different compensations only because the expropriating organs are different-one urban and another rural.

b. Perennial Crops

Unlike annual crops, perennial crops are crops that give fruit once or twice a year for many years.[103] For some farmers, perennial crops are supplementary crops while for others they are the main ones. For example, for farmers of southern and south-eastern Ethiopia, coffee is the main crop that sustains their livelihood. In northern Ethiopia, mango and orange trees are not the main products; but they do

---

[99] Article 11(13) of Amhara Valuation Directive; Article 16(8) of Addis Ababa Valuation Directive.

[100] See generally Article 13 of the Federal Compensation Regulation; Article 14.1.a of Amhara Valuation Directive; Articles 16(3)–16(7) of Addis Ababa Valuation Directive.

[101] Article 6(5) of the Federal Compensation Regulation. The usual types of annual crops that grow in Ethiopia are *Tef,* Wheat, Maize, Barley and Millet.

[102] This is especially true in urban areas where the market value of building materials is neither frequently updated (see supra note 16). Unlike the building materials, though, the inflation rate for consumer goods in Ethiopia, such as crops, is highly volatile. For example in 2008 it reached 44 percent, and lowered to single digit in the next 2 years only to increase again to 32 % in 2012 (see details from the Ethiopian Central Statistical Agency at http://www.csa.gov.et).

[103] For example orange, mango, sugar cane, coffee and *chat* trees are considered as perennial crops that give fruits from year to year.

exist in their field together with other trees. The reason this is mentioned is that in southern Ethiopia where farms are covered with coffee trees, the assessment of compensation is different from other perennial crops as discussed below.

Perennial crops are identified in the laws as *ripe* and *unripe* perennial crops. The compensation for *unripe* perennial crops is determined by "calculating the estimated cost incurred for growing the plants"; while the compensation for *ripe* perennial crops is assessed based on the "market price of average annual yield of the plants."[104] Therefore, there is no basic difference between annual crops and ripe perennial crops since the compensation is based on the market value of the annual yield collected from the land. The only exception, as mentioned above, is the assessment of compensation for coffee trees. This exception was observed in the Tulu Kapi Gold Mine Project of the Oromia Region.[105] In that project, the farmers who lost their land completely were provided with replacement land. If replacement land is given, the compensation for the crops (annual or perennial) should be based on one year's harvest only. But in the Tulu Kapi Project, the compensation for loss of the coffee trees was calculated on 10 years' basis. Such type of compensation modality is, of course, not recognized by the Federal Compensation Regulation. It is a mere practice since the Oromia region has not yet adopted a valuation regulation, like that of the Amhara Region. The assessment was based on 10 years yield because one year's compensation could not adequately compensate the loss.[106] One farmer from this project is said to have declared that he would prefer to retain his coffee land rather than giving it away for a 50 years' compensation.[107] The reason is simple: coffee brings higher income when compared to other perennial crops.

Another interesting case is one that is related to the palm trees grown in the Afar desert.[108] The palm trees were grown in the desert and the pastoral community used to collect fruit occasionally. Then when Allana Potash wanted to expropriate the land,[109] the community demanded compensation. The researcher was also asked to give his opinion on the matter. The issue was whether naturally grown perennial trees, which are found on the desert (open access) and untreated and unclaimed by a specific group could be compensable. Since there are other similar cases related to trees, this issue shall be raised and answered below.

---

[104] Article 6 cum. 13(3), (4) of the Federal Compensation Regulation; Similar principle is included in Amhara and Addis Ababa Valuation Regulations.

[105] Tulu Kapi, supra note 24 of Chap. 4.

[106] Interview with Ato Teshome, supra note 29 of Chap. 4. This was explained during the meeting held in Nekemt and dealing with the Tulu Kapi Valuation procedures, supra note 24 of Chap. 4.

[107] Ibid.

[108] Afar is the north eastern region in Ethiopia (see map.) It is known for its hostile and hot climate. The Afar is a desert but endowed with large deposit of Potash and other minerals. The Afar people are nomads and the resources (water and grazing land) are communally owned properties.

[109] See Allana, supra note 46 of Chap. 4.

C. Trees

The term "trees" refers to big trees like eucalyptus, acacia, *ficus vasta* or other indigenous trees. They grow by themselves or are planted by man for timber, construction or firewood purposes. Compensation for such trees is assessed based on "the type and level of growth of the tree and the current local price per square meter or per unit," but if the owner chooses, an alternative is given for the owner to "cut and collect the woods in lieu of compensation."[110] During calculation of compensation, three sizes of tree (big, medium and small) are identified for which market price is fixed.[111] So, in short, tree plants are compensated on the basis of the market value of the specific type and size of the trees.

One issue that we tried to identify during valuation of trees was whether all types of trees (natural or planted by man) would be considered as compensable. In Amhara region, except shrubs and the like, every tree is compensable. So long as the tree is found in one person's land and so long as it is protected by the person, compensation would be paid for it.[112] On the other hand, in Oromia region, the practice is that natural or indigenous trees are not considered during valuation. In the Tulu Kapi Gold Mining Project, one of the controversial issues was whether those naturally grown trees which the farmers used as sheds to their coffee plants would be valued for compensation or not. Owners and the local woreda administration argued that the trees should be considered as private property and qualified for compensation. But the regional land administration bureau adamantly rejected the idea of assessment of these trees. The reason given was that if they permit this, farmers would claim the whole forest around as their property and would inflate the compensation for the company.[113]

As already mentioned above, the same issue was also raised in the Afar region in relation to the Allana Potash's expropriation of palm trees grown on the desert land. The decision of the Regional government is not yet known. The reason for all the confusion is that unlike Addis Ababa and the Amhara region, the Oromia and Afar regions have failed to adopt valuation directives. Issues of this nature which are not covered in the Federal Expropriation proclamation and Compensation Regulation should be answered by detailed regional valuation directives.

But it seems unjustified to deny compensation in Oromia for trees which happens to be grown on one's land. The law does not discriminate on the basis of naturally grown or planted by a person. Whatever attachment found on the land and has a worth is considered as a private property and subject of compensation. Besides to being a clear violation of the constitution and the expropriation laws, the denial of compensation for naturally grown trees may cause one possible problem if

---

110 Article 7(1) of the Federal Compensation Regulation.

111 See for example Article 14(1)(a)(vi–vii) of the Amhara Valuation Directive.

112 Interview with Ato Mihret, supra note 11 of Chap. 4. See also Articles 11(11) and 19(2) of the Amhara Valuation Regulation.

113 Ato Teshome, supra note 29 of Chap. 4.

uncorrected: knowing such truth, farmers may tend to cut the trees and sell them as firewood or lumber that in turn causes environmental problems.

d. Grass

The other compensable plant is grass. Grass is used as forage for animals and for construction of houses. Farmers who have excess grass can also sell it to others. The value of grass is assessed based on the market value of grass collected from a given land.[114] The same law allows owners to collect the grass in lieu of receiving compensation. The problem identified with compensation for grass is that when the grass is held in common, compensation may not be paid. This happens mainly for two reasons: first, there may not be unity among the farmers to enforce their rights to receive compensation; and secondly, if the project is made in the interest of the rural community, compensation for common lands, such as grazing land, is usually waived. In our case study, in Rib Dam Project, the farmers who lost their grazing land for a campsite claimed that they did not receive compensation for the grazing land. Of course, they were compensated for grass found in their private holdings.

6.5.3.3 Compensation for Loss of Rural Land

In this section the following three modalities of compensations for loss of rural land are examined: full monetary compensation (displacement compensation), partial monetary compensation, and land to land compensation.

a. Full Monetary Compensation

A person who lost a landholding forever as a result of an expropriation procedure is entitled to displacement compensation (monetary compensation) for his/her loss. This is in addition to the compensation provided for the property situated on the land and the improvement s/he brought about on the land. As has been argued (Sect. 6.5.1.2), a displacement compensation is not as such a compensation that replaces the lost property, for land is not a private property. Displacement compensation is rather a kind of rehabilitative support provided to farmers until they are able to regain a capacity to put themselves in their original position.[115] Concerning this the law provides:

> A rural land holder whose land holding has been permanently expropriated shall, in addition to the compensation payable. … [for property on and improvements to the land], be paid displacement compensation which shall be equivalent to ten times the average annual income he secured during the five years preceding the expropriation of the land.[116]

[114] Article 8 of the Federal Compensation Regulation.

[115] To put one self into the original position is a rare incident for an Ethiopian farmer. Some farmers whose land was expropriated by urban municipality may be successful to regain their capacity because of the slightly different compensation package provided, as shall be seen soon.

[116] Article 8(1) of the Expropriation Proclamation.

A complete loss of land often happens when the land is required for the intended project. The assumption here is that unless the land is needed for temporary purposes such as building campsites or detour roads, the taking would be most probably forever. Thus, when the farmer is left without land, a monetary compensation equivalent to 10 years' compensation will be awarded. The amount of compensation is fixed at 10 years annual income, based on the average annual income earned in the preceding 5 years. The justification for fixing this amount is unknown, and probably baseless. Even the parliamentary discussion made during the adoption of the expropriation proclamation reveals nothing as to why the multiplier was made ten and the average income 5 years.

Nonetheless, a systematic search makes us to believe that the principle must have been copied from the Chinese Land Administration Law (LAL) of 1986 (as amended finally in 2004.).[117] Article 47 of the Chinese LAL provides for three types of compensations in the event of expropriation of cultivated land: *compensation for land*, *resettlement subsidies*, and *compensation for attachments and young crops on the requisitioned land.* Compensation for expropriated cultivated land is six to ten times the average annual output value of the expropriated land, calculated on the basis of 3 years preceding such requisition.[118] Resettlement subsidies for expropriated cultivated land is calculated according to the agricultural population needing to be resettled, and it shall be four to six times the average annual output value of the expropriated cultivated land calculated on the basis of 3 years preceding such expropriation, provided that it is not more than fifteen times of the average annual income.[119] Of course, the value of property and plants is also considered. The law further provides that if the land and resettlement compensations are not enough to enable the farmer to resettle, additional money could be given provided that the total compensation does not exceed 30 times the average annual output value of the expropriated land calculated on the basis of 3 years preceding such expropriation.[120]

There are slight differences between the Ethiopian and the Chinese compensation methods although the basic principle remains the same. The first difference is that the Chinese LAL provides additional cash compensation for the loss of the land. The second type of compensation termed as *resettlement compensation* is something similar to what is known as *displacement compensation* in Ethiopia. Unlike in China, there is no as such compensation given for loss of land in Ethiopia. The second difference is that while compensation is calculated on the basis of the preceding three years average value in China, in Ethiopia it is 5 years. Thirdly, while in China the multiplier is given in a range of 6–10 years, in Ethiopia it is fixed

[117] The People's Republic of China Land Administration Law, supra note 30.

[118] Ibid.

[119] Ibid.

[120] Ibid.

at 10 years. Finally, in China the compensation modality is elastic (it can go to a maximum of 30 times[121]), but in Ethiopia it is a rigid one.

In following this type of compensation modality, the Chinese LAL from the outset describes the principle it follows. The first sentence of Article 47 clearly declares that the "land expropriated shall be compensated on the basis of its original purpose of use."[122] This is the other side of the "highest and best use" principle already discussed (Sect. 6.3.3). One cannot be sure whether the Ethiopian compensation of rural land also follows this type of principle. Because the Ethiopian law does not give compensation for the loss of the land, it cannot be said the compensation is based on the *original purpose of use of the land.*

Coming back to the discussion at hand, it is already emphasized that the displacement compensation is an equivalent to the value of 10 years produce. The practice of computing the displacement compensation is discussed below.

Valuators first collect data about the types of crops growing in the area, the size of the land in hectare, productivity per hectare, productivity of the land per year (for example, once, twice, or thrice-in irrigable land). The data includes all such particulars of the past 5 years. By assuming that the land grows one type of crop per year, valuators take five kinds of crops with different value and production level. Using the market prices of the cereals witnessed during the past 5 years, the valuation committee calculates and derives an average annual income for the farmer and multiplies it by ten.

The general assessment is that the amount of displacement compensation provided for farmers is not enough. This assessment is based on the feelings of interviewed farmers, land administration experts, and my comparison of the actually paid compensation with the current food prices. By and large, one can look into the statistical data on inflation of food prices.[123] Legal and practical problems that make the displacement compensation principle contentious are identified and presented below.

The first legal problem stems from the constitutional right to the land itself. As already explained in Chap. 2, land belongs to the joint ownership of the state and the people. To ensure this right, the constitution and the rural land proclamations provide equal access to rural land and the protection against arbitrary eviction. Farmers are recognized as collective owners of the land and entrusted with *holding right* which is not limited in time and which provides all land rights except sale. But the protection and guarantee given to this right in terms of compensation is not

---

[121] Even then, the Chinese compensation amount was criticized for "low compensation standard that does not reflect soaring prices, rigid regulations and a lack of guarantee for the farmers' long-term livelihood and social security." For this reason, a move to amend the law was made in 2012, at least to remove then 30 years and to assess land based on market price. This however is still in debate in parliament, see the information at: (http://news.xinhuanet.com/english/china/2012-12/24/c_132060718.htm); (http://www.reuters.com//2013/03/07/us-china-landreform-idUSBRE9260CH20130307).

[122] The People's Republic of China Land Administration Law. Article 47.

[123] See supra note 80.

adequate. When land is taken for public purposes, the damage that is caused to the holders is not equally compensated by the average value of 10 years' production.

In simple terms, the loss sustained and the compensation given do not match, since the 10 years compensation does not replace a loss of a lifetime and even beyond. It is an acceptable fact now that the amount of displacement compensation to farmers cannot buy them an equal livelihood.[124] It would not even buy enough food for 3 years. On the other hand, the money awarded as compensation could be recovered within fewer years if the farmer were allowed to keep his land. The money could be easily recovered because firstly, the price of goods is always on the increase, and secondly, the yield of the land improves from year to year.[125]

The other flaw with the law is that the calculation is measured on the basis of the average annual income gained over the past 5 years. The question is whether it would be wiser to apply the value of 5 years back instead of the present market value. Besides, why did the legislator choose 5 years instead of, for example, two or three, like the Chinese one? This question is raised because inflation on food items is continuously increasing at a very high rate, and thus the money given now cannot buy for the farmers the same amount of food that they bought in the past. Most farmers interviewed, as well as people from the land administration organs, share this concern and criticize the rule on this ground. This means the price of goods two to 5 years ago does not reflect the current market situation, let alone that of the coming 10 years. It is like forcing the farmer to sell his crops today and tomorrow at yesterday's price. It should rather have considered the likely future increases in the inflation rate to calculate the present and future compensation to be paid.

A third problem has to do with the incompleteness of the law and the lack of practical support to the displaced farmers. Previously, it has been argued that the Ethiopian legislation does not clearly envisage the need for and the requirements of resettlement and rehabilitation programs. Although the displacement compensation is understood here as *rehabilitative support,* the law gives no additional assistance to the displaced farmers. The government does not either give any practical training or additional assistance to help the farmers on how to invest the money. Our

---

[124] Almost all interviewed farmers have confirmed that the amount of money they received as displacement compensation was finished within a maximum period of 2 years, and they would rather prefer retaining the land to any amount of compensation. This shows that the revision of the law to increase the multiplier (like what is proposed in China) or to change the valuation method is an imperative.

[125] The use of modern farming methods, inputs (e.g. fertilizer and pesticides) and development of irrigation systems enable farmers to increase the productivity of their land. For example, during my investigation of valuation of rural lands in Amhara Region, I observed that the productivity of land has been increasing with an average of 5 q/ha annually. This fact is also supported by many studies. For example, according the Ethiopian CSA data between 2004/05 and 2007/08 the average yield (annual increase of productivity per hectare) for five major grains Tef, barley, wheat, maize and sorghum was 6.2, 7.7, 4.5, 1.5, 7.8 and 8.9 % respectively (Seyoum, A., Dorosh, P. & Asrat, S. Year. Crop Production in Ethiopia: Regional Patterns and Trends. *In:* Ethiopia Strategy Support Program II, 2010 International Food Policy Research Institute, p. 11, http://www.ifpri.org/sites/default/files/publications/esspwp16.pdf).

argument is that onetime payment does not create a sustainable form of compensation because the sum is often squandered by farmers of little experience in handling cash capital. Hence, after expropriation, the farmers usually ended up in daily laboring that brings them very little income.

b. Partial Monetary Compensation

Sometimes, there is the possibility of dispossessing the farmer from his land for a temporary period of time. Farmers may be left for few years without land. The idea is that either their original land would be returned to them or a new replacement land would be given at the end of the project. For example, land may be taken provisionally for workers' campsite, storage, or detour during road construction. Moreover, land nearby a big project may be temporarily shut down by the project owner for health and safety reasons. Or farmers may be disrupted from cultivation because of a delay in the provision of replacement land. The mode of payment of compensation in this regard is given as follows:

> A rural landowner or holders of common land whose land holding has been provisionally expropriated shall, in addition to the compensation (for property on the land and improvement), be paid until repossession of the land, compensation for lost income based on the average annual income secured during the five years preceding the expropriation of the land.[126]

The insufficiency of compensation that I raised above is also more or less true to temporary dislocations. The other practical problem that surfaces in relation to this practice is that an agency that took the land provisionally may not give it back in the same condition as it was before. For example, road companies tend to spoil and destroy the fertility and usability of the land by mixing asphalt and other toxic substances which they used during the construction work. Fortunately, however, most of the land given for such purposes is communal or state owned. Nevertheless, there are cases which have even reached the courts. The nature of such cases is that a road construction company has left piles of stones and earth on their land after it has finished the work at hand. Courts usually decide either compensation be paid[127] or the land be reinstated to the original condition.[128] In other cases, road companies use excess land for detour road and refuse to pay compensation for the interruption.[129]

---

[126] Article 8(2) of Expropriation Proclamation.

[127] There are many cases of this nature reaching regional and federal courts. For example, in the case between Worku Teshager v. Sur Construction, (West Gojam High Court, Civ. Case No. 08569) and Worku Sime v. Sur Construction (West Gojam High Court, Civ. Case No. 08724), the allegation of both plaintiffs was that the defendant, a road construction company, had despoiled their land and made it uncultivable for the next 5 years. Accordingly, they asked for 5 years compensation.

[128] Mola Wondimagegn v. Sur Construction, (South Gonder High Court Civ. Case No. 29258). The court, instead of compensation money, ordered the removal of unused quarry, re-fill of pits, and the spread of topsoil.

[129] Tibebu Belay v. Sur Construction, (North Gonder High Court, Civ. Case No. 31057).

Sometimes, when project works continue for more than the intended period, the project owners are reluctant to pay additional compensation. A good example of this situation is the condition of the farmers in the area surrounding the Koga Irrigation project.[130] The Koga irrigation project was constructed with the aim of cultivating 7,000 ha of command area. The people displaced from the reservoir area would be compensated by land replacement in the cultivation (command) area after conducting redistribution (readjustment) of land. The original plan was that it would take the government 3 years to finish the construction and readjustment works. Therefore, the displaced farmers were given a 3 years compensation anticipating that after 3 years they would get new land for irrigation farming. But, it took the government more than 5 years to complete the process. Farmers complained at that time that compensation was not paid for the additional 2 years.[131]

c. Land-to-Land Compensation

A land to land compensation is the most preferable mode of compensation among Ethiopian farmers. The reason is that, for a farmer, land is not only a source of economy, but also a source of dignity and pride. To date, social status and prestige are determined based on the economic status of a person, and thereby on the size and fertility of land s/he holds. Land possession also enhances women's sense of freedom and self esteem. A landless person in rural areas is a wanderer without abode and social status. But most importantly, farming is the only skill and way of life farmers can understand and be confident of. Thus, even at a generous compensation, farmers do not prefer compensation in terms of money. A study for the purpose of valuation, made by BoEPLAU, showed that among 90 farmers who had been asked to make choice between the two modes of compensation, only one farmer showed an interest in monetary compensation.[132] Another study conducted by Beza Consultants, to identify compensation preference of displaced farmers from the Rib Irrigation Dam areas concludes that "field investigation result reveals that almost all Project-Affected People would like to have a land to land compensation than cash remuneration."[133] A similar question was raised by myself while interviewing forty five affected farmers in the Rib Irrigation dam, and 100 % of those queried favored land-to-land compensation.

This has nothing to do with the amount of compensation awarded, but with the ways of life and the general economic development of the country. Uneducated and alien to urban life, most farmers do not want to change their profession, for farming is the only skill they are good at. Lack of adequate alternative jobs in urban areas

[130] The Koga irrigation project was an Ethiopian and African Development Bank joint project constructed at more than half a billion birr. It is found in the Mecha woreda of Amhara region in Ethiopia.

[131] Daniel W. Ambaye, supra note 196 of Chap. 2, p. 27, 28.

[132] Interview with Ato Bayih Tiruneh, Deputy Head of BoEPLAU, Interview conducted in 2007 and confirmed in 2012.

[133] Beza Consulting, supra note 31 of Chap. 1, p. 27.

also makes them to stick to their farming job. Concerning the possibility of land to land compensation modality, the law provides:

> Where the woreda administration confirms that a substitute land which can be easily ploughed and generate comparable income is available for the land holder, the compensation to be paid … shall be only equivalent to the average annual income secured during the five years preceding the expropriation of the land.[134]

Unlike the above two situations where the farmer is awarded with compensation of 10 years or less for complete or temporary loss of land, farmers will get only one year's compensation since their land would be replaced immediately.

In practice, land-to-land compensation is effected when the woreda or kebele administration possesses extra land in the locality. Extra land may be collected by woredas through the conversion of communal lands to private holdings or the reclamation of land which is abandoned, left without an heir and other reasons.[135] This reserve land is supposed to be distributed to the youth and to people who lost their land by expropriation. In reality, however, since land is scarce, land-to-land compensation is applied less frequently, especially in northern Ethiopia (including Amhara region). Experts in the region have confirmed that there is no excess land in rural parts of most of the Amhara Region.[136]

Most implementing agencies (investors) favor this kind of compensation system in order to avoid the payment of displacement compensation. The reason is, as stated above, in the case of land-to-land compensation, monetary compensation is made only for property on the land and to the extent of one year's annual income. On the other hand, if no land is given as replacement, the implementing agency has to pay 10 years income. Neither is the investor obliged to pay a land value for the government if it gets the land without paying compensation to the farmers. So, from the implementing agency's perspective, this system of land-to-land compensation is preferable. The theoretical problem is that, at whose expense does such a system operate? Why should the community be the bearer of this burden, rather than the organ that benefits from the taking? This is especially true when the land is expropriated for pure private purposes, such as horticulture business. The land which was given as land-to-land compensation might be a common land, or one which could have been distributed to landless youth of the community.

Another practical problem associated with this provision is that implementing agencies use it as an excuse not to pay compensation. Implementing agencies, especially government agencies, require the rural woreda to give replacement land,

---

[134] Article 8(3) of the Expropriation Proclamation.

[135] Proclamation 133/2005 of the Amhara region under 21 provides the following as conditions of depriving holding rights: engaged in non-farming activity, disappeared from locality for 5 consecutive years, fallowed land for 3 consecutive years, caused gross damage to the land, notified the government for withdrawal from farming activity.

[136] Group discussion held with 10 senior land administration experts of the Amhara Region. They worked in each zonal administration of the region and they confirmed the realities of their respective administrative zones. The only available land in the region is in the low land areas of Jawi.

irrespective of its availability. In the study area in Amhara region, a notorious government agency that denies paying compensation is the region's Rural Roads Authority.

The Amhara Region Rural Roads Authority is empowered to construct roads that connect every village to the main highways. The 5 years' GTP of the regional government is to build 18,000 km of rural gravel roads with 4–10 m width. This program is known as Universal Rural Roads Access Program (URRAP). The construction of the roads also needs additional land for ditches and shoulders which sometimes require a total width of 30 m of land.[137] In the year 2011/12 only, the authority built 2,280 km of gravel roads across the region.[138]

What is worrying is that the regional roads authority does not pay compensation for the land it takes for the road construction. The regional government is said to be unwilling to allocate budget for compensation related to rural roads.[139] Therefore, neither the regional government nor the authority has the intention of paying compensation as the local community is expected to bear the burden.[140] The justification held is that since it is the rural community that raises the demand for a rural road, it must also share the burden. The researcher interviewed experts from the BoEPLAU and the affected farmers. The procedure that took place looked like the following.

Government representatives come to the village and call a meeting in which they raise the idea of road construction. People would be asked if they would support this and the people responded positively since road is their basic problem. But at this point the plan was not clear; whose land would be affected and whether compensation would be paid was not known. One thing which was clear during the meetings was that the rural community would support the development of roads.

Next, new plans for roads were put in place and the road authority (through its contractors) came and started cutting and tearing up the lands without any prior notice or compensation for the holders. When the affected farmers asked for compensation, the roads authority told them to ask their respective woredas for replacement land. When they asked the woreda for replacement land, it could not give them any for there was none. When they tried to block the construction work, they were arrested, and when they tried to speak out, they were labeled as *anti-development* and *anti-social*. A farmer on whose land a road passes would at least lose a quarter of a hectare.[141]

The argument of the government against paying compensation relies on two grounds. First, the government claims that it lacks adequate finance, and if it tries to pay compensation for every piece of land taken, the construction activity would be frustrated. Second, government authorities argue that since the rural community

137 Interview with Ato Akane, supra note 33 of Chap. 1.

138 Ibid.

139 Interview with Ato Mebit, supra note 20 of Chap. 4.

140 Ibid.

141 Group Discussion with land administration experts, supra note 136.

gave its consent to support (in terms of labor, money, land) the roads' construction, it was against the agreement to claim compensation afterwards.[142] Yet, our argument is that despite the community is claimed to have given its consent to forfeit compensation, unless the government secured individual landholder's consent to do so, the consent of the community at large could not serve as a binding one on the individual. Even if the agreement of the society can be said a binding one on the individual, why should one or few individuals be separated and forced to bear the burden, while it is the general community that benefits from it?

By contrast, the highways constructed by the federal government do not cause such problems. At least, in principle, the Federal Government Roads Authority pays compensation. This means, in one village area a farmer who lost his land for a highway construction shall be compensated, while another who lost the land for the Region's Rural Roads will be denied.

There are also other government organs which try to deny compensation for the land they took by shifting the burden to the nearby rural woreda. A good example is the cases of the Yibab Eyesus area farmers who lost their land for a military base. Yibab is a rural *kebele* found in the western escarpment of Bahir Dar City. Today the area is partly hosting the FDRE Defense Forces, Western Division. The army has in its control 257,277 ha of land, which had been held by 142 household farmers. In May 2003, the military suddenly started to fence the land and built base camp without notifying the farmers or paying them compensation. The farmers did not receive prior notification or information concerning the expropriation of their land for defense purpose. The army on its part claimed that it received the land by order of the Regional Urban Land Development Bureau. In any case, most of the farmers sued the Military for unlawful occupation of their land and 3 years' interrupted income. In the cases under review,[143] the plaintiffs alleged that the military occupied their land and denied them access to their farms and as a result they could not harvest for three consecutive years. Accordingly, they demanded for compensation of lost income. In all the cases, the court accepted their claim and ordered the Ministry of Defense to pay 3 years compensation.

Another practical and legal problem related to land-to-land compensation occurs when the replacement land is not similar to the expropriated land. Most often, the replacement land is not similar in size, fertility, access to roads and distance to facilities such as schools and clinics. Sometimes, the expropriated land might be an irrigable land which provides the holder three harvests a year, while the replacement property, dependent only on annual rain fall, may make harvest possible only once in a year. This shows that the expropriated farmer may not get comparable land in fertility, size and other benefits. The Federal Expropriation Proclamation is silent on the adjustment of these disparities.

---

[142] Interviews made with officials of Qunzila, Fagita, and Denbecha woredas.

[143] All the cases were handled by the West Gojam High Court. The cases are (Abeje Yitayew vs. Ministry of Defense, Western Division, Civ. File No. 9600), (Awoke Addis vs. Ministry of Defense, Western Division, Civ. File No. 9587), and (Tarekegn Eskemeche vs. Ministry of Defense, Western Division, Civ. File No. 9803).

My findings show the existence of two practices in this respect. In a bid to fill the gap, the Amhara Valuation Directive gives a solution to a difference in land size, stating "if the replaced land is not *comparable* with the previous one, displacement compensation shall be paid for the difference only."[144] For example, if the replacement land is five times less in size (ha) than the former one, then displacement compensation shall be given for the lost 5 ha. And yet this provision does not answer the whole problem. In the quoted rule above, the word "comparable" is not adequately defined, but the implication is comparability in land size. The implication is that even this provision (in Amhara) does not take account of differences in land fertility and in access to roads and water bodies.

When one looks into the experience in Oromia Region, irrespective of their previous land sizes, farmers receive whatever size is available. This means a farmer who had lost 10 ha of land may be compensated with equal or smaller size of land. If the land available is smaller in size and poor in fertility, there is no mechanism to redress the difference. The argument is that land belongs to the public (not private) and there is no justification for an individual to demand an equal replacement.[145] S/he shall be treated like everyone else in the locality.

6.5.4 Determination of Compensation in Peri-Urban Area

A peri-urban land is found in between rural administration and an urban one. Literally speaking, this is the land found in the peripheries of towns and cities. Originally, such land was part of the rural administration, but because of urban expansion, it was acquired by urban administration through expropriation process. The reason that this case is examined separately is because the modality of compensating landholding farmers is slightly different from that of the other rural farmer.

One of the common features of such area in Ethiopia is the widespread informal land transfers to urban speculators. In the anticipation of regularization of their possession at a later stage, many urban speculators and landless people informally buy land from the farmers. The farmers on their side, by weighing the compensation that they would be paid (upon the expropriation of the land) and the sales price they are receiving, prefer selling the land. The whole process is hazardous for the buyers compared to the sellers, since land sale is illegal.

A vacuum peri-urban is created when the urban administration adopts a revised master plan that includes the nearby rural farmlands without actually expropriating and adding them to its land bank. This new territory now falls under no one's

[144] Article 14(3) of Amhara Valuation Directive.

[145] Interview with Ato Teshome, supra note 29 of Chap. 4. He emphasized, "Farmers will be provided replacement land on the basis of the amount of land available and the policy of the region. It is not mandatory and necessary to replace the same size of land if the former holding was bigger in size."

jurisdiction. For this reason, farmers try to transform their agricultural lands to residential area by subdividing and then selling the plots without any interference from government bodies.[146] Sometimes, city officials bulldoze the built area in fear of later contentions with residents.[147]

When one looks into the compensation modalities, farmers are compensated for their properties on the land and the improvements they bring about to the land, in the manner discussed above. Further, farmers get displacement compensation calculated at 10 year's income. Except in small and emerging towns, land-to-land compensation is not used. The usual practice is rather to absorb the farmers into the urban life by providing them residential plots on the site or somewhere within the urban expansion zone.

Concerning the size of the land and other requirements, one may look into the Addis Ababa City valuation Directive as a guiding rule. The Directive identifies two types of rural dwellers: those who have farmland and those who do not. The latter are people who are mainly engaged in handicraft and similar non farming activities. Farmers who have land and house on the expropriated land shall receive plots of land on the expansion zone.[148] The size of the land to be provided ranges from 200 to 500 m^2 based on the size of the farmland they had possessed previously (details are given in Annex A-VIII).

With regard to the non-farming rural residents, the Directive allows them 150 m^2 of residential plots, provided they can prove their landlessness.[149] Further, the law permits married children who live with their parents in the same compound but in a separate house, to get 105 m^2 of land for residential purpose.[150]

This rule may be different in regional cities. For example, in the Amhara region, irrespective of the land size, any farmer who lost land to the urban center is given 250 m^2 of land, while his married children who live with him get 105 m^2 of land.[151]

The Directive is not clear on one point, though. It is not clear whether residential land will be given to those farmers whose farmland is expropriated but who own residential house elsewhere. The law is clear about non-farming rural residents; it requires a proof from the rural woreda administration that shows they do not hold land or any house. In any case, it seems that what matters is-not owning a house in another place of the rural woreda, but holding a land. This is because it is the land that is the source of income, not the house. Therefore, the rational way should be to check whether the farmer has another land, enough to feed and sustain his family.

This rule has two legal ramifications worth discussing. The first one is that it creates a double treatment of farmers who lose their land for urban development on

---

146 This is the case in Addis Ababa City as well as in Bahir Dar.

147 In Bahir Dar City, City municipality uses this system to discourage informality.

148 Addis Ababa City Valuation Directive, Articles 13.1.7 cum. 20.9 cum. Annex Six.

149 Id., Articles 20.10 cum. 13.1.8.

150 Id., Articles 20.11 cum. 13.1.9.

151 Group Discussion with Addisu Begashaw, Begiziew Tsehayu and Fasil Simeneh, supra note 45 of Chap. 4.

the one hand and for rural development on the other. Farmers who lose their land for rural development will get only the compensations package discussed previously (Sect. 6.5.3). But a farmer who is expropriated by an urban administration is awarded an urban residential plot, besides all the other compensation packages. Therefore, the mere luck of expropriation of one's land by an urban administration, instead of by a rural administration creates a gap that is worth the whole compensation. This is said because the urban residential plot has more value than the whole compensation given for the land and property on the land together.

The second legal ramification is that farmers who anticipate the expropriation of their land by urban administration will either subdivide and sell their farm land or demolish their old houses and construct a better house on it. Those who buy land informally and build houses on them will not be compensated excepting the existence of corruption and lack of evidence. So, this is not as such a legal problem by itself. The problem comes with the second aspect, demolition and construction of better houses. The researcher has witnessed practices in Bahir Dar in which old farm houses are replaced by new and better ones and where farmers change their residence from the deep rural areas to the land in the city periphery and build better houses.

The problem is similar to what is raised by some economists. Some economists oppose payment of compensation on the basis that property owner intentionally makes initial investment on a given land, knowing that there is some probability of a future taking of the property by the government. When a taking occurs, the initial investment is rendered worthless.[152] The argument is that land owners would make inefficient and useless investments. Likewise, the fear of the writer is that because of the speculations of the expropriation of peri-urban land by the urban administration, farmers may tend to invest much on building houses that would only be demolished upon expropriation of the land.

6.6 Appeal and the Role of Courts

6.6.1 Appeal Process and Appealable Cases

As already mentioned previously (Sect. 5.4.5), of all the expropriation procedures, courts have clear mandate in hearing cases related to compensation. Of course, this power is limited to the denial or inadequacy of compensation. Further, the courts can hear some of the cases only by appeal, not as first instances as shall be shown below.

As a matter of principle, urban and rural administrations are required to establish an administrative "grievance hearing organ" to hear complaints related to

[152] Innes, R. 2000. Economics of Taking and Compensation When Land and its Public Use Value Are in Private Hands. *Land Economics,* 76, p. 2.

landholdings. In urban centers it is formally known as "Municipal Court", while in rural areas it is known as "Social Court." If such organs are not established, complaints related to landholding shall be submitted to regular courts having jurisdiction.[153]

Be it a municipal, social or a regular court that has the jurisdiction to hear land related disputes, when it comes to compensation, the plaintiff must submit it first to another internal administrative body. For example, in Bahir Dar and Addis Ababa, Arada Sub-city, the internal body is usually known as "compensation hearing committee." A person who has complaint on the amount of compensation must first express the complaint to a "Valuation and Compensation Auditor Expert" in writing.[154] The expert is most likely a property valuator, and if there are visible irregularities or errors committed during inventory of assets, the expert may correct them. If the expert insists on her/his previous judgment, s/he may refuse to make changes. Afterwards, the complainant can go one step upwards and lodge his complaint to another senior valuation expert. And the senior officer would refer it to a "Compensation Grievance Hearing Committee."[155] This committee has the power to investigate all the procedures which were followed during valuation, and if it thinks fit, it may order the re-evaluation of the assets. The same procedure is followed in rural areas as well.[156]

A party that is dissatisfied by the decision of the "Compensation Grievance Hearing Committee" has the right to appeal the case to a regular or municipal court within 30 days from the day of decision.[157] Municipal courts are found only in larger cities with a specific jurisdiction to hear cases related to civil and criminal matters. In Addis Ababa, the municipal court has an appellate high court as well. In Bahir Dar City, it is only a first instance court and this means the decision is appealable to the regular high court.

Many cases related to inadequacy of compensation reach the Federal Supreme Court Cassation Division, the highest appellate court in the country. Even though people have the right to go to the highest court by way of appeal, it is nonetheless mandatory for them to start first with the administrative organ, i.e., the "valuation committee". This has been recently confirmed by a decision of the Federal Cassation Court when it reversed all decisions and ordered the initiation of the case with the administrative organ[158] which is the valuation committee.

The other type of complaint entertained by courts is the denial of compensation, or as discussed under Sect. 4.3.6, the *non consideration of property for*

---

[153] Article 11(1) of Federal Expropriation Proclamation.

[154] Addis Ababa Valuation Directive, 29.

[155] Id., Article 30.

[156] See for example Article 40 of the Amhara Rural Valuation Directive. Complaint is first submitted to the "Valuation Committee". If not satisfied, the complaint may go to "Compensation Grievance Hearing Committee" established at woreda level.

[157] Article 11(4) of Federal expropriation Proclamation.

[158] Ethiopian Roads Authority v. Jada Biru, (Federal Supreme Court Cassation Division, Cass. File No. 57271), Dec 2010.

compensation. Since denial of compensation is not about valuation and inadequacy of compensation, but rather about violation of property right, it falls under the jurisdiction of a municipal or regular court, as the case may be. To support this with a case law, the Federal Cassation Court differentiates between cases based on “insufficiency of compensation” and those based on “denial of compensation” and underlines that the later type of cases would fall under the jurisdiction of regular or municipal courts.[159]

Denial of compensation occurred for various reasons, such as absence of possession or ownership title to the property taken, or due to a mere violation of rights by the government. Most of the cases lodged to the municipal court of Bahir Dar City, for instance, have to do with absence of clear titles to the expropriated land.[160] One of the cases that reached the Federal Supreme Court Cassation Division was of this nature. In the case between Tolesa Wirtu v. Ethiopian Electric Power Corporation,[161] the appellant claimed that the respondent denied him compensation for land taken from him for dam construction by the latter. The court rejected the claim because the land for which compensation was claimed was outside of his legal holdings. The appellant has been using land which was not given to him by respective government authorities. Similar incidents also happen in urban areas in a variety of ways, when people carry out construction either on government land or expand construction beyond their legitimate holdings.

On the whole, the power of courts in respect to compensation is encouraging. Yet, their power on the valuation part is limited since the courts totally rely on the expertise of the land authorities. Absence of alternative expert valuators and private companies contributes to the limited exercise of power by courts.

6.6.2 *Incidental and Consequential Damages*

Incidental loss refers to a loss that is sustained as a result of an indirect action of the expropriation of the land. Such losses are typified by damage or destruction of good will, expenses incurred in moving to a new location and profits lost because of business interruption or inability to relocate.[162] Whereas, consequential damages is caused as a result of partial taking and works carry out near to the property. A good example in this case is when part of one’s land is expropriated for road construction and the person loss business income because of the construction.

---

159 Solomon Mehari v. Mekelle City Administration, (Federal Supreme Court Cassation Division, Cass. File No. 81159), Dec 2012. In this case, the appellant alleged for the expropriation of his land by the respondent without payment of compensation. So the issue was not about insufficiency of compensation, but about payment of compensation.

160 Interview with Ato Birhanu, supra note 33 of Chap. 4.

161 Federal Supreme Court Cassation Division, (Cass. File No. 75763), Jan 2013.

162 Comments: 1958, supra note 53, p. 62.

Although the law allows the payment of relocation compensation, there are still other costs which are not compensable. As mentioned earlier, the additional cost (e.g. transportation cost) and the lost income (e.g. income that was generated from home based businesses), both of which are caused due to relocation are clear examples of incidental damages. Further, the most common type of loss is the interruption of business and thereby loss of income as a result of road construction.[163] This may of course be referred as consequential damage since it is not related to the total expropriation of one's land.

Another similar issue, which surfaces in courts and which needs to be settled is the delay in payment of compensation and the damages caused as a result. Most implementing agencies pay compensation long after they acquire the land. The problem associated with this is whether the displaced people could claim compensation for lost income or for additional costs they are exposed to. In a case that reached the Federal Supreme Court Cassation Division,[164] the Ethiopian Roads Authority (now appellant) expropriated land and ordered the demolition of a warehouse belonging to the respondent. The demolition sign was marked on the house in June and the demolition was carried out 6 months later, without payment of compensation. The present respondent lodged a suit against the roads authority claiming a compensation of birr 166,155 which was assessed by the roads authority and an additional birr 178,500 as interrupted income for 17 months. The plaintiff argued that since the demolition mark was put on his house, he closed his business and as a result he lost income. Had he been allowed to keep opening the business, he could have earned that amount of money. Although the lower courts consistently accepted the claim and decided in favor of the plaintiff, the Cassation Court reversed it by saying that additional payments in the form of incidental damages is not recognized by the expropriation proclamation. The proclamation recognizes only the replacement cost of a lost building and nothing else, like lost income.

6.7 Conclusion

Valuation and compensation stage is the most important and equally the most contentious part of an expropriation process. People may be less resistant to the land expropriation on grounds of absence of public purpose or other requirements, but mostly on the amount of compensation. The issues and arguments raised in this

[163] Although there is no data available that shows the amount of loss, there are many people in Addis Ababa who either closed down or temporarily interrupt their business because of road constructions. Road constructions in the city take 24–48 months to finish and business such as restaurants, shops (clothing, butcher, barber) and supermarkets are usually closed for lack of customers. Only those who own the shops/houses can manage to reopen them. Those who rent usually close and forced to relocate to other places and start afresh.

[164] Ethiopian Roads Authority v. Tule Abdo (Federal Supreme Court Cassation Division, Cass. File No. 63352) July, 2011.

chapter lead us to the conclusion that amount of compensation is not fair. Although the assumption is that the Ethiopian compensation system is based on the indemnity principle, this is frustrated by the different valuation regulations and techniques.

The constitution guarantees a *commensurate* amount of compensation for property on the land. Further, the expropriation proclamation states that the valuation of a property shall be based on replacement cost method. Because the principle of cost replacement was wrongly conceived, it leads now to low level compensations. On top of that, the government does not frequently update the prices of material and labor, while inflation is galloping. Urban properties are estimated by valuators without considering the location value and this left the owners in disadvantageous position. Urban property owners do not get a compensation which they could otherwise get it from the market. On the contrary, it is the state that reaps the profit of the developed location. There is a very huge price difference between the voluntary sales price of properties and the compensation values and this big disparity shows that the system is not healthy.

The displacement compensation provided for complete loss of rural land is found to be arbitrary and without scientific justification. This is said because it does not rectify the lifetime land right of peasants they loss as a result of expropriation. Unaided and unassisted, peasants and their families are ended up in low level livelihood as compared to their previous position.

Taking in Ethiopia is not land resumption like in China, wherein farmers use land upon fixed lease period. In Ethiopia farmers are joint holders and given a limitless right by time. And it is unjust to deny compensation for this lost. Displacement compensation is not a compensation for the loss of the land.

Absence of clear resettlement and rehabilitation laws in the country exacerbates the condition of the displaced farmers after the expropriation.

Chapter 7
Conclusions and Recommendations

7.1 Introduction

This research is based on two aspects of Ethiopian land law: land rights and expropriation. By land rights, it refers to those entitlements and privileges a holder or an owner of a land enjoys and which are recognized and enforced by court of law. These could range from ownership, the widest and "absolute" right, to a mere right of use, such as tenancy. The idea of discussing land rights was necessitated because without it the nature of expropriation as limitation on property right and the adequacy of compensation paid to owners could not be fully appreciated.

Expropriation is fully addressed in this thesis as a sovereign power of the state and as a limitation on the constitutionally recognized property rights. And yet, the state is not with absolute liberty to take property by expropriation without limit and justification. To the contrary, the state expropriation power is restricted on two important grounds: that the taking of the property must be to the satisfaction of public interest and that fair compensation must be paid to the owner. Besides these two important provisos, there are also other conditions which the state is supposed to follow, such as service of notice.

This chapter presents a summary of the most important findings of the study, as well as the conclusions drawn from this, and ends with some recommendations for policy change and legal reform. The summary is not intended to be a complete recapitulation of the entire contents of the thesis, but rather attempts to points out the most important aspects of the research work.

D.W. Ambaye, *Land Rights and Expropriation in Ethiopia*,
Springer Theses, DOI 10.1007/978-3-319-14639-3_7

7.2 Summary and Conclusions on Issues of Land Rights

7.2.1 Land Rights in Retrospect

In Chap. 2, land rights in Ethiopia were discussed with a particular emphasis on the current land rights as envisaged in the present rural and urban land laws. Historical aspect of land rights that covers the entire period up to 1991 were also included. The significance of the historical background is imperative because in the absence of that it is difficult to fully grasp the arrangement that Ethiopia has today and the ups and downs that it has been passing through. The political instability and the dynamism of land laws that come with it have been the main causes for tenure insecurity in Ethiopia. Therefore, having stable laws and political system are of paramount importance to the stability of rights and tenure security of land holders. Perhaps, conversely speaking, stability of land rights and laws may also contribute a lot to the political stability; people who have real property may not want war and political instability that may affect and destroy their interests.

Before the eruption of the Ethiopian Revolution in 1974, rural land was significantly under the control of the state and the upper elites. In the northern part of the country, of course, the *rist* system permitted the peasant population to claim part of the rural land for subsistence. Since the *rist* land had been claimed based on lineage relationship, land was highly fragmented and land dispute between new claimants and the lineage was rampant. In spite of the fact that peasants were said to be the ultimate owners of their land, they, nonetheless, were burdened with numerous obligations by the state and the nobility. Besides the usual tax obligations that exacted a fifth and a tenth of their produce, the local nobility, *gult* holders, demanded from the peasant special gifts and manual services that strained significant part of the latter's economy.

Similarly, but on a worst form, most of the land in the southern part of Ethiopia was controlled by the state, the church and the elite. The elite included the nobility and the military. After the re-annexation of the southern territories into the present Ethiopia, in the latter half of nineteenth century, the native peasants were completely evicted from their land. Because of the resistance they showed to the entry of imperial forces, their land was taken as punishment and they were left as *gabbars*, landless laborers. This injustice was perpetrated for the next 100 years until the removal of the imperial power from the throne by the revolution.

It does not mean, however, that the state was indifferent to the misery of the *gabbars* and peasants, especially of the southern territories. Starting from as early as the 1930s, the government had been trying to introduce some reforms that aimed at lessening the burdens of the peasantry. Different decrees and proclamations pertaining to land tax and abolition of manual services, imposed by the nobility on the *rist* holders and *gabbars*, were promulgated although they had little effect. The desired land reform that could enable the *gabbar* of the south as the owner of land was aborted and systematically frustrated by many actors during the imperial regime. Starting from the royal family, all the way through, the landlords in both houses of the parliament, many of whom were from the church and the military were against any land reform that might take away and reduce their land holdings.

The land ownership in urban centers was neither different from that of the rural one. Much of the urban land, especially in Addis Ababa, was controlled by the elite capitalists. The poor were forced to live in substandard and dilapidated rental houses, built by the elite for such purpose.

The significant characteristic of land ownership rights in the pre 1974 Ethiopia was that all urban land was owned privately. Although it was in practice as early as the seventeenth century, private ownership of urban land was formally recognized by law in the 1908 Addis Ababa Land Charter that allowed the holding of land in private ownership and its free transfer to others by sale or other modalities. Similarly, rural land in southern Ethiopia was held in private ownership, including ownership by the church and the state, both of which operated at the same time. Rural land was bought and sold freely in the south unlike that of northern Ethiopia. In northern Ethiopia, rural land was a lineage property owned by a family, and individuals were only given *rist* right, a right to use, rent, donate, and inherit to family members. Selling land outside the lineage was prohibited.

One of the fundamental reasons for the eruption of the revolution was the unjust land holding system in the country. Hence, the bold and unforgettable rallying-motto of the revolution, carried by university students and others, was read as "Land to the Tiller." Since the burden of the system was heavy and the suffering of the peasant population deep, the effect of the revolution was similarly radical. In order to root out the feudo-capitalist political system, the new military government, the Derg, nationalized all land and distributed to the landless.

The Marxist military junta (a.k.a. Derg) passed two proclamations pertaining to the nationalizations of "all rural land and natural resources" and "all urban land and extra houses". Proclamation No. 31/1975 that nationalized all rural land and natural resources abolished by a single stroke the age old land tenure system in the country and transferred all rural land to state ownership. The state became the sole owner of all rural land and it distributed it to the peasants of the north and south equally. Big landlords lost their land without any compensation and were treated equally like their peasants and *gabbars* by receiving equal size of land. On top of that, they were prohibited from using hired labor, which indeed was a very radical shift. The proclamation provided all peasants a lifetime inheritable land use rights over their possession. But, they were forbidden from selling, renting, mortgaging, bartering, or donating the land. Therefore, in spite of its equitability in terms of creating access to rural land to all, the proclamation was restrictive on the freedom of using the land rights. In this way, the motto "Land to the Tiller" was said to be aborted because the Derg that came to power under the slogan has paradoxically ended up itself as the sole owner.

The Derg had also passed a proclamation that nationalized all urban land and extra houses, Proclamation 47/1975. Just like the rural land, all urban land became under state ownership. Big urban land owners lost their land without getting compensation for it. Furthermore, the proclamation nationalized extra rentable houses from those who owned more than one residential and one business houses.

Although the proclamation promised that compensation would be paid for the nationalized extra houses, in reality, the Derg paid nothing.

The Derg's land policy was generally supported by the majority of the people, since land was from the beginning controlled by insignificantly few people. The proclamations were indeed rewarding to the many rural and urban poor who were landless and homeless all of their lives. It also eradicated the old system and its landed elites, which consequently triggered resistance and armed clashes. Especially, in northern Ethiopia, supporters of the old regime and *rist* owners, who were unhappy about the restrictive nature of the proclamation, refuted the proclamation and declared war on the Derg.

Another significant characteristic of this period was that the Derg started to take erroneous land policy measures such as repeated land distribution, forced villagization and grain requisition (that denies market value for the farmer), which ultimately became the reasons for the loss of the support the government had gained at the beginning. As a consequence of all these, the Derg's 17 years rule was remembered as a period of famine, civil war and instability.

7.2.2 Existing Land Rights

The Ethiopian history of land policy is still traumatized by the land tenure system of the imperial era. After coming to power in 1991, the current government could not bring about basic land policy change to that of its predecessor, the Derg. It seems the then Marxist students (later guerilla fighters and now government officials), who struggled under the slogan "Land to the Tiller" forgot about its true meaning and ended up in "state and public ownership of land", when they adopted the new constitution in 1995.

The present land rights are incorporated basically in the current FDRE Constitution, the Rural Land Administration and Use Proclamation, and the Urban Land Lease Proclamation. Therefore, there are dual land laws governing rural and urban land. Today, the Constitution as well as the Federal and Regional rural land laws allow free access to rural land by any adult person who is a resident and wishes to engage in agriculture. As compared to proclamation 31/1975 of the Derg era, the land rights provided today to rural farmers have been liberalized. The land right is specifically termed as "holding right" that provides the holder prerogatives of using, renting/leasing, inheriting, and donating the land.

This, indeed, is a significant development as compared to the land rights incorporated in the previous Proclamation 31/1975. Nevertheless, the current land policy has also its own shortcomings which are concluded in the following criticisms: the land law promotes insecurity of tenure because it allows, among other things, periodic land redistribution; it is inefficient because it constrains land transactions and has inhibited the emergence of a dynamic land market; it promotes fragmentation of land and growing pressure on land resources because it discourages rural people from leaving their farms for other employment opportunities; it also gives the state immense power over the farming population because land is state property and the state may use that as a political weapon.

Even if the current rural land law liberalizes most of the land rights, it completely forbids that sale and exchange of land. It further imposes restrictions on lease and rental, inheritance and donation of rights. For instance, with due regard to the difference among regions, peasants cannot rent the entire size of their land; not more than half of the land may be rented out to fellow farmers or investors. A farmer may bequeath land only to family members, and children who have other occupation and income cannot benefit from it.

The equitability of access to land, underlined by the laws, is idealistic for there is shortage of land in rural Ethiopia. Most farmers live in the highlands where there is high population pressure and hence shortage of land. In the low lands of Ethiopia, where there is abundant arable land, the population is sparse. But the land policy and political environment do not encourage the movement of people from the highlands to the lowland areas or from rural areas to urban centers for the following specific reasons.

First, the residence requirement in the regional rural land laws obliges farmer to live in the same place continuously without any other additional income. This makes people to sit and wait in the rural area for fear of losing their land. Secondly, the residency requirement has been abused and wrongly interpreted by regional officials and is equated to "ethnicity" or "nativity" requirement, and thereby halting any future movement of farmers from other regions. Thirdly, since farmers cannot rent or lease the whole of their farm land to others, they cannot move to urban cities or other regions fallowing their land. Fallowing one's land for three consecutive years entails the loss of the land. Fourthly, since farmers would lose their land if they get an income above some limit, they do not dare to search for alternative income by moving to the urban centers and other regions.

For this reason, there is a high population pressure in the highland rural areas and this creates three further problems: firstly, in order to accommodate the many landless people, the possibility of future land distribution hovers on the air and this creates tenure insecurity; secondly, kebele and woreda officials are giving land from communal lands such as grazing and protected forest lands to landless youth in the village, and this affects the environment; and thirdly, since many people are not moving out of their villages, land fragmentation is being exacerbated.

Urban land has been governed by a lease proclamation starting from 1993. The current proclamation No. 721/2011 was the third lease proclamation following the repeal of its two predecessors adopted after 1993. Although there are still significant amount of land properties acquired under the old permit system (Derg period), the intention of the law is to convert all urban land possessions into lease system. Lease is the cardinal system of urban land tenure. In urban centers, land can be acquired from government through auction, save a small chance of incorporating oneself into self-help housing associations and thereby getting a chance to a home. This means, most of the land required for housing and business will be transferred only through auction.

Because of this, there is a fear that the poor will be marginalized if it is only the highest bidders can get access to urban land. Latest data about the lease auction price showed that the price is extremely high which makes it unaffordable not only to the low income groups but also to the middle income ones. My argument is that the urban land lease proclamations' focus is on generating income rather than also creating equitable land access for all, in a way that reflects the common ownership of land by the people and the state.

Because speculators were said to be beneficiaries of the old lease system by transferring lease right only to third persons, the law discourages the transfer of lease right (bare land) and lease rights with less than half completed constructions. If such right is to be transferred by sale, 95 % of the profit will go to the state. The sole justification behind this rule is to encourage people to complete construction before they transfer it to third parties. In a similar fashion, the law restricts the mortgage money one can borrow from banks. The amount of money one can borrow from banks by securing the lease right is made equal to the actual paid lease price on the land. Location is not to be considered for mortgage purpose. Further, people who are found to be transferring lease right without completing construction shall be barred from future auctions if they do so three times.

The absurdity of this rule is that the government's wish to see more constructed houses comes at the expense of the violation of the constitutional right of property. The constitution under Article 40(1) cum (7) guarantees the full ownership of any construction on the land and the free transfer of it at any price to third parties. It is grossly unfair for the government, after receiving its price for the lease, to again claim profit from the sale. By and large, this practice will again harm the poor since the poor people are the ones who may be forced to sell their property before finishing construction. Lack of adequate funds, family and health reasons might force them to sell their property, and they do not usually get the full value of their property. It may also be the poor who is at the other spectrum of the transaction. This means, poor people may want to buy only bare land or unfinished properties for lack of finance. If the available houses in the market are only those finished ones, the poor, for sure, cannot afford to buy them.

The proclamation indirectly shows that land has no value for the holder. In addition to denying owners the full profit of sales price, the proclamation also denies people getting the best of a loan by mortgaging their properties. If the loan amount is equal or less than the paid lease price, where is then the worth of urban property? If location is not considered during valuation of assets for mortgage, and if buildings shall be valued based only on their cost replacement, then, what is the point of buying land and constructing buildings? If the business man is expected "to reap only what he sows", then what is the wisdom of investment and profit? The whole idea behind this rule is odd and singular and does not have any feasible justification.

In general, the current urban land lease system impedes the free transfer of lease right and defies the very purpose of revising the former lease proclamation in that it exacerbates the concentration of land in the hands of the rich, while denying access to the poor.

7.2.3 Equity and Liberty in Land Rights in the Three Regimes

The Imperial era was better in terms of the freedoms or liberties of land use that it gave to owners, as it allowed the free transfer of land by sale or any other means. Even the *rist* land in the northern part of the country could be sold to lineage members. Yet, the system was inequitable since land was generally controlled by the elites. The Derg's land tenure system was equitable since it created access to land for all people and prohibited the concentration of land in the hands of few. But, it restricted the freedom of using one's land property rights. Now the mission for the current government, when it came to power in 1991, should have been to solve the problems encountered by its predecessors: how to ensure equity in land holding, while at the same time liberalizing the land use rights of the people. From the foregoing discussion, it can be concluded that the current government is not successful in solving both problems. It should do more in creating access to land rights, especially in urban areas, and in liberalizing the land use rights in the country within the given constitutional framework (state and public ownership of land.).

7.3 Summaries and Key Problems in Expropriation

Expropriation has been defined in this thesis as a forced taking of land by the state for public purpose activities and upon advance payment of fair compensation. Expropriation has been exercised starting from time immemorial, although it was after the seventeenth century that it got its present form. European jurists and philosophers gave justifications for the eminent domain power of the state but upon two important provisos, payment of compensation and existence of public interest. Historical documents from European countries, before the seventeenth century, also show that both aspects were respected, even though they were not incorporated into legal documents.

In Ethiopia, expropriation traces back its history to the 1908 Menelik's Addis Ababa Land Charter wherein it is stated that the government may expropriate private land for public purpose activities and upon payment of compensation. Other sources, although very few, have also shown that in earlier periods there were a tendencies to compensate in situations where the kings took land that belonged to private individuals. But, of course, evidences are rare and it cannot be conclusively said that this was the general practice. In fact, the contrary view seems also true because there are other sources which show that the power of the kings to take and give land was extremely absolute.

Expropriation is justified on the primacy of social interest over that of the individual. And yet, the interest of the individual is not completely disregarded as mechanisms are set to recompense the loss at the expense of society. This theory was consistently held by all philosophers and jurists, irrespective of their difference on the sanctity or otherwise of private property. No one wants the individual to be "sacrificed at the altar" in the interest of society. With the development of modern laws and constitutions as well as court decisions, it has become clear now that the state may freely exercise its eminent domain power, provided that the taking serves some social interest and fair compensation is paid in advance. The determination of the fairness of the compensation and the real existence of public purpose requires, in most countries, the intervention of courts. In other words, individual property right may not be totally left to the will and judgment of the administrative authorities only, for there may be the tendency of violating such rights.

For this reason, expropriation is made to pass through a certain procedure so as, on the one hand, to avoid arbitrariness in practice, and on the other, to safeguard the interest of the individual. The procedure generally includes public discussion, notice, valuation, compensation and appeal.

The FDRE Constitution is the source of expropriation power of the state in Ethiopia. Detailed laws and regulations are provided in the FDRE Expropriation Proclamation No. 455/2005 and Regulation No. 135/2007. A review of the proclamation shows that expropriation power is provided to the woreda or urban administration, although the decisions for expropriation might also come from above. The rural and urban administrations operate separately and are responsible for all the procedures starting from public discussion to payment of compensation.

With regard to the procedures that should be followed during expropriation, the law lacks clarity in many respects. What is clearly envisaged so far is that it is the woreda and urban administrations that are empowered with expropriation right, and the fact that notice shall be given after the completion of valuation. It does not tell whether public discussion should be conducted during the planning stage, although in practice it is being done. Yet, since it is not put in the law as a mandatory procedure, there is no way to assert whether people should always be consulted, although consultation is a wise idea.

As a matter of principle, notice should have been considered as part of the public discussion aiming at creating awareness about a potential expropriation action. In Ethiopia, however, it is used entirely for different purposes. It serves as a warning to inform the person about the amount of money he would receive as compensation and the timeframe within which he is supposed to vacate from the place.

Another gap in the law is that it does not clearly fix the cut-off date, the date beyond which no improvement on the land is possible. The logical timeframe for cut-off date is the date on which the inventory of assets has been completed. But, the indirect meaning of the law shows that the cut-off date is the same as the date of notice. If one tries to follow this line of argument, then one falls into a trap of endless processes of inventories and improvements. This was clearly exemplified in the Nyota case wherein coffee farmers tried to plant new coffee seedlings after inventory of all coffee trees and assets was completed.

The other discrepancy identified in this study was that although the law requires the presence of owners during inventory of assets for valuation purpose, there were cases where inventories were taken in their absence.

Resettlement and rehabilitation program as a mandatory procedure is not boldly and sufficiently put in the expropriation laws. For this reason, today, one cannot be sure about the obligations of the state in providing rehabilitation support to displaced farmers. Whereas in projects that are supported by the World Bank the state and private investors are trying to carryout resettlement and rehabilitation programs, in most other cases, there are no such practices performed either by a public or private operators. Only in selected huge public projects does the state try to give resettlement and rehabilitation assistances. This creates a double treatment of displaced people in the absence of clear and comprehensive guidelines as to when and how this should be provided. The result of this disregard leaves farmers untended with all the cash money in their hands and unwise decisions in their "minds". This eventually leads to a spendthrift behavior of the farmers which made them end up in poverty.

It has been mentioned in this thesis once and again that public purpose is one form of limitation on the government's power of expropriation. Land may not be expropriated unless it is found to be very important to society. Legislations try to define this importance either strictly, by listing down the potential activities for which land might be wanted, or broadly, by providing a general principle that serves as a spring board for the government to justify its takings. On top of that, courts may also involve in deciding whether a certain project indeed meets the public purpose requirement or not.

The Ethiopian Expropriation Proclamation defines public purpose in its widest meaning as one that gives "direct or indirect" benefit to society, and relates to the "urban structural development" and the country's general economic "development strategy". These parameters invite for a variety of limitless projects and activities, which in effect, leave the "public purpose" requirement in vain. There is no visible limit to the state's power of expropriating private property, even for private use purposes. It may not openly be said that land which belongs to *individual A* can be expropriated for transfer to *individual B*. But it is perfectly possible to take the land from *individual A* and transfer it to *individual C*, provided that the latter would put the land to *better use*, such as building a hotel or horticulture. So, unlike the Civil Code, which prohibited land expropriation for *pure economic gains*, the present law entertains economic gain as one of the attributes of public purpose.

The implication of this rule is that it puts all properties, which are found within the city center and the peripheries at the risk of expropriation. There is no clear limitation on the power of the government that protects people's land and property right. If a new road is constructed in a neighborhood, for example, the city may demand the land owners either to upgrade their buildings according to the master plan, which most of the time is beyond their ability, or else the land would be transferred to those who can afford. It is common for people in cities to cede their land for the construction of hotels, and for farmers to do the same for the establishment of horticulture farms. The notorious case we mentioned in the thesis was that of the Sheraton Addis Hotel, which acquired 42 ha of land by expropriation just to expand its business.

To exacerbate the situation, the role of courts in these matters is ambiguous, if not interpreted as none. The Expropriation Proclamation does not in clear terms provide the courts power to review an administrative decision concerning the public purpose decision. Theoretically, it may be possible to argue that courts do have such power, but it is difficult to be sure, for lack of case law. In simple terms, it would be an ideal protection for the property rights of the people if courts could be given an explicit power to review an administrative decision concerning public purpose.

The other issue addressed in this study is compensation. Payment of fair compensation is another limitation on the expropriation power of the state. Fair compensation is believed to exist if the compensation made is equal to the market value of the property. Market value of a property is roughly understood as the price gained on the open market when a willing buyer and seller reach agreement after negotiation. In short, market value is the price at which the contracting parties to the sale contract give their consent[1] to transact. Expropriation is a forced sale, and if the state wants genuinely to recompense the loss, then the compensation must reflect the price of the victim of the expropriation. This price is presumed to enable the loser to go to the market and fetch similar property of comparative utility.

To get a market value of a property, appraisers mostly employ three methodologies, namely: comparative sales approach, income capitalization approach and replacement cost approach. Since enough has already been said about the nature of the three methods in Chap. 6, it is suffice here to mention that it is the third method which is employed in Ethiopia.

The state, as a matter of principle, follows cost replacement to recompense the damage caused as a result of expropriation. Although the other two approaches may not be readily applied now, for lack of data and infrastructure, they may be used so long as the state can allow that in legislation, and fulfills the necessary data and infrastructure. These are, especially, related to full-fledged property registration, upkeep of all property transactions, and availability of analyzed market prices data. In the absence of full market data, the only means of estimating the value of real property is cost replacement.

Even though it is possible to reach market value through the use of replacement cost approach, the Ethiopian replacement cost approach is defective as compared to the international practice. It does not at all give market value for the displaced people. For example, it does not consider the value of the land or the location on which the building rests. Secondly, it disregards all incidental and consequential damages, such as additional cost incurred as a result of change in location, reduction in market value for property leftover after partial expropriation, lost income because of delay in expropriation process, and business closure as a result of public construction works.

The valuation technique does not bother to narrow the difference between the market value (voluntary sale) and the expropriation value of urban property. In most cases, the difference is more than tenfold and it is always the state that fully captures

[1] Consent in the law of contract assumes the free will (willingness) of the parties without any duress (violence), mistake or error. While duress shows absence of any coercion that forces the parties to enter into the contract, error and mistake shows that the parties had full information and knowledge about the nature of the subject of sale and the prevailing values they give for it.

the profit. Farmers in the fringes of towns and cities, anticipating expropriation, tend to subdivide and informally sell their farm land, by realizing that the sales price is more compensating than the one paid by the state during expropriation.

Our evidences show that under the existing circumstances, the money paid as compensation to replace a demolished house is short of the necessary sum. It could not replace any standard house as per the requirements of the city regulations. One reason is that the prices of materials and labor, the two most important components of valuation calculation, are not frequently updated in a way that reflects the existing market and inflation rates. The other reason is that the depreciation allowance deducted from the estimated value takes away more than half of the sum. That is why cost replacement approach is said to be unsuitable for valuation of old properties. Owners of urban property are found today in "between a rock and a hard place"; the state denies location value and rather reduces depreciation allowance from the estimated compensation value, and yet it demands the people to construct standard houses.

The nature of the compensation given for loss of rural land is not clear, although we classified it in this paper as resettlement compensation. Although the source of the law concerning the compensation for loss of rural land seems the Chinese LAL, the Ethiopian expropriation does not follow it to the full. Unlike the Chinese LAL, the Ethiopian Expropriation Proclamation does not provide compensation for the loss of the land itself. In other words, although peasants are guaranteed with life-time land right to the land (as opposed to the 30 years lease right in China), they do not get compensation when they lose it. It is not possible to argue that the 10 years displacement compensation provided replaces the loss of the land, except that it can indeed be considered as a form of rehabilitation support. In China, farmers receive a maximum of 13 years value of produce as compensation for loss of land and compensation for displacement (rehabilitation).

When we come to the computation of the value of the 10 years' displacement compensation, we do not know for sure the exact justification for selecting 10 years. Furthermore, during calculation, appraisers are required to go 5 years back to get an average value on which to base the displacement compensation; they just multiply the average price by 10. If one accepts the displacement compensation as real compensation for the loss of the land, then in the face of galloping inflation, it is grossly unfair to base the calculation on the market value of the past, instead of the present or the future likely values.

The practice of compensation payment suffers mainly from the following problems. The first one has to do with the reluctance or refusal to compensate. As in the case of the Amhara Rural Roads Authority, there are government agencies that refuse to pay compensation for no apparent reasons. Further, small towns which expropriate land from the nearby farmers are reluctant to pay compensation on the ground of lack of finance. Secondly, in most cases, payments of compensation are protracted and delayed. Especially, rural farmers complained that the compensation was paid a year after they vacated from their land. And the government did not make good the inflation loss that came as a result of the delay in payment.

Land to land compensation is an alternative compensation method provided that excess land is available in the locality. The laws are not clear and detailed about its applicability, though. The laws are silent, for example, as to what will happen if the replacement land is not comparable to the expropriated land in terms of size, location, and fertility. Only the Amhara Valuation Directive tries to answer issues related to difference in land size, though it does not consider the other differences of location and fertility. Other regions have not come up with their respective valuation and compensation directives and as a result the practice is different in different regions.

The Ethiopian valuation system also suffers from the lack of qualified experts and consultants. All valuations in the rural area are conducted by unskilled local elders and representatives of different government offices. In urban areas, non-professional and unskilled people, such as geographers, economists, lawyers, accountants and civil engineers are being assigned as valuators of real property. In some cases, there are also allegations of corruptions by these valuators. One fact in relation to this point is that there are no private valuation consultation companies in the country that could serve as alternative valuators. Consequentially, even if cases are brought to courts on grounds of insufficiency of compensation amounts, the courts could not be of much help since there are no experts who can give second opinion on the matter. What happens is rather the same valuator who had made the previous valuation may be ordered for second opinion, which yields to little change.

7.4 Recommendations

7.4.1 Legal and Policy Reform Recommendations on Land Rights

Based on the above conclusions and findings, the following specific recommendations are forwarded:

1. The government should revise the rural land proclamations and liberate some of the restrictions imposed on rights such as rent, donation and inheritance. Sharecropping or cash based land rents for longer periods may attract investors with better money and farming technology. The laws may also be designed in such a way that they benefit peasants through lease contract. There are cases of informal land sales in the name of lease across the country, and since these are being done outside of the law, the rights of the contracting parties are always at risk.
2. The requirement for farmers to reside in the farm area is not necessary, because it hampers the peasants from searching alternative income by staying for longer periods in urban areas. The residence requirement creates unnecessary pressure and an increase in population presence in rural areas, for fear of loss of land. This accelerates fragmentation and lesser productivity of the land. Coupled with

this, the shadow of the possibility of land distribution creates strong insecurity on farmers, and abolishment of this possibility is imperative. Instead of carrying out redistribution, landless employees should be encouraged to farm in the vast lowland areas, or to look for other livelihood alternatives in urban areas. Nevertheless, this can be done, if and only if, the government can guarantee the safe movement of people across regions and the opportunity of working as farmers there. If ethnicity and regionalism continues to serve as a requisite by politicians to get land in Ethiopia, the problem of social pressure and land fragmentation will continue forever. The cases of the Gura Farda and Beni Shangul evictions have sent strong insecurity sentiment among people who are living outside of the regions of their birth.

3. Much care is needed in the event of land transfer for large-scale agricultural investment. Among others, care should be made on the amount of land transferred, the lease period granted, and the effect it may cause to the environment.
4. Efficient and equitable land distribution in urban Ethiopia should get the attention of policy makers. There is no doubt that the new urban land lease proclamation will boost the urban revenue as a result of land lease transfer; but it will leave the urban poor unaided. An equitable system that creates free access to urban land should be designed (such as lot). There is no doubt that land will be, in the future, concentrated in the hands of a few, who can afford to offer much during auction. The argument is that the constitutional principle that declares the state and public ownership of land is less reflected in urban areas than in the rural scenario. Farmers are given all rights except sale and exchange. In urban areas, except for the narrow opportunity of getting condominium houses, poor and middle income people do not have alternative to get land.
5. The restrictions made on urban land transfer have to be lifted. Government should fight land speculation by supplying more land or, by imposing urban land tax (so as to discourage those who collect idle land in anticipation of profit) rather than restricting transaction. Especially, the restriction imposed on banks not to lend more than the paid-up lease price is likely to have a damaging effect on the economy, since the business community cannot get enough capital from banks.

7.4.2 Legal and Policy Reform Recommendations on Expropriation

With the rapid economic development and urbanization witnessed in recent years, large amount of urban and rural land has been taken by expropriation. Even if expropriation is accepted as the only tool to acquire land for development and urbanization purposes, two conditions have to be fulfilled: firstly, the procedure has to follow due process of law, and secondly, owners must be compensated fully. If people are denied justice or the value (market value or replacement value) of their property, the development that comes is not worth having since it is based on the involuntary scarifications of individuals and violation of their rights. From morality point of view, it is not different from a wealth which is collected through theft, child labor, slavery, gross violation of human right or other similar unethical conducts. Therefore, in order to ensure justice and the equal ownership right of the people with that of the state, a constitution and proclamation level legislative reform is imperative.

1. It has been concluded that the compensation amount which is paid today is short of standard. The controversy on inadequacy of compensation arises primarily from the constitution itself. The FDRE Constitution embraces two seemingly conflicting Sub-Articles under Articles 40 and 40(3)[2] guarantees the equal ownership of land by the state and the people. On the other hand, Article 40(8)[3] gives compensation only to the *private property* on the land, not the land itself. The conflict seems also to continue when one looks into the Expropriation Proclamation and Regulations. The subsidiary legislations follow an ambiguous approach by giving compensation in cash (replacement cost) for the loss of the private property on the land, and a land to land compensation, or cash in the case of rural areas, for the loss of the land. It seems the Expropriation Proclamation and the Regulation, to a limited level, follow the ownership right of the people to the land as embedded in Article 40(3).
   Therefore, if the intention of the Constitution is to ensure equal ownership of the land by the people and the state, then this equality must also be reflected in the compensation modality as well. Hence, Article 40(8) must be revised in such a way that it is harmonized with Article 40(3). One possible way to do this is to state in clear terms that during expropriation, commensurate compensation would be paid to the land and other properties thereon.
2. When it comes to compensation, the state denies the people the right to get compensation for the land, as if it is the sole owner of all the land. It has been mentioned that in urban areas it is the state that captures the enhanced land value or location value by transferring the space through lease to others. On the other hand, the owners of real property are left with insignificant amount of money as replacement cost. In this case, the recommended solution is: even if appraisers insist on the application of depreciation allowance, let the state share the profit it reaps with the condemnee. In this way it is possible to render justice and to enable the owner to have sufficient fund to finish the construction of the replacement house. The reason that we recommend half and not full of the

[2] "The right to ownership of rural and urban land, as well as of all natural resources, is exclusively vested in the State and in the peoples of Ethiopia. Land is a common property of the Nations, Nationalities and Peoples of Ethiopia and shall not be subject to sale or to other means of exchange" Article 40(3) of FDRE Constitution.

[3] "Without prejudice to the right to private property, the government may expropriate private property for public purposes subject to payment in advance of compensation commensurate to the value of the property" Article 40(8) of FDRE Constitution.

market value of the location is because half of the ownership right of the land goes to the state.

3. The cost replacement approach is sanctioned in the law as the only valuation approach, and we already saw some of its problems. It cannot fairly value old properties. It is, therefore, necessary to introduce all types of valuation approaches so that the valuator can choose one which is scientifically suitable to reach fair value.
4. In situations where part of urban land is expropriated and where the holder insists to retain the rest of the land, compensation is not paid for the land taken. This emanates from the misconceived idea of the sole proprietorship of land by the state. But, land belongs to both the holder and the state equally. Therefore, the partial taking of land that causes value reduction on the remaining part of the land must be, somehow, compensated. This can be done either by calculating the market lease value of the land taken or by calculating the reduction on the market value of the retained property. In the short period, since it may be difficult to determine the market value of the real property because of lack of market data, it will be easier to follow the first way of calculating the compensation in such occurrences.
5. The compensation given for rural farmers is marred by the application of the illogical previous 5 years average values, in order to determine the future loss. This makes the compensation amount unfair. Hence, one of the primary areas of concern for reform is this very provision. The 10 years' displacement compensation must be calculated based on, at least, the current market prices of crops, if not the future likely price by considering the possible increase in inflation.
6. The nature of the displacement compensation that is calculated at 10 years' produce and given to the farmer in lieu of land to land compensation is not clear. It is vague whether it is compensation for loss of the land or a rehabilitation support for displacement, although we inclined to argue in this thesis in favor of the latter. The most probable origin of the Ethiopian expropriation proclamation, the Chinese LAL, allows two kinds of compensations for complete loss of land: compensation for the loss of the land and displacement compensation. This is fair and I recommend that the same procedure be followed in Ethiopia. Therefore, as a legislative reform I recommend that an additional compensation computed at 10–15 years' current value of produce be introduced.
7. The Expropriation Proclamation does not unequivocally list down the procedural steps that the government should follow during expropriation. What I have tried to put in Chap. 3 is just based on the existing practice and the logical sequence of things that should come one after the other. In the absence of clear guidelines, authorities tend to do the work arbitrarily, and this may cause the violation of people's right. Therefore, as a legal reform, the law must come up with the logical arrangement of steps or procedures that must be followed. Chief among these, planning, notice, public discussion, inventory and valuation of assets, payment of compensation and appropriation of land should be

included on priority level. Planning, among others, should include the request for land by the project owner and the consideration and approval of public purpose nature of the project. Further, the cut-off date which is missed in the current law must be clearly included in the inventory stage. Cut-off date must be fixed as the date of the completion of the inventory of assets for valuation purpose. Public discussion must give room for detailed consultation with private owners and the chance to negotiate on some compensation modalities.

8. The roles of valuation committee and inventory committee must be clear. It is important that the two committees should either be brought down to one, or should be given clear responsibilities in order to avoid confusion and establish accountability.
9. The scope and limitation of public purpose is unknown since the power of expropriation given to the state is a broader one. This creates tenure insecurity on all urban and rural land holders. Although there are not many case laws, neither the affected people nor the courts seem to challenge the government's decision on public purpose. Therefore, the only effective means to delimit the state expropriation power is through legislative revision and inclusion of limiting factors. In this regard, there are several possibilities that could be followed. One way is to list down the potential activities which are considered as benefiting the society in general. This was, in fact, the course of action which was followed by the previous Expropriation proclamation 401/2004. The second possibility is to maintain the present generalist approach but with a limitation of some sort. For example, it may be said that the government may expropriate land for a public purpose that gives direct or indirect benefit, provided that it is not intended for pure private economic gain. At least, in this way, it is possible to avoid expropriation for pure private gains such as hotels and the like, which investors could otherwise secure the land through purchase from private owners or through lease auction from the government.
10. The role of courts must be improved if a legislative reform has to be done on the present expropriation legislation. Courts should have roles on all the expropriation procedures. For example, courts must hear grievances related to the violation of the steps in the expropriation process, such as absence of notice, consultation and inventory of assets without one's presence. Courts must have a clear say on the public purpose nature of a project, if the administrative decision happens to be challenged. Clarity on the laws avoids any fear or confusion on parts of judges, as the courts in today's Ethiopia are not "free" from political influence.
11. The legislative reform should not be limited only to the federal level. All regional states must be encouraged to come up with detailed implementing regulation, having similar approaches in the process.
12. It is recommendable to include clear and comprehensive resettlement and rehabilitation legislation in the reform. Except the policy intention, envisaged under Article 44 of the FDRE Constitution, there is not much said in the current expropriation proclamation about the need and applicability of resettlement and rehabilitation programs and the responsibilities of public and private actors.

For this reason, displaced people in rural areas and urban centers are left without support that could help them to regain their former livelihood. Therefore, the inclusion of such a program in the laws is of paramount importance.

7.4.3 Recommendations to Improve the Practice

With all due regard to the acceptability of the above recommendations, it may not be easy to initiate and accelerate a legislative reform on the expropriation legislations within a short period of time. Therefore, another set of recommendations which can be applied within the existing legislative framework are given as follow:

1. The expropriation process should be, as far as possible, transparent and participatory. Most people's claim was that during public discussions, politicians of higher caliber usually come and provide undelivered promises. The other problem is that valuators are not honest and transparent enough when they take inventory, especially in rural areas. Therefore, this practice shall be curbed by being honest and open in the dealings and discussions with the affected people.
2. Despite the legal requirement for a written notice to be delivered in person to the affected people, in practice authorities do not follow it. Notices are just posted on notice boards, and they might be missed by the affected people. The urban and rural administrations are, therefore, required to correct this practice.
3. Leaving aside the urban people with uncertain titles, many rural farmers affected by rural roads construction projects are complaining of denial of compensation. This is deeply felt by them when especially they see that the Federal Roads Authority pays compensation, while the Regional Rural Roads Authority refuses them the compensation. This action of the government is unjustified by any standard of the law. Even if the road construction brings about benefit to the affected people as well, there is no moral or legal justification to make them alone to bear the burden. Therefore, the government must allocate fund for this purpose and solve the problem, and thereby avoid the double treatments of farmers whose land has been taken by the regional government.
4. In several areas, farmers have complained some of their properties were not counted during inventory. The practice in Oromia Region is, of course, peculiar in that it denies compensation to naturally grown (indigenous) trees. This practice is obviously causing two apparent problems: firstly, not to give compensation for indigenous trees grown on one's land is a clear violation of the law, as the trees are also properties recognized by the constitution; and secondly, if farmers are denied compensation, it is likely that farmers will cut all the trees, which eventually causes deforestation and harms the environment
5. Delays in compensation payments, which are rampant in many areas, should be corrected by the state. Because of bureaucratic practices, farmers and urban residents have to wait as long as a year to receive the compensation after they

are displaced from their land. The problem here is that the money after a year will lose some value for inflation. Inflation on food staff and properties do usually register double digit growth. Therefore, delay in compensation payment leads to reduction in compensation amount and thus, unfair compensation.

6. Literally, the valuation profession is not yet created; the state has a great task to strengthen the few education centers to provide it with such professionals. It also has to encourage those who are in the market, but are unknown and unrecognized, to come to light and work as professionals. Repeated and continuous short term training on property valuation is necessary to those who are engaged in the practice as valuators of the different woredas and urban administrations.
7. The government and courts must encourage people to go by appeal whenever there are grievances and injustices done by the administration. Administration wrongs and injustices committed by low level officials are general maladministration problem of the state, which can be solved by the administrative apparatus. But, there might be other injustices which are sanctioned from above, such as an expropriation decision by a Federal or State organs. Such kind of injustice can be solved only by involving the legislator (in the long run) or courts in the near future. The freedom of courts should be respected at any time, and in the absence of any limitation to the contrary, the courts should consider themselves as fully empowered to review administrative decisions of the state concerning expropriation.
8. No uniform and consistent valuation and compensation regulations are enacted across all regions in Ethiopia. Only the Amhara Region and Addis Ababa City have adopted such laws. The absence of detailed regulations in the Regional States created differences in valuation techniques and formulas which lead to unfair compensation in some regions. Since the Federal Expropriation Proclamation and Compensation Regulation are not comprehensive enough to cover all aspects of valuation, the regions were supposed to come up with some gap filling provisions of their own. Those gap filling provisions are in legislation in Amhara and Addis Ababa, but remain in practice in the other regions. We recommend them as short term strategies, since it takes only few months if the responsible organs are willing to do so.

Annex A

Table A.1 Replacement of land for residential purpose

Size of land taken in m^2	Replacement land at redevelopment area in m^2	Replacement in condominium housing in m^2	Replacement land at expansion area in m^2	Type of building
50 and below	–	25	75-in housing association	According to city plan
51–100	–	30	90-in housing association	According to city plan
100–150	–	35	125	According to city plan
151–200	–	50	175	According to city plan
201–250	105	–	200	According to city plan
251–300	150	–	250	According to city plan
301–350	175	–	300	According to city plan
351–400	200	–	350	According to city plan
401–450	225	–	400	According to city plan
451–500	250	–	450	According to city plan
Above 501	350	–	500	According to city plan

D.W. Ambaye, *Land Rights and Expropriation in Ethiopia*,
Springer Theses, DOI 10.1007/978-3-319-14639-3

Table A.2 Replacement of land for business purpose

Size of land taken in m^2	Replacement land at redevelopment area in m^2	Replacement in condominium housing in m^2	Replacement land at expansion area in m^2	Type of building
150 and below	–	50	150	According to city Plan
151–250	–	75	210	According to city plan
251–350	150	–	300	According to city plan
351–450	200	–	400	According to city plan
451–550	250	–	500	According to city plan
551–650	300	–	600	According to city plan
651–750	350	–	700	According to city plan
751–850	400	–	800	According to city plan
851–950	450	–	900	According to city plan
951–1,050	500	–	1,000	According to city plan
1,051–1,250	525	–	1,050	According to city plan
1,251–1,450	550	–	1,100	According to city plan
1,451–1,650	575	–	1,150	According to city plan
1,651–1,850	600	–	1,200	According to city plan
1,851–2,000	625	–	1,250	According to city plan
2,000 and above	650	–	1,300	According to city plan

Table A.3 Replacement of land for industry and workshop

Size of land taken in m^2	Replacement land at redevelopment area in m^2	Replacement in condominium housing in m^2	Replacement land at expansion area in m^2	Type of building
250 and below	–	–	250	According to city plan
251–550	–	–	500	According to city plan
551–750	–	–	750	According to city plan
751–950	–	–	950	According to city plan
951–1,150	–	–	1,000	According to city plan
1,151–1,250	–	–	1,250	According to city plan
1,251–1,500	–	–	1,500	According to city plan
1,501–1,700	–	–	1,700	According to city plan
1,701–2,000	–	–	2,000	According to city plan
2,001–2,500	–	–	2,500	According to city plan
2,501–3,000	–	–	3,000	According to city plan
3,001–3,500	–	–	3,500	According to city plan
3,501–4,000	–	–	4,000	According to city plan
4,001–4,500	–	–	4,500	According to city plan
4,501–5,000	–	–	5,000	According to city plan
5,001 and above	–	–	5,500	According to city plan

Table A.4 Replacement land for garage and warehouse purpose

Size of land taken in m^2	Replacement land at redevelopment area in m^2	Replacement in condominium housing in m^2	Replacement land at expansion area in m^2	Type of building
150 and below	–	–	150	According to city plan
151–250	–	–	250	According to city plan
251–350	–	–	350	According to city plan
351–450	–	–	450	According to city plan
451–550	–	–	550	According to city plan
551–650	–	–	650	According to city plan
651–750	–	–	750	According to city plan
751–850	–	–	850	According to city plan
851–950	–	–	950	According to city plan
951–1,150	–	–	1,150	According to city plan
1,151–1,250	–	–	1,250	According to city plan
1,251–1,500	–	–	1,500	According to city plan
1,501–1,700	–	–	1,700	According to city plan
1,701–2,000	–	–	2,000	According to city plan
2,001 and above	–	–	2,250	According to city plan

Table A.5 Replacement of land for public entertainment

Size of land taken in m^2	Replacement land at redevelopment area in m^2	Replacement in condominium housing in m^2	Replacement land at expansion area in m^2	Type of building
250 and below	250	–	250	According to city plan
251–350	350	–	350	According to city plan
351–450	450	–	450	According to city plan
451–550	550	–	550	According to city plan
551–650	650	–	650	According to city plan
651–750	750	–	750	According to city plan
751–850	850	–	850	According to city plan
851–950	950	–	950	According to city plan
951–1,150	950	–	1,150	According to city plan
1,151–1,500	1,250	–	1,500	According to city plan
1,501–2,000	1,500	–	1,750	According to city plan
2,001–2,500	1,600	–	2,250	According to city plan
2,501 and above	1,650	–	2,500	According to city plan

Table A.6 Replacement of land for religious institutions

Size of land taken in m^2	Replacement land at redevelopment area in m^2	Replacement in condominium housing in m^2	Replacement land at expansion area in m^2	Type of building
250 and below	250	–	250	According to city plan
251–350	350	–	350	According to city plan
351–450	450	–	450	According to city plan
451–550	550	–	550	According to city plan
551–650	650	–	650	According to city plan
651–750	750	–	750	According to city plan
751–850	850	–	850	According to city plan
851–950	950	–	950	According to city plan
951–1,150	950	–	1,150	According to city plan
1,151–1,500	1,250	–	1,500	According to city plan
1,501–2,000	1,500	–	1,750	According to city plan
2,001–2,500	1,600	–	2,250	According to city plan
2,501 and above	1,650	–	2,500	According to city plan

Table A.7 Replacement of land for educational and health centers

Size of land taken in m^2	Replacement land at redevelopment area in m^2	Replacement in condominium housing in m^2	Replacement land at expansion area in m^2	Type of building
851–950	950	–	950	According to city plan
951–1,150	950	–	1,150	According to city plan
1,151–1,500	1,250	–	1,500	According to city plan
1,501–2,000	1,500	–	1,750	According to city plan
2,501 and above	1,750	–	2,000	According to city plan

Table A.8 Replacement of land for residential purpose to farmers who are incorporate into a city

S. No.	Land held by the Farmer in m^2	Replacement land for housing in expansion area	Building type
1	Up to 10,500	200	According to city plan
2	10,501–30,000	250	According to city plan
3	30,001–40,500	300	According to city plan
4	40,501–60,000	350	According to city plan
5	60,001–70,500	400	According to city plan
6	70,501–90,000	450	According to city plan
7	Above 90,001	500	According to city plan

News Papers

Addis Fortune (http://www.addisfortune.net)
Capital (http://www.capitalethiopia.com)
The Reporter (http://www.thereporterethiopia.com)
Reporter (Amharic Version) (http://www.ethiopianreporter.com)
African Review (http://www.africareview.com)

D.W. Ambaye, *Land Rights and Expropriation in Ethiopia*,
Springer Theses, DOI 10.1007/978-3-319-14639-3

Interviews

Interview Made with Ato Mihretu Dagnew, Senior Valuation Expert, at the Amhara BoEPLAU, January 8, 2013, Bahir Dar.
Interview Made with Ato Daniel, Property Valuator at Arada Sub-City of Addis Ababa City, Addis Ababa, October 31, 2012.
Interview Made with Ato Mikias Goitom, Property Valuator at Yaka Sub-City of Addis Ababa City, Addis Ababa, November 1, 2012.
Group interview made with Fasil Simeneh, Addissu Begashaw and Begiziew Tsehayu, Property Valuators at Bahir Dar City Municipality, Bahir Dar, October 15, 2012.
Interview Made with Ato Essayas Kebede, Director of the Agricultural Investment Support Directorate, Ministry of Agriculture, Addis Ababa, December 2011.
Interview with Ato Adem Nuri, Head of Valuation and Compensation Section at the Addis Ababa City Land Bank and Urban Renewal Project Office, September 12, 2012
Interview made with Ato Dereje Gebrie and Samson Mekonnen, Representatives of Displaced People from Arada Sub-City, October 30, 2012, Addis Ababa
Interview made with Ato Birhanu Andualem, Judge at Bahir Dar Municipal Court, Bahir Dar, November 22, 2012.
Interview made with Ato Sintayehu Dires, head of Land Administration Work Flow, ANRS Bureau of Environmental Protection Land Administration and Use (BoEPLAU), December 26, Bahir Dar, 2012.
Interview made with Ato Yalew Abate, former head of the ANRS Urban Works and Development Bureau, Bahir Dar, May 2011.
Interview With Ato Mebit Admass, Deputy General Manager of ANRS Rural Roads Authority, Bahir Dar, January 2, 2013.
Interview with Ato Akane, represented head of Universal Rural Roads Access Program (URRAP) of Amhara Rural Roads Authority, Bahir Dar, January 2, 2013.

D.W. Ambaye, *Land Rights and Expropriation in Ethiopia*,
Springer Theses, DOI 10.1007/978-3-319-14639-3

Interviews

Cases

Ethiopian Roads Authority v. Jada Biru, (Federal Supreme Court Cassation Division, Cass. File No. 57271), December 2010.
Solomon Mehari v. Mekelle City Administration, (Federal Supreme Court Cassation Division, Cass. File No. 81159), December 2012.
Tolesa Wirtu v. Ethiopian Electric Power Corporation, (Federal Supreme Court Cassation Division, Cass. File No. 75763), January 2013.
Ethiopian Roads Authority v. Tule Abdo, (Federal Supreme Court Cassation Division, Cass. File No. 63352) July 2011.
Abeje Yitayew v. Ministry of Defense Western Division, (West Gojam High Court, Civ. File No. 9600).
Awoke Addis v. Ministry of Defense Western Division, (West Gojam High Court, Civ. File No. 9587)
Tarekegn Eskemeche v. Ministry of Defense Western Division, (West Gojam High Court, Civ. File No. 9803)
Tsegaye Meseret & et al. v. Federal Roads Authority, (Federal Supreme Court Cassation Division, Cass. File No. 50810), October 2010

D.W. Ambaye, *Land Rights and Expropriation in Ethiopia*,
Springer Theses, DOI 10.1007/978-3-319-14639-3

References

A Proclamation to Amend the Land Tax Proclamation of 1944. (1966). Proclamation No. 230/1966. *Negarit Gazeta*. Year 25, No. 9.

AACA. (2012). *Addis Abbeba: Ye2003 Ametawi Metsihaf* (Addis Ababa: 2011/12 Year Book). Addis Ababa: Addis Ababa City Administration Communication Affaira Bureau.

Abdissa, F., & Degefa, T. (2011). Urbanization and changing livelihoods: The case of farmers' displacement in the expansion of Addis Ababa. In C. Teller & A. Hailemariam (Eds.) *The demographic transition and development in Africa: The unique case of Ethiopia*. London: Springer.

Abera, M. (2012). *Ye Eethiopia Meseretawi ye Lease Hig Hasabochna Yemiasketlachew Chigroch (Fundamentals of the Ethiopian lease law and its problems)*. Far East Trading: Addis Ababa.

Addis Ababa Valuation and Compensation of Replacement Land and Housing. *Directive No. 3/2010*. Addis Ababa City Council.

Admassie, Y. (2000). *Twenty years to nowhere: Property rights, land management and conservation in Ethiopia*. Asmara: The Red Sea Press Inc.

Alabama-section. (1976). Eminent domain: A survey of alabama law. *Alabama Law Review, 28*.

Amhara Valuation and Compensation Directive. *Directive 5/2011*. ANRS Regional Council.

Appropriation of Land for Government Works and Payment of Compensation for Property Proclamation, Proclamation 401/2004. *Negarit Gazeta*. Year 10, No. 42.

Allen, T. (2007). Compensation for property under the european convention of human rights. *Michigan Journal of International Law, 28*, 287–335.

Allen, T. (2008). Control over the use and abuse of eminent domain in England: A comparative view. In R. P. Malloy (Ed.) *Private property, community development, and eminent domain*. Hampshire: Ashgate Publishing Limited.

Alterman, R. (2011). Regulatory takings and the role of comparative research. In R. Alterman (Ed.) *Takings international: A comparative perspective on land use regulations and compensation rights*. Chicago: American Bar Association.

Alvarez, F. (1970). *Narrative of the Portuguese Embassy to Abyssinia During the Years 1520–1527*. London: The Hakluyt Society. (Originally translated by John Stanley in 1881).

Amendola, F. C., et al. (Eds.) (2006). *Eminent domain Corpus Juris Secondum* (Vol. 29A). C.J.S: Thomson West.

Ambaye, D. W. (2009a). Land valuation for expropriation in Ethiopia: Valuation methods and adequacy of compensation. In *7th FIG regional conference*. Hanoi, Vietnam, Retrieved October 19–22, 2009 from (http://www.fig.net/pub/vietnam/papers/ts04c/ts04c_ambaye_3753.pdf).

Andargachew-Tiruneh. (1993). *The Ethiopian revolution, 1974–1987: A transformation from an aristocratic to a totalitarian autocracy*. New York: Cambridge University Press.

Appraisal-Institute. (2001). *The apprisal of real estate*. Chicago: Apprisal Institute.

Aregawi-Berhe. (2008). *A political history of the tigray people's liberation front (1975-1991): Revolt, ideology and mobilisation in Ethiopia*. Amesterdam: Amesterdam University.

D.W. Ambaye, *Land Rights and Expropriation in Ethiopia*,
Springer Theses, DOI 10.1007/978-3-319-14639-3

Aristotle [Translated]. (1984). *The Athenian constitution*. London: Penguin Books.

Arko-Adjei, A. (2011). *Adapting land administration to the institutional framework of customary tenure: The case of Peri-urban Ghana*. Amsterdam: TUDelft.

Aubry & Rau. (1966). *Droit Civil Francis -Property*. (Translated by the Louisiana State Law Institute West Publishing Co).

Author. (2004). E.C. Sefafi ye gibrina investment le Ethiopia min Yifeyidal? (What is the benefit of large scale agricultural investment for Ethiopia?) Reporter.

Awotash-Alemu. (2003). *The impact of expropriation on investment: The case of Ethiopia*. Unpublished Senior Thesis, Law Faculty, Addis Ababa University.

Bahru-Zewde. (1991). *A history of modern Ethiopia, 1855–1974*. Addis Ababa: Addis Ababa University Press.

Benson, B. L. (Ed.). (2010). *Property rights: Eminent domain and regulatory takings re-examined*. New York: Palgrave Macmillan.

Benson, B. L., & Brown, M. (2010). Eminent domain for private use: Is it justified by market failure or an example of government failure? In B. L. Benson (Ed.) *Property rights: Eminent domain and regulatory takings re-examined*. New York: The Independent Institute.

Bentham, J. (2000). *An introduction to the principles of morals and legislation*. London: Batoche Books, Kitchener. (Original 1781).

Betts, R. M., & Ely, S. J. (2008). *Basic real estate appraisal: Principles and procedures*. New York: Thomson South-Western.

Beza-Consulting. (2011). Ethiopian nile irrigation and drainage project. Ministry of Water Resources.

Bhatia, H. L. (2003). *Public finance*. Mumbai: Vikas Publishing House Pvt. Ltd.

Bin, Z. X. (2002). Compensation system in the people's republic of China. In T. Kotaka & D. L. Callies (Eds.) *Taking land: Compulsory purchase and regulation in Asian-Pacific countries*. Honolulu: University of Hawai'i Press.

Birks, P. (1985). The Roman law concept of dominium and the idea of absolute ownership. *Acta Juridica, 28*, 1–37.

Bjerken, T. (1990). Expropriation in Sweden. In G. M. Erasmus (Ed.) *Compensation for expropriation: A comparative study*. Oxford: St. Edmund Hall University of Oxford.

Black, H. C. (1991). *Black's law dictionary* (6th ed.). St, Paul, Minn: West Group.

Blackstone, W. (1825). *Commentaries on the laws of England*, London: A. Strahan Law Printer.

Blanc, H. (2007). *A narrative of captivity in Abyssinia: With some account of the late emperor theodore, his country and people*. Harvard: Harvard University. (Original 1868).

Bourassa, S. C., & Hong, Y.-H. (2003). *Leasing public land: International experiences*. Cambridge: Massachusetts Lincoln Institute of Public policy.

Bouvier, J. (1984). *Bouvier's law dictionary* (4th ed.). New York: William S. Hein & Co.

Boynton, S. (1962). Components of eminent domain: An ancient tool for contemporary use. *South Carolina Law Review, 15*, 943–975.

Bruce, J. (1790). *Travels to discover the source of the nile in the years 1768, 1769, 1770, 1771, 1772 & 1773*. Edinburgh: Printed by J. Ruthven for G.G.J & J. Robinson, Paternoster-Row.

Bryman, A., & Bell, E. (2003). *Business research methods*. Oxford: Oxford University Press.

Buchanan, A., & Mathieu, D. (1986). Philosophy and justice. In R. L. Cohen (Ed.) *Justice*. New York and London: Plenum Press.

Budge, E. A. W. (1922). *The kibre negest: The glory of kings*. London.

Caulk, R. A. (1978). Armies as preditors: Soldiers and peasants in Ethiopia c. 1850–1935. *The International Journal of African Historical Studies, 11*, 457–493.

Chan, N. (2003). Land acquisition compensation in China—problems and answers. *International Real Estate Review, 6*.

Clapham, C. (1988). *Transformation and continuity in revolutionary Ethiopia*. Cambridge: Cambridge University Press.

Clarke, A., & Kohler, P. (2005). *Property law: commentary and materials*. Cambridge: Cambridge University Press.

Clawson, M. (1968). Land. In D. L. Sills (Ed.) *International encyclopedia of the social sciences.* USA: The Macmillan Company and The Free Press.

Cohen, J. M. (1977). Rural and urban land reform in Ethiopia. *African Law Studies, 14*, 3–61.

Constitution of the Federal Demecratic Republic of Ethiopia, Proclamation No. 1/1995. *Negarit Gazeta.* Year 1 No. 1.

Comments (1948–1949). The public use limitation on eminent domain: An advance requiem. *Yale Law Journal, 58*, 599–614.

Comments (1956). What use is a public use in eminent domain? *Saint Louis University Law Journal, 4*, 316.

Comments (1958). Eminent domain valuations in an age of redevelopment: Incidental losses. *Yale Law Journal, 67*, 61–92.

Cook, K. S., & Hegtvedt, K. A. (1983). Distributive justice, equity and equality. *Annual Review of Sociology, 9*, 217–241.

Council-of-Europe. (1952). Protocol No. 1 to the convention for the protection of human rights and fundamental freedoms. Paris.

Crabtree, S. (1983). Public use in eminent domain: Are there limits after Oakland raiders and poletown? *California Western Law Review, 20*, 82.

Crummey, D. (1969). Tewodros as reformer and modernizer. *The Journal of African History, 10*, 457–469.

Crummey, D. (2000). *Land and society in the christian kingdom of Ethiopia: From the thirteenth to the twentieth century.* USA: University of Illinios Press.

Crummey, D., & Sishagne, S. (1991). Land tenure and the social accumulation of wealth in eighteenth-century Ethiopia: Evidencefrom the qwesqwam land register. *The International Journal of African Historical Studies, 24*, 241–258.

Dana, D. A. (2007). The law and expressive meaning of condemning the poor after Kelo. *Northwestern University Law Review, 101*, 365.

Davies, M. (2007). *Property: Meanings, histories, theories.* New York: Routledge-Cavendish.

Deininger, K. (2003). *Land policies for growth and poverty reduction. A world bank policy research report.* Oxford: World Bank and Oxford University Press.

Deininger, K., Ayalew, D., & Alemu, T. (2009). Impacts of land certification on tenure security, investment, and land markets: Evidence from Ethiopia. *Environment for Development, Discussion Paper Series, EfD DP 09-11* [Online]. http://siteresources.worldbank.org/NEWS/Resources/land_eegistration_in_ethiopia.pdf.

Deininger, K., Ayalew, D., Holden, S., & Zevenbergen, J. (2007). Rural land certification in ethiopia: process, initial impact, and implications for other African Countries. *World Bank Policy Research Working Paper 4218.* World Bank.

Demsetz, H. (1967). Toward a theory of property rights. *The American Economic Review, 57*, 347–359.

Denscombe, M. (2007). *The good research guide.* New York: Open University Press.

Dessalegn, R. (1970). Condition of the Ethiopian peasantry. *Challenger,* X.

Dessalegn, R. (1993). Agrarian change and agrarian crisis: State and peasantry in post-revolution Ethiopia. *Africa: Journal of the International African Institute, 63*, 36–55.

Dessalegn, R. (2006). From heterogeneity to homogeneity: agrarian class structure in Ethiopia since the 1950s. In R. Dessalegn & A. Taye (Eds.) *Land and the challenge of sustainable development in Ethiopia.* Addis Ababa: Forum for Social Studies.

Dessalegn, R. (2009a-a). Land and agrarian unrest in wollo: From the imperial regime to the derg. In R. Dessalegn (Ed.) *The peasant and the state: Studies in agrarian change in Ethiopia 1950s–2000s (collection of articles by same author).* Addis Ababa: Addis Ababa Univrsity Press.

Dessalegn, R. (2009a-b). Land registration and tenure security: A critical assessment. In R. Dessalegn (Ed.) *The peasant and the state: studies in agrarian change in Ethiopia 1950s–2000s.* Addis Ababa: Addis Ababa University Press.

Dessalegn, R. (2009b). An assessment on the Ethiopian agricultural policy. In A. Taye (Ed.) *Digest of Ethiopian national policies, strategies and programmes (amharic)*. Addis Ababa: Forum for Social Studies and The European Union.
Dessalegn, R. (2011). *Land to investors: Large-scale land transfer in Ethiopia. FSS policy debate series*. Forum for Social Studies: Addis Ababa.
Desta, G. (1975). *Expropriation: Law and practice*. Unpublished senior thesis at the Faculty of Law of Addis Ababa University.
Dobinson, I., & Johns, F. (2007). Qualitative legal research. In M. Mcconville & W. H. Chui (Eds.) *Research methods for law*. Edinburgh: Edinburgh University Press.
Dunning, H. C. (1970). Land reform in Ethiopia: A case study in non-development. *UCLA L. Rev, 18*, 271–307.
Dworkin, R. (1977). *Taking rights seriously*. Harvard: Harvard University Press.
Dwyer, P. G., & McPhee, P. (Eds.). (2002). *The French revolution and Napoleon: A source book*. London: Routledge.
EEA, EEPRI. (2002). *A research report on land tenure and agricultural development in Ethiopia*. Addis Ababa: Ethiopian Economic Association/Ethiopian Economic Policy Research Institute.
Epstein, R. A. (1985). *Takings, private property and the power of eminent domain*. Cambridge: Harvard University Press.
Epstein, R. A. (1993). *Bargaining with the state*. New Jersey: Princeton University Press.
Erasumes, G. M. (1990). *Compensation for expropriation: Comparative study*, Oxford: Jason Reese in association with The UK National Committee of Comparative Law.
Ewing, W. H. (Ed.) (1972). *Consolidated laws of Ethiopia*, (Vol. I). Addis Ababa: The Law Faculty of Haile Sellassie I University.
Ethiopian Civil Procedure Code. *Negarit Gazeta-Extraordinary*. Decree No. 52/1965, Year 25, No. 3.
FAO. (2002). *Land tenure and rural development*. Rome: United Nations Food and Agriculture Organization.
FAO. (2008). *Compulsory acquisition of land and compensation. FAO Land Tenure Studies* (Vol. 10). Rome: Food and Agriculture Organization of the United Nations.
FDRE Expropriation of Landholdings for Public Purposes and Payment of Compensation Proclamation, Proclamation No. 455/2005. *Negarit Gazeta*. Year 11, No. 43.
FDRE Investment Proclamation, Proclmation No. 769/2012. *Negarit Gazeta*. Year 18, No. 63.
FDRE Rural Land Administration and Land Use Proclamation, Proclamation No. 456/2005. *Negarit Gazeta*. Year 11, No. 44.
FDRE Urban Lands Lease Holding Proclamation, Proclamation No. 721/2011. *Negarit Gazeta*. Year 18, No. 4.
FDRE Urban Planning Proclamation, Proclamation No. 574/ 2008. *Negarit Gazeta*. Year 14, No. 29.
Federal Courts Proclamation No. 25/1996. *Negarit Gazetta*. Year 2, No. 13.
Federal Courts Proclamation Re-amendment Proclamation No 454/2005. *Negarit Gazetta*. Year 11, No. 42.
Federal Democratic Republic of Ethiopia Rural Land Administration and Land Use Proclamation, Proclamation No. 456/2005. *Negarit Gazeta*. Year 11, No. 44.
Fitha Negest (Amharic and Geez Version). Addis Ababa: Tesfa-Gebre-Sellassie Printing Press.
Fisher, W. (1990). Ideology, religion and the constitutional protection of private property: 1760–1860. *Emory Law Journal, 65*, 104.
Fleischacker, S. (2004). *A short history of distributive justice*. Massachusetts: Harvard University Press.
Fletcher, W. M. (2011). Eminent domain. *Fletcher cyclopedia of the law of corporations*. 6A Fletcher Cyclopedia Corporations, § 2905.
Garnett, N. S. (2003). The public-use question as a takings problem. *George Washington Law Review, 71*, 934.

Garnsey, P. (2007). *Thinking about property from antiquity to the age of revolution*. Cambridge: Cambridge University Press.

Gilkes, P. (1975). *The dying lion: Feudalism and modernization in Ethiopia*. London: Julian Friedman Publishers.

Grant, J. A. C. (1930). The "higher law" background of the law of eminent domain. *Wisconsin Law Review, 6*, 68–85.

Gravelle, H., & Rees, R. (2004). *Microeconomics*. Essex: Prentice Hall.

Green, B. D. (2009). *Compulsory purchase and compensation*. London: EG Books.

Grotius, H. (1625) [orig.] *On the law of war and peace* A.C. Campbell translation, De Jure Belli ac Pacis.

Gebreselassie, S. (2006). Land, land policy and smallholder agriculture in Ethiopia: Options and scenarios. *Future agricultures consortium meeting*. Brighton: The Institute of Development Studies.

Government Ownership of Urban Land and Extra Houses, Proclamation No. 47/1975. *Negarit Gazeta*. Year 34, No. 41.

Gebre-Wold-ingida, W. (1962). Ethiopia's traditional system of land tenure and taxation. *Ethiopia Observer, 5*, 302–339.

Gebru, T. (1991). *Ethiopia: Power and protest: Peasant revolts in the twentieth century*. Cambridge: Cambridge University Press.

Haddad, N. W. (2006). Public use or private benefit? The post-Kelo intersection of religious land use and the public use doctrine. *Fordham Law Review, 75*, 1105.

Hardin, G. (1968). The tragedy of the commons. *Science, 162*, 1243–1248.

Harrington, M. P. (2001). "Public use" and the original understanding of the so-called "Taking" clause. *Hastings Law Review, 53*, 1245–1301.

Harris, C. (1844). *The highlands of Ethiopia*, London: Longman, Brown, Green, and Longmans.

Henze, P. B. (2000). *Layers of time: History of Ethiopia*, London: C. Hurst & Co Publishers Ltd.

Herring, P. (1968). Public interest. In D. L. Sills (Ed.) *International encyclopedia of the social sciences*. USA: The Macmillan Company & The Free Press.

Ho, P. (2005). *Institutions in transition: Land ownership, property rights, and social conflict in China*. New York: Oxford University Press.

Hobbes, T. (1996). *Leviathan*, New York: Oxford University Press. (J. C. A. Gaskin (Ed.), Originally published 1651).

Hoben, A. (1973). *Land tenure among the amhara of Ethiopia: The dynamics of cognatic descent*. Chicago: University of Chicago Press.

Honoré, A. M. (1961). Ownership. In A. G. Guest (Ed.) *Oxford essays in jurisprudence*. Oxford: Oxford University Press.

Horne, F. (2011). *Understanding land investment deals in Africa: Country report Ethiopia*. Oakland, USA: The Oakland Institute.

Huntingford, G. W. B. (1965). *The land charters of Northern Ethiopia*. Addis Ababa: Institute of Ethiopian Studies and the Faculty of Law, Haile Sellassie I University.

IFC (2002). *Handbook for preparing a resettlement action plan*. International Finance Corporation, A Member of World Bank Group.

IFC (2012). *Policy and performance standards on environmental and social sustainability*. International Finance Corporation, World Bank Group.

Innes, R. (2000). Economics of taking and compensation when land and its public use value are in private hands. *Land Economics, 76*.

Issac, D. (2012). *Property valuation principles*. New York: Palgrave.

Johanson, D. C., & Edey, M. A. (1981). *Lucy, the beginning of human kind*. New York: Simon & Schuster.

Johnson, C. (1999). The developmental state: Odyssey of a concept. In M. Woo-Cumings (Ed.) *The developmental state*. New York: Cornell University Press.

Johnston, D. (1999). *Roman law in context*. Cambridge: Cambridge University Press.

Jones, J. W. (1972). Expropriation in Roman laws. *Law Quarter Review, 45*, 512–527.

Jones, S. D. (2006). That land is your land, this land is my land..until the local government can turn it for a profit: A critical analysis of Kelo v. city of New London. *BYU Journal of Public Law, 20*, 139.

Kahr, J., & Thomsett, M. (2005). *Real estate market valuation and analysis.* New Jersey: Wiley.

Kalbro, T. (2000). Compulsory purchase and restrictions on land use: Principles of compensation in Swedish law. *Property development and compulsory purchase.* Stockholm: Royal Institute of Technology (KTH).

Kalbro, T. (2003). Private compulsory purchase and the public interest. In T. Kalbro (Ed.) *Urban land management: Papers on property development and compulsory purchase.* Stockholm: KTH.

Kitay, M. G. (1985). *Land acquisition in developing countries: Policies and procedures of the public sector.* Boston: Oelgeschlager, Gunn & Hain, Publishers Inc.

Kivell, P., & McKay. (1988). Public ownership of urban land. *Transactions of the Institute of British Geographers, New Series, 13*, 165–178.

Kivell, P. (1993). *Land and the city: Patterns and processes of urban change.* London: Routledge.

Kratovil, R., Frank, J., & Harrison, J. (1954). Eminent Domain-Policy and concept. *California Law Review, 42*, 596–652.

Land Tax Proclamation, Proclamation No. 70/1944. *Negarit Gazeta.* Year 4, No. 2.

Lapiso-G-Delebo (1983) EC. *Ye Ethiopia Ye Gebar Sireat-na Jimir Capitalism: 1900–1966 (Ethiopian gabar system and the beginning of capitalism: 1908–1974).* Addis Ababa.

Larebo, H. M. (1994). *The building of an empire: Italian land policy in Ethiopia 1935–1941.* Oxford: Clarendon Press.

Lenhoff, A. (1942). Development of the concept of eminent domain. *Columbia Law Review, 42*, 596.

Locke, J. (1980). *Second treatise of civil governmnet* (C. M. Macpherson (Ed.) Orginally published 1690). Cambridge: Hackett Publishing Company Inc.

Locke, J. (1986). *The second treatise on civil government.* New York: Prometheus Books. [Original 1690].

Layne, T. (1991). *Ethiopian transitional period economic policy.* Addis Ababa: Office of Prime Minister.

Mahteme-Selassie, W. M. (1957). The land system of Ethiopia. *Ethiopia Observer, 1.*

Mahteme-Sellassie, W. M. (1970). *Zekre Neger* (2nd ed.). Addis Ababa.

Marcus, H. G. (1994). *A history of Ethiopia.* Los Angeles: University of California Press.

Marcus, P. (1942). The taking and destruction of property under a defense and war program. *Cornell Law Quarterly, 27*, 476.

Markakis, J. (2006). *Ethiopia: Anatomy of a traditional polity.* Addis Ababa: Shama Books.

Mathis, K. (2009). *Efficiency instead of justice? Searching for the philosophical foundations of the economic analysis of law.* New York: Springer.

Matthews, N. (1920). The valuation of property in the Roman law. *Harvard Law Review, 34*, 229–259.

McCormick, C. T. (1932). The measure of compensation in eminent domain. *Minnesota Law Review, 17*, 461–498.

McCrudden, C. (2006). Legal research and the social sciences. *Law Quarterly Review, 122* 632–650.

McNulty, W. D. (1912). Eminent domain in continental Europe. *The Yale Law Journal, 21*, 555–570.

Meidinger, E. E. (1981). The "Public uses" of eminent domain: History and policy. *Environmental Law, 11.*

Merrill, T. W. (1987). The economics of public use. *Cornell Law Review, 72*, 61–116.

Merrill, T. W., & Smith, H. E. (2010). *The Oxford introductions to U.S. law: Property.* New York: Oxford University Press.

Mariam, W. M. (1966). Problems of urbanization. In *Proceeding of the third international conference of Ethiopian studies*, 1970. Addis Ababa: Institute of Ethiopian Studies, Haile Sellassie I University.

Mesganaw K. (2009). The current urban land tenure system in Ethiopia. In A. Muradu (Ed.) *Land law and policy in Ethiopia since 1991: Continuities and changes.* Addis Ababa: Ethiopian Business Law Series, Faculty of Law, Addis Ababa University.

Michelman, F. I. (1966). Property, utility, and fairness: Comments on the ethical foundations of "just compensation" law. *Harvard Law Review*, *80*, 1165–1258.

Mikkelsen, S. D. (2006). Eminent domain after Kelo v. city of New London: Compensating for the supreme court's refusal to enforce the fifth amendment. *Duke Journal of Constitutional Law & Public Policy Sidbar* 2, 11.

Ministry-of-Information (1968). *Yemeret Yizota be Hibretesebawit Ethiopia (Land possession in the republic of Ethiopia),* Addis Ababa.

Mofed. (2010). *federal democratic republic of Ethiopia growth and transformation plan (GTP): 2010/2011–2014/2015.* Addis Ababa: Ministry of Finance and Economic Development.

Moipad. (2001). *Federal democratic republic of ethiopia rural development policies, strategies and instruments (amharic).* Addis Ababa: Ministry of Information, Press and Audiovisual Department.

Mengistu, M. (2009). The ethiopian urban landholding system: An assessment of the governing legal regime. In A. Muradu (Ed.) *Land law and policy in Ethiopia since 1991: Continuities and changes.* Addis Ababa: Law Faculty, Addis Ababa University.

Moore, V. (1990). Compulsory purchase in the united kingdom. In G. M. Erasmus (Ed.) *Compensation for expropriation: A comparative study.* Oxford: National Committee of Comparative Law.

Munch, P. (1976). An economic analysis of eminent domain. *Journal of Political Economy, 84*, 473.

Munteanu, C. (2005). Historical remarks on the legal notion of property. *Acta Universitatis Lucian Blaga, 54*.

Munzer, S. R. (1990). *A theory of property.* New York: Cambridge University Press.

Muradu, A. (2007). Review of decisions of state courts over state matters by the federal supreme court. *Mizan Law Review, 1*, 61.

Ndjovu, C. E. (2003). *Compulsory purchase in tanzania: Bulldozing property rights.* Ph.D Thesis, Kungl Tekniska Hogskolan.

Niguse, K. (2012). *Land tenure and tenure security among somali pastoralists: Within the context of dual tenure system.* L.L.M Thesis, Bahir Dar University, School of Law.

Nichols, P. (1940). The meaning of public use in the law of eminent domain. *Boston University Law Review, 20*, 615.

Nichols, P., Sackman J., et al. (Eds.) (2007). *1 Nichols on eminent domain.* New York: Matthew Bender & Company, Inc.

Norell, L. (2008). *Is the market value a fair and objective measure for determining compensation for compulsory purchase. Land reform.* Rome: FAO.

Nozick, R. (1974). *Anarchy, state, and Utopia.* Oxford: Blackwell.

Oromia Rural Land Use and Administration, Proclamation 130/2007.

Olika, T. (2006). Ethiopia: Politics of land tenure policies under the three regimes, a carrot and stick rulling strategy in Ethiopian politics. In T. Olika (Ed.) *Ethiopia: Politics, policy making and rural development.* Addis Ababa: Department of Political & International Relations, Addis Ababa University.

Ostrom, E. (1990). *Governing the commons: The evolution of institutions for collective action.* Cambridge: Cambridge University Press.

Palm, L. (2010). Quick and cheap mass land registration and computerisation in Ethiopia. *Facing the challenges—building the capacity.* Sydney, Australia: FIG Congress.

Pankhurst, R. (1961). Menelik and the foundation of Addis Ababa. *The Journal of African History,* 2, 103–117.

Pankhurst, R. (1966). *State and land in Ethiopian history*. Addis Ababa: The Institute of Ethiopian Studies and the Faculty of Law, Haile Sellasie I University.

Pankhurst, R. (1968). *Economic history of Ethiopia 1800–1935*. Addis Ababa: Haile Sellassie I University Press.

Pankhurst, R. (1990). *A social history of Ethiopia*. Addis Ababa: Institute of Ethiopian Studies, Addis Ababa University.

Paul, E. F. (1987). *Property rights and eminent domain*. New Brunswick and London: Transaction Publishers.

Paul, J. C. N., & Clapham, C. (1972). *Ethiopian constitutional development i, a source book*. Addis Ababa: Haile Sellassie I University and Oxford University Press.

Pausewang, S. (1982). *Peasants, land and society: A social history of land reform in Ethiopia*. Weltforum-Varlag: Munchen.

Picard, E. (1990). Expropriation in France. In G. M. Erasmus (Ed.) *Compensation for expropriation: A comparative study*. Oxford: St. Edmund Hall University of Oxford.

Pierre, B. (1997). Classification of property and conceptions of ownership in civil and common law. *Revue Generale De Droit, 28*, 235–274.

Posner, R. (2002). *Economic analysis of law*. New York: Aspen Publishers.

Pound, R. (1939). The law of property and recent juristic thought. *ABA Journal, 25*, 993–998.

Pufendorf, S. V. (1673). *De Officio Homines et Civis (On the duty of man and citizen according to the natural law)*.

Public Ownership of Rural Lands, Proclamation No. 31/1975. *Negarit Gazeta*. Year 34, No. 26.

Rawls, J. (1999). *A theory of justice*. Massachusetts: The Belknap Press of Harvard University Press.

Rescher, N. (1966). *Distributive justice: A constructive critique of the utilitarian theory of distribution*. Indianapolis, IN: Bob Merrill.

Reynolds, S. (2010). *Before eminent domain: Toward a history of expropriation of land for the common good*. Chapel Hill: The University of North Carolina Press.

Rousseau, J. J. (1762). *The social contract* (Translated by Christopher Betts-1994). Oxford: Oxford University Press.

Re-enactment of Urban Lands Lease Holding Proclamation, Proclamation No. 272/2002. *Negarit Gazeta*. Year 8, No. 19.

Sax, J. (1964). Takings and the police power. *Yale Law Journal, 74*, 36.

Sayce, S., Smith, J., Cooper, R., & Rowland, P. V. (2006). *Real estate appraisal: From value to worth*. Oxford: Blackwell Publishing.

Schultz, D. (2009). *Evicted! Property rights and eminent domain in America*, Praeger.

Scott, A. D. (1955). The fishery: The objectives of sole ownership. *Journal of Political Economy, 63*, 116–124.

Seyoum, A., Dorosh, P. & Asrat, S. (2010). Crop production in Ethiopia: Regional patterns and trends. In *Ethiopia strategy support program II*. Washington: International Food Policy Research Institute.

Shiferaw, B. (1995). The evolution of land tenure in the imperial era. In B. Shiferaw (Ed.) *An economic history of Ethiopia: The imperial era 1941–1974*. Dakar: Codesria.

Simmonds, N. E. (2008). *Central issues in jurisprudence: Justice, law and rights*, London: Sweet & Maxwell and Thomson Reuters.

Simpson, S. R. (1961). Towards a definition of "absolute ownership": II. *Journal of African Law, 5*, 145–151.

Snare, F. (1972). The concept of property. *American Philosophical Quarterly, 9*, 200–206.

Somin, I. (2010). The limits of backlash: Assessing the political response to Kelo. In Benson, B. L. (Ed.) *Property rights: Eminent domain and regulatory takings re-examined*. New York: Palgrave Macmillan.

Stake, R. E. (1995). *The art of case study research*. Thousand Oaks, California: Saga Publication.

Stevenson, G. G. (1991). *Common property economics: A general theory and land use applications*. Cambridge: Cambridge University Press.

Stiglitz, J. E., & Driffill, J. (2000). *Economics*. New York, London: W. W. Norton & Company.

Stoebuck, W. B. (1972). A general theory of eminent domain. *Washington Law Review, 47*, 553–608.

Sullivan, R. M. (1990). Eminent domain in the united states: An overview of federal condemnation proceedings. In G. M. Erasmus (Ed.) *Compensation for expropriation: A comparative study*. Oxford: St. Edmund Hall University of Oxford.

Sellasie, T. T. G. (1959) (EC). *Tarik Zemen ze Dagmawi Menelik Nuguse Negest Ityopia (History of the lives and times of menelik II king of kings of Ethiopia)*. Addis Ababa, Artistic Ltd.

Tamrat, T. (1972). *Church and state in Ethiopia, 1270–1527*. Oxford: Clarendon Press.

The People's Republic of China Land Administration Law.

The Constitution of the People's Democratic Republic of Ethiopia, Proclamation 1 of 1987. *Negarit Gazetta*. Year 47, No. 1.

The Civil Code of Ethiopia. *Negarit Gazeta: Gazette Extraordinary*. Proclamation No. 165/1960.

The Revised Amhara National Regional State Rural Land Administration and Use Proclamation, Proclamation No. 133/2006. *Zikre Hig*. Year 11, No. 18.

The Revised Constitution of the Empire of Ethiopia. (1955). *Negarit Gazetta*.

The Revised Tigray National Regional State Rural Land Administration and Use Proclamation, Proclamation No. 136/2007. *Tigray Negarit Gazeta*. Year 16 No. 1.

The Southern Nations, Nationalities and Peoples Regional State Rural Land Administration and Utilization Proclamation, Proclamation 110/2007. *Debub Negarit Gazeta*. Year No.

The Civil Code of Ethiopia. (1960). *Negarit Gazeta: Gazette Extraordinary*. Proclamation No. 165/1960.

UN-HABITAT. (2008). *Ethiopia: Addis Ababa urban profile*. Nairobi: United Nations Human Settlements Programme.

UN-HABITAT. (2010). *The Ethiopia case of condominium housing: The integrated housing development programme*. Nairobi: United Nations Human Settlements Programme.

UNECE. (1996). *Land administration guidelines*. Geneva: United Nations Economic Commission for Europe.

Urban Lands Lease Holding Proclamation, Proclamation No. 80/1993. *Negarit Gazeta*. Year 53, No. 40.

Urban Lands Lease Holding Proclamation, Proclamation No. 721/2011. *Negarit Gazeta*. Year 18, No. 4.

Urban Land and Extra House: From Yesterday to Today (Amharic). (1978). Addis Ababa: Committee established for the Fourth Anniversary of the Revolution.

Urmson, J. (1998). *Aristotle's Ethics*. Oxford: Blackwells Publishers.

Ventolo, W. L., & Williams, M. R. (2001). *Fundamentals of real estate appraisal*. Chicago: Dearborn Financial Publication.

Viitanen, K. (2002). Just compensation in expropriation. *FIG XXII international congress*. Washington, D.C. USA: International Federation of Surveyor.

Viitanen, K., Falkenbach, H., & Nuuja, K. (2010). *Compulsory purchase and compensation recommendations for good practice*. Helsinki International Federation of Surveyors: FIG Policy Statement.

Vranken, J. (2012). Exciting times for legal scholarship. www.bjutijddschriften.nl/tijdschrift/rem/2012/2/ReM_2212_002_002_004.pdf.

Waldron, J. (1988). *The right to private property*. Oxford: Clarendorn Press.

Wegren, S. K. (Ed.) (1998). *Land reform in the former Soviet Union and Eastern Europe*, London, Routledge.

West's Encyclopedia of American Law. (2005a). In J. Lehman, & S. Phelps (Eds.) *Foundations of the U.S law: Magna charta*. San Francisco: Thomson Gale.

West's Encyclopedia of American Law. (2005b). In J. Lehman., et al. (Ed.) *Eminent Domain* (2nd ed., Vol. 4). San Francisco, London and Munich: Thomson Gale.

Wright, R. R., & Gitelman, M. (2000). *Land use in a nutshell*. Minnesota: West Groups.

Wyatt, P. (2005). *Property valuation in an economic context*. Oxford: Wiley-Blackwell.

Young, J. (1997). *Peasant revolution in Ethiopia the tigray people's liberation front, 1975–1991*. New York: Cambridge University Press.

Zewde B. (2008a). The city center: A shifting concept in the history of Addis Ababa. In B. Zewde (Ed.) *Society, state and history: Selected essays*. Addis Ababa: Addis Ababa University Press.

Zewde B. (2008b). Economic origins of the absolutist state in Ethiopia (1916–1935). In B. ZEWDE (Ed.) *Society, state and history: Selected essays*. Addis Ababa: Addis Ababa University Press.

MIX
Papier aus verantwortungsvollen Quellen
Paper from responsible sources
FSC® C105338

If you have any concerns about our products,
you can contact us on
ProductSafety@springernature.com

In case Publisher is established outside the EU,
the EU authorized representative is:
Springer Nature Customer Service Center GmbH
Europaplatz 3, 69115 Heidelberg, Germany

Printed by Libri Plureos GmbH
in Hamburg, Germany